# Arizona Real Estate: Practice & Law

Consulting Editor
TERRENCE M. ZAJAC, DREI

SIXTH EDITION

**Real Estate Education Company**
a division of Dearborn Financial Publishing, Inc.

Publisher: Carol L. Luitjens
Senior Development Editor: Cheryl D. Wilson
Development Editor: Robert A. Porché
Art and Design Manager: Lucy Jenkins

Published by Real Estate Education Company®,
a division of Dearborn Financial Publishing, Inc.®
155 North Wacker Drive
Chicago, IL 60606-1719
(312) 836-4400

Printed in the United States of America.

10  9  8  7  6  5

**Library of Congress Cataloging-in-Publication Data**

Arizona real estate : practice and law — 6th ed. / Terrence M. Zajac, consulting editor
    p.       cm.
  Rev. ed. of : Arizona supplement for Modern real estate practice.
  5th ed. c1988.
    Includes index.
    ISBN 0-7931-0106-9
    1. Real estate business—Law and legislation—Arizona. 2. Vendors and purchasers—Arizona. 3. Real property—Arizona. 4. Real estate business—Arizona. I. Zajac, Terrence M. II. Miler, Charles E.
  KF2042.R4G34     1993 Arizona
  346.79104'37—dc20
  [347.9106437]
                               96-13851
                                 CIP

# Contents

# Preface

## THE TOTAL LEARNING SYSTEM™

*Arizona Real Estate: Practice and Law*, Sixth Edition, represents a major step forward in modern real estate education. In the past, the *Arizona Supplement* was just that: a supplementary volume tied to the nation's best-selling real estate principles text, *Modern Real Estate Practice*. This new edition, however, is now a key component of Real Estate Education Company's "Total Learning System™." This system offers students and educators a complete turnkey package for prelicense real estate courses, continuing education and professional enrichment. As the demographics and structure of the real estate industry change, Real Estate Education Company® is helping students, instructors and practitioners adapt to this new environment by providing more accessible and versatile educational tools.

### Introducing *Arizona Real Estate: Practice and Law*

This book can be used with equal effectiveness with *any* of our principles products:

- *Modern Real Estate Practice,* 13th Edition
- *Modern Real Estate Practice,* 14th Edition
- *Real Estate Fundamentals,* 4th Edition Revised
- *Mastering Real Estate Principles*
- *SuccessMaster* software—National Edition

*Arizona Real Estate* also offers current real estate professionals a practical handbook of Arizona's real estate law and rules, along with the most current developments. Every effort has been made to ensure that the information contained in this book is both relevant and current. There are also numerous references to state statutes and the Commissioner's Rules, so readers can look up the law themselves in most public and university libraries.

Readers using *Arizona Real Estate* to prepare for the state real estate licensing examination should note that this book does not address the national topics that constitute 80 percent of the real estate examination. Students are advised to first read the relevant material in one of the main principles products, then turn to *Arizona Real Estate* for a focus on Arizona's particular laws and practices as they relate to that subject. This book is designed to discuss the statutes, rules and practical real estate issues that arise in the state of Arizona.

## HOW TO USE THIS BOOK

The conversion table below provides a quick and easy reference for using *Arizona Real Estate: Practice and Law* in conjunction with various principles books. For instance, *Arizona Real Estate*'s Chapter 14, "Closing the Real Estate Transaction," may be read in conjunction with Chapter 23 in *Modern Real Estate Practice*, 13th Edition; Chapter 22 in *Modern Real Estate Practice*, 14th Edition; Chapter 15 in *Real Estate Fundamentals*; Chapter 12 in *Mastering Real Estate Principles;* and Lesson 12 in *SuccessMaster* software.

| *Arizona Real Estate: Practice and Law,* 6th Edition | *Modern Real Estate Practice,* 13th Edition | *Modern Real Estate Practice,* 14th Edition | *Real Estate Fundamentals,* 4th Edition Revised | *Mastering Real Estate Principles* | *SuccessMaster* (National) software |
|---|---|---|---|---|---|
| 1. Real Estate Brokerage | 4 | 4, 5 | 8 | 13 | 13 |
| 2. Listing Agreements | 5 | 6 | 6 | 15 | 15 |
| 3. Interests in Real Estate | 6 | 7 | 2 | 7 | 7 |
| 4. How Ownership Is Held | 7 | 8 | 4 | 9 | 9 |
| 5. Legal Descriptions | 8 | 9 | 1 | 6 | 6 |
| 6. Real Estate Taxes and Other Liens | 9 | 10 | 9 | 5, 25 | 5, 26 |
| 7. Real Estate Contracts | 10 | 11 | 6 | 14 | 14 |
| 8. Transfer of Title | 11 | 12 | 3 | 10 | 10 |
| 9. Title Records | 12 | 13 | 5 | 11 | 11 |
| 10. Real Estate License Laws | 13 | — | — | 16 | 16 |
| 11. Real Estate Financing | 14, 15 | 14, 15 | 11 | Unit VII | Unit 7 |
| 12. Leases | 16 | 16 | 7 | 8 | 8 |
| 13. Subdividing and Property Development | 20 | 19 | 13 | — | — |
| 14. Closing the Real Estate Transaction | 23 | 22 | 15 | 12 | 12 |

## ACKNOWLEDGMENTS

The publisher is particularly grateful to Terrence M. Zajac, DREI, who is the consulting editor for the sixth edition. Mr. Zajac is president and owner of Terry Zajac Seminars in Scottsdale. He is national past-president of the Real Estate Educators Association and was former secretary of the National Association of Master Appraisers. Mr. Zajac was also coauthor of the fifth edition of this text and a contributing writer on an earlier edition of *Modern Real Estate Practice*.

Appreciation is also expressed to Kathryn J. Haupt of North Bend, Washington, who served as development writer for this edition. Ms. Haupt is an attorney and a member of the Washington State Bar Association. Specializing in real estate education, she has developed several real estate courses. She has also authored interactive real estate education computer programs and has edited and authored numerous real estate textbooks for Real Estate Education Company.

Special thanks go to the following people for their invaluable assistance in preparing this edition: Stuart M. Bernstein, Best School of Real Estate, Sedona/Flagstaff; Rex R. Denham, NorthWestern School of Real Estate, Bullhead City; John Foltz, Realty Executives, Phoenix; E. Ray Henry, Arizona Institute of Real Estate, Flagstaff/Prescott; Marge Lindsay, John Hall & Associations, Inc., Phoenix; Dr. James L. McNett, Glendale Community College, Glendale; Nick J. Petra, Priority One Educational Systems, Scottsdale; Jim Sexton, John Hall & Associates, Inc.

Contributions to earlier editions came from Beverly Beddow; Marcia J. Busching, Esq.; Paul Corrington; Harry L. Dickey; Diane Flanningan; Jerry Froment, Esq.; William Gray; Michael J. Klotzman; Stella Nightingale; Kim Schultz; Matthew E. Shannon, Esq.

ACKNOWLEDGEMENTS

# 1
# Real Estate Brokerage and Agency

Arizona law requires a person to obtain a real estate broker's license before offering real estate brokerage services and collecting commissions (ARS Section 32–2122). The owner of the brokerage business does not need to be licensed, however, as a licensed broker can be employed to manage the brokerage on the owner's behalf.

Arizona real estate licenses are granted and regulated by the Arizona Real Estate Commissioner under the provisions of the Arizona Real Estate Code (Arizona Revised Statutes, Title 32, Chapter 20). This law and the Commissioner's Rules (which have the same force and effect as law) also regulate and place restrictions on the activities of brokers and salespersons. Some of the provisions of both the Real Estate Code and the Rules were created to implement and enforce the law of agency in broker-client relationships. The specific provisions of these regulations are discussed in Chapter 10.

## THE BROKER AS AGENT

In many cases, the broker is the agent of the person who has contracted for the broker's services and agreed to pay for those services. However, compensation alone does not determine the existence of an agency relationship. In fact, an agency relationship can exist even if there is no fee involved (this is called a **gratuitous agency**). Whether an agency relationship has been created and who the agent represents are critical issues in the life of a real estate licensee. That is why it is so important for a licensee to understand the general principles of agency law and the specific agency requirements that Arizona law imposes on a licensee.

An agent is classified as either a **general agent** or a **special agent**, based on the extent of the authority granted. A general agent is authorized to represent a principal in all matters concerning one area of interest, such as the principal's business affairs. A special agent is authorized to represent a principal in one specific transaction or piece of business, such as the sale of a piece of real property. A real estate broker is typically a special agent.

A salesperson works for, and is associated with, his or her employing broker and can act only on the behalf of that broker. A salesperson cannot act as the agent of a buyer or seller (even though he or she may be incorrectly referred to as the "agent" of the broker's clients).

A broker who is employed by a property owner to market the owner's property is generally given authority to advertise the property, show the property to prospective purchasers and receive offers to purchase the property. The broker may not, however, accept or reject offers on behalf of the principal (here, the property owner) without written permission. The Commissioner's Rules require a broker to submit all offers promptly to the principal, regardless of their merit.

As an agent of the seller, the broker assumes a special legal responsibility to care for the seller's interests. There are five basic fiduciary duties involved in an agency relationship. First, the agent must exercise a reasonable degree of *care* while transacting business on behalf of the principal. The agent must be *obedient* to the principal; that means obeying all instructions, as long as they are both lawful and ethical and pertinent to their professional relationship. The agent must *account* for all money received from or on behalf of the seller, and must be *loyal* to the principal's interests above anyone else's—including the agent's own personal interest. Finally, the agent is obligated to *disclose* to the principal any material facts regarding the transaction. Together, these fiduciary duties may be remembered by the acronym COALD.

Historically, there has been a great deal of confusion on the part of many home buyers, who may believe that the real estate broker represents them, and not the home seller. This confusion stems from the personal, often fairly long-term relationship that develops between a home buyer and his or her real estate agent. As the broker or licensee shows the home buyer various properties and discusses his or her various needs and desires, the buyer (and, indeed, the agent as well) may begin to believe that the real estate agent is acting in the buyer's best interests. The buyer forgets, if he or she ever really understood, that in this situation the real estate agent represents the seller. (Note that if the agent's action causes a buyer to believe that an agency relationship exists between the agent and the buyer, such an agency relationship may be deemed to exist by a court of law. This type of inadvertent agency relationship adds to the real estate agent's dilemma.)

There are two common solutions to this dilemma; one is buyer brokerage, and the other is full and accurate agency disclosure.

**Buyer brokerage** has become increasingly common in Arizona. Buyer brokerage occurs when a real estate broker represents a property buyer. In the past few years, the concept of buyer brokerage has expanded from use primarily in nonresidential real estate markets to acceptance in the residential market. Potential buyers may employ their own brokers to obtain the best property on the most favorable terms.

Agents who represent buyers generally prefer to have "exclusive" agency agreements. That is, the buyer agrees to work exclusively with that particular agent, and that agent will be compensated if the buyer purchases a property, regardless of who helps the buyer find the property. The benefits of an exclusive buyer agency agreement are similar to the benefits of an exclusive listing agreement. The exclusiveness of the agreement gives the agent greater protection and encourages the agent to work harder on behalf of the buyer. The agent does not have to worry about the buyer changing his or her mind and working with someone else.

Buyer-agency agreements help eliminate the potential problems that can occur when the parties—the buyer, the seller, and the real estate agent—are unsure about who is representing whom. Given that an owner and potential buyer have conflicting interests, buyer brokerage will probably become even more widely used in residential transactions in the coming years.

**Full agency disclosure** is also used to avoid confusion over who is representing whom. Many states have adopted very specific requirements relative to agency disclosure. For these states, disclosures regarding whom the broker is representing are required to be in writing and signed or initialed by the buyer and seller. While Arizona does not currently require mandatory disclosure, a broker would be wise to implement an office policy of disclosure.

Both seller brokerage and buyer brokerage are types of **single agency**. That is, the broker is representing only one party to the transaction. However, in some circumstances, a broker may be a dual agent and represent both the buyer and the seller in the same transaction. **Dual agency** is sometimes intentional (the broker fully intends to represent both parties) and is sometimes unintentional (the broker's dual representation is caused by the broker's actions or words).

Arizona law states that a broker may not represent and receive a commission from both parties to a transaction unless both parties are informed and agree in writing to the arrangement. The broker's attorney should be consulted in such situations, however, as it is extremely difficult to fulfill the fiduciary obligations to both parties in a real estate transaction.

All real estate licensees should note that their responsibilities to both client and customer are defined in Rule R4–28–1101, "Duties to client," paragraph A, which reads:

> A licensee owes a fiduciary duty to his client and shall protect and promote the interests of the client. The licensee shall also fairly deal with all other parties to a transaction.

## Creating an Agency

Agencies are typically created by contract (an **express agency**). They may also be created by the actions of the parties (an **implied agency**). The seller-agency relationship is created between a broker and property seller through a written listing agreement, which employs the broker as the seller's agent. An agency may also be created by contract between a broker and a prospective purchaser, as previously described, or between a broker and property owner, through a management agreement.

The Arizona Statute of Frauds provides that a listing agreement (defined as an agreement authorizing a broker to sell real estate belonging to others) is unenforceable unless it is in writing and signed by the parties or their authorized representatives. This means that no legal action may be brought to enforce the agreement (usually, the payment of the broker's commission) unless the agreement is in writing and properly signed.

Arizona law also includes requirements for written listing agreements and their contents. These provisions are discussed in Chapter 2. Note that the scope of the broker's responsibility and authority as an agent is determined by both the specific provisions of the listing agreement and the Arizona Real Estate Code and the Commissioner's Rules. For example, the law provides that a broker cannot place a For Sale sign on an owner's property without the owner's written permission, which typically would be included as a provision of the listing agreement.

## Dealing with Customers

In dealing with customers (prospective purchasers or sellers, depending on the type of agency involved), the broker and his or her salesperson must fulfill their fiduciary obligations to their principal. He or she must also comply with Rule RA–28–1101, which requires every licensee to disclose all known material information to all the parties to a transaction, including any information about

- the fact that the seller may be unable to perform due to defects in his or her title,
- the fact that the buyer may be unable to perform due to insolvency or other financial problems,
- any material defects existing in any property being transferred and
- the possible existence of any lien or encumbrance on any property being transferred.

**Figure 1.1 The Agency Relationship**

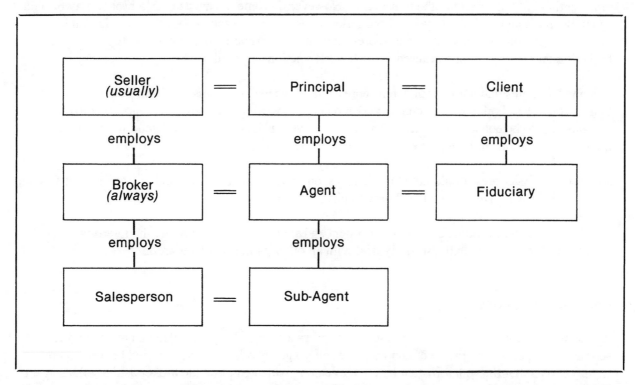

A real estate agent cannot avoid these disclosure duties by claiming that he or she did not know about the material information. All "known" material information, as mentioned in the rule, is really more of an objective standard. If a competent real estate agent should have known about a particular defect, all real estate agents will be held to that standard.

On the topic of disclosures, note that recent amendments to Arizona law provide that no action can be brought against a seller who fails to disclose that the property was the site of a homicide or other felony or was owned or occupied by an AIDS victim.

**Example:** The commissioner has determined that all real estate agents must disclose to prospective buyers whether property is located over a superfund site. Agent Brown fails to discover that a property his customer is interested in is located over contaminated groundwater. Agent Brown did not actually know about that material fact, but he was not relieved of the duty to disclose it. (All competent agents should know where superfund sites are.) If Agent Brown fails to disclose this fact and the customer buys the property, Agent Brown could be liable later for failure to disclose.

Note that while a broker representing a seller must disclose all material information he or she learns about a purchaser, the broker must not violate, or encourage the seller to violate, any federal or state fair housing laws.

While the broker must act fairly toward all the parties, certain confidential information obtained from a principal can be divulged only with the principal's permission. For example, a broker should never indicate to a prospective purchaser, without the principal's permission, that the principal might accept a lower price for the property or that there is an urgency to sell.

In dealing with customers, the broker must also remember that he or she is liable for any false statements, misrepresentations of fact, or omissions of material fact, especially if such statements result

**Figure 1.2 The Broker's Compensation**

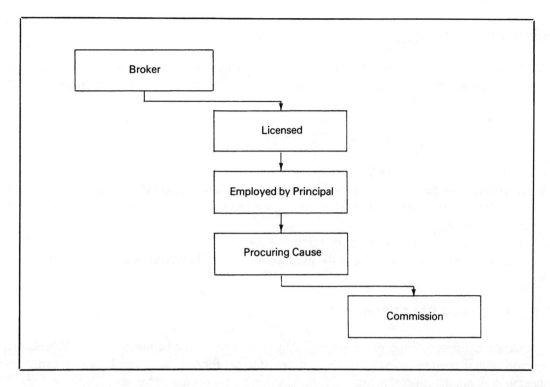

in damage to a customer who relied upon them. The broker may also be held liable for such statements made by his or her salesperson if the broker had knowledge of the salesperson's actions or if the broker had reason to believe, based on the salesperson's past history, that the salesperson might make such statements.

## The Broker's Compensation

The broker's commission, usually a specified percentage of the final sales price, is one of the main terms of the listing agreement. The amount or exact percentage that the broker will receive is a matter to be negotiated between the listing broker and seller in each transaction.

The broker is entitled to payment for his or her services upon fulfilling the terms of the employment contract. Generally, when a broker procures a qualified buyer who is "ready, willing and able" to purchase on the seller's terms as set forth in the listing agreement (often referred to as a "mirror image" offer), the broker has earned a commission, whether or not the sale is actually consummated. The broker cannot force the seller to accept the buyer and complete the sale, but when the broker has produced a buyer who meets the requirements set forth in the listing agreement, he or she has acquired a legal claim to the agreed-upon commission.

Some listing agreements condition the broker's right to payment upon the actual close of the sale. In other words, the listing agreement states that the commission is due and payable upon the closing of the transaction or is to be paid from the proceeds of the closing. This condition means that the broker is entitled to payment only if the sale actually occurs.

Whenever there is a question over the broker's right to a commission, the final answer will be determined by the courts. Generally, the broker will be able to collect the commission if it can be proven that he or she was properly licensed, had a valid written employment agreement and had, in fact, procured a "ready, willing and able" buyer or located the property he or she was hired to locate under the terms of a buyer agency agreement.

## Termination of Agency

A broker's employment as an agent may be terminated in a number of ways. With the exception of an agency coupled with an interest, agency may be terminated for any of the following reasons:

1. The death or incapacity of either party (a notice of death is not required)
2. The destruction or condemnation of the property
3. The expiration of the agency term
4. Mutual agreement to terminate the agency
5. Revocation by the principal or renunciation by the agent (note that the party who is terminating the relationship is not relieved of the obligation to pay a commission or fulfill any other contractual obligations)
6. The bankruptcy of the principal or agent
7. The completion or fulfillment of the purpose for which the agency was created

## THE REAL ESTATE SALESPERSON

In Arizona, a real estate salesperson is employed by or on behalf of a licensed real estate broker. A salesperson cannot operate unless he or she is licensed to act for one particular broker. Furthermore, a salesperson may not accept compensation from any person except his or her employing broker  (ARS Section 32–2155). If a salesperson goes on to acquire a broker's license, he or she may then set up his or her own brokerage. Alternatively, a broker may also become an **associate broker**. An associate broker is affiliated with a broker, just as a salesperson is, and cannot act directly for a principal or hire affiliated salespeople.

All listings, advertisements, statements and other actions of a salesperson (or associate broker) are performed in the employing broker's name. The broker is responsible for the activities of his or her salespeople and for their impact on clients and customers. In fact, the broker is explicitly given the responsibility of supervising his or her salesperson's actions.

The issue of whether a real estate salesperson (or associate broker) is an employee or an independent contractor is determined by a strict interpretation of the law. According to the Internal Revenue Code, a licensee may be an independent contractor under a written contract with the employing broker. Under such an arrangement, the licensee is responsible for all of his or her income and payroll taxes, and the broker cannot provide employee benefits (such as health insurance coverage, paid vacations or company cars) or directly or indirectly control the activities of the licensee. (The Internal Revenue Service has a history of successful prosecution of brokers who have provided employee benefits while claiming that their associates were independent contractors.) Brokers should have their associates sign independent contractor agreements to avoid the potential tax liabilities they would incur if their licensees were determined to be employees by the IRS.

The Arizona Department of Real Estate takes a different approach to the employee/independent contractor issue. According to the department, an employer-employee relationship always exists between the broker and his or her affiliated licensees regarding the activities undertaken and the statements made by those licensees. This is due to the professional liability that is incurred when a broker hires a salesperson to act on his or her behalf. Should a licensee act inappropriately or illegally when representing the employing broker, that broker could be held liable for failing to properly supervise the licensee.

Thus, a licensee can be both an employee and an independent contractor at the same time. Both the IRS and the Arizona Department of Real Estate agree that the status of a licensee for purposes of taxation is unaffected by the status of the licensee for purposes of professional liability.

## QUESTIONS

1. In Arizona, a salesperson can represent a

   a. broker.
   b. principal.
   c. fiduciary.
   d. customer.

2. Typically, a broker has earned a commission when the

   a. seller signs the listing contract.
   b. buyer makes any offer for the property.
   c. seller accepts any offer for the property.
   d. transaction closes escrow.

3. In Arizona, for a broker to establish a claim for commission, he or she must first show

   a. proof of employment and that he or she was properly licensed.
   b. that he or she was the procuring cause and had a valid written employment agreement.
   c. proof that he or she was properly licensed and the procuring cause of the sale.
   d. that he or she was the procuring cause, had a valid written employment agreement and was properly licensed.

4. A real estate salesperson may

   a. accept a commission directly from the principal.
   b. be employed by two brokers at the same time.
   c. enter the brokerage business on his or her own.
   d. solicit listings on behalf of his or her broker.

5. The amount of commission to be charged by a broker is determined by

   a. local custom.
   b. the multiple-listing service.
   c. the Department of Real Estate.
   d. negotiation.

6. A person who is responsible for the results of his or her work using his or her own methods, but is not subject to the control of another, is a/an

   a. employee.
   b. independent contractor.
   c. fiduciary.
   d. principal.

7. Arizona law requires a licensee to disclose material defects in a property to

   a. the buyer only.
   b. the seller only.
   c. all parties to a transaction.
   d. his or her broker only.

8. Salesperson *E* acted in an unethical manner in successfully completing a large sale. His broker, *M,*

   a. may be liable for a failure to supervise.
   b. is not liable if he had no knowledge of *E's* actions.
   c. should ignore the problem.
   d. should immediately suspend *E's* license.

9. Broker *W* was employed by the sellers to market their home. Because of her agency relationship with the sellers, *W* may perform all of the following functions *except*

    a. receive offers to purchase the property.
    b. show the property to potential purchasers.
    c. accept or reject offers on behalf of the sellers.
    d. employ an advertising agency to write her ad copy.

10. Broker *T* had an oral agreement with the *L*s to market their property. After *T* sold the property, he asked the *L*s for his 6 percent commission, which they refused to pay. Which of the following statements is true?

    a. *T* can sue the *L*s for not paying his commission.
    b. *T* can place a lien on the *L*s property for the amount of the commission.
    c. *T* will receive the customary amount of commission for his market area.
    d. *T* has no valid claim for a commission.

# 2
# Listing Agreements

## THE LISTING AGREEMENT

Arizona law imposes several requirements for listing agreements. For instance, no legal action may be brought to enforce a listing agreement unless that agreement or a memorandum of it is in writing and signed by the parties or their representatives (ARS Section 44–101). In other words, to be enforceable, a listing agreement must be in writing and signed by the parties. In addition, all listing agreements must include beginning and ending dates.

If the amount or percentage of compensation to be paid to the broker is not specifically stated in the agreement, the broker is not entitled to a commission even though he or she may fulfill the terms of the agreement. When the commission amount is not stated in the listing, the property owner may choose to pay the broker's commission, but the broker cannot force the seller to pay through a court action. In a lawsuit for commission, the courts will not supply such a vital contract term for a deficient listing agreement.

While most listings are obtained by salespeople, it is the broker who "owns" the listings and who is obligated to use his or her best efforts to find a buyer for the listed real estate. Therefore, brokers must review and approve every listing taken by their personnel within five days of the date the listing was taken. As evidence of his or her approval, the broker must initial and date the agreement. This duty to review listing agreements may be delegated to a branch manager, provided the delegation is in writing.

Note that a listing agreement is a contract for the broker's personal services. As such, it may not be assigned to another broker without the express written consent of the principal. However, the terms of many multiple-listing-service forms expressly authorize the broker to submit the listing to the multiple-listing service so that other brokers and their salespeople can find buyers for the listed property.

### Types of Listings

Arizona brokers may use open (nonexclusive), exclusive agency or exclusive right to sell listings. Net listings are also legal. In a *net listing*, the seller agrees to receive a predetermined net amount of money from a sale. The listing broker keeps any amount above the seller's net as his or her commission. Net listings are used only when the seller insists that he or she wants to receive a stipulated amount for the listed property.

Standard printed forms are available for both nonexclusive and exclusive listings (including multiple-listing-service forms). The state does not require the use of any particular form. However, multiple-listing services are not obligated to accept open listings.

## Problems Involving Listing Agreements

Difficulties can arise in situations where an owner gives one or more open, or nonexclusive, listings for a property and then gives an exclusive listing for the same property to another broker. Giving an exclusive listing to a broker does not cancel or terminate any nonexclusive listings given to other brokers for the same property. If the property is sold by a broker who has a nonexclusive listing, the owner will be obligated to pay a full commission both to the selling broker and to the broker who held the exclusive listing for the property.

A broker must try to avoid situations in which the principal may be liable for two full commissions. If a broker who has obtained an exclusive listing learns that the principal has previously given a nonexclusive listing for the property to another broker, the exclusive broker must advise the principal to cancel the nonexclusive listing.

Many listing agreement forms used in Arizona include a **broker protection** clause (sometimes called a 90-day clause). This clause provides that the owner will pay the broker a commission if, within a specified number of days after the listing expires, the owner sells or otherwise transfers an interest to a buyer whom the owner originally met or made contact with through the broker or his or her salesperson. The specified period is negotiable between the parties. Ninety days is a common time period.

The purpose of the broker protection clause is to protect a broker who shows a property to a prospective buyer during the listing term, only to have the parties enter into an agreement and complete the transaction after the listing has expired. The courts generally rule that a broker protection clause gives the broker the right to a commission from a transaction that is entered into after the listing term expires if it can be proven that the broker put the purchaser in touch with the seller during the listing term, and the purchaser consummated a transaction within the protection period.

A broker protection clause can create situations in which an owner becomes liable for paying a commission to two separate brokers. This can occur if the seller immediately relists the property with another broker and that broker finds a buyer within the original broker's protection period. Therefore, many exclusive right to sell listings include a provision that nullifies the broker protection clause if the owner enters an exclusive right to sell listing agreement with another broker during the protection period.

## Listing Forms

Arizona does not mandate the use of state-drafted forms as some states do, so theoretically brokers may draft their own listing contract forms. However, most brokers belong to a multiple-listing service and use that service's forms. In this way, a broker's listing agreements will automatically be acceptable to the multiple-listing service. Furthermore, these standard forms generally address all the potentially troublesome situations that regularly occur in real estate listing transactions. License applicants should study the forms reproduced in this book to familiarize themselves with their provisions.

The largest multiple-listing service in Arizona is the Arizona Regional Multiple Listing Service or ARMLS. ARMLS operates in central Arizona, primarily in the Maricopa County market (which includes Phoenix and its surrounding cities). The ARMLS listing form is divided into two parts (Figure 2.1). The first part of the form is the employment agreement between the broker and the seller. It specifies the rights and obligations of the parties and sets forth the terms of the broker's employment, including the commission to be paid, the listed price of the property, the expiration date of the contract and other pertinent contractual information. There is a statement printed above the signature lines that concerns the determination of the broker's commission—it emphasizes that the commission in any transaction is determined by the broker and the seller, and it cannot be set by a multiple-listing service or an association or Board of REALTORS®.

The second part of the form allows data on the listed property to be entered easily into the multiple-listing-service computer system. This information is then available to other brokers who belong to the service and is used to help the listing broker market the property. These data assist other brokers in developing a mental picture of the property and are helpful when a licensee is looking for a property with specific features. A licensee can search the computer's data banks to obtain complete details of all the listed properties that meet the prospective buyer's criteria.

Another type of exclusive-right-to-sell listing contract is that used by the Tucson Association of REALTORS® Multiple Listing Service (TARMLS) (Figure 2.2). TARMLS operates in southern Arizona, primarily in the Pima County market, which serves Tucson. Note that many of the provisions of each contract, although worded differently, have the same effect. Other types of listing contracts are also available, including an open listing contract (Figure 2.3).

## Taking the Listing

When taking a listing, the licensee should obtain as much information as possible about the property. Not only will this help the licensee market the property, it will also minimize the problems that might occur once a sales contract has been entered into and the contract placed into escrow.

Information about the items in the following list should be gathered when a listing is taken. This list is by no means exhaustive, so the licensee should obtain additional instructions from his or her broker before listing a property.

1. The name(s) and address(es) of the owner(s)
2. The street address and legal description of the property (as well as the tax parcel number, when required by the broker or the multiple-listing service)
3. The size (square footage) of the improvements
4. The age of the improvements and type of construction
5. The number and dimensions of the rooms
6. The size and dimensions of the lot
7. Information on any existing financing, including the name and address of the lender, the type of loan, the loan balance, the interest rate, the total monthly payment, whether the payment includes property tax and insurance impounds, whether the loan may be assumed by a buyer and under what circumstances, and whether the loan may be prepaid without penalty
8. The possibility of seller financing
9. The amount of any outstanding special assessments and whether they will be paid by the sellers or assumed by the buyers
10. The zoning classification of the property
11. The current (or most recent) year's property taxes

12. Information concerning the neighborhood (schools, parks and recreational facilities, transportation)
13. The proposed date of possession for the buyers
14. Any real property to be removed from the premises by the sellers and any personal property to be included in the sale (both the listing and the subsequent purchase contract should be explicit on these points)
15. Any special features that make the property more appealing and marketable

It is worth mentioning that a substantial percentage of buyer complaints are related to inaccurate information in the listing agreement. Real estate agents should stress to the seller the importance of providing accurate information about the condition of the property.

All licensees must deliver a copy of the listing agreement to the sellers immediately after it is signed by all parties.

After the listing agreement has been entered into, the licensee should check the county records for any existing mortgages, deeds of trust or agreements of sale to verify the information given by the sellers. This information may also be obtained through a preliminary title report from a title insurance company. When the sellers are unsure of the information they give or are not aware of certain factors that might affect the marketability of the property, the licensee must obtain and verify the required data, including whether a survey exists, whether there are any deed restrictions or zoning limitations affecting the property, and the actual distances to local schools and shopping areas.

## SELLING AND ADVERTISING

Arizona law sets forth definite guidelines regarding advertising and other promotional practices that may be used by brokers and salespeople in their businesses. Generally, a licensee cannot solicit, sell or offer to sell any real property by offering free lots or by conducting lotteries or contests in order to influence a purchaser or prospective purchaser of the property being marketed. (NOTE: some drawings or contests may be used in the sale of subdivision properties.)

Any offer of a "free" gift or item made in connection with a sales promotion must be without conditions. Furthermore, any gift or item offered (even if not labeled "free") must be clearly described, including the approximate retail value, and any costs or conditions associated with the receipt of the item must be clearly disclosed before anyone participates in the offer. Any offer of reduced-price or free travel, accommodations, meals or entertainment cannot be described as "awards" or "prizes" or by similar phrases; and any costs, limitations or restriction must be fully disclosed.

A licensee cannot advertise a property or offer it for sale or lease without the written permission of the owner or the owner's representative. In addition, a licensee may place a sign on the property offering it for sale, rent, lease or exchange only with the written consent of the owner. Any sign so placed must be removed immediately upon the owner's request.

A licensee cannot advertise in a manner that indicates that the offer is being made by an individual who is not engaged in the real estate business. This type of advertisement is referred to as a "blind ad," and it is misleading and deceptive to the public. Advertisements that give only a post office box number, street address or telephone number are also prohibited.

## Figure 2.1 Exclusive Right to Sell (Page 1 of 5)

Type **ER**     **EXCLUSIVE RIGHT TO SELL/RENT**     Legal I.D. **196460**
(LISTING CONTRACT LEGAL LANGUAGE)

THIS IS INTENDED TO BE A LEGALLY BINDING CONTRACT. NO REPRESENTATION IS MADE AS TO THE LEGAL VALIDITY OR ADEQUACY OF ANY PROVISION OR THE TAX CONSEQUENCES THEREOF. IF YOU DESIRE LEGAL OR TAX ADVICE, CONSULT YOUR ATTORNEY OR TAX ADVISOR.

1. **EXCLUSIVE RIGHT TO SELL AND RENT.** In consideration of the acceptance by the undersigned licensed Arizona real estate broker ("Broker") of the terms of this Listing Contract ("Listing") and Broker's promise to endeavor to effect a ☐ sale or rental   ☐ sale   ☐ rental of the property described below ("Property"), I or we, as owner(s) ("Owner"), employ and grant Broker the exclusive and irrevocable right commencing on _____ , 19____ , and expiring at 11:59 p.m. _____ , 19____ , to sell, rent, exchange, or option the Property described in Paragraph 2.

2. **THE PROPERTY.** For purposes of this Listing, the "Property" means the real property in _____ County, Arizona described below, plus all fixtures and improvements thereon, all appurtenances incident thereto and all personal property described in Paragraphs 4 and 9.

    Street Address _____ City/Town _____

    Legal Description _____

3. **PRICE.** The listing price shall be:   Sale: $ _____

    Rental: $ _____ per month, plus all applicable lease or rental (transaction privilege) taxes to be paid as described in the Owner's Profile Sheet ("Data Entry Form"), or such other price and terms as are accepted by Owner.

4. **FIXTURES AND PERSONAL PROPERTY.** The Property includes personal property and excludes leased equipment as described in the Data Entry Form. Except as provided in the Data Entry Form, the Property also includes all of the following existing fixtures or personal property: storage sheds; heating and cooling equipment; built-in appliances; attached light fixtures and ceiling fans; window and door screens; sun screens; storm windows and doors; towel, curtain and drapery rods; draperies and other window coverings; attached carpeting; attached fireplace equipment; pool and spa equipment (including any mechanical or other cleaning systems); garage door openers and controls; attached TV antennas (excluding satellite dishes); attached plant watering, fire suppression and misting systems; water treatment systems; smoke detectors and fire warning systems; security systems and fences.

5. **ACCESS AND LOCKBOX.** Owner ☐ does   ☐ does not authorize Broker to install and use, on the Property, a lockbox containing a key to the Property. Owner acknowledges that a lockbox and any other keys left with or available to Broker will permit access to the Property by Broker or any other broker, with or without potential purchasers or tenants ("Prospects"), even when Owner and occupant are absent. If the Property is occupied by someone other than Owner, Owner will provide to Broker the occupant's written permission for the installation of the lockbox and the publication and dissemination of the occupant's name and telephone number. Owner acknowledges that neither the Arizona Regional Multiple Listing Service ("ARMLS"), nor any Board or Association of REALTORS®, nor any broker, is insuring Owner or occupant against theft, loss or vandalism resulting from any such access. Owner is responsible for obtaining appropriate insurance.

6. **AGENCY RELATIONSHIPS.**
    a. Owner understands that Broker is Owner's agent with respect to this Listing. Owner understands that a Prospect may also wish to be represented by Broker in connection with the purchase or rental of the Property. In that event, Broker would be serving as the agent for both Owner and the Prospect. Since Owner does not wish to limit the range of Prospects at this time, Owner agrees to work with Broker to resolve any potential agency conflicts that may arise.
    b. Owner initially authorizes Broker to cooperate with other brokers ☐ in any manner whatsoever   ☐ as subagents only   ☐ without offering subagency . This election does not relieve Broker of his obligation to present all offers except as provided in Paragraph 28.

7. **COMPENSATION TO BROKER.** Owner agrees to compensate Broker as follows:
    a. **RETAINER.** Broker acknowledges receipt of a non-refundable retainer fee of _____ payable to Broker for initial consultation, research and other services.
    b. **COMMISSIONS.** If Broker produces a ready, willing and able purchaser or tenant in accordance with this Listing, or if a sale, rental, option or exchange of the Property is made by Owner or through any other agent, or otherwise, during the term of this exclusive listing, for services rendered, Owner agrees to pay Broker a commission of

    | Sale: | Rental: |
    |---|---|

    With respect to any holdovers or renewals of rental, regardless of whether this Listing has expired, Owner agrees to pay a commission of _____ .The amount of the sale or rental commission shall be due and payable to Broker if, without the consent of Broker, the Property is withdrawn from this Listing, otherwise withdrawn from sale or rental or rented, transferred, or conveyed by Owner.

    c. **PURCHASE BY TENANT.** If during the terms of any rental of the Property, including any renewals or holdovers, or within _____ days after its termination, any tenant, or his heirs, executors, or assigns shall buy the Property from Owner, the sale commission described in Paragraph 7(b) shall be deemed earned by and payable to Broker.

    d. **AFTER EXPIRATION.** After the expiration of this Listing, the same commissions, as appropriate, shall be payable if a sale, rental, exchange, or option is made by Owner to any person to whom the Property has been shown or with whom Owner or any broker has negotiated concerning the Property during the term of this Listing (1) within _____ days after the expiration of this Listing, unless the Property has been listed on an exclusive basis with another broker, or (2) during the pendency, including the closing, of any purchase contract or escrow relating to the Property that was executed or opened during the term of this Listing, or (3) as contemplated by Paragraph 7(c).

    e. **FAILURE TO COMPLETE.** If completion of a sale or rental is prevented by default of Owner, or with the consent of Owner, the entire sale or rental commission, as appropriate, shall be paid to Broker by Owner. If any earnest deposit is forfeited for any other reason, Owner shall pay a brokerage fee equal to the lesser of one-half of the earnest deposit or the full amount of the commission.

    f. **PAYMENT FROM ESCROW OR RENT.** Owner instructs the escrow company, if any, to pay all such compensation to Broker in cash as a condition to closing or upon cancellation of the escrow, and to the extent necessary, irrevocably assigns to Broker all money payable to Owner at the closing or cancellation of the escrow. Broker is authorized to deduct compensation from any rent or other monies received on behalf of Owner.

    g. **OTHER BROKERS.** Owner authorizes Broker to divide all such compensation with other brokers in any manner acceptable to Broker.

    h. **NO LIMITATION.** Nothing in this Listing shall be construed as limiting applicable provisions of law relating to when commissions are earned or payable.

8. **HOME PROTECTION PLAN.** Owner acknowledges that home protection plans are available and that such plans may provide additional protection and benefits to Owner and any purchaser of the Property. Owner ☐ does   ☐ does not agree to provide at his expense a home protection plan for the purchaser that will be effective at the close of escrow.

9. **ADDITIONAL TERMS.** _____

10. THE TERMS AND CONDITIONS ON THE REVERSE SIDE HEREOF PLUS ALL INFORMATION ON THE DATA ENTRY FORM ARE INCORPORATED HEREIN BY REFERENCE. COMMISSIONS PAYABLE FOR THE SALE, RENTAL OR MANAGEMENT OF PROPERTY ARE NOT SET BY ANY BOARD OR ASSOCIATION OF REALTORS' OR MULTIPLE LISTING SERVICE OR IN ANY MANNER OTHER THAN BY NEGOTIATION BETWEEN THE BROKER AND THE CLIENT. BY SIGNING BELOW, OWNER ACKNOWLEDGES THAT HE HAS READ, UNDERSTANDS AND ACCEPTS ALL TERMS AND PROVISIONS CONTAINED HEREIN AND THAT HE HAS RECEIVED A COPY OF THIS LISTING.

    Print Name of Owner _____    Print Name of Owner _____

    Street _____    City/Town _____ State ____ Zip ____

    Phone _____    Fax Phone _____

11. Owner's Signature _____ Mo/Da/Yr    Owner's Signature _____ Mo/Da/Yr

    In consideration of Owner's representations and promises in this Listing, Broker agrees to endeavor to effect a sale, rental, exchange, or option in accordance with this Listing and further agrees to provide this Listing for publication by a local Board or Association of REALTORS' and dissemination to the users of ARMLS.

    Firm Name (Broker) _____    Office Phone _____

    By: _____    Fax Phone _____
        Agent's Signature    Date

    Copyright February 1993 by Arizona Regional Multiple Listing Service, Inc.     For Use with Data Entry Forms 1, 2, 3.

    For Broker's office use only:

    Broker's File/Lot No.: _____ Manager's Initials: _____ Broker's Initials: _____ Date: _____

    **BROKER**

# Figure 2.1 Exclusive Right to Sell (Page 2 of 5)

12. **MULTIPLE LISTING SERVICE.** A Multiple Listing Service is a means by which authorized participants make blanket unilateral offers of cooperation and compensation to other participants. Broker is a member of a local Board or Association of REALTORS®, which is a shareholder or client of ARMLS. The information on the Data Entry Form will be provided to ARMLS to be published and disseminated to its users even after the cancellation or expiration of this Listing. Broker is authorized to report the sale, exchange, option or rental of the Property, and its price, terms and financing, to a local Board or Association of REALTORS® for dissemination to authorized ARMLS users and to the public and for use by authorized ARMLS users.

13. **ROLE OF BROKER.** Owner acknowledges that Broker is not responsible for the custody or condition of the Property or for its management, maintenance, upkeep or repair.

14. **TITLE.** If there is a sale of the Property, Owner agrees to furnish marketable title by warranty deed and an Owner's policy of title insurance in the full amount of the purchase price.

15. **DOCUMENTS.** In connection with any sale or rental of the Property, Owner consents to the use of the standard form of purchase or rental contract used by Broker and all other standard documents used by the escrow and title companies.

16. **COOPERATION BY OWNER.** Owner agrees to make available to Broker and Prospects all data, records and documents pertaining to the Property. Owner authorizes Broker, and any other broker authorized by Broker, to preview and show the Property at reasonable times and upon reasonable notice and agrees to commit no act which might tend to obstruct Broker's performance hereunder. If the Property is occupied by someone other than Owner, Owner will provide to Broker the occupant's written consent to cooperate in connection with the showing of the Property. Owner shall not deal directly with any Prospect or other broker during the term of this Listing and shall refer all Prospects and other brokers to Broker during the term hereof.

17. **SIGN.** Broker is authorized to place Broker's appropriate signs on the Property until the later of any close of escrow by a purchaser or occupancy by a tenant.

18. **GENERAL WARRANTIES BY OWNER.** Owner represents and warrants:

    a. **CAPACITY.** Owner has the legal capacity, full power and authority to enter into this Listing and consummate the transactions contemplated hereby on his own behalf or on behalf of the party he represents, as appropriate.

    b. **ADVERSE INFORMATION.** Owner will disclose to any Prospect and Broker all material facts known to him concerning adverse conditions or latent defects in, or affecting the Property.

    c. **CORRECT INFORMATION.** All information concerning the Property in this Listing, including the Data Entry Form relating to the Property, or otherwise provided by Owner to Broker or to any Prospect is, or will be at the time provided, and shall be at close of escrow or occupancy by a tenant, true, correct and complete. Owner agrees to notify Broker promptly if there is any material change in such information until the latest to occur of the expiration of this Listing, any close of escrow or occupancy by a tenant.

19. **WARRANTIES BY OWNER ON THE SALE OF THE PROPERTY.** Owner represents and warrants:

    a. **CONDITION OF PROPERTY.** Except as otherwise provided in this Listing, Owner warrants that, at the earlier of possession by a purchaser or the close of escrow: the roof will have no known leaks; all heating, cooling, mechanical, plumbing, watering and electrical systems and built-in appliances will be in working condition; if the Property has a swimming pool and/or spa, the pool and/or spa will be clean and in proper chemical balance and the motors, filter systems, cleaning systems and heaters, if so equipped, will be in working condition; and the Property shall otherwise be in substantially the same condition as on the effective date of this Listing. Owner agrees to maintain and repair the Property, as necessary, to fulfill the warranties described in this Paragraph 19(a). Prior to the close of escrow, Owner shall grant the purchaser or purchaser's representatives reasonable access to enter and inspect the Property for the purpose of satisfying purchaser that the Property is as warranted by Owner.

    b. **PAYMENTS FOR IMPROVEMENTS.** Prior to the close of escrow, payment in full will have been made for all labor, professional services, materials, machinery, fixtures or tools furnished within the 120 days immediately preceding the close of escrow in connection with the construction, alteration or repair of any structure on or improvement to the Property.

    c. **SANITATION SYSTEM.** The information in this Listing, if any, regarding connection to a public sewer system, septic tank or other sanitation system is correct.

    d. **AVAILABILITY OF UTILITIES.** Owner is obligated to deliver all utility service equipment and appliance hook-ups in a condition that will enable the purchaser to connect all utility services that are available on the effective date of this Listing without repairs or additional improvement expense.

    e. **WOOD INFESTATION REPORT.** Owner will, at his expense, place in escrow a wood infestation report by a qualified, licensed pest control operator, which, when considered in its entirety, indicates that all residences and buildings attached to the Property are free from evidence of current infestation and damage from wood destroying pests or organisms. Owner agrees to pay up to one percent of the purchase price for the extermination of such pests and organisms, the treatment of the Property, the repair of the damages caused by infestation and the correction of any conditions conducive to infestation. If such costs exceed one percent of the purchase price, (1) the purchaser may elect to cancel the sale unless Owner agrees in writing to pay all of such costs, and (2) Owner may elect to cancel the sale unless the purchaser agrees in writing to accept the Property together with the one percent that the Owner has agreed to pay.

    f. **TRANSFER OF WATER.** Owner agrees to execute, acknowledge and deliver, or cause to be executed, acknowledged and delivered, such additional documents and instruments, including without limitation, any deeds, assignments, grants or conveyances of water rights, use rights, vested rights, licenses, easements, or rights of way necessary for the purchaser to acquire the rights to use any water rights and any wells which serve or are located on the Property (subject to the interests of persons other than the Owner, which interests shall be disclosed to the purchaser) as well as all easements, licenses or rights of way which may be necessary or convenient for the use of such water rights or wells.

20. **RELIEF OF LIABILITY.** Broker is hereby relieved of any and all liability and responsibility for everything stated in Paragraphs 18 and 19.

21. **INDEMNIFICATION.** Owner agrees to indemnify and hold Broker, all Boards or Associations of REALTORS®, ARMLS and all other brokers harmless against any and all claims, liability, damage or loss arising from any misrepresentation or breach of warranty by Owner in this Listing, any incorrect information supplied by Owner and any facts concerning the Property not disclosed by Owner, including without limitation, any facts known to Owner relating to adverse conditions or latent defects.

22. **OTHER OWNERS AND PROSPECTS.** Owner understands that other owners may make offers to sell or rent or may sell, rent, exchange or option properties similar to the Property through Broker. Owner consents to any agency representation by Broker of such other owners before, during and after the expiration of this Listing and understands that the Property probably will not be presented or shown to every Prospect encountered by Broker.

23. **ATTORNEYS' FEES.** In any action or proceeding to enforce any provision of this Listing, or for damages sustained by reason of its breach, the prevailing party shall be entitled to receive from the other party reasonable attorneys' fees, as set by the court or arbitrator and not by a jury, and all other related expenses, such as expert witness fees, fees paid to investigators and court costs. Additionally, if any Broker reasonably hires an attorney to enforce the collection of any commission payable pursuant to this Listing, and is successful in collecting some or all of such commission without commencing any action or proceeding, Owner agrees to pay such Broker's reasonable attorneys' fees and costs and Owner also agrees to pay interest at the legal rate on all compensation and other amounts owed or due to Broker from the time due until paid in full.

24. **DEPOSITS.** Owner authorizes Broker to accept earnest deposits on behalf of Owner and to issue receipts for such earnest deposits.

25. **DISPUTE RESOLUTION.** If such system is reasonably available to the parties, Owner agrees to request from the purchaser or tenant of the Property written confirmation that any dispute or claim arising from or relating to the purchase or rental contract, the breach of the purchase or rental contract or services provided in relation to the purchase or rental contract shall be submitted to mediation in accordance with the Rules and Procedures of the REALTORS® Homesellers/Homebuyers Dispute Resolution System. Subject to certain exclusions, disputes subject to mediation shall include, in part, representations made by Owner, purchaser, tenant, or any broker or other person or entity in connection with the sale, rental, purchase, financing or condition or any other aspect of the Property, including without limitation any allegation of concealment, misrepresentation, negligence or fraud. If the purchaser or tenant of the Property consents to mediation, Owner agrees to submit disputes as described in such Rules and Procedures to mediation.

26. **RECOMMENDATIONS.** If any broker recommends a builder, contractor, escrow company, title company, pest control service, appraiser, lender, home inspection company, home warranty company or any other person or entity to Owner for any purpose, such recommendation shall be independently investigated and evaluated by Owner, who hereby acknowledges that any decision to enter into any contractual arrangement with any such person or entity recommended by any broker will be based solely upon such independent investigation and evaluation. Owner understands that said contractual arrangement may result in a commission or fee to a broker.

27. **FIRPTA.** If applicable, Owner agrees to complete, sign and deliver to escrow company a certificate indicating whether Owner is a foreign person or non-resident alien pursuant to the Foreign Investment in Real Property Tax Act of 1980 (FIRPTA).

28. **SUBSEQUENT OFFER.** Once there is a fully executed rental contract with respect to the Property, Owner waives his right to receive any subsequent rental offers with respect to the Property until after forfeiture by the offeror or other nullification of the rental contract. Once there is a fully executed purchase contract with respect to the Property, Owner waives his right to receive any subsequent purchase or rental offers with respect to the Property until after forfeiture by the offeror or other nullification of the purchase contract.

29. **EQUAL HOUSING OPPORTUNITY.** Properties will be presented in compliance with federal, state and local fair housing laws and regulations.

30. **TIME OF ESSENCE.** Time is of the essence in the performance of the obligations contained in this Listing.

31. **COUNTERPARTS AND FACSIMILE.** This Listing may be executed in any number of counterparts by the parties hereto. All counterparts so executed shall constitute one Listing binding upon all parties hereto, notwithstanding that all parties do not sign the same counterpart. A facsimile copy of the entire Listing which indicates that the Listing was fully executed shall be treated as an original Listing.

32. **CONSTRUCTION OF LANGUAGE AND GOVERNING LAW.** The language of this Listing shall be construed according to its fair meaning and not strictly for or against either party. Words used in the masculine, feminine or neuter shall apply to either gender or the neuter, as appropriate. All singular and plural words shall be interpreted to refer to the number consistent with circumstances and context. The headings or captions of paragraphs in this Listing are for convenience and reference only and do not define, limit or describe the scope or intent of this Listing or the provisions of such paragraphs. If this Listing is used for a rental, exchange, or option instead of a sale of the Property, all language in this Listing relating to the sale of property shall be construed to apply as appropriate, to a rental, exchange or option. For example, Owner shall be deemed to be Exchanger, Optionor, or Landlord respectively. This Listing shall be governed by the laws of the State of Arizona.

33. **TAX LIABILITY.** Landlord acknowledges that his rental property may be subject to a sales tax on gross receipts and a special rental classification for property taxes. Landlord agrees to obtain appropriate licenses and pay fees and taxes when due. Landlord agrees to indemnify and hold Broker harmless for any such tax liability, including penalties and interest.

34. **ENTIRE AGREEMENT.** This Listing, the Data Entry Sheet and any attached exhibits and any addenda or supplements signed by the parties, shall constitute the entire agreement between Owner and Broker and supersede any other written or oral agreements between Owner and Broker. This Listing can be modified only by a writing signed by Owner and Broker.

# Figure 2.1 Exclusive Right to Sell (Page 3 of 5)

**ARIZONA REGIONAL MULTIPLE LISTING SERVICE, INC.**
**RESIDENTIAL PROFILE SHEET (CLASS 1)**
PAGE 1 OF 3

REALTOR®

R Denotes Required Entries for Adding a Listing

R**AREA** — Area  R**GRID** — Map Code/Grid  R**TYPE** — Type of Listing (ER/EA)

R**HSN** — House Number  R**CP** — Compass Pt  R**STR** — Street Name  R**SC** — (ST/RD/LN/ETC) (See User Sheet)  **UN** — Unit Number

R**BL** — Hundred Block  R**BC** — N/S/E/W  R**CT** — City/Town Code (See User Sheet)  R**ZP** — Zip Code Prefix  **Z4** — Zip Code + 4  R**COU** — County Code  **BU** — Building Number

R**BK** — Assessor's Book Number  R**MA** — Assessor's Map Number  R**PN** — Parcel Number  **PL** — Parcel Letter  **TWN** — Township  **RNG** — Range  **SCT** — Section  **MPG** — WWMAP Page  **MPX** — WWMAP Top Coordinate  **MPY** — WWMAP Side Coordinate

R**SBD** — Subdivision Name/Balance of Legal (or Metes & Bounds)

**LT** — Lot Number  **BOOK_PG** — County Record Book & Page #  **CTRCT** — Census Tract  **GLAT** — Geo Sync Latitude  **GLNG** — Geo Sync Longitude

R**BR** — Bedrooms (Studio=0)  R**BATHS** — Bathrooms  **SQ** — Approx. Square Feet  R**SS** — Source of Square Footage  T=County Assessor / A=Appraiser / M=Agent Measured / B=Builder / X=Blank SQ.  **LS** — Lot Size Dimensions (or IRR)

R**FE** — **F DXPSTHQALN** — Encoded Features (See User Sheet) (Insert Data or Circle When Applicable)  R**HORS** — Horses (Y/N)  R**PHY** — Physically Challenged Features (Y/N)

**MD** — Model  R**YR** — Year Built (or NEW/UNK/UC)  R**BD** — Builder

**PCN** — Planned Community Name  **MNM** — Marketing Name

R**ES** — Elementary School  R**JH** — Junior High School  R**HS** — High School  R**ESD** — Elem. School District #  R**HSD** — High School District #
(See User Sheet for School Codes)

R**MB** X — Master Bedroom None = 0 x 0  R**2B** X — 2nd Bedroom None = 0 x 0  R**3B** X — 3rd Bedroom None = 0 x 0  R**4B** X — 4th Bedroom None = 0 x 0  R**5B** X — 5th Bedroom None = 0 x 0

R**LR** — Living Room None = 0 x 0  R**DR** — Dining Room None = 0 x 0  R**FR** X — Family Room None = 0 x 0  R**KT** X — Kitchen None = 0 x 0  R**DN** — Den/Other Room None = 0 x 0

R**LP** — List Price  **EQ=LP - TO** Computer will Calculate Equity  R**DP** — Down Payment For Assumption or Carryback Purposes Only (None = 0)  R**TA** — Total Assumable Monthly Payments (None = 0)

R**1E** — 1st Encumbrance (None = 0)  R**1A** — 1st Loan Assum. (Y/N) (None = N)  R**1Q** — 1st Loan Qualify (Y/N) (None = N)  R**1R** — 1st Interest Rate (None = 0)  R**1P** — 1st Monthly Payment (None = 0)

R**2E** — 2nd Encumbrance (None = 0)  R**2A** — 2nd Loan Assum. (Y/N) (None = N)  R**2Q** — 2nd Loan Qualify (Y/N) (None = N)  R**2R** — 2nd Interest Rate (None = 0)  R**2P** — 2nd Monthly Payment (None = 0)

R**3E** — 3rd/All Encumbrances (None = 0)  R**3A** — 3rd Loan Assum. (Y/N) (None = N)  R**3Q** — 3rd Loan Qualify (Y/N) (None = N)  R**3R** — 3rd Interest Rate (None = 0)  R**3P** — 3rd Monthly Payment (None = 0)

**TO = 1E + 2E + 3E** Computer will Calculate Total Encumbrances  **TP** **PITIMF** Monthly Payment Includes (Circle Where Applicable)  R**TX** — Taxes  R**TY** — Tax Year  **WK** — Week Available (Timeshares)

R**HOA** — Homeowner's Association (Y/N)  R**HO** — Homeowner's Association Fee None = 0  **HF** Paid — M = Monthly / Q = Quarterly / S = Semi-Annually / A = Annually  R**PD** — Pad Fee None = 0  **PF** Paid — M = Monthly / Q = Quarterly / S = Semi-Annually / A = Annually  R**LL** — Land Lease Fee None = 0  **LF** Paid — M = Monthly / Q = Quarterly / S = Semi-Annually / A = Annually

R**TN** — Occupant  V = Vacant / O = Owner / T = Tenant / I = Interim Occ.  R**ON** — Owner/Occupant Name  **OT** — Owner/Occupant Phone

R**SBA** — Subagents (Y/N)  R**CS** — Comp. to Subagent  R**BB** — Buyer Broker (Y/N)  R**CB** — Comp. to Buyer Broker  **XC** — Other Compensation  R**VCOM** — Variable Commission (Y/N)

R**LO** — List Office Code  **OPH2** — Office Other Phone Number  **OFAX** — Office Fax Phone Number

R**LA1** — Agent 1 Code  List Agent Name  R**LD** — List Date  R**EXP** — Expire Date

**HP1** — Agent 1 Home Phone  **MB1** — Agent 1 Mobile Phone  **PAG1** — Agent 1 Pager Phone

**LA2** — Agent 2 Code  **HP2** — Agent 2 Home Phone  **MB2** — Agent 2 Mobile Phone  **PAG2** — Agent 2 Pager Phone

**MLS #** — Field Entered Y ___ N ___ — Legal ID

The undersigned Owner acknowledges and reaffirms that this Profile Sheet is an integral part of the Listing Contract between Owner and Broker, that all information in the Profile Sheet is true, correct and complete, that the Owner will promptly notify Broker if there is any material change in such information during the term of this Listing and that Owner will indemnify other persons for inaccuracies in such information as further provided in the Listing Contract. If there is a conflict between the Listing Contract and this Profile Sheet, the terms of this Profile Sheet shall prevail. Owner agrees to indemnify and hold Broker, all Boards or Associations of REALTORS®, ARMLS and all other brokers harmless against any and all claims, liability, damage or loss arising from any misrepresentation or breach of warranty by Owner in this Listing, any incorrect information supplied by Owner and any facts concerning the Property not disclosed by Owner, including without limitation, any facts known to Owner relating to adverse conditions or latent defects.

_____   _____
OWNER SIGNATURE            DATE

The undersigned Broker represents and warrants that the information in and manner of execution of this Profile Sheet and the related Listing Contract comply in all respects with the Rules and Regulations of ARMLS and the Broker's Board or Association of REALTORS®.

_____   _____
BROKER SIGNATURE           DATE

## Figure 2.1 Exclusive Right to Sell (Page 4 of 5)

---

**CLASS 1 - PAGE 2 OF 3**

(FEATURES: For Adding a Listing, underline the proper feature selections. (R) denotes required entries for Adding a Listing. All required Features must be entered for a new listing.)

**RDTYP   Dwelling Type**
A.   Single Family-Detached (SF DET)
B.   Patio Home (PATIO)
C.   Townhouse (TOWNHS)
D.   Apartment Style (APT)
E.   Gemini/Twin Home (GEMINI)
F.   Mobile Home (MOBILE)
G.   Manufactured Housing (MNFACT)

**ROWNS   Ownership**
A.   Fee Simple (FEE)
B.   Leasehold (LEASE)
C.   Condominium (CONDO)
D.   Timeshare (TSHAR)
E.   Co-Operative (COOP)

**RARCH   Architecture**
A.   Single Level (SNGL)
B.   Multi-Level (MULT)
C.   Ranch (RNCH)
D.   Territorial (TERR)
E.   Spanish (SPAN)
F.   Contemporary (CONT)
G.   Other (See Remarks) (OTHR)

**BSTY   Building Style**
A.   2-3-4 Plex (234P)
B.   Clustered (CLUST)
C.   String (STRNG)
D.   High-Rise (HRISE)

**RAPSF   Approx. Sq. Ft. Range**
A.   <1,000 (<1,000)
B.   1,001-1,200 (1,001,1,200)
C.   1,201-1,400 (1,201-1,400)
D.   1,401-1,600 (1,401-1,600)
E.   1,601-1,800 (1,601-1,800)
F.   1,801-2,000 (1,801-2,000)
G.   2,001-2,250 (2,001-2,250)
H.   2,251-2,500 (2,251-2,500)
I.   2,501-2,750 (2,501-2,750)
J.   2,751-3,000 (2,751-3,000)
K.   3,001-3,500 (3,001-3,500)
L.   3,501-4,000 (3,501-4,000)
M.   4,001-4,500 (4,001-4,500)
N.   4,501-5,000 (4,501-5,000)
O.   5,001 + (5,001 +)

**RMBTH   Master Bathroom**
A.   3/4 Bath Master Bedroom (3/4 MSTR)
B.   Full Bath Master Bedroom (FULL MSTR)
C.   Separate Shower and Tub (SEP SH/TB)
D.   Double Sinks (2 SINKS)
E.   2 Master Baths (2 MST BTH)
F.   Tub with Jets (TUBJET)
G.   Bidet (BIDET)
H.   None (NONE)

**BED   Additional Bedroom Information**
A.   Master Bedroom Split (MSPLT)
B.   Other Bedroom Split (OSPLT)
C.   2 Master Bedrooms (2MBR)
D.   Master Bedroom Upstairs (MBRUP)
E.   Master Bedroom Downstairs (MBRDN)
F.   Master Bedroom Sitting Room (MBSIT)
G.   Separate Bedroom Exit (EXIT)
H.   Master Bedroom Walk-In Closet (MWLKN)
I.   Other Bedroom Walk-In Closet (OWLKN)

**RFP   Fireplace**
A.   1 Fireplace (1)
B.   2 Fireplaces (2)
C.   3+ Fireplaces (3+)
D.   Fireplace in Family Room (FM)
E.   Fireplace in Living Room (LR)
F.   Fireplace in Master Bedroom (MB)
G.   Two Way Fireplace (2W)
H.   Gas Fireplace (GS)
I.   Freestanding Fireplace (FS)
J.   Exterior Fireplace (EX)
K.   Firepit (PT)
L.   No Fireplace (NO)
M.   Other (See Remarks) (OT)

**RPPOL   Pool - Private**
A.   Pool-Private (PVT)
B.   Fenced Pool (FNC)
C.   Diving Pool (DIV)
D.   Heated Pool (HTD)
E.   Play Pool (PLY)
F.   Lap Pool (LAP)
G.   Above Ground Pool (AGD)
H.   No Pool (NO)

**RPSPA   Spa - Private**
A.   Spa Private (SPA)
B.   Above Ground Spa (AGS)
C.   Spa-Heated (SPH)
D.   None (NO)

**CPOL   Pool - Community**
A.   Community Pool (PL)
B.   Community Pool - Heated (PLH)
C.   Community Spa (SP)
D.   Community Spa - Heated (SPH)

**RDIN   Dining Area**
A.   Formal (FORML)
B.   Eat-In Kitchen (EATIN)
C.   Breakfast Room (BRKRM)
D.   Dining in Living/Great Room (LR/GR)
E.   Dining in Family Room (FAM)
F.   Breakfast Bar (BRKBR)
G.   Other Dining (See Remarks) (OTHR)

**RKFEA   Kitchen Features**
A.   Range/Oven (RG&OV)
B.   Dishwasher (DISH)
C.   Disposal (DSPL)
D.   Microwave (MICRO)
E.   Compactor (CMPAC)
F.   Refrigerator (REFRG)
G.   Pantry (PNTRY)
H.   Kitchen Island (ISLND)
I.   None (NONE)
J.   Other (See Remarks) (OTHR)

**RLNDRY   Laundry**
A.   Washer Included (WASHER)
B.   Dryer Included (DRYER)
C.   Stacked Washer/Dryer Included (STACKD)
D.   Washer/Dryer Hook-Up Only (HOOKUP)
E.   Inside Laundry (I-LND)
F.   Community Laundry (C-LND)
G.   Laundry in Garage (G-LND)
H.   Coin-Op Laundry (COINOP)
I.   None (NONE)
J.   Other (See Remarks) (OTHR)

**RFEA   Features**
A.   Fix-Up (FIXUP)
B.   Remodeled (See Remarks) (REMODL)
C.   Skylight(s) (SKYLIT)
D.   Vaulted Ceiling(s) (VAULTD)
E.   Central Vacuum (CNTVAC)
F.   Wet Bar(s) (WETBAR)
G.   Intercom (INTCOM)
H.   Roller Shields (ROLLSH)
I.   Fire Sprinklers (FIRESP)
J.   Elevator (ELEVTR)
K.   Security System (Owned) (SECOWN)
L.   Security System (Leased) (SECLSD)
M.   Cable TV Available (CABLE)
N.   Furnished (See Remarks) (FURNSH)
O.   None (NONE)
P.   Other (See Remarks) (OTHR)

**RMS   Other Rooms**
A.   Family Room (FAMRM)
B.   Great Room (GRTRM)
C.   Library/Den (LB/DN)
D.   Basement (BSMNT)
E.   Game/Rec Room (GAME)
F.   Arizona Room/Lanai (AZ RM)
G.   Loft (LOFT)
H.   Guest Qtrs-Sep Entrance (GSTQTR)
I.   Exercise/Sauna Room (SAUNA)
J.   Separate Workshop (SEPWK)
K.   Clubhouse (CLUBHS)

**RXFEA   Exterior Features**
A.   Separate Guest House (GSTHSE)
B.   Tennis Court(s) (TENNIS)
C.   Handball/Racquetball Court(s) (HNDRAC)
D.   Sport Court(s) (SPORT)
E.   Patio (PATIO)
F.   Covered Patio(s) (CPATIO)
G.   Balcony/Deck(s) (BAL/DCK)
H.   Gazebo/Ramada (GAZRAM)
I.   Storage Shed(s) (STGSHD)
J.   Circular Drive (CIRDRV)
K.   Private Street(s) (PVT ST)
L.   Private Yard(s)/Courtyard(s) (PVTYRD)
M.   Yard Watering System-Front (WTRFRT)
N.   Yard Watering System-Back (WTRBCK)
O.   Children's Play Area (KIDPLY)
P.   None (NONE)
Q.   Other (See Remarks) (OTHR)

**MH   Mobile Home Features**
A.   Single Wide (SINGL)
B.   Multi Wide (MULTI)
C.   Built after 1976 (1976+)
D.   In Subdivision (INSUB)
E.   Affidavit of Fixture (AFFID)
F.   Mobile Home - 5+ Acres (5+ AC)
G.   Mobile Home - Waterline Hookup (WTRHU)
H.   Mobile Home - Financing Available (FINAV)

**RPRK   Parking**
A.   1 Car Garage (1G)
B.   2 Car Garage (2G)
C.   3 Car Garage (3G)
D.   4+ Car Garage (4+G)
E.   1 Car Carport (1C)
F.   2+ Car Carport (2+C)
G.   Detached (DETACH)
H.   Slab (SLAB)
I.   Assigned Parking (ASSN)
J.   Unassigned Parking (UNASN)
K.   Side Vehicle Entry (SIDE)
L.   Rear Vehicle Entry (REAR)
M.   RV Parking (RVPKG)
N.   RV Gate (RVGATE)
O.   Electric Door Opener(s) (ELEOPN)
P.   Separate Storage Area(s) (SEPSTG)
Q.   Other (See Remarks) (OTHR)

**RCNST   Construction**
A.   Block (BLOCK)
B.   Frame - Wood (FRMWD)
C.   Frame - Metal (FRMMT)
D.   Brick (BRICK)
E.   Slump Block (SL-BLK)
F.   Adobe (ADOBE)
G.   Other (See Remarks) (OTHR)

**RFNSH   Construction - Finish**
A.   Painted (PAINT)
B.   Stucco (STUCCO)
C.   Brick Trim/Veneer (BKTRIM)
D.   Stone (STONE)
E.   Siding (SIDING)
F.   Other (See Remarks) (OTHR)

**CSTA   Construction - Status**
A.   To-Be-Built (BEBULT)
B.   Under Construction (UNCNST)
C.   Completed Spec Home (SPECHM)

**RROOF   Roofing**
A.   Comp-Shingle (COMP)
B.   Built-Up (BLT-UP)
C.   All Tile (TILE)
D.   Partial Tile (P-TILE)
E.   Rock (ROCK)
F.   Shake (SHAKE)
G.   Concrete (CONCRT)
H.   Foam (FOAM)
I.   Rolled (ROLLED)
J.   Metal (METAL)
K.   Other (See Remarks) (OTHR)

**RCOOL   Cooling**
A.   Refrigeration (REF)
B.   Evaporative (EVAP)
C.   Both Refrg & Evap (BOTH)
D.   Window/Wall Unit (W/W)
E.   No Cooling (NONE)

**RHEAT   Heating**
A.   Electric Heat (ELEC)
B.   Gas Heat (GAS)
C.   Wall/Floor Heat (WFLR)
D.   No Heat (NONE)
E.   Other (See Remarks) (OTHR)

**EGY   Energy Features**
A.   Solar Hot Water (S-HWTR)
B.   Sunscreen(s) (SUNSCR)
C.   Ceiling Fan(s) (C-FAN)
D.   Multi-Pane Windows (MLTPAN)
E.   Load Controller (LDCONT)
F.   Multi-Zones (M-ZONE)

**RUTIL   Utilities**
A.   APS (APS)
B.   SRP (SRP)
C.   SW Gas (SW GAS)
D.   City Electric (C-ELE)
E.   City Gas (C-GAS)
F.   Other Electric (O-ELE)
G.   Other Gas (O-GAS)
H.   Butane/Propane (BUTANE)
I.   Other (See Remarks) (OTHR)

**RWTR   Water**
A.   City Water (C-WT)
B.   Private Water Comany (P-WT)
C.   Well - Privately Owned (WLPO)
D.   Well - Shared (WLSH)
E.   Hauled (HAUL)
F.   Water Softener (Owned) (WS-O)
G.   Water Softener (Leased) WS-L)
H.   Irrigation (IRR)
I.   Drinking Water Filtering System (FILT)

Owner acknowledges receipt of copy of this page, which constitutes Page 2 of 3 Pages. Owner's Initials (_____) Broker's Initials (_____)

# Figure 2.1 Exclusive Right to Sell (Page 5 of 5)

| CLASS 1 - PAGE 3 OF 3 |
|---|

(FEATURES: For Adding a Listing, underline the proper feature selections. (R) denotes required entries for Adding a Listing. All required Features must be entered for a new listing.)

**RSWR** Sewer
A. Sewer - Public (PUBL)
B. Sewer - Private (PRIV)
C. Sewer - Available (AVAL)
D. Sewer in and Connected (SCON)
E. Septic (SEPT)
F. Septic in and Connected (SPIN)
G. No Sewer/Septic (NONE)
H. Other (See Remarks) (OTHR)

**SERV** Services
A. City Service (CIT)
B. County Services (COU)
C. Other (See Remarks) (OTHR)

**RFNC** Fencing
A. Block (BLOK)
B. Wood (WOOD)
C. Chain Link (LINK)
D. Concrete Panel (CONC)
E. Wire (See Remarks) (WIRE)
F. Partial (PART)
G. None (NONE)
H. Other (See Remarks) (OTHR)

**PROP** Property Description
A. Borders Preserve/Public Land (PUBLD)
B. Waterfront Lot (WFRNT)
C. Lake Subdivision (LAKE)
D. Golf Course Lot (GLFLT)
E. Golf Course Subdivision (GLFSB)
F. Hillside Lot (HILSD)
G. Cul-De-Sac Lot (CDSAC)
H. Corner Lot (CORNR)
I. Desert Front (DSFRT)
J. Desert Back (DSBCK)
K. Historic District (HDIST)
L. City Light View(s) (CTYVW)
M. Mountain View(s) (MTNVW)
N. Gated Community (GATED)
O. Guarded Entry (GUARD)
P. North/South Exposure (N/S)
Q. Alley (ALLEY)
R. Street(s) Not Paved (NOPAV)
S. Adjacent to Wash (WASH)
T. Borders Common Area (BDCOM)

**HRSE** Horses
A. Corral (CORL)
B. Stall (STAL)
C. Barn (BARN)
D. Tack Room (TACK)
E. Arena (ARNA)
F. Auto Water (AWTR)
G. Hot Walker (WLKR)
H. Commercial Breed (CBRD)
I. Commercial Board (CBOA)
J. Bridle Path Access (BPTH)
K. Other (See Remarks) (OTHR)

**LTSZ** Lot Size
A. 1-7,500 (1-7,500)
B. 7,501-10,000 (7,501-10,000)
C. 10,001-12,500 (10,001-12,500)
D. 12,501-15,000 (12,501-15,000)
E. 15,001-18,000 (15,001-18,000)
F. 18,001-24,000 (18,001-24,000)
G. 24,001-35,000 (24,001-35,000)
H. 35,001-43,559 (35,001-43,559)
I. 1 to 1.9 Acres (1 TO 1.9 AC)
J. 2 to 4.9 Acres (2 TO 4.9 AC)
K. 5 to 9.9 Acres (5 TO 9.9 AC)
L. 10 + Acres (10+ AC)

**RSHOW** Show Instructions
A. Alarm Activated (ALRM)
B. Call Lister (LSTR)
C. Special Instr/Pets (CLO) (PETS)
D. Call Occupant (OCC)
E. Subagent-Use Lockbox (LBSA)
F. Buyer Broker-Use Lockbox (LBBB)
G. Lockbox-Occupied (LBOC)
H. Lockbox-Vacant (LBVA)
I. Lockbox - Not ARMLS (LBNA)
J. Vacant (VAC)
K. KILO or Courtesy Key (KILO)
L. Key at Guard Gate (KAGG)
M. Tenants Rights (TRGT)

**RPOS** Possession
A. By Agreement (AGREE)
B. Close of Escrow (COE)
C. Close of Escrow +2 days (COE+2)
D. Tenants Rights (T/RGT)

**USTY** Unit Style
A. All on One Level (1LVL)
B. Two Levels (2LVL)
C. Three or More Levels (3+LVL)
D. No Common Walls (NCMWAL)
E. One Common Wall (1CMWAL)
F. Two Common Walls (2CMWAL)
G. Three Common Walls (3CMWAL)
H. Neighbors Above (NABOVE)
I. Neighbors Below (NBELOW)
J. End Unit (END)
K. Poolside (PLSIDE)
L. Ground Level (GLVL)

**RFEES** Association Fees Include
A. Exterior Maintenance of Unit (EXTU)
B. Roof Maintenance - Partial (ROFP)
C. Roof Mainenance - Full (ROFF)
D. Blanket Insurance Policy (INSR)
E. Water (WTR)
F. Sewer (SWR)
G. Garbage Collection (GRBG)
H. Pest Control (PEST)
I. Air Conditioning/Heating (ACHT)
J. Electric (ELEC)
K. Gas (GAS)
L. Cable or Satellite TV (CBTV)
M. Front Yard Maintenance (FYRD)
N. Common Area Maintenance (CAM)
O. Street Maintenance (STMT)
P. No Fee (NONE)
Q. Other (See Remarks) (OTHR)

**RREST** Association Restrictions
A. Pets OK (See Remarks) (PETS OK)
B. No Trucks, Trailers, or Boats (NO TRK)
C. Separate RV Parking (SEP RV)
D. HOA Approval of Buyer Required (HOA BYR)
E. None (NONE)
F. Other (See Remarks) (OTHR)

**RINFO** Association Information
A. FHA Approved Project (FHAOK)
B. VA Approved Project (VAOK)
C. Special Assessment Pending (SPASMPD)
D. Professionally Managed (PRO-MGD)
E. Self Managed (SLF-MGD)
F. Not Managed (NOT-MGD)
G. Club, Membership Optional (CLUB)
H. None (NONE)
I. Other (See Remarks) (OTHR)

**RLN1** Existing 1st Loan
A. FHA (FHA)
B. VA (VA)
C. Conventional (CONV)
D. Farm Home (FMHA)
E. Private (PRIV)
F. Wrap (WRAP)
G. Treat as Free and Clear (F&C)
H. Other (See Remarks) (OTHR)

**TRM1** Existing 1st Loan Terms
A. Assume - No Qualify (NOQUAL)
B. Assume - Qualify (ASSM-Q)
C. Non Assumable (NOASUM)
D. Balloon/Call Provision (BALOON)
E. No Prepay Penalty (NOPRE)
F. Interest Only (INTONL)
G. Financial Information Subject to Verification (VERIFY)
H. All Assumable Existing Encumberances-No Qualify (ALLNQ)
I. Not Applicable (N/A)

**TYP1** Existing 1st Loan Type
A. Fixed (FIX)
B. Adjustable/Graduated (ADJ)
C. Not Applicable (N/A)

**TRMO** Existing Other Loan Terms
A. Interest Only (INTO)
B. Balloon - Call Provision (BALL)
C. Other (See Remarks) (OTHR)
D. Not Applicable (N/A)

**MISC** Miscellaneous
A. Retirement Only (RETIRE)
B. Owner/Agent (OWN/AGT)
C. Court Approval Required (COURT APP)
D. Lender/Corp Approval Required (LENDR APP)
E. REO Property (REO PROP)
F. Exclusions (See Remarks) (EXCLUSION)
G. Flood Plain (FLOOD PLN)
H. Home Warranty (HOME WTY)
I. Have 1st Right/Accepting Backups (1RGHT/BU)

**RNFIN** New Financing
A. Cash (CASH)
B. CTL (CTL)
C. VA (VA)
D. FHA (FHA)
E. Conventional (CONV)
F. Farm Home (FMHA)
G. Buy Down Subsidy (BUYD)
H. Seller to Approve Points (SAPP)
I. No Carry (NCAR)
J. Seller May Carry (MCAR)
K. Wraparound (WRAP)
L. Lease Option (LSOP)
M. Lease Purchase (LSPU)
N. Also For Rent (RENT)
O. Equity Share (EQSH)
P. Exchange (EXCH)

**RDISC** Disclosures
A. Seller Disclosure Available (SPDS)
B. Super Fund/WQARF/DOD Area (SFND)
C. Agency Disclosure Required (AGCY)
D. Special Assessment District (SAD)
E. None (NONE)

**PHO** Photo Code
A. Take Photo (TAKE)
B. Photo Submitted (SUBM)
C. Sketch Submitted (SKTC)
D. No Photo Requested (NON)
E. Extra Photos/Sketches Submitted (EXTR)

**EXM:** ⬚⬚⬚ ⬚⬚⬚
For Office Use Only

**DIRECTIONS:** Enter up to 159 Characters Maximum (including spaces and punctuation) to detail directions to the property.

XST Cross Street

DIR1 (Line 1)

DIR2 (Line 2)

**REMARKS:** 560 Characters Maximum (including spaces and puntuation) to specify any additional information.

RM1 (Line 1)

RM2 (Line 2)

RM3 (Line 3)

RM4 (Line 4)

RM5 (Line 5)

RM6 (Line 6)

RM7 (Line 7)

Owner acknowledges receipt of copy of this page, which constitutes Page 3 of 3 Pages. Owner's Initials ( ) Broker's Initials ( )

## Figure 2.2 Exclusive Right to Sell (Page 1 of 3)

### EXCLUSIVE RIGHT TO SELL
(Employment Agreement)

THE PRINTED PORTION OF THIS EMPLOYMENT AGREEMENT (AGREEMENT) HAS BEEN APPROVED BY THE TUCSON ASSOCIATION OF REALTORS®MULTIPLE LISTING SERVICE, INC. THIS IS INTENDED TO BE A BINDING AGREEMENT. NO REPRESENTATION IS MADE AS TO THE LEGAL VALIDITY OF ANY PROVISION OR THE TAX CONSEQUENCES THEREOF. IF YOU DESIRE LEGAL OR TAX ADVICE, CONSULT YOUR ATTORNEY OR TAX ADVISOR.

1   **EXCLUSIVE RIGHT TO SELL:** I/We, the Owner(s) of the Premises described below, are the Owner(s) of record (hereafter referred to as "Seller") and have
2   the legal capacity and authority to and hereby give the Broker named on line 161 (hereafter referred to as "Listing Broker") the Exclusive Right to Sell the
3   Premises.

4   **TERM:** This Exclusive Right to Sell the Premises begins on _____MONTH_____DAY_____YEAR and shall end at midnight
5   on _____MONTH_____DAY_____YEAR, except that the Agreement shall continue in full force and effect through the completion of sale
6   of the Premises if the offer to sell was entered into before the expiration time stated above.

7   **THE PREMISES:** The Seller warrants to the Brokers, Agents. Tucson Association of REALTORS®/Multiple Listing Service, Inc. (hereafter referred to as
8   "MLS"), and Buyers that the information being provided is complete, true and accurate and agrees to offer for sale the following described property, together
9   with all fixtures. improvements and appurtenances incident thereto, including personal property listed below (collectively referred to herein as the "Premises"):

9   Property Address: _____ Assessor's # _____

10   City _____ County _____ , AZ Zip Code _____

11   Legal Description _____

12   _____

13   **FIXTURES AND PERSONAL PROPERTY:** All existing fixtures attached to the Premises: including storage sheds: electrical, plumbing. heating and cooling
14   equipment: built-in appliances; light fixtures: ceiling fans: window and door screens: sun screens: solar systems: storm windows and doors: shutters: awnings:
15   water misting systems: fire detection/suppression systems: towel, curtain and drapery rods: draperies and other window coverings: attached floor coverings:
16   air cooler(s) and/or conditioner(s): attached fireplace equipment: wood burning stoves: pool and spa equipment (including any mechanical or other cleaning
17   systems); garage door openers and controls: security systems and/or alarms: timers: mailbox: attached TV antennas (excluding satellite dishes): and all
18   existing landscaping including trees. cacti and shrubs shall be left upon and included with the Premises.

19   Additional Existing Personal Property Included: _____

20   _____

21   Fixtures and Leased Equipment NOT Included: _____

22   _____

23   **LISTED PRICE:** The Premises shall be offered for sale at $_____ and upon such terms and conditions as provided for in the
24   Property Profile Sheet, signed by Seller, which shall be considered part of this Agreement, or at such other price, terms and conditions as subsequently agreed
25   by Seller and Listing Broker. Seller authorizes the Listing Broker to update and correct information in the Property Profile Sheet as necessary.

26   **BROKERAGE FEE:** COMMISSIONS PAYABLE FOR THE SALE. LEASING OR MANAGEMENT OF PROPERTY ARE NOT SET BY ANY BOARD OR
27   ASSOCIATION OF REALTORS® OR MULTIPLE LISTING SERVICE OR IN ANY MANNER. COMMISSIONS ARE NEGOTIATED BETWEEN THE BROKER

28   AND CLIENT. Seller shall owe the Listing Broker a fee of: _____

29   upon the occurrence of any of the following events:

30   A.   During the term of this Agreement. the Listing Broker, or other real estate Broker cooperating with the Listing Broker, produces a Buyer ready, willing
31       and able to purchase the Premises according to price and terms offered in this Agreement or at such other price, terms and conditions as subsequently
32       agreed by Seller; or
33   B.   Seller sells/transfers/leases/auctions the Premises. unilaterally terminates this Agreement or otherwise makes the Premises unavailable to the Listing
34       Broker for sale during the term of this Agreement; or
35   C.   An offer to sell is signed by the Seller within _____days of the termination of this Agreement. for the sale, exchange or other conveyance
36       of title to any person(s) shown the Premises during the term of this Agreement by the Listing Broker. any other Cooperating Broker or the Seller, unless
37       the Premises has been relisted during this period on an exclusive basis with any other Broker; or
38   D.   If the completion of the sale is prevented by the Seller.

39   With regard to a sale of the Premises through the Listing Broker. said fee shall be paid at the time of and as a condition of closing; in all other cases said fee
40   shall be paid at the time of such event. Delivery of a copy of this Employment Agreement to escrow company shall constitute instructions to escrow agent
41   to pay Listing Broker and any Cooperating Broker as provided herein. If the earnest deposit is forfeited for any reason. Seller shall pay, at the exclusive option
42   of the Listing Broker, a brokerage fee equal to one-half of the earnest deposit, provided such payment shall not exceed the full amount of the brokerage fee.
43   Nothing in this paragraph shall be construed as limiting applicable provisions of law relating to when brokerage fees are earned or payable.

44   **REPRESENTATION/COOPERATION:** Brokers and their Agents may represent the Seller, the Buyer or both. By signing this Agreement, the Listing Broker
45   and his Agents become the Agent of the Seller (Seller's Agent) and have the fiduciary duties of loyalty, obedience, disclosure, confidentiality and accounting
46   to the Seller. Seller may be responsible for the actions and representations of Seller's Agents. The Listing Broker is directed to place this listing in MLS and
47   extend an offer of cooperation and compensation to other participants of the service as indicated below:

SOURCE: Copyright Tucson Association of REALTORS® Multiple Listing Service, Inc.

# Figure 2.2 Exclusive Right to Sell (Page 2 of 3)

48  **Subagents:** Subagents are those Brokers and their Agents who elect to represent the Seller and not the Buyer. Subagents have the fiduciary duties of loyalty,
49  obedience, disclosure, confidentiality and accounting to the Seller. The Subagent receives compensation from the Listing Broker. Seller may be responsible
50  for the actions and representations of Subagents.

51  Seller authorizes Listing Broker to offer cooperation and compensation to Subagents:  [  ] Yes    [  ] No

52  **Buyer's Agents:** Buyer's Agents are those Brokers and their Agents who elect to represent the Buyer and not the Seller. A Buyer's Agent has the fiduciary
53  duties of loyalty, obedience, disclosure, confidentiality and accounting to the Buyer. The Buyer's Agent may receive compensation from the Buyer and/or
54  from the Listing Broker.

55  Seller authorizes Listing Broker to offer cooperation and compensation to Buyer's Agents:  [  ] Yes    [  ] No

56  **Dual Agents (also known as "limited agents"):** A dual agency (or limited agency) may occur when the Listing Broker procures a Buyer for the Premises.
57  In this situation, the same real estate company may be representing the Seller's interest and the Buyer's interest. A dual agency may occur in this or in other
58  ways. Brokers and their Agents can legally represent both the Seller and the Buyer with the knowledge and written consent of both the Seller and Buyer.
59  A Dual Agent has the duties of loyalty, obedience, disclosure, confidentiality and accounting to both the Seller and the Buyer. Seller recognizes that in a dual
60  agency situation, the duties normally owed the Seller by the Listing Broker and his Agents may be limited in that confidential information pertaining to the Buyer
61  may not be disclosed to the Seller (and likewise, confidential information concerning the Seller may not be disclosed to the Buyer). Seller agrees that the
62  Listing Broker and his Agents shall not be liable for failing or refusing to disclose confidential information. The Dual Agent may receive compensation from
63  the Buyer and/or from the Listing Broker.

64  Seller authorizes Listing Broker to offer cooperation and compensation to Dual Agents:  [  ] Yes    [  ] No

65  **NOTE:  Compensation offered to Cooperating Brokers and Agents is indicated on the Property Profile Sheet.**

66  **CONDUCT:** Regardless of representation, Brokers and their Agents have the following obligations to both the Seller and the Buyer:
67  a)  to treat all parties to a transaction fairly as required by law. REALTORS® are obligated by the Code of Ethics to treat all parties to a transaction honestly.
68  b)  a duty to disclose all facts known to the Broker which may materially and adversely affect the consideration to be paid for the Premises.

69  **SIGNS:** Seller [  ] agrees [  ] does not agree to the placement of a "For Sale" sign together with appropriate name riders etc., and upon acceptance of an
70  offer for the Premises, a "Sold" sign or sign rider that indicates the property is in escrow. Seller agrees to remove all other 'For Sale" signs upon effective
71  date of this Agreement.

72  **ACCESS AND KEYSAFE:** Seller [  ] does [  ] does not authorize Listing Broker to install and use at the Premises a keysafe containing a key to the Premises.
73  A keysafe permits access to the Premises, not only to the Listing Broker, but also to any member of the Tucson Association of REALTORS®/Multiple Listing
74  Service, Inc., together with potential Buyers. even when Seller is not present. Seller authorizes and agrees to cooperate with Listing Broker and any other
75  Cooperating Brokers and Agents to preview and show the premises at reasonable times and upon reasonable notice. Seller shall provide Listing Broker with
76  written permission for access from the occupant of the Premises, if occupant is a person other than the Seller.

77  **HOME PROTECTION PLAN:** Seller [  ] agrees [  ] does not agree to provide, at Seller's expense, a home protection plan promptly after signing this contract.
78  Home protection plans may provide benefits to the Seller and the Buyer of the Premises.

79  **SELLER'S OBLIGATIONS:** Seller agrees to complete and return to Listing Broker a Seller Property Disclosure form as supplied by Listing Broker within five
80  (5) calendar days after receipt of form. Seller agrees to make available all pertinent data, records and documents pertaining to the Premises. Seller
81  acknowledges Seller's duty to disclose all facts known to Seller concerning any adverse conditions. including hidden defects or defects not readily visible
82  affecting the Premises. Seller is unaware of any hazardous substance problems at or affecting the Premises and will disclose any such problem upon
83  discovery. Seller is aware that Seller may be responsible for failing to disclose such information and for misrepresenting the condition of the Premises. Seller
84  shall inform Listing Broker, in writing, of any and all changes of any nature that could affect the value or marketability of the Premises or would render incorrect
85  or incomplete, information contained in the Property Profile Sheet or Seller Property Disclosure Form. as soon as possible after such changes occur. Seller
86  shall also inform Listing Broker, in writing, of any subsequently acquired information which makes inaccurate or incomplete, any information previously
87  disclosed, as soon as possible after such information is acquired.

88  **Property Condition:** Seller is responsible for the care. repair, custody, management or condition of the Premises and agrees to maintain the Premises
89  in the same or better condition as on the effective date of this Agreement.

90  **Insurance:** Seller is responsible for maintaining appropriate insurance to cover possible liability and losses from access, including liability for bodily injury
91  and losses due to theft and vandalism.

92  **Septic System:** If the Premises are served in whole or in part by a septic disposal system, Seller shall, at Seller's expense, place in escrow a document
93  of certification as may be required by the local Health Department or other regulatory body. If a public sewer line of sufficient capacity exists within 200
94  feet of the Premises, the lender or local health authority may require connection upon any transfer of ownership.

95  **Pool Disclosure:** The State of Arizona, Pima County and the City of Tucson have laws and ordinances regarding pool safety and enclosures. Seller
96  may be required to bring property into compliance with enclosure/barrier laws and must give the Buyer a notice explaining safety education and
97  responsibilities of pool ownership as approved by the Department of Health Services.

98  **Wood Infestation:** Seller may, at his expense, be required to place in escrow a Wood Infestation Report of all residences and buildings included in this
99  sale prepared by a pest control licensee consistent with the Rules and Regulations of the Structural Pest Control Commission of the State of Arizona.

100  **Homeowner's Association Information:**  If the Premises is located within a Homeowner's Association/Condominium/Planned Unit Development, the
101  Seller agrees to provide as soon as practical, copies of covenants, conditions and restrictions, articles of information, bylaws, other governing documents,
102  current financial statement, budget and all additional information and to complete a Homeowner's Association Information form as supplied by Listing
103  Broker.

104  **Title:** Seller shall furnish good and marketable title, evidenced by a Standard Owner's Title Insurance Policy, at time of closing.

105  **Closing:** Seller agrees that close of escrow shall be defined as recordation of the closing documents. Seller shall sign all appropriate closing documents
106  prior to recordation. Seller will pay a prorated portion of taxes, assessments, homeowner's association fees, insurance premiums and other costs related
107  to the property. Seller shall direct the escrow company handling the closing to pay any brokerage fee due Listing Broker as a condition of closing. Any
108  proceeds shall be distributed after recordation.

109  **FIRPTA:** Upon Listing Broker's request, Seller agrees to complete, sign and deliver to escrow company a certificate concerning whether Seller is a foreign
110  person or nonresident alien pursuant to the Foreign Investment in Real Property Tax Act of 1980 (FIRPTA).

## Figure 2.2 Exclusive Right to Sell (Page 3 of 3)

111   **INDEMNIFICATION:** Tucson Association of REALTORS®, Inc. and the Tucson Association of REALTORS®/Multiple Listing Service, Inc. are not parties to
112   this Agreement. As a condition of this Agreement, Seller agrees to indemnify and hold harmless the Tucson Association of REALTORS®, Inc. and the Tucson
113   Association of REALTORS®/Multiple Listing Service, Inc., their employees and volunteers, the Listing Broker and his Agents, Subagents, Buyer's Agents
114   and all other Cooperating Brokers against any and all claims, liability, damage or loss (including attorney's fees) arising from any misrepresentation or breach
115   of warranty by Seller or from any incorrect information supplied by Seller or from any facts concerning the Premises not disclosed by Seller, including without
116   limitation, any facts known to Seller relating to adverse conditions or latent defects or hazardous substances located in, on or adjacent to the Premises.

117   **RECOMMENDATIONS:** If the Listing Broker or Cooperating Brokers or Agents should recommend a contractor, service or any other person or entity to the
118   Seller for any purpose, such recommendation shall be independently investigated by the Seller and Seller shall not hold the Listing Broker or Cooperating
119   Brokers or Agents legally accountable for making such recommendation. Seller understands that said recommendation may result in compensation to Listing
120   Broker or Cooperating Brokers or Agents and such compensation shall be disclosed in writing to all parties.

121   **OTHER SELLERS AND PROSPECTS:** Seller understands that other owners may employ Listing Broker to sell, exchange or option properties similar to that
122   of the Seller. Seller consents to any agency representation by Listing Broker of such other owners before, during and after the expiration of this Agreement.
123   Seller further understands that the Premises may not be presented or shown to every prospect encountered by Listing Broker and his Agents.

124   **EQUAL OPPORTUNITY:** The Premises is offered to all persons without respect to their ancestry, race, religion, color, sex, sexual preference, handicap,
125   marital status, familial status, age or national origin or any other category mandated by prevailing federal, state or local laws, statutes or ordinances as may
126   be amended from time to time.

127   **SUBSEQUENT OFFER:** Seller shall have the right to receive subsequent Offer(s) to Purchase the Premises unless otherwise agreed in an accepted Offer
128   to Purchase.

129   **MEDIATION/ARBITRATION:** The Tucson Association of REALTORS®, Inc., may provide for resolution of disputes through mediation and/or arbitration.

130   **ATTORNEY'S FEES:** In any action or proceeding to enforce any provision of this Agreement, or for damages caused by a default, the prevailing party shall
131   be entitled to reasonable attorneys' fees and to related expenses, such as expert witness fees, fees paid to investigators and court costs. Additionally, if the
132   Listing Broker hires an attorney to enforce the collection of any brokerage fee and is successful in collecting some or all of said brokerage fee with or without
133   commencing a legal action or proceeding, Seller agrees to pay such attorneys' fees and costs.

134   **CONSTRUCTION OF LANGUAGE:** The language of this Agreement shall be construed according to its fair meaning and not strictly for or against either party.
135   Words used in the masculine, feminine or neuter shall apply to either gender or the neuter, as appropriate. All singular and plural words shall be interpreted
136   to refer to the number consistent with circumstances and context.

137   **ORIGINAL DOCUMENTS:** Seller agrees that a facsimile of this Agreement and other documents made reference to herein, or in a subsequent writing, or
138   are required to be signed as a condition of closing, shall constitute an original and may be signed in counterpart.

139   **ENTIRE AGREEMENT:** This Agreement, the Property Profile Sheet, any attached exhibits and any addenda or supplements signed by the parties, shall
140   constitute the entire agreement between Seller and Listing Broker and supersede any other written or oral agreements between Seller and Listing Broker and
141   will be in full force and effect until the expiration date. Any release prior to the agreed upon expiration date is at the option of the Listing Broker including any
142   conditions that may be part of a release. Seller agrees not to advertise or market, in any way, the Premises without the express written permission of the
143   Listing Broker. The pre-printed portions of this Agreement may not be modified without the express written permission of the Tucson Association of
144   REALTORS®/Multiple Listing Service, Inc. Any other modifications must be in writing and signed by Listing Broker and Seller.

145   **NOTE: Seller acknowledges that signing more than one Exclusive Right to Sell Agreement for the same term could expose the Seller to multiple
146   liability for additional brokerage fees.**

147   **ADDITIONAL TERMS, PROVISIONS OR INFORMATION:** _____

148   _____

149   *AGREED*

150   _____          _____
151   Owner/Seller - Printed Name                          Owner/Seller - Printed Name

152   _____          _____
153   Owner/Seller - Signature              (mo/da/yr)    Owner/Seller - Signature              (mo/da/yr)

154   _____          _____
155   Address                                              Phone - Home                      FAX

156   _____          _____
157   City                     State      Zip            Phone - Office                    FAX

158   _____          _____
159   Listing Agent - Printed Name                         Listing Agent - Signature            (mo/da/yr)

160   *ACCEPTED*

161   _____          _____
162   Designated Broker - Printed Name                     Designated Broker - Signature        (mo/da/yr)

163   _____          _____
164   Firm Name                                            Address

165   _____          _____
166   Phone                    FAX                        City                     State      Zip

167   _____
168   File No.

**Figure 2.3 Open Listing Agreement**

OPEN LISTING AGREEMENT

DATE: _____

OWNER herein grants unto _____, BROKER, the right to sell for a period of _____ days from the date hereof, which will terminate as of the _____ day of _____, 19 _____, the following property:

_____

_____

for a gross sales price of $ _____ on the following terms:

_____

_____

or at such other terms and price as the OWNER shall accept. It is understood that OWNER has a right to list this property with other Brokers only on a nonexclusive basis or may sell as Owner on the same terms, condition and duration as this agreement.

COMMISSION: OWNER agrees to pay BROKER a commission of _____% _____, if BROKER procures a purchaser during the terms of this agreement at the above price or any other price or terms agreeable to OWNER; of if the property is sold, transferred, leased, rented or exchanged by any person within _____ days after the expiration of this agreement, to any person, firm or corporation, with whom BROKER has negotiated for the purchase of this property, during the term herein, and if BROKER supplies OWNER with a list of such parties within a reasonable time after the expiration of this agreement.


_____          _____
OWNER                                    BROKER


_____          _____
OWNER                                    BY


_____          _____
ADDRESS

While business may be conducted under fictitious business names or trade names, the commissioner may refuse to issue licenses to entities who want to do business under names that are potentially misleading or detrimental to the public interest.

For more information on advertising, see Chapter 10, "Real Estate License Laws."

## TERMINATION OF LISTINGS

A listing contract may be terminated by any of the following occurrences:

1. Performance by the broker
2. The expiration of the contract term
3. Revocation by the principal
4. Cancellation (renunciation) by the broker
5. Mutual consent
6. The bankruptcy, death or incapacity of either the broker or the principal
7. The destruction of the property
8. A change in property use by outside forces beyond the control of the principal and the broker (such as condemnation under eminent domain)

## BUYER BROKERAGE

As the residential real estate market gradually recognizes the fact that buyers may separately employ and compensate brokers to represent them in real estate transactions, contracts to accommodate such situations have been developed both by individual brokers and by trade associations. The exclusive retainer agreement (Figure 2.4) developed by the Arizona Association of REALTORS® is representative of this type of contract.

Some buyers may hesitate to enter into an exclusive buyer agency agreement. However, a nonexclusive buyer agency agreement has many of the same problems as an open listing. Exclusiveness gives the broker more control of the transaction, greater assurance of client loyalty and a bigger incentive for working hard on the client's behalf. (Note that an exclusive buyer agency agreement will generally require the agent to use "due diligence" in trying to find a property for a buyer, just as an exclusive listing agreement requires the agent to use due diligence in finding a buyer for a property.) Exclusive buyer agency agreements also reduce the risk of controversy over who was the procuring cause of a purchase.

While the employment and compensation to be earned are the result of working for the buyer rather than for the seller, the contract contains provisions governing the actions and the liabilities of the employed broker similar to those contained in the exclusive-right-to-sell agreement. Before any licensee attempts to use such a contract, however, he or she should consult with the employing broker about the potential benefits and pitfalls of creating such a fiduciary relationship with a buyer.

Note that a nonexclusive buyer agency may arise inadvertently, for example, when the agent causes the buyer to believe that the agent is representing the buyer, when in fact the agent is officially representing the seller. These implied buyer agency relationships are nonexclusive. Because there is no written buyer agency agreement at all, the potential for misunderstandings and conflicts of interest is enormous.

## Figure 2.4 Buyer-Broker Exclusive Employment Agreement

 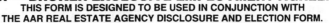 

**BUYER — BROKER EXCLUSIVE EMPLOYMENT AGREEMENT**
THIS FORM IS DESIGNED TO BE USED IN CONJUNCTION WITH
THE AAR REAL ESTATE AGENCY DISCLOSURE AND ELECTION FORM.

THE PRINTED PORTION OF THIS AGREEMENT HAS BEEN APPROVED BY THE ARIZONA ASSOCIATION OF REALTORS®. NO REPRESENTATION IS MADE AS TO THE LEGAL VALIDITY OR ADEQUACY OF ANY PROVISION OR THE TAX CONSEQUENCES THEREOF. IF YOU DESIRE LEGAL OR TAX ADVICE, CONSULT YOUR ATTORNEY OR TAX ADVISOR.

1. _____ ("Buyer") hereby exclusively employs and grants to
2. _____ called ("Broker") and its agent _____
   (FIRM NAME)                                                              (AGENT'S NAME)
3. the irrevocable right, commencing on _____ , 19____ , and expiring at midnight on _____ , 19____ ,
4. to locate property and negotiate terms and conditions acceptable to Buyer for purchase, exchange, option, or lease as follows:
5. **General Nature of Property:** Buyer represents that he intends to acquire an interest in one or more properties meeting the
6. following general description:
7. Type: ☐ Residential ☐ Land ☐ Commercial ☐ Other: _____
8. **Broker Compensation:** Unless otherwise stated below, Broker's compensation shall be paid at the time of and as a condition of
9. closing, as follows:
10. a. The amount of compensation shall be:_____.
11. b. Buyer agrees to compensate Broker if the Buyer or any other person acting on the Buyer's behalf enters into an agreement
12. to purchase, exchange, option, or lease any property of the general nature described herein.
13. c. Buyer authorizes Broker to accept compensation from seller or seller's broker, which compensation shall be credited
14. against any compensation owed by Buyer to Broker under this Agreement.
15. d. If completion of any transaction is prevented by Buyer's default or with the consent of Buyer, the total compensation due
16. under this Agreement shall be immediately due and payable by Buyer.
17. e. Buyer agrees to pay such compensation if Buyer within _____ calendar days after the termination of this Agreement enters
18. into an agreement to purchase, exchange, option or lease any property shown to or negotiated on behalf of the Buyer by
19. Broker during the term of this Agreement, unless Buyer enters into a subsequent buyer-broker exclusive employment
20. agreement with another Broker.
21. **Retainer Fee:** Buyer agrees to pay and Broker acknowledges receipt of a non-refundable retainer fee in the amount of $_____
22. payable to Broker for initial counseling, consultation and research, which retainer fee shall be credited against any other
23. compensation owed by Buyer to Broker as provided above on Line 10.
24. **New Home/Lot Sales:** Buyer acknowledges that many new home/lot sellers will not compensate Broker if Broker does not
25. accompany Buyer on the first new home/lot visit. Buyer agrees that if Buyer makes a first visit to a new home/lot or model home
26. without Broker, resulting in a seller's refusal to compensate Broker, that Buyer will compensate Broker as provided above on Line 10.
27. **Buyer's Duties:** Buyer agrees to work exclusively with Broker and to provide to Broker or lender, upon request, information
28. necessary to assure Buyer's ability to acquire property described above. Buyer further agrees to view or consider property of the
29. general type set forth in this Agreement, and to negotiate in good faith to acquire such property.
30. **Equal Housing Opportunity:** It is the policy of the Broker to abide by all local, state, and federal laws prohibiting discrimination
31. against any individual or group of individuals. The Broker has no duty to disclose the racial, ethnic, or religious composition of any
32. neighborhood, community, or building, nor whether persons with disabilities are housed in any home or facility, except that the
33. agent may identify housing facilities meeting the needs of a disabled buyer.
34. **Addenda Incorporated:** ☐ Real Estate Agency Disclosure & Election; ☐ Other: _____
35. **Additional Terms:** _____
36. _____
37. _____
38. _____
39. COMMISSIONS PAYABLE FOR THE PURCHASE, EXCHANGE, OPTION OR LEASE OF PROPERTY ARE NOT SET BY ANY
40. BOARD OR ASSOCIATION OF REALTORS® OR MULTIPLE LISTING SERVICE OR IN ANY MANNER OTHER THAN AS
41. NEGOTIATED BETWEEN BROKER AND BUYER.
42. **Other Potential Buyers:** Buyer consents and acknowledges that other potential buyers represented by Broker may consider,
43. make offers on, or acquire an interest in the same or similar properties as Buyer is seeking.
44. **Mediation:** Any dispute or claim in law or equity arising out of this Agreement shall be submitted to mediation in accordance with
45. the mediation procedures of the local REALTOR® association or, if not available, another mediation provider.
46. **Attorneys' Fees:** In any action, proceeding or arbitration arising out of this Agreement, the prevailing party shall be entitled to
47. reasonable attorneys' fees and costs.
48. **Capacity:** Buyer warrants that Buyer has the legal capacity, full power and authority to enter into this Agreement and
49. consummate the transaction contemplated hereby on Buyer's own behalf or on behalf of the party Buyer represents, as
50. appropriate.
51. **Entire Agreement:** This Agreement, any attached exhibits and any addenda signed by the parties shall constitute the entire
52. agreement between Broker and Buyer, and shall supersede any other written or oral agreement between Broker and Buyer. This
53. Agreement can be modified only by a writing signed by Broker and Buyer. A fully executed facsimile copy of this Agreement shall
54. be treated as an original Agreement.
55. **Acceptance:** Buyer hereby agrees to all of the terms and conditions herein and acknowledges receipt of a copy of this
56. Agreement.
57. _____ _____  _____ _____
    Buyer's Signature                 MO-DA-YR      Buyer's Signature                 MO-DA-YR
58. _____ _____  _____ _____ _____
    Street                                          City                      State    Zip
59. ( _____ )_____  ( _____ )_____
    Telephone                           Fax
60. _____ _____ _____
    Firm Name                           Agent Signature                   MO-DA-YR
61. | **For Broker Use Only** _____ |
    |          Brokerage File/Log No.        Manager's Initials    Broker's Initials    MO-DA-YR |

This form is available for use by the entire real estate industry. The use of this form is not intended to identify the user as a REALTOR®. REALTOR® is a registered collective membership mark which may be used only by real estate licensees who are members of the NATIONAL ASSOCIATION OF REALTORS® and who subscribe to its Code of Ethics.         ®1995 Arizona Association of REALTORS® BUYER-BROKER 8/95)

**SOURCE:** Permission granted by Arizona Association of REALTORS®.

## LIMITING THE LICENSEE'S LIABILITY

Because of the confusion that can result when sellers and buyers do not understand the agency obligations of real estate licensees, the Arizona Association of REALTORS® has developed two forms for use by the real estate industry as a whole.

The "Real Estate Agency Disclosure and Election" (Figure 2.5) aids in explaining to prospective clients and customers the level of service they are entitled to, and assists brokers in confirming their agency relationships.

The "Limited Dual Representation Agreement" (Figure 2.6) helps a broker create a disclosed dual agency relationship. This eliminates the implications of an illegal undisclosed dual agency while it explains to both clients the representation that they will receive from the broker.

As always, care should be exercised by the broker when using these forms, and competent legal advice should be sought in more difficult situations.

# Figure 2.5 Real Estate Agency Disclosure and Election

## REAL ESTATE
## AGENCY DISCLOSURE AND ELECTION

THE PRINTED PORTION OF THIS DOCUMENT HAS BEEN APPROVED BY THE ARIZONA ASSOCIATION OF REALTORS® AND IS BEING PROVIDED IN COMPLIANCE WITH THE REALTOR® CODE OF ETHICS. NO REPRESENTATION IS MADE AS TO THE LEGAL VALIDITY OR ADEQUACY OF ANY PROVISION THEREOF. IF YOU DESIRE LEGAL ADVICE, CONSULT YOUR ATTORNEY.

### DISCLOSURE

1. BEFORE A SELLER OR A BUYER ENTERS INTO A DISCUSSION WITH A REAL ESTATE BROKER OR BROKER'S SALESPERSON, THE
2. SELLER OR THE BUYER SHOULD UNDERSTAND WHAT TYPE OF AGENCY RELATIONSHIP OR REPRESENTATION THEY HAVE WITH THE
3. BROKER IN THE TRANSACTION. THE SELLER OR THE BUYER SHOULD CAREFULLY READ ALL AGREEMENTS TO INSURE THAT THE
4. AGREEMENTS ADEQUATELY EXPRESS THEIR UNDERSTANDING OF THE TRANSACTION. **THE DUTIES OF THE BROKER IN A REAL**
5. **ESTATE TRANSACTION DO NOT RELIEVE A SELLER OR A BUYER FROM THE RESPONSIBILITY TO PROTECT THEIR OWN INTEREST.**

6. **I. Buyer's Broker:** A Broker other than the Seller's Broker can agree with the Buyer to act as the Broker for the Buyer only.  In these situations,
7. the Buyer's Broker is not representing the Seller, even if the Buyer's Broker is receiving compensation for services rendered, either in full or in
8. part, from the Seller or through the Seller's Broker.  A Buyer's Broker has the following obligations:
9. To the Buyer:
10. (a) The fiduciary duties of loyalty, obedience, disclosure, confidentiality, and accounting in dealings with the Buyer.
11. To the Buyer and the Seller:
12. (a) Diligent exercise of reasonable skill and care in the performance of the Broker's duties.
13. (b) A duty of honest and fair dealing.
14. (c) A duty to disclose all facts known to the Broker which materially and adversely affect the consideration to be paid for the property.

15. **II. Seller's Broker:** A Broker under a listing agreement with the Seller or as a subagent of the Seller acts as the Broker for the Seller only.  A
16. Seller's Broker has the following obligations:
17. To the Seller:
18. (a) The fiduciary duties of loyalty, obedience, disclosure, confidentiality, and accounting in dealings with the Seller.
19. To the Buyer and the Seller:
20. (a) Diligent exercise of reasonable skill and care in the performance of the Broker's duties.
21. (b) A duty of honest and fair dealing.
22. (c) A duty to disclose all facts known to the Broker which materially and adversely affect the consideration to be paid for the property.

23. **III. Broker Representing both Seller and Buyer (Limited Dual Representation):** A Broker, either acting directly or through one or more
24. licensees within the same brokerage firm, can legally represent both the Seller and the Buyer in a transaction, but only with the knowledge
25. and consent of both the Seller and the Buyer. The parties understand that:
26. a) the Broker represents both the Buyer and the Seller with limitations of the duties owed to the Buyer and the Seller, such as:
27. 1) The Broker will not, without written authorization, disclose to the other party that the Seller will accept a price or terms other than
28. stated in the listing or that the Buyer will accept a price or terms other than offered;
29. 2) There will be conflicts in the duties of loyalty, obedience, disclosure and confidentiality.  Disclosure of confidential information may be
30. made only with written authorization.  This does not, relieve the Broker of the obligation to disclose all known facts which materially
31. and adversely affect the consideration to be paid by any party.
32. b) The Broker shall exercise reasonable skill and care in the performance of the Broker's duties.
33. c) The Broker shall be obligated at all times to deal honestly and fairly with all parties.

### ELECTION

34. **Buyer Election** (Complete this section only if you are the Buyer.)
35. The undersigned elects to have the Broker (Check any that apply)

36. ☐ represent the Buyer as Buyer's Broker (See Section I)

37. ☐ represent the Seller as Seller's Broker. (See Section II)

38. ☐ show Buyer properties listed with Broker's firm. As a result, Buyer agrees that Broker shall act as agent for both Buyer and Seller provided that the
39. Seller consents to dual representation (See Section III).  Buyer's and Seller's consent should be acknowledged in a separate writing other than the
40. purchase contract.

41. **Seller Election** (Complete this section only if you are the Seller.)
42. The undersigned elects to have the Broker: (Check any that apply)

43. ☐ represent the Seller as Seller's Broker. (See Section II)

44. ☐ show Seller's property to buyers represented by  Broker's firm and Seller agrees that Broker shall act as agent for both Seller and Buyer provided
45. that Buyer consents to the dual representation (See Section III). Seller's and  Buyer's consent should be acknowledged in a separate writing other
46. than the purchase contract.

47. THE UNDERSIGNED    ☐ BUYER(S)  OR  ☐ SELLER(S)   ACKNOWLEDGE RECEIPT OF A COPY OF THIS DOCUMENT.

48. _____   _____   _____   _____
    SIGNED             MO/DA/YR        SIGNED            MO/DA/YR

49. _____   _____   _____   _____
    FIRM NAME (BROKER)             LICENSEE'S SIGNATURE       MO/DA/YR

This form is available for use by the entire real estate industry. The use of this form is not intended to identify the user as a REALTOR®. REALTOR® is a registered collective membership mark which may be used only by real estate licensees who are members of the NATIONAL ASSOCIATION OF REALTORS® and subscribe to its Code of Ethics.
©ARIZONA ASSOCIATION OF REALTORS® FORM 1587-1555 READAE MAY 94

SOURCE: Permission granted by Arizona Association of REALTORS®.

## Figure 2.6 Limited Dual Representation Agreement

### LIMITED DUAL REPRESENTATION AGREEMENT
**BROKER REPRESENTS BOTH SELLER AND BUYER OR BOTH LANDLORD AND TENANT**

THE PRINTED PORTION OF THIS CONTRACT HAS BEEN APPROVED BY THE ARIZONA ASSOCIATION OF REALTORS®. THIS IS INTENDED TO BE A BINDING CONTRACT. NO REPRESENTATION IS MADE AS TO THE LEGAL VALIDITY OR ADEQUACY OF ANY PROVISION THEREOF. IF YOU DESIRE LEGAL ADVICE, CONSULT YOUR ATTORNEY.

1. BUYER/TENANT ("BUYER") _____

2. SELLER/LANDLORD ("SELLER") _____

3. SUBJECT PROPERTY ("PROPERTY") _____ _____

4. "BROKER" _____
                                           NAME OF FIRM                             NAME OF LICENSEE(S)

5. **Broker Authorization:** The Broker in this transaction, together with the Broker's licensees collectively referred to as "Broker," is autho-
6. rized to represent both Seller and Buyer in this transaction. Seller and Buyer understand that Broker cannot represent the interests of one
7. party to the exclusion or detriment of the other party.

8. **Additional Disclosures:** The parties understand that:
9.    a) The Broker represents both the Buyer and the Seller with limitations of the duties owed to the Buyer and the Seller, such as:
10.       1) The Broker will not, without written authorization, disclose to the other party that the Seller will accept a price or terms other than
11.         stated in the listing or that the Buyer will accept a price or terms other than offered;
12.       2) There will be conflicts in the duties of loyalty, obedience, disclosure and confidentiality. Disclosure of confidential information may
13.         be made only with written authorization. This does not relieve the Broker of the obligation to disclose all known facts which materi-
14.         ally and adversely affect the consideration to be paid by any party to the transaction.
15.    b) The Broker shall exercise reasonable skill and care in the performance of the Broker's duties.
16.    c) The Broker shall be obligated at all times to deal honestly and fairly with all parties.
17.    d) The duties of the Broker in this transaction do not relieve the Seller or the Buyer from the responsibility to protect their own interests.

18. **Compensation:** Compensation to the Broker shall be paid pursuant to separate agreement(s). Compensation in and of itself does not
19. necessarily establish representation of any party.

20. **Indemnification:** Seller and Buyer agree to indemnify and hold Broker harmless against any and all claims, damages, losses, expenses or
21. liabilities including attorneys' fees and costs incurred by Broker in any defense thereof arising from Broker's role of limited dual representation.

22. **Prior Agreements:** Seller and Buyer understand this document does not replace prior agreements entered into with Broker to represent
23. Buyer or Seller . However, in any areas where this Limited Dual Representation Agreement contradicts or conflicts with prior agreements,
24. this Limited Dual Representation Agreement shall supersede.

25. **Automatic Cancellation:** If the Seller and Buyer do not enter into an agreement relating to the Property or if the transaction between the
26. Seller and the Buyer fails to close, Buyer and Seller agree that this Agreement is automatically canceled and the Broker's role of limited
27. dual representation is terminated.
28. THE UNDERSIGNED PARTIES ACKNOWLEDGE  THAT THEY HAVE THOROUGHLY READ AND APPROVED THIS AGREEMENT
29. AND ACKNOWLEDGE RECEIPT OF A COPY.

30. Dated: _____    Dated: _____
               MO/DA/YR                                     MO/DA/YR

31. Seller(s) _____    Buyer(s) _____
              PRINT                                    PRINT

32. Seller(s) Signature: _____    Buyer(s) Signature: _____

33. Seller's Signature: _____    Buyer's Signature: _____

SOURCE: Permission granted by Arizona Association of REALTORS®.

## QUESTIONS

1. A listing taken by a real estate salesperson belongs to the

   a. salesperson.
   b. salesperson and employing broker equally.
   c. employing broker.
   d. seller.

2. All of the following are requirements of the Commissioner's Rules *except*

   a. a seller must receive a copy of the listing agreement upon signing it.
   b. a broker must, within five days of the date of the contract, approve all listing contracts taken by his or her salespeople.
   c. all listing contracts for real property must be in writing and signed by all parties.
   d. all listing contracts must be accompanied by a market analysis for the proper pricing of the property.

3. All of the following would terminate a listing contract *except* the

   a. expiration of the contract.
   b. death or incapacity of the broker.
   c. nonpayment of the commission by the owner.
   d. destruction of the improvements on the property.

4. An Arizona licensee advertises a property in her own name and does not include her broker's name or mention that she is a real estate licensee. Which of the following is true?

   a. The licensee has placed a blind ad and may be subject to disciplinary action.
   b. The licensee has done nothing wrong.
   c. If the licensee sells the property through the ad, the seller will not owe the licensee a commission.
   d. If the licensee sells the property through the ad, the buyer will be able to back out of the transaction with no penalties.

5. A listing contract specifically states that the broker is not to accept an earnest money deposit of less than $5,000 and that the earnest money is to be only in cash or by certified check. A buyer wants to write an offer and use a $1,000 personal check as earnest money. The broker may

   a. accept the deposit but not submit the offer.
   b. refuse to accept the deposit but submit the offer.
   c. accept the deposit as an agent of the buyer.
   d. refuse to accept the deposit.

6. *D* had his property under an exclusive agency listing with Broker *W*. If *D* sells his property during the listing term without using *W*'s services, he owes *W*

   a. the full commission.
   b. a partial commission.
   c. *W*'s costs.
   d. nothing.

7. Broker *S* takes a listing on *P*'s home, not knowing that *P* is married to *J* and the home is community property. After *S* secures a "ready, willing and able" buyer for the property on *P*'s terms, *P* says that he does not have to sell because his wife, *J*, did not sign the listing contract. Which of the following statements is true regarding *S*'s possible actions?

   a. He can collect his commission from *P* and *J*.
   b. He can place a lien against the property for his commission.
   c. He can retain the earnest money from the buyer in lieu of his commission.
   d. He can collect his commission from *P*.

8. *W* hired *M* as his broker under an open listing. While that listing was still in effect, *W*—without informing *M*—hired *A* under an exclusive listing for the same property. If *M* procures a buyer for the property, then *W* must pay a

   a. full commission only to *M*.
   b. full commission only to *A*.
   c. full commissions to both *M* and *A*.
   d. half commission to both *M* and *A*.

9. A listing contract

   a. is an employment contract for the personal and professional services of the broker.
   b. obligates the seller to convey the property if the broker produces a "ready, willing and able" buyer.
   c. obligates the broker to work diligently for both the seller and the buyer.
   d. automatically requires the payment of a commission while the broker protection clause is in effect.

10. *G* listed her condominium unit with Broker *H*. *H* brought an offer from the *R*s that met all the terms of the listing, and the *R*s were able to pay cash for the unit. However, *G* changed her mind and rejected the *R*s' offer. In this situation, *G*

    a. does not have to sell her unit.
    b. does not owe a commission to *H*.
    c. is liable to the *R*s for specific performance.
    d. is liable to the *R*s for compensatory damages.

# 3
# Interests in Real Estate

## LEGAL LIFE ESTATES

### Marital Life Estates

The marital life estates of dower and curtesy have never been recognized in Arizona, which is a community property state. See Chapter 4, "How Ownership Is Held," for a full discussion of community property.

### Homestead

In Arizona, the homestead exemption, which is statutory and thus requires no recording, is the only legal life estate recognized by law. The homestead exemption is intended to protect the equity that a homeowner has in his or her residence against the execution of judgment liens (ARS Section 33–1101 through Section 33–1105). Note that the homestead exemption does not protect a homeowner from the foreclosure of voluntary liens, such as a mortgage or deed of trust.

Every homeowner who resides in Arizona, whether single or married, who is at least eighteen years old, has the right to a homestead on his or her residence. A residence may be a single-family dwelling, a condominium unit or a mobile home (regardless of whether the land under the mobile home is leased or owned). Note that only one homestead exemption is allowed at a time. The homestead exemption automatically attaches to the person's equity interest in homestead property.

The amount of the homestead exemption is $100,000. This means that up to $100,000 of the homeowner's equity will be protected in the event of a judgment execution (the homestead exemption may not exceed the homeowner's equity in the residence). The homeowner's equity is determined by deducting the amount of any outstanding mortgage liens, trust deed liens, mechanic's liens and real estate tax liens from the value of the property.

The amount of exemption that a homeowner may actually receive in the case of a court-ordered sale of the residence is not necessarily $100,000. For example, suppose a home is sold at a court-ordered sale for $157,000 and there is a mortgage lien on the property with an unpaid balance of $105,000. After the $105,000 is paid to the lender, the owner will receive only the $52,000 remainder.

Some people mistakenly believe that a homestead exemption will prevent the sale of their residences. This is not true. If a judgment creditor wants to execute his or her judgment lien, a homestead exemption will not prevent a judge from ordering the sale of the property; it will only protect up to $100,000 of the homeowner's equity.

Once established, a homestead exemption may be terminated in one of three ways:

1. The claimant may record a document called an "Abandonment of Homestead."
2. The sale of the property will terminate the homestead (the property ceases to fulfill the "residence" requirement, and the homeowner receives his or her equity at the close of escrow). When a homestead exemption is terminated by the sale of the property, Arizona law (ARS Section 33–1101, paragraph C) provides that the homestead exemption automatically attaches to the identifiable cash proceeds from the sale of the home for a period of 18 months after the close of escrow, or until the individual establishes a new homestead with the proceeds. So, although a homestead exemption technically is not transferable from one residence to another, the protection afforded by the exemption permits an individual to sell one residence and purchase another without fear of losing the equity.
3. Because the homestead exemption protects only the equity in the homeowner's residence, a permanent move from the state of Arizona is considered to be a physical abandonment of the property, thus terminating the homestead exemption. The law allows the homeowner to leave the homesteaded residence for up to two years before the absence becomes a "physical abandonment."

## EASEMENTS

An easement is the right acquired by one person to use land owned by another for a specific purpose. While the text provides a general discussion of the various types of easements—all of which are valid in Arizona—easements by necessity and easements by prescription require a more detailed discussion.

### Easement by Necessity

Under Arizona law, all property owners are supposed to have ingress and egress rights to their property; in other words, all property owners are to have some type of permanent access to their land. If a property is landlocked—that is, completely surrounded by property owned by others—the owner may file a lawsuit and ask the court to condemn enough land on an adjoining parcel to allow for ingress and egress. The court proceeding is similar to a public taking under a government exercise of eminent domain; however, the suit is filed by an individual rather than by a government entity. If the court action is successful, the landowner will receive the right to cross the adjoining parcel of land by virtue of an easement by necessity. In many cases, the owner of the adjoining parcel must be compensated for the value of the easement; such compensation is fixed by the court.

The Arizona Real Estate Code specifically prohibits the sale of any subdivided or unsubdivided property without permanent access to a public road (ARS Section 32–2185.02, paragraph A, and Section 32–2195, paragraph B7). However, there are thousands of landlocked parcels throughout the state, primarily located along the borders of government lands (such as land owned by the Bureau of Land Management, U.S. Forest Service and Bureau of Indian Affairs). These parcels were created by inaccurate surveying and questionable land sales that occurred before any subdivision regulations were enacted. While it is impossible to obtain an easement by necessity on any lands regulated by the subdivision requirements, it is still possible to obtain such an easement on unregulated land.

## Easement by Prescription

Prescriptive easements in Arizona are an extension of the concept of acquiring the title to property through adverse possession (discussed in Chapter 8). A person may acquire an easement by prescription across the land of another after **ten years** of continuous use. During that time, the claimant's use of the land must be **continuous** (uninterrupted), **open and notorious** (obvious for all to see) and **hostile** (without the knowledge or permission of the owner).

An easement by prescription involves a lawsuit, and if the court grants the easement, the claimant must continue to use the easement so granted. An easement by prescription runs with the land and is transferable when the property is sold. But if the easement rights are not used for five continuous years, then the person on whose land the easement is located (the **servient tenement**) may apply to the court to have the easement removed.

## WATER RIGHTS

Arizona has both surface water and groundwater, and each is governed by a separate section of the Arizona Revised Statutes.

## Surface Water

Arizona law defines surface water as "waters from all sources, flowing in streams, canyons, ravines, or other natural channels, or in definite underground channels, whether perennial or intermittent, flood, waste, or surplus water, and of lakes, ponds, and springs on the surface." Water flowing in the Central Arizona Project system is also considered to be surface water and regulated as such.

Surface water is governed by the doctrine of **prior appropriation**: "first in time, first in right." Because there may not be sufficient water available to satisfy the needs of all potential users, permits for the right to use surface water must be obtained from the Arizona Department of Water Resources. Generally, the first permit applicant will receive the right to use the water from the resource identified in the application first; subsequent applicants will receive rights to use whatever water is still available from that source. Therefore, the user holding the permit with the oldest date has the legal right to satisfy his or her needs from the specified source before anyone else. The holder of the permit with the next-oldest date can then satisfy his or her needs from the surplus, and so on, until there is no surplus remaining.

When multiple applications are pending for water from the same resource, the priority for permits is as follows:

- Domestic and municipal uses (domestic use including irrigation of up to a one-half acre parcel)
- Irrigation and stock watering
- Power generation and mining uses
- Recreation and wildlife, including fish
- Artificial groundwater recharge

Once a permit is granted, the right to use the water cannot be terminated except by five years of continuous nonuse without cause by the holder of the permit, voluntary abandonment of the permit or eminent domain. Only permits given in conjunction with power generation (such as a hydroelectric facility) must be renewed, with a preferential right of renewal every 40 years.

**Riparian rights** as they existed at common law do not exist in Arizona, because of the scarcity of water. However, when a parcel of land is bordered by surface water, riparian rights (including the principles of "navigable" and "nonnavigable" water) will determine the extent of that land ownership. In general, rivers and lakes that form interstate boundaries are considered navigable. Owners of land along navigable bodies of water have title only to the mean high watermark, and the water in the river and the land below the mean high watermark belong to the federal government. Owners of land along nonnavigable waters have title to the land up to the center of the water source (such as the centerline of a riverbed or streambed). The water rights that pertain to nonnavigable rivers and streams, however, can still be controlled by the state or federal government.

Surface water rights in Arizona are under review in a legal action known as the "Arizona General Adjudication." This is a suit between the state of Arizona and Arizona Indian tribes, and concerns the rights to all surface waters in the state. It was filed in 1974 and is expected to last well into the 21st century. It will not be known for many years what the final effect on surface water rights will ultimately be, or whether any groundwater rights will be affected by this litigation.

## Groundwater

Arizona law defines groundwater as "water under the surface of the earth, regardless of the geologic structure in which it is standing or moving. Groundwater does not include water flowing in underground streams with ascertainable beds and banks."

More than 40 percent of Arizona's water is groundwater. Because of the rapid development of the state, groundwater traditionally has been pumped from underground storage areas, called "aquifers," faster than it could be replaced naturally. This phenomenon is known as "overdraft." Years of overdraft have led to significant groundwater level declines—as much as 600 feet in some areas. Continuous overdraft results in increased drilling and pumping costs, as well as the deterioration of water quality (because water from greater depths contains more salts and minerals). Overdraft also causes subsidence—cracks and fissures in the earth that can damage roads, buildings and other structures. (Sinkholes are a good example of the damage that can be caused by overdrafts.)

As a result of continuous overdrafts, in 1980 Arizona enacted the Groundwater Management Code, which is a comprehensive law designed to monitor and regulate the use of groundwater. The objectives of the code are to minimize overdraft throughout the state, to allocate Arizona's limited groundwater supply more effectively and to encourage the development of supplemental sources of water. Supplemental source development has led to innovations such as the use of effluent for watering and irrigation (thus conserving potable water supplies) and on-site rainwater retention for nonresidential buildings (which allows run-off to percolate through the soil to the water table rather than burdening public storm drains and contributing to flooding).

Administered by the Arizona Department of Water Resources, the Groundwater Management Code sets limits on who can use groundwater, where and how it can be used and how much may be withdrawn from the aquifers. Toward these ends, Irrigation Nonexpansion Areas (INAs) and Active Management Areas (AMAs) have been established where water management programs are most needed.

In INAs, where irrigation use threatens to exceed the limited water supply, irrigated acreage is restricted; but specific water conservation measures are not required. There are three INAs in the state: Douglas, Harquahala and Joseph City.

Four AMAs have been created where the overdraft problem is critical: Phoenix, Pinal, Prescott and Tucson. More than 84 percent of the state's population currently resides in the AMAs, and projections show as much as 92 percent of the population could reside in the AMAs by the year 2025. Therefore, more rigorous water management requirements are necessary.

Municipalities or private water companies supply the water to most urban properties located in the AMAs. Generally, any water rights belonging to these properties have been subrogated to the water provider so that continuous service from a common water source can be provided to each site.

Many suburban and rural properties in the AMAs still have their water rights intact. But the owners of these properties do not automatically have the right to withdraw groundwater. Unless a proposed well qualifies as an **exempt well** (which is defined below), in order to withdraw groundwater, the property owner must have

- grandfathered water rights,
- a withdrawal permit (one of the seven types available),
- a service area permit or
- a storage and recovery permit.

The Arizona Department of Water Resources has many pamphlets available that give the specific requirements for those types of rights or permits.

An exempt well within an AMA is a well with a maximum pump capacity of 35 gallons per minute that is used to withdraw groundwater only for nonirrigation purposes. (However, the watering of less than two acres of garden or grass is allowed.) This type of well is sometimes referred to as a **domestic use well**. Only one exempt well may serve the same use at the same location, so an owner may not drill multiple exempt wells to serve the same purpose. (However, one well can be drilled to serve multiple properties.) Anyone who wants to drill an exempt well must file a Notice of Intent to Drill with the Arizona Department of Water Resources and receive the department's approval before drilling. Exempt well owners are not required to measure groundwater pumpage, file annual water use reports or pay withdrawal fees.

The Arizona Department of Water Resources is required by the code to develop **management plans** for each AMA, with each plan containing specific water conservation requirements aimed at achieving the management goal for that AMA. The department has the statutory authority to implement and enforce these plans.

The management goal for the three urban AMAs—Phoenix, Prescott and Tucson—is **safe yield** by the year 2025. Safe yield means that the annual groundwater withdrawals do not exceed the annual groundwater recharge. In the Pinal AMA, which is predominantly an agricultural economy, the goal is to maintain the economy as long as feasible while recognizing the need to preserve groundwater for future nonirrigation uses. As time passes, the management plans for each AMA will become more stringent as conservation requirements become more rigorous.

A word of warning: because of the comprehensive regulation of water use throughout Arizona (which is the result of an increasing demand on a decreasing supply), before a licensee attempts to market real estate that has accompanying water rights, he or she should get written confirmation of those water rights from the Arizona Department of Water Resources.

**Figure 3.1 Summary of Freehold Interests**

Freehold Estates
A.     Fee Simple Estates—*pass in perpetuity*
      1.     Fee Simple Absolute
      2.     Fee Simple Determinable (*base fee*)—defeasible
      3.     Fee Simple on Condition Subsequent—defeasible
      4.     Fee Simple Conditional (*fee tail*)—illegal

B.     Life Estates—*indefinite, but limited*
      1.     Conventional Life Estates (based on common law)
          a.     Ordinary Estate in Reversion
          b.     Pur Autre Vie Estate in Reversion
          c.     Ordinary Estate in Remainder
          d.     Pur Autre Vie Estate in Remainder
      2.     Legal Life Estates (based on statutory law)
          a.     Dower—not used in Arizona
          b.     Curtesy—not used in Arizona
          c.     Homestead

## Assured Water Supplies and Adequate Water Supplies

Water is a critical issue in land development, and the state has jurisdiction over both the certification of water supplies and the requirements for any related disclosures.

Developers wanting to offer to the public subdivided property within a groundwater AMA must have an **assured water supply**, which is a minimum 100-year supply. This supply can be certified either by a contract with a municipal provider who allows the developer to tie-in to that municipality's existing water distribution system, or by a Certificate of Assured Water Supply issued by the director of the Arizona Department of Water Resources.

Developers offering subdivided property outside of a groundwater AMA or offering unsubdivided property must have an **adequate water supply**, which is a disclosure only of whatever water supplies, if any, are available. This determination is made by the director of the Arizona Department of Water Resources, and its disclosures in public reports are required and enforced by the commissioner of the Arizona Department of Real Estate.

## QUESTIONS

1. To acquire an easement by prescription under Arizona law, the claimant must perform all of the following *except*

    a.   use the property openly.
    b.   pay the taxes on the property.
    c.   be there without the owner's permission.
    d.   use the property for ten continuous years.

2. All of the following would terminate a homestead exemption in Arizona *except* the

    a.   signing and recording of an abandonment of homestead.
    b.   permanent physical abandonment of the property.
    c.   filing for bankruptcy by the owners.
    d.   sale of the property.

3. The two types of water rights that are regulated in Arizona are

   a. navigable and nonnavigable.
   b. surface and ground.
   c. riparian and littoral.
   d. flowing and static.

4. All of the following are required for a homeowner to be entitled to a homestead exemption in Arizona except the homeowner must

   a. own the property on which the exemption is allowed.
   b. be at least eighteen years of age.
   c. record the declaration of homestead.
   d. be a legal resident of Arizona.

5. If two individuals own property on opposite sides of a nonnavigable stream, their ownership interests extend to the

   a. high watermark of the stream, but not the water.
   b. low watermark of the stream, but not the water.
   c. center of the stream, but not the water.
   d. center of the stream, and the right to use all of the water.

6. The creation of a life estate also creates a/an

   a. allodial interest.
   b. remainder or a reversion.
   c. determinable fee interest.
   d. defeasible fee interest.

7. An easement is terminated by all of the following *except*

   a. a merger.
   b. a sale in which the deed does not reference the easement.
   c. the physical destruction of the servient tenement.
   d. a quitclaim deed from the holder of the dominant tenement to the holder of the servient tenement.

8. The owner's equity in his or her home is protected by a homestead exemption up to

   a. $50,000.
   b. $75,000.
   c. $100,000.
   d. $125,000.

9. As the result of a car accident, *S* recorded a judgment against the *N*s for $19,000. A title search indicated that the *N*s had a mortgage lien for $53,000 and a lien for the construction of a swimming pool for $13,500. If the court ordered the sale of the *N* residence to satisfy the judgment lien, and the property brought $181,500, what would *S* receive?

   a. Nothing
   b. $5,000
   c. $15,000
   d. $19,000

10. All of the following requirements must be met for an exempt well *except* that

    a. it must be located outside of a groundwater active management area.
    b. it must be used only for domestic purposes.
    c. the maximum capacity cannot exceed 35 gallons per minute.
    d. it cannot serve a parcel larger than two acres.

# 4

# How Ownership Is Held

The last chapter described what estates or interests in real estate may be owned; this chapter explains how real estate may be owned.

In Arizona, real estate may be owned in **severalty** (by a single owner), **concurrently** (by two or more owners) or in **trust**. Concurrent ownership of real estate can take the form of a joint tenancy, a tenancy in common, community property or community property with the right of survivorship. Any legal entity, such as a partnership or corporation, can own real estate in severalty or as a tenant in common with other firms or individuals. Obviously, they cannot own real estate as community property or as joint tenants, because as legal entities they never marry or die.

## TENANCY IN COMMON

According to Arizona law, a deed of conveyance to two or more persons automatically creates a tenancy in common, except conveyances to married couples (who own property as community property) and conveyances to trustees, executors and administrators (who receive title to the property in joint tenancy).

With a tenancy in common, there are no unities of time, title or interest. Therefore, tenants in common may acquire title through separate deeds, may have unequal interests in the property and may freely convey their interests by sale, gift or will. The recipient of such an interest may also hold title as a tenant in common with the other owners.

## COMMUNITY PROPERTY

In Arizona, unless otherwise specified, all property owned by a married person is either **separate property** or **community property**. A person's separate property consists of all personal and real property that was acquired by him or her before the marriage, as well as any property acquired by gift, by will or by inheritance during the marriage, except for property for which one of the spouses signs a disclaimer deed, disclaiming any community property interest. Community property is defined as all property, real and personal, acquired by either spouse during the marriage, except for property acquired by only one of them as a gift, through a will or by inheritance.

Both personal and real property that is brought into the marriage remains the separate property of the owner-spouse. Income and profits produced by such property during the marriage also remain that spouse's separate property.

Both personal and real property acquired during the marriage belongs to the married couple (often referred to as the "marital community") equally. The income and profits produced by community property during the marriage belong to the married couple equally. Also, the personal earnings of each spouse (such as wages or salary) are community property, even if the spouses are legally separated.

Either spouse may also acquire real property as his or her sole and separate property, even though married at the time of acquisition. This may be accomplished by having the nonowner spouse sign a disclaimer deed when the property is purchased. In effect, this deed disavows the signer's spousal interest in the property. It should be noted, however, that any financial encumbrances placed against the property remain a marital community obligation.

When managing separate property, each spouse is responsible for his or her own debts, and one spouse cannot be held liable for the debts created by the other. However, either spouse may authorize the other to act on his or her behalf by granting such authority through a power of attorney.

The community is liable for any debts created by either spouse during the marriage. It is also liable for any separate debts incurred by either spouse before the marriage up to the value of that spouse's contribution to the community property.

Each spouse has equal authority over all community property; that is, each has equal authority to manage, control and dispose of community property. Either spouse can contract debts or otherwise act for the benefit of the community. However, neither spouse can convey or encumber any community real property (except for an unpatented mining claim) unless they both sign and acknowledge all the contracts or other documents involved in the transaction. Any conveyance or encumbrance of community real property that is not signed and acknowledged by both spouses is invalid.

Upon the death of either spouse, one-half of the community property automatically belongs to the surviving spouse. The other half of the property is distributed according to the decedent's will. If the decedent has no will, his or her estate is distributed according to Arizona's statutes governing descent and distribution (the Uniform Probate Code). If the decedent has no will and no apparent heirs, his or her half of the community property reverts to the surviving spouse.

There is also another type of community property: **community property with right of survivorship**. Under this type of ownership, if one spouse dies, the surviving spouse automatically acquires sole ownership in the community property. There is no necessity for probate. The right of survivorship is discussed in more detail in the following section on joint tenancy.

When dealing with property owned by a married person, the real estate licensee should be particularly careful to ascertain the status of that property (whether it is separate or community property). Any married person who deliberately represents himself or herself as being able to individually encumber or convey real property and then does so, when a spouse's signature is required for such an action, has committed a felony under Arizona law.

Married couples are not strictly limited to community property ownership in Arizona. Quite often, they elect to take title to their real property as **tenants in common**. By owning property as tenants in common, a married couple can provide for unequal ownership interests.

**Figure 4.1 Summary of Concurrent Ownership**

| | Tenancy in Common | Community Property | Joint Tenancy |
|---|---|---|---|
| Unities: | 1. Possession | 1. Possession | 1. Time<br>2. Title<br>3. Interest<br>4. Possession |
| Created by: | Arizona Statute | Arizona Statute | Action of the Parties |
| Individual Interests Salable? | YES | NO | YES |
| Individual Interests Devisible? | YES | YES | NO |
| Multiple Deeds Permitted? | YES | NO | NO |
| Equal Interests Required? | NO | YES | YES |

Remember, a licensee is not qualified or allowed to give advice on how a married couple should take title. Property buyers should always obtain the appropriate tax and legal advice before making a decision regarding the method of taking title.

NOTE: Tenancy by the entirety, a special type of marital ownership available in some noncommunity property states, does not exist in Arizona.

## JOINT TENANCY

Joint tenancy with rights of survivorship is created when the grantees sign a **joint tenancy deed**, a special type of deed through which they waive their community property rights and tenancy in common interests in favor of joint tenancy. Any two or more natural persons (regardless of whether they are married) may take title as joint tenants. Because a corporation is not a natural person, it cannot take title as a joint tenant. (Corporations never die; therefore, survivorship rights would never take effect.)

The principal benefit of joint tenancy is the right of survivorship (sometimes referred to as the **grand incident**)—the automatic transfer at death of a decedent's interest to the surviving joint tenants. Although a joint tenancy interest may be separately conveyed by sale or gift, such an interest cannot be willed. The joint tenancy deed provides that a joint tenancy interest transfers at its owner's death to the survivors. Thus, the agreement created by the joint tenancy supersedes any provisions of a will. (Remember, now spouses can take advantage of the right to survivorship when they own property as community property with right of survivorship.)

## CONDOMINIUM OWNERSHIP

Arizona's Condominiums Act (Title 33, Chapter 9) regulates the creation, management and termination of condominiums. A condominium is defined by Arizona law as

real estate, portions of which are designated for separate ownership and the remainder of which is designated for common ownership solely by the owners of the separate portions. Real estate is not a condominium unless the undivided interests in the common elements are vested in the unit owners.

A condominium can only be created pursuant by recording a condominium declaration in each county in which any portion of the condominium is located. The declaration is recorded in the same way a deed is recorded; the declaration is indexed in the name of the condominium and in the name of the condominium association and otherwise as required by law.

The declaration must contain

- the name of the condominium and the name of the association;
- the name of every county in which any portion of the condominium is located;
- a legal description of the real estate included in the condominium;
- a description of the boundaries of each unit created by the declaration;
- a description of any limited common elements;
- a description of any development rights and other special declarant rights, together with a legal description of the real estate to which each of those rights applies, any time limit within which each of those rights must be exercised and any other conditions or limitations under which the rights described may be exercised or will lapse;
- the allocation of the common interests, votes and common expense liabilities;
- any restrictions on use, occupancy and alienation of the units;
- a statement that the assessment obligations of the unit owner is secured by a lien on the owner's unit;
- the condominium plat; and
- any other matters deemed appropriate or required by law.

## Management

The condominium is managed by a unit owner's association, which must be organized no later than the date the first condominium unit is conveyed. Only unit owners may belong to the association.

The unit owners' association has the power to adopt and amend bylaws and rules, adopt and amend budgets, hire and fire managing agents and other employees, institute or defend litigation, make contracts and incur liabilities, regulate the use and maintenance of common elements, make improvements and grant easements. The activities are carried out by the association's board of directors.

To prevent developers from retaining control of a condominium, or from profiting unduly from management or employment contracts, there are strict limits on the developer's ability to manage the condominium. According to Arizona law, a condominium **declarant** (developer) can only control the unit owner's association for up to 90 days after the conveyance of 75 percent of the units, or four years after ceasing to offer units for sale, whichever comes first. Furthermore, any management or employment contracts entered into by the declarant on behalf of the association may be canceled at any time without penalty after the board of directors elected by the unit owners takes office.

## Termination

A condominium may be terminated only by a vote of an 80 percent majority (or any larger percentage specified in the declaration). The termination agreement must be recorded in each county in which any portion of the condominium is located. The termination agreement may provide that all of the common elements and units will be sold following termination. However, if the real estate constituting the condominium is not to be sold following termination, title to all the real estate vests in the unit owners as tenants in common in proportion to their respective interests.

## TIME–SHARES

In Arizona, a time-share project is defined as

> a project in which a purchaser receives the right in perpetuity, for life or for a term of years to the recurrent, exclusive use or occupancy of a lot, parcel, unit or segment of real property, annually or on some other periodic basis, for a period of time that has been or will be allotted from the use or occupancy periods into which the project has been divided.

Arizona law (Title 32, Chapter 20, Article 9) regulates the creation and sale of time-shares (interests in time-share projects). Arizona's time-share law is essentially a consumer protection law: it requires the issuance of a public report before time-shares can be offered for sale or lease, it gives time-share buyers or lessees seven-day rescission rights after the initial purchase and it regulates time-share advertising. The time-share statutes apply to any time-share offering in Arizona of 12 or more intervals to Arizona residents, regardless of where the project is located. The law strictly regulates the use of promotions, prizes and other inducements in the marketing of time-share intervals.

## Public Reports

A public report on a time-share project must be obtained before any time-shares can be offered for sale or lease. The application for a public report is submitted to the commissioner and must contain a good deal of information about the project, including (but not limited to)

- the name and address of the owner and developer;
- a comprehensive statement of the time-share program;
- the legal description and location of the land;
- a recorded map of the project;
- a description of the total facility in terms of the number of buildings, number of stories and common areas;
- a true statement of assurances for the installation of off-site improvements;
- proof of adequate financial arrangements for any improvements;

- a complete disclosure as to the operating costs of the time-share program;
- a current preliminary title report;
- a statement of the provisions made for the management of the project (including a copy of the management agreement); and
- copies of all contracts and promotional materials to be used.

Once the application for the public report has been submitted, the commissioner examines the time-share project, makes his or her findings public and (unless there is cause for denial) issues a public report to the developer that authorizes the sale or lease of the time-shares in Arizona. Time-shares sold or leased prior to the issuance of a public report may be voidable by the purchaser.

Arizona law requires all inducement-based promotional and advertising material used in connection with the sales of time-shares to be filed with the commissioner, to be approved or disapproved within 15 days. Furthermore, any advertising, communication or sales literature of any kind (including oral statements) may not contain

- any untrue statements of material fact or any omissions of material fact that would make such statements misleading;

- any statement or representation that the time-share is offered without risk or that loss is impossible; and

- any statement or representation or pictorial presentation of proposed improvements or nonexistent scenes without clearly indicating that the improvements are proposed and the scenes do not exist.

Under Arizona's time-share law, purchasers have the right to rescind the purchase or lease of a time-share without cause for a period of seven days after the execution of the sale or lease documents. The rescission must be made in writing.

## QUESTIONS

1. Two brothers buy property. They are automatically

   a. joint tenants with rights of survivorship.
   b. community property owners.
   c. tenants in common.
   d. tenants by the entirety.

2. Which of the following best describes a condominium?

   a. Individual ownership of an individual unit and the common areas
   b. Individual ownership of an individual unit; common ownership of the common areas
   c. Common ownership of an individual unit and the common areas
   d. Common ownership of an individual unit; individual ownership of the common areas

3. A condominium is created by

   a. recording a declaration.
   b. signing and acknowledging the articles and bylaws.
   c. agreement by all of the unit owners.
   d. a vote of 80 percent of the board of directors.

4. All of the following statements about community property are true *except*

   a. the profits, interests and rents earned by a person's separate property remain as part of his or her separate property.
   b. if one spouse dies, then the entire property automatically belongs to the surviving spouse's children.
   c. community property can be conveyed only if both the husband and wife sign all the pertinent contracts and documents.
   d. community property consists of all property acquired by a husband and wife (except by gift, will or inheritance) during their marriage.

5. A joint tenancy between two single men would become a tenancy in common upon

   a. the death of one of the men.
   b. one selling his interest to the other.
   c. the marriage of one of the men.
   d. one selling his interest to a third party.

6. Can *J* and *M*, husband and wife, buy property as tenants in common?

   a. This is impossible, as a married couple cannot own property as tenants in common.
   b. *J* and *M* would have to sign a special disclaimer statement in order to do so.
   c. *J* and *M* can own property as tenants in common, but they cannot will their share of the property to their heirs.
   d. *J* and *M* can own property as tenants in common, as long as they make their wishes clear.

7. Mr. *M* is purchasing a home in Arizona while Mrs. *M* is selling their farm in Iowa. When the deed of conveyance is issued, it has only Mr. *M*'s name on it. The interest in the home in Arizona belongs to

   a. Mr. *M* only, as separate property.
   b. Mr. *M* and Mrs. *M* as tenants by the entirety.
   c. Mr. *M* and Mrs. *M* as joint tenants with rights of survivorship.
   d. Mr. *M* and Mrs. *M* as community property.

8. A management contract entered into by a condominium declarant

   a. must be honored by the unit owners for at least four years.
   b. can be canceled by the unit owners without penalty at any time.
   c. is automatically void.
   d. must provide for the declarant to be the property manager.

9. Mr. and Mrs. *K* each have children by their previous marriages. Mrs. *K* wills her community property with right of survivorship to her daughter. If Mrs. *K* dies, her daughter will receive

   a. no interest in the property.
   b. one-half interest in the property with Mr. *K*.
   c. one-quarter interest in the property with Mr. *K*.
   d. one-half interest with Mr. *K* as a tenant in common.

10. A purchaser has how many days to rescind a time-share purchase?

   a. Four
   b. Five
   c. Six
   d. Seven

# 5
# Legal Descriptions

## LEGAL DESCRIPTIONS IN ARIZONA

Land in Arizona is described by **metes and bounds**, by the **government** or **rectangular survey system**, and by the **lot and block** or **recorded plat system**. Although most properties are described using only one of the three methods available, often two or even three of the methods are incorporated into the description of a particularly difficult-to-describe parcel of property.

In general, an acceptable legal description is considered by the courts to be one from which a competent surveyor can establish the boundaries of a parcel of property. It doesn't matter which method is used by the surveyor. A reference to a recorded document, such as a deed that already contains a complete legal description of the property in question, is also considered an acceptable property description. A street address by itself is not an adequate property description as it does not accurately describe the property but only refers to an arbitrary determination by the U.S. Postal Service. Also, because much of the state is undeveloped, street addresses are not always available.

## Tax Parcel Number

Caution must be exercised when using a tax parcel number as a means of identifying property. This number is assigned for convenience by the county assessor. A tax parcel number is subject to periodic changes, especially when a large tract of land is divided into smaller parcels. Any descriptions of land containing references to a tax parcel number must always include the particular year the parcel number appears on the county tax assessment rolls. (Tax parcel numbers are not considered a form of legal description.)

## Government or Rectangular Survey System

Government or rectangular survey descriptions in Arizona are based upon a monument located where the Gila River and the Salt River formerly converged, approximately 20 miles southwest of the Phoenix area in Maricopa County. The Gila and Salt River Base and Meridian (G&SRB&M) is the basis of all survey descriptions in the state, with the exception of a tract in northeast Arizona (the Navajo Base and Meridian).

The Gila and Salt River Base Line extends east and west across the state, from New Mexico to California, and Baseline Road follows the base line through most of Maricopa County. The Principal

Meridian runs north and south through the state, from Utah to Mexico, and 115th Avenue is located on it in western Maricopa County.

The original survey marker, placed in 1867 and reset in 1962, is near the intersection of 115th Avenue and Baseline Road near Goodyear.

A special survey, called the Navajo Base and Meridian, was established in New Mexico in 1869 to survey and legally describe a portion of the Indian reservation land located in the northeast corner of Arizona and the adjacent northwest corner of New Mexico. The only Arizona land surveyed in this system falls within Ranges Six West to Ten West of the Navajo Meridian and Townships One North to Fourteen North of the Navajo Base Line. Although the land in Arizona is still described by the Navajo Base and Meridian, the portion of the survey in New Mexico has long been abandoned and the land absorbed into the New Mexico Base and Meridian.

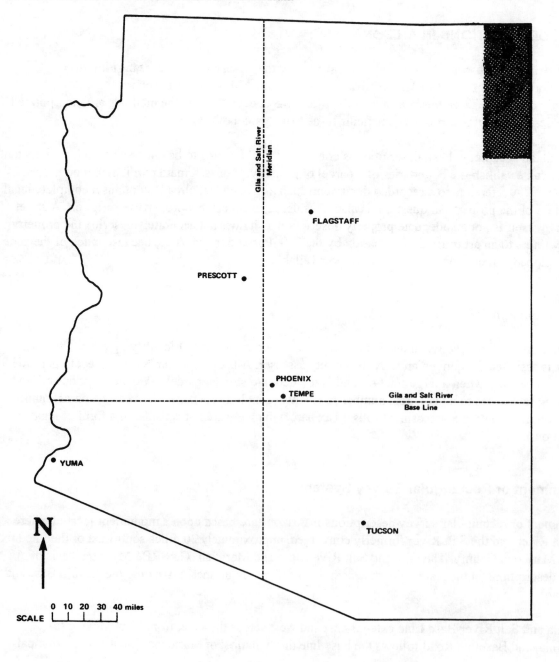

## Lot and Block or Recorded Plat System

Plat maps, particularly for subdivided property, are recorded in the county in which the property is located. Initially, a large parcel of land is described either by metes and bounds or by a government or rectangular survey system. Once this large parcel is surveyed, it may be broken down into smaller parcels. A specific parcel may then be identified by the lot and block number as shown on the recorded plat map. The "lot" refers to the numerical designation of any particular parcel; the "block" refers to the name of the subdivision or part of the subdivision under which the map is recorded. The "block" reference is drawn from the early 1900s when a city block was the most common type of subdivided property.

All property owners or developers who subdivide a tract of land into six or more parcels must submit a subdivision plat to the real estate commissioner before it is recorded and before any parcels are sold or offered for sale. This requirement is part of the subdivision disclosure laws, which are discussed in detail in Chapter 14.

## QUESTIONS

1. The legal description, "The Northwest 1/4 of the Southwest 1/4 of Section 6, Township 4 North, Range 7 West" is defective because there is no reference to

   a. lot numbers.
   b. boundary lines.
   c. baseline and meridian.
   d. a record of survey.

2. To keep the Principal Meridian and range lines as nearly as possible 6 miles apart, a correction known as a government check is made every

   a. 3 miles.
   b. 6 miles.
   c. 12 miles.
   d. 24 miles.

3. Fractional sections in a rectangular survey system that are less than a quarter-section in area are known as

   a. fractional parcels.
   b. government lots.
   c. hiatus.
   d. fractional townships.

4. How many acres are contained in the following parcel: "Beginning at the NE corner of the SW 1/4 of Section 23; then, one mile, more or less, in a northerly direction to the NW corner of the SE 1/4 of Section 14; then, one mile, more or less, in a southeasterly direction to the NW corner of the SE 1/4 of Section 24; then, one mile, more or less, in a westerly direction to the point of beginning"?

   a. 160
   b. 320
   c. 640
   d. 1,280

5. A property was ten acres. How many 50-foot by 100-foot lots would fit on the property if 26,000 square feet were dedicated for roads?

   a. 80
   b. 81
   c. 82
   d. 83

6. *M* owns 4.5 acres of land for which he paid $78,400. Adjoining owners want to buy a strip of *M*'s land measuring 100 feet by 150 feet. What should this strip cost if *M* were to sell it for the same price as he originally paid?

   a. $3,000
   b. $6,000
   c. $7,800
   d. $9,400

7. A parcel of land is 400 feet by 640 feet. The parcel is cut in half diagonally by a stream. How many acres are there in each half of the parcel?

   a. 2.75
   b. 2.94
   c. 5.51
   d. 5.88

8. A man owns the NW 1/4 and the SW 1/4 of Section 17, and his neighbor owns the NE 1/4 and the SE 1/4 of Section 18. If they agree to each install one half of a common fence, how many rods of fencing would each install?

   a. 160
   b. 220
   c. 320
   d. 440

9. Mr. *W* was estimating the cost of building a patio in his backyard. The 60-foot by 15-foot by 4-inch thick slab would cost $78.40 per cubic yard of concrete, and the finishing would cost $.38 per square root. The total cost for *W*'s patio would be

   a. $875.33.
   b. $1,045.33.
   c. $1,182.13.
   d. $1,213.11.

10. The section due West of Section 18, Township 5 North, Range 8 West is

   a. Section 19, Township 5 North, Range 8 West.
   b. Section 17, Township 5 North, Range 8 West.
   c. Section 13, Township 5 North, Range 9 West.
   d. Section 12, Township 5 North, Range 7 West.

## REAL ESTATE TAXES

### Levy and Assessment

Real estate taxes in Arizona are **ad valorem** taxes (ad valorem is Latin for "according to value"). Ad valorem property taxes are based on the assessed value of the property. The tax year is a calendar year—January through December.

Real estate taxes give rise to a tax lien. The annual real estate tax lien is a statutory lien against all privately owned real property in the state. The lien takes effect on the first Monday of each January. Real estate tax liens have priority over all other liens in Arizona, except for those held by the state, and are sometimes referred to as **prior liens** because of their automatic, statutory nature.

Arizona uses a single tax billing system; a single tax bill includes levies made by the state, the county, the municipality, the community college district, the school district and any other authorized special districts (such as those established for flood control and water conservation). Tax bills are issued to all property owners in September, although for properties subject to any mortgage or trust deed liens, the tax bill is usually sent to the first recorded lienholder (the lender).

Real estate taxes are determined by applying a statistical model to the market value of each parcel. The county assessor's office is responsible for estimating the market value of all properties in the county's jurisdiction. This is accomplished in two ways. First, there is continuous on-site appraisal of properties throughout the county. Second, an "Affidavit of Property Value" must be filed with the assessor's office each time a conveyance deed is recorded with the county recorder's office. These methods allow the assessor's office to monitor current property values as reflected in the marketplace.

The assessment process is continuous throughout the year, but those values determined by the county assessor as of January 1 of each year will be used to compute the tax bills issued during the following September.

Notices of valuation (Figure 6.1) are supposed to be mailed no later than November 15, or December 15 with a special exemption from the director of the Arizona Department of Revenue. A property owner who believes that his or her property's assessment is too high has the right to appeal that assessment to the county assessor within 45 days after the mailing date of the notice of valuation. An owner who does

**Figure 6.1 Notice of Valuation**

```
                                                              23219-C  F·BL SEG·0
   129-29-071          RESIDENTIAL NOTICE OF VALUE        ┌─────────────────────┐
 F  PETE CORPSTEIN            THIS IS NOT A TAX BILL      │   PRESORTED         │
 R  MARICOPA COUNTY ASSESSOR                              │ FIRST CLASS MAIL    │
 O  301 W. JEFFERSON                                      │ U.S. POSTAGE PAID   │
    PHOENIX, AZ  85003                                    │ PHOENIX, AZ         │
 M  (602) 506-3406                                        │ PERMIT# 359         │
                                                          └─────────────────────┘
 See Reverse Side for Definitions and Instructions.   Your Appeal Deadline Is APRIL 15, 1996
```

| Property In The County of: | Year | Parcel ID | BK | MP | Parcel | Notice Date 02/15/96 |
|---|---|---|---|---|---|---|
| MARICOPA | 1997 | | | | | |

| | LEGAL CLASS | 1996 VALUATION VALUE | ASST. RATIO | ASSESSED VALUE | LEGAL CLASS | 1997 VALUATION VALUE | ASST RATIO | ASSESSED VALUE |
|---|---|---|---|---|---|---|---|---|
| FULL CASH VALUE | 5 | 93440 | 10.0 | 9344 | 5 | 99281 | 10.0 | 9928 |
| LIMITED VALUE | 5 | 93440 | 10.0 | 9344 | 5 | 99281 | 10.0 | 9928 |

THIS PROPERTY IS CLASSIFIED AS OWNER OCCUPIED RESIDENTIAL (LEGAL CLASS 5). IF THIS PROPERTY IS BEING USED AS A RENTAL UNIT, THE OWNER MUST NOTIFY THE COUNTY ASSESSOR OF THE RENTAL USE. FAILURE TO DO SO MAY RESULT IN A CIVIL PENALTY.

```
                  SEC/LOT 71        TWNS/BLOCK        RANGE/TRACT
LEGAL             VILLAGE GROVE 2
DESCRIPTION

        ‖‖‖‖‖‖‖‖‖‖‖‖‖‖‖‖‖‖‖‖‖‖‖‖‖‖‖‖‖‖‖‖‖

        TO:
```

---

All property must be valued at full cash value. Your property also has a limited value that cannot exceed the full cash value. The limited assessed value is the basis for computing primary taxes for the maintenance and operation of school districts, cities, community college districts, counties, and the state. The assessed value derived from the full cash value is the basis for computing secondary taxes for bonds, budget overrides, and special districts such as fire, flood control, and other limited purpose districts. The assessed value divided by 100, times the tax rate (set in August of each year), determines property taxes billed in October. The assessment ratio for owner-occupied residential (legal class 5) property is 10%.

The legal description on the face of this notice may be incomplete due to space limitation. Please notify your assessor of any address changes.

## APPEAL INSTRUCTIONS

If you feel that this property has been improperly valued or erroneously listed, you may petition the assessor for review within 60 days of the NOTICE DATE on the front of this card. A "Petition For Review of Valuation" with filing instructions can be obtained from the assessor's office.

Completed petitions for review must be filed with the assessor's office by the APPEAL DEADLINE DATE printed on the front of this notice.

(97 BL)

SOURCE: Maricopa County Assessor/Maricopa County Treasurer.

not receive a satisfactory response from the assessor may present his or her case to the county board of equalization within 15 days of the mailing date of the assessor's decision. An appeal of an unfavorable decision from the board of equalization may be made to the state tax appeal board within 15 days of the mailing date of the board of equalization's decision. The tax appeal board must render a decision within 30 days of any hearing on the appeal, but generally no later than July 25. Any unfavorable decision from the tax appeal board must be made to the superior court for the county in which the appeal property is located no later than November 1, which is the deadline for all appeals. Note that the tax payment, which is due on October 1, must be paid for the appeal process to continue.

Under Arizona law, valuations for tax purposes cannot be increased by more than 10 percent per year, resulting in a limited value figure. (However, if 25 percent of the difference between the full cash value for the current year and the limited value for the prior year exceeds the 10 percent increase, the larger figure will be used.) The limited value is frequently—but not always—less than the full cash value. An exception to this rule may be made for taxes that voters have approved separately to cover the costs of items such as bond issues and budgetary overrides. Thus, tax notices in Arizona indicate two valuations for real property, the limited value and the full cash value. The limited value of the property is the basis for the primary property taxes—those used to support normal government operations. The full cash value of the property is the basis for secondary property taxes—those used for bond interest, bond redemption, budgetary overrides and other self-imposed expenditures.

The limited value, used to calculate the primary property tax obligation of the property owner, is multiplied by a **tax assessment ratio**, which is based on the property usage. The resulting figure is the **assessed valuation**, which becomes the basis for the annual tax bill. The eleven classifications of property established by the legislature are given below with their appropriate tax assessment ratios:

| | |
|---|---|
| Class 1: | mining claims and producing mines and their related mills and smelters; standing timber: 28% in 1995, reducing by one percent per year down to 25% |
| Class 2: | telecommunications company property; gas, water, electric utility and pipeline company property: 28% in 1995, reducing by one percent per year down to 25% |
| Class 3: | commercial and industrial property; standing timber: one percent of its full cash value up to $50,000; 25% of its full cash value over $50,000 |
| Class 4: | agricultural property; vacant land, all other property not included in other classes: 16% |
| Class 5: | owner-occupied residential property; residential facilities and licensed care institutions for the handicapped and the elderly: 10% |
| Class 6: | residential rental property: 10% |
| Class 7: | railroad company property (except for that in Class 9); private car company property; airport and flight property: to be determined annually by the director of the Arizona Department of Revenue (per statutorily specified formulas) |
| Class 8: | historic property: 5% |
| Class 9: | scenic or historic railroad property, commercial historic property: to be determined annually by the director of the Arizona Department of Revenue (per statutorily specified formulas) |
| Class 10: | residential historic property: to be determined by the director of the Arizona Department of Revenue (per statutorily specified formulas) |
| Class 11: | leasehold improvements on government-owned land: one percent of its full cash value |

**Figure 6.2 Tax Bill Calculations**

$$\frac{\text{state \$ needed}}{\text{state tax base}} \quad = \qquad + \quad \text{state tax rate}$$

$$\frac{\text{county \$ needed}}{\text{county tax base}} \quad = \qquad + \quad \text{county tax rate}$$

$$\frac{\text{municipality \$ needed}}{\text{municipality tax base}} \quad = \qquad + \quad \text{municipality tax rate}$$

et cetera . . .

$$\qquad\qquad\qquad\qquad\qquad = \quad \text{combined tax rate}$$

| **Primary Values and Taxes** (funds for government operations) | **Secondary Values and Taxes** (funds for self-imposed expenditures) |
|---|---|
| limited value | full cash value |
| × tax assessment ratio | × tax assessment ratio |
| = assessed valuation | = assessed valuation |
| assessed valuation | assessed valuation |
| × combined tax rate | × special tax rate |
| = annual tax bill for government operations | = annual tax bill for self-imposed expenditures |

annual tax bill for government operations + (annual tax bill for self-imposed expenditures, if any) = total annual tax bill

The tax rate is expressed as dollars of tax per $100 of assessed valuation. The tax rate for each taxing authority is determined by the budgetary process. When the operating budget of each authority is set, the amount to be funded with real estate taxes is divided by the total assessed valuation of all the property in that authority's jurisdiction. The result is converted to a percentage basis: dollars of tax per $100 of assessed valuation.

The taxing authorities then combine their individual tax rates into a "combined tax rate" for each parcel in the state. Thus, each property owner will pay the amount of taxes that is necessary to support each taxing authority that provides services to the parcel being taxed.

## Figure 6.3 Sample Tax Bill

FULL YEAR

FIRST HALF

PLEASE CHECK WHICH PAYMENT APPLIES

U.S. FUNDS ONLY

PRINT THE ABOVE PARCEL
NUMBER ON YOUR CHECK

PARCEL NUMBER

MAKE CHECK PAYABLE TO:
Maricopa County Treasurer
P O Box 78574
Phoenix, AZ  85062-8574

1995 FULL YEAR PAYMENT STUB OR
1995 FIRST HALF PAYMENT STUB
DUE OCTOBER 1, 1995

MAKE CHANGES TO MAILING ADDRESS BELOW:

DETACH AND RETURN WITH PAYMENT

PARCEL NUMBER   MTG. CODE   LOAN NUMBER

PROPERTY DESCRIPTION
SEC/LOT   TWN/BLK   RNG/TR

**MARICOPA COUNTY
TREASURER**
DOUG TODD, TREASURER
P O BOX 29214
PHOENIX, AZ  85038-9214
(602)506-8511

**MARICOPA COUNTY
1995 CONSOLIDATED
PROPERTY TAX
STATEMENT**

NOTICE: SEE REVERSE SIDE FOR
IMPORTANT INFORMATION.

$25.00 CHARGE IF CHECK
FAILS TO CLEAR BANK.

YOUR CHECK IS YOUR RECEIPT.

| | LIMITED (PRIMARY) VALUES | | | PRIMARY | COMPARATIVE 1994 AMT | 1995 DISTRIBUTION | | FIRST HALF TAX AMOUNT |
| TYPE | LIMITED | % | ASSESSED | | | RATE / 100 | 1995 AMT | |
| LAND/BLDG PERSONAL EXEMPTION | | | | STATE COUNTY CITY SCHOOL CO. EDUC. COMM. COL. | | | | |
| PRIM. TOT. | | | | | | | | DUE OCT. 1, 1995 DELINQUENT AFTER NOV. 1, 1995 |
| AREA CODE | | | | SUBTOTAL | | | | INTEREST ON LATE PAYMENT IS 16% PER YEAR PRORATED MONTHLY AS OF THE FIRST DAY OF THE MONTH.  ARS 42-342 |

| | FULL CASH (SECONDARY) VALUES | | | SECONDARY | | | | SECOND HALF TAX AMOUNT |
| TYPE | FULL CASH | % | ASSESSED | | | | | |
| LAND/BLDG PERSONAL EXEMPTION | | | | FLOOD CAWCD BONDS OVERRIDES VOL. FIRE LIBRARY | | | | |
| SEC. TOT. | | | | SUBTOTAL | | | | DUE MARCH 1, 1996 DELINQUENT AFTER MAY 1, 1996 |

SPECIAL DISTRICT (VALUE/ACRES/SQ FT)= ASSESSED   DIST#

INTEREST ON LATE PAYMENT
IS 16% PER YEAR PRORATED
MONTHLY AS OF THE FIRST DAY
OF THE MONTH. ARS 42-342

**KEEP THIS
PORTION FOR
YOUR RECORDS**

IF NOT PAID BY DELINQUENT DATES, CALL OR WRITE
FOR INTEREST AMOUNT. SEE NOTE NO. 3 ON REVERSE SIDE

TOTAL 1995 TAX
(MAY BE PAID IN FULL)

Valuations and property classifications are established by the County Assessor.

Please send written inquiries to: Doug Todd, Maricopa County Treasurer, Room 100, 301 W. Jefferson Street, Phoenix, AZ  85003-2199

DETACH AND RETURN WITH PAYMENT

**1995 SECOND HALF PAYMENT STUB
DUE MARCH 1, 1996**

MAKE CHECK PAYABLE TO:
**Maricopa County Treasurer
P O Box 78574
Phoenix, AZ  85062-8574**

PARCEL NUMBER

PRINT THE ABOVE PARCEL
NUMBER ON YOUR CHECK

**U.S. FUNDS ONLY**

SECOND HALF

MAKE CHANGES TO MAILING ADDRESS BELOW:

Two other restrictions establish maximum limits on individual assessments. First, the actual amount of tax levied against a property cannot increase by more than two percent per year. Second, the total tax levy on an owner-occupied residence or any other Class 5 property cannot exceed one percent of its limited value. The state pays any excess over that amount and credits it to the local school district.

## Payment, Delinquency and Redemption

Tax bills (Figure 6.3) are generally issued in September. Property taxes can be paid in two installments. The first one-half payment is due and payable on October 1 and is delinquent if not paid by November 1. A penalty of 16 percent per year, prorated monthly from the first day of each month, is imposed on all delinquent taxes. The second one-half payment is due and payable on March 1 of the following year and is delinquent if not paid by May 1. A property owner must be notified of the delinquency by mail by the following September 1.

The sale of a property for delinquent taxes, penalties and fees can occur only during the February following the owner's notification of the delinquency. Before the sale can occur, the notice of the sale must be mailed to the property owner at his or her address of record, and the notice must be published once each week for two consecutive weeks in a newspaper of general circulation in the county where the property is located.

Tax sales are held by the county treasurer. There are three possible outcomes of a tax sale. First, there may be no bids for a property, in which case the tax lien is assigned to the state. Second, there may be only one bid for the property. In this situation, the successful bidder will receive a certificate of purchase for the property upon payment of the delinquent taxes, penalties and filing fees. Third, there may be multiple bids for the property. Should this happen, a certificate of purchase is issued to the bidder who accepts the lowest rate of interest on the certificate should the delinquent property owner want to redeem the certificate. The interest rate bidding will start at the maximum of 16 percent per year and will be bid down until the bidding stops—which may be all the way to a rate of 0 percent.

The successful bidder at a tax sale then records the certificate of purchase with the county recorder, which creates a lien against the property in favor of the successful bidder. (The delinquent property owner continues to own and possess the property.) Once the certificate of purchase has been recorded, the delinquent property owner—or any other person having a legal or equitable claim against the property (such as a mortgage lienholder, a trust deed lienholder or a mechanic lienholder)—may redeem the certificate of purchase. To do so, he or she must pay an amount equal to

- the sales price of the certificate of purchase,
- interest on the sales price at the rate specified in the certificate of purchase (between 16 and 0 percent),
- all taxes accruing on the real estate after the tax sale that were paid by the purchaser of the certificate and were endorsed on the certificate, and
- interest on the subsequent taxes at the same rate as specified in the certificate.

In other words, the person redeeming the certificate of purchase must pay the sales price plus interest, as well as all accruing real estate taxes. (A person having a partial interest in the property may redeem a certificate of purchase lien against that interest by paying the proportionate part of the whole amount due.) A redemption of the certificate of purchase must occur within three years of the date of the tax sale.

**Figure 6.4 Tax Dates Time Line**

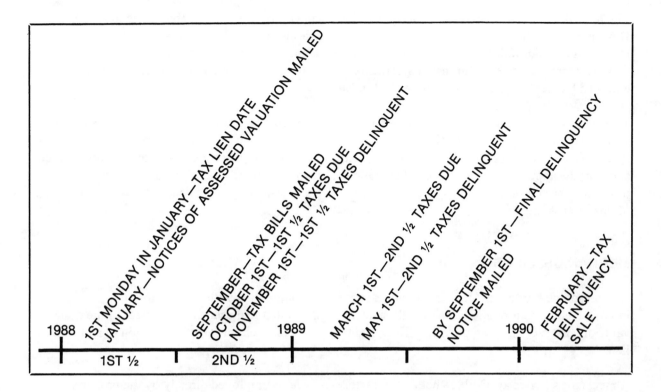

If the certificate of purchase is not redeemed by the delinquent property owner or other lienholder within the three-year period, the holder of the certificate of purchase may foreclose his or her lien by filing a suit to quiet title in the superior court of the county in which the property is located. If the court finds the tax sale valid and the certificate unredeemed, it will enter a judgment in favor of the plaintiff and order the county treasurer's office to prepare and issue a treasurer's deed (a type of bargain and sale deed) to the party in whose favor the judgment was entered. (The total time for this process may be as long as five years from the original tax delinquency.)

If the certificate is not redeemed and a suit to quiet title is not filed within five years of the date of the tax sale, the holder of the certificate of purchase may apply for and receive a treasurer's deed directly from the county treasurer's office. This process involves advertising a notice of nonredemption in four consecutive weekly issues of a newspaper of general circulation in that county, as well as the payment of a filing fee. The holder of the certificate must also pay the county treasurer's expenses for issuing the deed. (The total time for this process may be as long as seven years from the original tax delinquency.)

## Tax Parcel Numbers

The county assessor's office in each county assigns a tax parcel number to each parcel under the assessor's jurisdiction. This tax number refers—by book, map and parcel number—to a specific description listed in the assessor's records. However, this tax parcel number may be changed. For example, when a parcel is subdivided, new tax parcel numbers are assigned to each of the smaller subdivided parcels. If reference is made to a tax parcel number for the sake of convenience, the reference must include the specific year that the parcel number appears in the assessor's records.

## SPECIAL ASSESSMENTS

The procedures for special assessments outlined in Chapter 6 of this text are applicable in Arizona. However, while the term "special assessments" usually brings to mind payments for street paving, curbs, gutters, sidewalks, street lights, storm sewers, sanitary sewers and the like, many of these types of assessments have been eliminated in Arizona by the stringent subdivision requirements written and enforced by the Arizona Department of Real Estate.

Title 48 of the Arizona Revised Statutes—which govern Special Taxing Districts—addresses the various types of **improvement districts** that can be created (there are currently more than 20 different types). The details regarding the creation of a district, and its authority to contract for the improvements and levy the appropriate charges, and their payment schedules, interest rates and delinquency procedures are tailored to each specific type of district. Consequently, such details are beyond the scope of this discussion.

## MECHANICS' LIENS

Any person who provides labor, materials or services in conjunction with the construction, improvement, repair or alteration of real estate has rights in that real estate to the extent of the dollar value of whatever has been provided. These rights can be exercised through the creation of a mechanic's lien.

A mechanic's lien is available to both a contractor (one who is employed directly by the property owner) and a subcontractor (one who is employed by the contractor rather than by the property owner). To secure a mechanic's lien, the contractor must record a notice and claim of lien with the county recorder in the county where the property is located within 90 days after the completion of the work. Any subcontractor (such as a laborer or supplier) must record a notice and claim of lien within 60 days after the completion of the work. A copy of that notice must also be given to the owner of the property.

Completion of the work is usually considered to be the earliest of the following events:

- The physical completion of the work
- The use of the improvement by the owner
- The written acceptance of the improvement by the owner
- The final inspection and written acceptance of the improvement by the government agency that issued the original building permit (normally evidenced by a certificate of occupancy)

However, completion of the work may also be construed to mean the voluntary cessation of work for 60 consecutive days, with the exceptions of labor strikes, material shortages and acts of God.

Most liens in Arizona are given priority according to the date and time they were recorded. However, a properly completed and recorded notice and claim of mechanic's lien creates a lien that reverts back to the date on which the contractor's work commenced. Thus, a mechanic's lien is given priority as of the date that the work was started (which is known as the **effective date**), and all mechanics' liens in favor of the contractor or any subcontractors on the same project will be given priority as of the same date.

In most situations, a mechanic's lien must be preceded by a preliminary 20-day notice. This notice is required of potential claimants of mechanic's liens, particularly those who provide materials and services as subcontractors (as opposed to those who provide physical labor). This 20-day notice informs the property owner that the property could be lost through a judicial foreclosure if the subcontractors are not fully paid by the contractor. For a mechanic's lien to be valid, the potential claimant must give the property owner, the contractor and the construction lender (if any) one copy of this notice within 20 days after the materials or services are first made available on the property. Any recipient of a 20-day notice must provide a written receipt for such notice.

The property owner can shorten the time period for enforcing a mechanic's lien by issuing and recording a **notice of the completion of work**. This notice, which must be recorded with the county recorder and sent to the contractor (as well as any other persons from whom the owner has received a preliminary 20-day notice), will shorten the filing time of the contractor from 90 days to 45 days and will shorten the filing time of any subcontractors from 60 days to 30 days. This notice can be drafted by the property owner at any time after the work has ceased or has been completed, and should be recorded immediately.

Once a mechanic's lien has been created by recording the notice and claim of lien, the lienholder must initiate a lawsuit for judicial foreclosure within six months after the date of recordation. If the lawsuit is filed, the property can be sold under a court order by the county sheriff; the land and the improvements may be sold either as one parcel or separately, depending on the amount of money owed and the instructions from the court. If the lawsuit is not filed within the required six-month time frame, the mechanic's lien will automatically expire. A mechanic's lien will also terminate if the property owner pays the money owed, if the lienholder releases the claim or if the attempt at foreclosure is unsuccessful.

Within 30 days after the satisfaction of a mechanic's lien, the lienholder must issue a **release of the claim of lien** to the property owner. Failure to do so subjects the lienholder to a civil penalty of $1,000 plus the actual damages caused to the owner by the lienholder's neglect or refusal.

Under Arizona law, a mechanic's lien against an owner-occupied residence is allowed only by contractors with whom the owner of the property has a written contract, and by subcontractors who have written contracts with the property owner, the contractor, the architect or the engineer. An owner-occupied residence is defined as either a single-family dwelling, a duplex or a single-family condominium unit.

It is possible for a property owner to avoid mechanics' liens by requiring the contractor whom he or she has employed to purchase a payment bond (a performance bond) and then record the bond and a copy of the employment contract with the county recorder. Once the bond and the contract have been recorded, no mechanics' liens are allowed to be claimed by anyone other than that contractor. **Lien waivers** may also be obtained by the property owner as proof of payment and a waiver of any further lien rights by the contractor.

## JUDGMENTS

A judgment is the result of a civil suit brought either for a personal wrong (a tort) or for a breach of contract. The plaintiff (the person who files the suit) asks the court to compensate him or her for damage caused by the wrongful actions of the defendant (the person against whom the suit is filed). If the court finds in favor of the defendant, the suit will be dismissed. But if the court finds in favor of the plaintiff, it will issue a judgment against the defendant, and the plaintiff will become a judgment creditor and the defendant will become a judgment debtor.

The judgment issued by the court does not automatically create a lien against the property of the debtor. It must first be recorded with the county recorder in the county in which it was issued. The lien affects all of the property owned by the debtor in that county when the judgment is recorded, as well as any property that the debtor may later acquire in that county.

If the debtor owns property in other counties, that property can also be made subject to the judgment lien if the creditor records a transcript of the judgment with the county recorder in the county or counties in which that property is located.

A judgment lien is valid for five years from the date it was entered by the court. The lien can be renewed if the creditor records an affidavit of renewal with the county recorder in all of the appropriate counties within 90 days before the expiration of the original judgment. Once renewed, the judgment continues as a lien for an additional five years.

A judgment lien may be extinguished by a release by the creditor, by the nonrenewal of the judgment, by the voluntary payment by the debtor or by foreclosure on the debtor's property by the creditor.

If no interest rate is agreed to by the parties to the suit, and if no interest rate is specified in the contract over which a suit is filed, then the court can award the legal rate of interest (10 percent simple) on the judgment.

Note that execution of a judgment lien is affected by Arizona's homestead law, which is discussed in Chapter 3.

## QUESTIONS

1. To claim a mechanic's lien for labor provided, a subcontractor must record a notice of the lien within how many days after the completion of the project?

   a. 30
   b. 60
   c. 90
   d. 120

2. In Arizona, the annual real estate tax lien takes effect on

   a. October 1.
   b. the first Monday in January.
   c. March 1.
   d. the first Monday in May.

3. When a property is sold for back taxes, the delinquent taxpayer has how long to redeem the property?

   a. 90 days
   b. 6 months
   c. 1 year
   d. 3 years

4. During the statutory redemption period following a tax sale, the delinquent taxpayer

   a. must vacate the premises.
   b. is allowed undisturbed possession.
   c. must continue to pay the real estate taxes.
   d. has five years in which to redeem the property.

5. Once a mechanic's lien has been recorded, the contractor has how long to file a foreclosure action?

    a. 60 days
    b. 90 days
    c. 6 months
    d. 1 year

6. All of the following statements concerning real estate taxes are true *except*

    a. a sheriff's deed is issued when the redemption period expires.
    b. the redemption period following the treasurer's sale is three years.
    c. a certificate of purchase can bear less than 16 percent interest.
    d. the delinquent property owner may have as long as five years to redeem the property.

7. *W* hired *C* to build a swimming pool on her property, but the agreement was only oral. After *W* paid *C* for the job, one of *C*'s subcontractors, *L*, called *W* to say that *C* had not paid him. *L* threatened *W* with a suit to collect the money due him. Which of the following best describes this situation?

    a. *W* should pay *L* to avoid the suit.
    b. *W* should call *C* and ask him to pay *L*.
    c. *L* could collect his money from *W*, but not the costs of the suit.
    d. *L* cannot collect his money from *W*.

8. The *W*s will pay their current year's real estate tax bill in two equal installments. The final payment is due on

    a. March 1 of next year.
    b. May 1 of this year.
    c. October 1 of next year.
    d. November 1 of this year.

9. *C* obtained a judgment against *H*, which *C* subsequently recorded. All of the following would terminate *C*'s lien on the property *except*

    a. the sale of *H*'s property to satisfy the debt.
    b. the nonrenewal of the judgment lien by *C*.
    c. the mortgaging of *H*'s property to satisfy the debt.
    d. the release of the judgment lien by *C*.

10. *P* successfully appealed for a reduction in her assessed valuation, which reduced her property value from $9,428 to $8,745. If *P*'s tax rate is $9.87, how much were her semiannual tax payments reduced?

    a. $33.71
    b. $431.57
    c. $465.27
    d. $683.00

# 7

# Real Estate Contracts

## LICENSEE'S AUTHORITY TO PREPARE DOCUMENTS

Under Article XXVI of Arizona's state constitution, real estate licensees are authorized to draft or complete any documents incidental to their real estate activities, including purchase agreements, earnest money receipts, land contracts, bills of sale, deeds, mortgages, leases, assignments and releases. Note, however, that under Arizona law, a licensee may not discourage any party to a real estate transaction from consulting an attorney, nor is he or she authorized to give legal advice.

### Unilateral Contracts

The only unilateral (one-sided) contracts that real estate licensees need to be concerned about are options and first right of refusal.

**Options.** An option is the right to buy (or rent, lease, sell or exchange) a property by a future date at a specified price. The option binds only the optionor (the person who gives the option); there are no obligations on the part of the optionee. In other words, the optionor must sell the property to the optionee should the optionee decide to purchase it. However, the optionee may freely choose whether or not to purchase the property. A good analogy for an option is a rain check obtained from a supermarket for an advertised but out-of-stock item—the grocery store must sell the product to the rain-check holder for the advertised price, but the rain-check holder does not have to purchase the item if he or she does not wish to.

When a property owner gives a prospective purchaser an option, the owner must be sure the property is available to the optionee. Should the prospective purchaser decide to exercise the option, the owner must sell the property according to the terms of the option. The optionee, however, is under no obligation to exercise the option.

For example, suppose an optionor agrees to sell her property to the optionee for $95,000 if the option is exercised (or "called") within 60 days. During that 60-day period, the optionor must make sure the property is available to the optionee and, if the optionee calls the option, convey the property for the agreed $95,000. The optionee is not obligated to call the option, however; and after the 60 days have passed, the optionee has no claim against the property.

If the owner were to sell the property to another during the option period, the sale must be made subject to the option. In other words, the new owner must honor the terms of the option agreement should the optionee decide to exercise the option.

In Arizona, options must be in writing and signed by the optionor, and valuable consideration must be tendered by the optionee. Usually, the optionee will record the option to protect his or her rights under the option.

**First Right of Refusal.** A holder of a first right of refusal has the right to match any incoming offer to purchase, rent, lease, sell or exchange the property in question. A first right of refusal gives the holder a certain time period in which to exercise that right after proper notification. For example, many condominium projects require that when a unit owner has received a bona fide offer for his or her unit, he or she must then offer the unit at the tendered price to the other unit owners in the project and perhaps even the association. The other owners then have the opportunity to either purchase the unit by matching the offer or allow the owner to consummate the sale.

## Statute of Frauds

The Arizona Statute of Frauds provides, in part, that certain contracts are unenforceable unless they are in writing and signed by the parties. These contracts include

- agreements for the sale of real estate or an interest in real estate;
- agreements authorizing or employing an agent or broker to purchase or sell real estate or mines for compensation; and
- leases for a term of more than one year.

## Contracts on Weekends or Holidays

A few states have laws that prohibit the execution of a contract on a Saturday, Sunday or holiday. Arizona has no such law, sometimes called a blue law; any contract properly executed is valid and binding regardless of the day.

## CONTRACTS FOR THE PURCHASE OF REAL ESTATE

In Arizona, a real estate purchase contract is known as a "real estate purchase contract and receipt for deposit," an "earnest money receipt" or simply a "purchase contract." Although a broker may develop a contract for use by his or her office, numerous forms are readily available. One of the most commonly used forms is reproduced in this book (Figure 7.1).

## Completing the Contract

A real estate licensee is prohibited from preparing any document, including a purchase contract, that states a false or misleading purchase price for a property. And every purchase contract must state the form of any earnest money received, that is, whether the earnest money received by the licensee was in the form of cash, a check, a promissory note or some other item of value.

The designated broker must review every purchase contract within five days of the date of its execution. After reviewing the contract, he or she must initial and date the contract's signature page. As the expert in real estate, the broker is responsible for the "form and content" of the document; the contract must be accurate and complete. The designated broker can authorize (in writing) an associate broker or manager to review and initial contracts.

### Figure 7.1 Purchase Contract (Page 1 of 7)

PAGE 1

## RESIDENTIAL RESALE REAL ESTATE
## PURCHASE CONTRACT AND RECEIPT FOR DEPOSIT

THE PRINTED PORTION OF THIS CONTRACT HAS BEEN APPROVED BY THE ARIZONA ASSOCIATION OF REALTORS®. THIS IS INTENDED TO BE A BINDING CONTRACT. NO REPRESENTATION IS MADE AS TO THE LEGAL VALIDITY OR ADEQUACY OF ANY PROVISION OR THE TAX CONSEQUENCES THEREOF. IF YOU DESIRE LEGAL, TAX OR OTHER PROFESSIONAL ADVICE, CONSULT YOUR ATTORNEY, TAX ADVISOR OR PROFESSIONAL CONSULTANT.

# RECEIPT

1. **Received From:** _____ ("Buyer")
2. **Agency Confirmation:** Broker named on Line 16 is the agent of (check one):
3. ☐ the Buyer exclusively; or   ☐ the Seller exclusively; or   ☐ both the Buyer and Seller
4. **Title:** The manner of taking title may have significant legal and tax consequences. Therefore, please consult your legal or tax advisor if you have any questions.
5. Buyer will take title as:  ☐ Determined before Close of Escrow   ☐ Community Property   ☐ Joint Tenants with Right of Survivorship
6. ☐ Sole and Separate Property   ☐ Tenants in Common   ☐ Other: _____
7. **Earnest Money:** Earnest money shall be held by Broker until offer is accepted. Upon acceptance, Broker is authorized to deposit the earnest money with
8. any Escrow Company to which the check is payable. If the check is payable to Broker, Broker may deposit the check in Broker's trust account or endorse
9. the check without recourse and deposit it with a duly licensed Escrow Company. Buyer agrees that, if Buyer breaches this Contract, any earnest money is
10. subject to forfeiture. All earnest money is subject to collection. In the event any check for earnest money is dishonored for any reason, at Seller's option,
11. Seller shall be immediately released from all obligations under this Contract notwithstanding any provisions contained herein. Unless otherwise provided
12. herein, all earnest money is considered to be part of the purchase price for the Premises described below.

13. a. Amount of    b. Form of   ☐ Personal Check    c. Deposited   ☐ Broker's Trust Account
14. Deposit $ _____   Earnest Money:  ☐ Other: _____   With:   ☐ Escrow Company: _____

15. **Received By:** _____
     (PRINT SALESPERSON'S NAME)          (SALESPERSON'S SIGNATURE)          MO/DA/YR
16. _____
     (PRINT NAME OF FIRM)

# OFFER

17. **Property Description and Offer:** Buyer agrees to purchase the real property and all fixtures and improvements thereon and appurtenances incident there-
18. to, plus personal property described below (collectively the "Premises").

19. Premises Address: _____ Assessor's #: _____
20. City: _____ County: _____ AZ, Zip Code: _____
21. Legal Description: _____

22. **Fixtures and Personal Property:** All existing fixtures attached to the Premises: including storage sheds, electrical, plumbing, heating and cooling equip-
23. ment; built-in appliances; light fixtures; ceiling fans; window and door screens, sun screens; solar systems; storm windows and doors, shutters, awnings;
24. water-misting systems; fire detection/suppression systems; towel, curtain and drapery rods; draperies and other window coverings; attached floor coverings;
25. air cooler(s) and/or conditioner(s); attached fireplace equipment; wood-burning stoves; pool and spa equipment (including any mechanical or other cleaning
26. systems (if owned by Seller); garage door openers and controls; security systems and/or alarms (if owned by Seller); timers; mailbox; attached TV
27. antennas (excluding satellite dishes); and all existing landscaping, including trees, cacti and shrubs shall be left upon and included with the Premises.

28. **Additional Existing Personal Property Included:** _____
29. _____
30. **Fixtures and Leased Equipment NOT Included:** _____

31. **Addenda Incorporated:**  ☐ AAR Addendum   ☐ Other _____

32. $ _____ **Full Purchase Price**, payable as follows:
33. $ _____ Earnest money as indicated above. _____
34. $ _____
35. $ _____
36. _____
37. _____
38. _____
39. _____
40. _____
41. _____
42. _____
43. _____
44. _____

45. **Closing Date:** Seller and Buyer will comply with all terms and conditions of this Contract and close escrow on [ MO/DA/YR ] . Any earlier closing
46. date requires mutual agreement of Seller and Buyer. Seller and Buyer hereby agree that the Close of Escrow shall be defined as recordation of the docu-
47. ments. If escrow does not close by such date, this Contract is subject to cancellation as provided in Lines 348-356.

48. **Possession and Keys:** Possession and occupancy shall be delivered to Buyer **at Close of Escrow, or** ☐ _____
49. _____
50. Seller shall provide keys and/or means to operate all locks, mailbox, security system/ alarms, and access to all common area facilities.
51. **IF THIS IS AN ALL CASH SALE, GO TO LINE 194.**

SOURCE: Permission granted by Arizona Association of REALTORS®.

## Figure 7.1 Purchase Contract (Page 2 of 7)

# FINANCING OPTIONS
## NEW CONVENTIONAL FIRST LOAN

52. **This sale is contingent upon Buyer qualifying for a new first loan.**

53. **Loan Amount:** $ _____  **Term of Loan:** _____

54. **Type Of Loan** ☐ Conventional Fixed Rate  ☐ Conventional Adjustable Rate  ☐ Other _____

55. **Interest Rate:** Interest rate shall not exceed _____ %  as an annual rate for a fixed rate loan or an initial rate for an adjustable rate loan.
56. Buyer agrees to establish the interest rate and "points" by separate written agreement with the lender at the time of the loan application.
57. **Loan Application:** Buyer agrees to file a substantially complete loan application within five (5) calendar days after the acceptance of this Contract and to
58. promptly supply all documentation required by the lender. Buyer agrees to pay such fees as required by the lender.

59. **Conditional Loan Approval:** Within **fifteen (15) calendar days** or ☐ _____ **calendar days**  after acceptance of this Contract, Buyer must place in
60. escrow a written conditional (preliminary) loan approval from the lender based on a completed loan application and preliminary credit report. If such condi-
61. tional (preliminary) loan approval is not received within the time specified, then Seller may give Buyer a five (5) calendar day written notice to perform. If
62. Buyer does not deliver to Escrow Company written conditional (preliminary) loan approval within said five (5) calendar days, then this Contract shall be
63. deemed cancelled and all earnest money shall be released to Buyer without further written consent of the parties and without regard to cancellation provi-
64. sions provided for elsewhere in this Contract. Buyer instructs lender to send copies of such approval to Brokers and Seller. Buyer authorizes the lender to
65. provide loan status updates to Brokers.

66. **Loan Costs:** Private Mortgage Insurance is required for certain types of loans. The cost will be paid by Buyer at the Close of Escrow in a manner acceptable to
67. lender. The following may be paid by either party:

68. **Discount points paid by:**  **Discount points shall not exceed:** _____
69. ☐ Buyer  ☐ Seller  ☐ _____  _____ total points. (does not include origination fee)

|  | Buyer | Seller |  | Buyer | Seller |
|---|---|---|---|---|---|
| 70. |  |  |  |  |  |
| 71. A.L.T.A. Lender Title Insurance Policy | ☐ | ☐ | Loan Origination Fee (Not to exceed ____ % of loan amount) | ☐ | ☐ |
| 72. Escrow Fees | ☐ | ☐ |  |  |  |
| 73. Appraisal Fee | ☐ | ☐ | ☐ ....Paid by Buyer and | ☐ .....Paid by Seller and |  |
| 74. |  |  | reimbursed by Seller at closing | reimbursed by Buyer at closing |  |

75. Any additional costs not otherwise agreed upon by Seller shall be paid by Buyer.

76. **Appraisal:** This sale is contingent upon an appraisal of the Premises by an appraiser acceptable to the lender for **at least the sales price or**

77. ☐ _____ . The party responsible for paying for the appraisal shall do so within **five (5) calendar days of**

78. **Contract acceptance or** ☐ _____ . Buyer and Seller acknowledge that the appraisal is an opinion
79. of value for lending purposes only, and may be different from the full purchase price.

## NEW FHA FIRST LOAN OR VA FIRST LOAN

80. **This sale is contingent upon Buyer qualifying for a new FHA or VA first loan:**

81. **Loan Amount:** $ _____ (excluding MIP, or Funding Fee)  **Term of Loan:** _____

82. **Type Of Loan:** ☐ FHA  ☐ VA

83. **FHA Mortgage Insurance Premium (MIP) or VA Funding Fee:** Amount $ _____  To be financed by Buyer which will increase the loan

84. amount to: $ _____ , or to be paid by Buyer in cash at Close of Escrow.

85. **Interest Rate:** Interest rate shall not exceed _____ %  as an annual rate for a fixed rate loan or an initial rate for an adjustable rate loan.
86. Buyer agrees to establish the interest rate and "points" by separate written agreement with the lender at the time of the loan application.
87. **Loan Application:** Buyer agrees to file a substantially complete loan application within five (5) calendar days after the acceptance of this Contract and to
88. promptly supply all documentation required by the lender. Buyer agrees to pay such fees as required by the lender.

89. **Conditional Loan Approval:** Within **fifteen (15) calendar days** or ☐ _____ **calendar days**  after acceptance of this Contract, Buyer must place in
90. escrow a written conditional (preliminary) loan approval from the lender based on a completed loan application and preliminary credit report. If such condi-
91. tional (preliminary) loan approval is not received within the time specified, then Seller may give Buyer a five (5) calendar day written notice to perform. If
92. Buyer does not deliver to Escrow Company written conditional (preliminary) loan approval within said five (5) calendar days, then this Contract shall be
93. deemed cancelled and all earnest money shall be released to Buyer without further written consent of the parties and without regard to cancellation provi-
94. sions provided for elsewhere in this Contract. Buyer instructs lender to send copies of such approval to Brokers and Seller. Buyer authorizes the lender to
95. provide loan status updates to Brokers.

96. **Loan Costs:** When maximizing the Buyer's loan amount under FHA "acquisition method," the Buyer's new loan amount **may** be reduced and additional
97. cash required at closing from the Buyer if the Seller pays for any of the items on Lines 98-105. The following may be paid by either party:

98. **Discount points paid by:**  **Discount points shall not exceed:** _____
99. ☐ Buyer  ☐ Seller  ☐ _____  _____ total points. (does not include origination fee)

|  | Buyer | Seller |  | Buyer | Seller |
|---|---|---|---|---|---|
| 100. |  |  |  |  |  |
| 101. A.L.T.A. Lender Title Insurance Policy | ☐ | ☐ | Loan Origination Fee | ☐ | ☐ |
| 102. Credit Report | ☐ | ☐ | Recording to Vest Title in Buyer | ☐ | ☐ |
| 103. Escrow Fees (V.A. - All by Seller) | ☐ | ☐ |  |  |  |
| 104. Appraisal Fee | ☐ | ☐ | ☐ ....Paid by Buyer and | ☐ .....Paid by Seller and |  |
| 105. |  |  | reimbursed by Seller at closing | reimbursed by Buyer at closing |  |

106. **Mandatory Costs:** FHA regulations require the Buyer to pay for the following items: Reserves (impounds) for property taxes and hazard insurance, plus adjusted
107. interest. Both FHA and VA require that the Seller must pay for the following fees, if applicable: assignment, flood certification, recordings to clear title, bringdown
108. endorsement, document preparation, photo/inspection, tax service and warehousing. In addition, VA requires the Seller to pay all escrow fees.
109. Any additional costs not otherwise agreed upon by Seller shall be paid by Buyer.

# Figure 7.1 Purchase Contract (Page 3 of 7)

110. **Appraisal:** The party responsible for paying for the appraisal shall do so within **five (5) calendar days or** ☐ _____ **calendar days** of Contract
111. acceptance. Buyer and Seller acknowledge that the appraisal is an opinion of value for lending purposes only, and may be different from
112. the full purchase price.
113. **VA Amendatory Clause:** It is expressly agreed that notwithstanding any other provision of this Contract, the Purchaser shall not incur any penalty by forfei-
114. ture of earnest money or otherwise be obligated to complete the purchase of the property described herein if the Contract purchase price or costs exceeds
115. the reasonable value of the property established by the Veterans Administration. The Purchaser shall, however, have the privilege and option of proceeding
116. with the consummation of this Contract without regard to the amount of the reasonable value established by the Veterans Administration.
117. **FHA Amendatory Clause:** It is expressly agreed that notwithstanding any other provisions of this Contract, the purchaser shall not be obligated to complete
118. the purchase of the property described herein or to incur any penalty by forfeiture of earnest money deposits or otherwise unless the purchaser has been
119. given in accordance with HUD/FHA or VA requirements a written statement by the Federal Housing Commissioner, Veterans Administration, or a Direct
120. Endorsement lender setting forth the appraised value of the property of not less than $ _____ .The purchaser shall have the
121. privilege and option of proceeding with consummation of the contract without regard to the amount of the appraised valuation. The appraised valuation is
122. arrived at to determine the maximum mortgage the Department of Housing and Urban Development will insure. HUD does not warrant the value nor the
123. condition of the property. The purchaser should satisfy himself/herself that the price and condition of the property are acceptable.
124. **Notice To Buyer:** If the residence was constructed prior to 1978, the U.S. Department of Housing and Urban Development requires that the Buyer receive
125. and sign a copy of "Notice to Purchasers of Housing Constructed Prior to 1978" before signing any purchase contract contingent upon FHA financing. The
126. notice explains potential risks if the residence contains lead-based paint.

## ASSUMPTION OF EXISTING FIRST LOAN

127. **Buyer agrees to assume the existing loan(s) and pay all payments subsequent to Close of Escrow.**
128. **Assumption:** This sale ☐ is ☐ is not contingent upon the Buyer qualifying for assumption of the existing first loan.
129. **Release of Seller's Liability:** This sale ☐ is ☐ is not contingent upon Seller being released by lender from liability for loan being assumed. If
130. Seller is not released from liability, Seller acknowledges that there may be continuing liability in the event of a Buyer default.

131. **Type Of Loan:** ☐ Conventional ☐ VA ☐ FHA _____ ☐ Other _____

132. **Current Interest Rate:** **Current Payment Amount:**
133. ☐ Fixed ☐ Adjustable _____ % $ _____ ☐ PITI ☐ PI ☐ Other _____

134. **Loan Balance:** $ _____
135. The balance of any encumbrance being assumed is approximate. Any difference shall be reflected in the:
136. ☐ Cash Down Payment ☐ Seller Carryback ☐ Other: _____

137. **Impounds:** Buyer shall ☐ reimburse Seller for any impounds transferred to Buyer or ☐ _____

138. **Loan Transfer and Assumption Fees:** To be paid by ☐ Buyer ☐ Seller ☐ _____ [All other lender charges shall be paid by Buyer.]
139. If more than one loan is being assumed, go to Additional Terms and Conditions (Lines 194-205).
140. **Credit Evaluation:** This sale ☐ is ☐ is not contingent upon Seller's approval of Buyer's credit. If applicable, Buyer shall provide to Seller a current
141. credit report from a credit reporting agency and a completed loan application on the current FNMA form within five (5) calendar days after acceptance of this
142. Contract. Disapproval of Buyer's credit requires written notice from Seller to Escrow Company within five (5) calendar days after receipt by Seller of current
143. credit report and completed loan application. Approval will not be unreasonably withheld. Escrow Company is directed to record a Notice of Request for
144. Sale on behalf of the Seller and at Seller's expense.
145. **Lender Requirements:** Buyer and Seller agree to cooperate fully with lender and supply the necessary documentation to complete the assumption.
146. **Mortgage Insurance:** The loan amount assumed may include mortgage insurance, which Buyer also assumes and agrees to pay exclusive of life insurance.

## SELLER CARRYBACK FINANCING

147. **A portion of the purchase price shall be financed by the Seller and paid by the Buyer as follows, with the first payment due** [ _____ ] .
MO/DA/YR

148. **Loan Amount:** $ _____ as adjusted, if necessary, pursuant to lines 134-136.

149. **Priority Of Loan:** ☐ First ☐ Second ☐ _____

150. **Type Of Financing Instrument:** Buyer shall execute a promissory note and deed of trust in favor of Seller and record the deed of trust against the Premises.

151. **Interest Rate:** The unpaid balance shall bear interest at the rate of _____ % per year, beginning at the Close of Escrow.

152. **Payment Intervals:** ☐ Monthly ☐ Quarterly ☐ Semi-annually ☐ Annually ☐ Other _____

153. **Collection Fees:** Collection setup fees and servicing costs shall be paid by ☐ Buyer ☐ Seller ☐ _____

154. Collection account to be handled by _____

155. **Payment Amount:** $ _____ , or more, including the above stated interest.
156. If an adjustment in the loan amount is necessary pursuant to line 148, parties agree to adjust the: ☐ Payment amount ☐ Term

157. **Loan Term:** ☐ Amortizing over _____ years ☐ If balloon payment, principal balance due on or before _____
158. ☐ Interest-only payments, with principal balance due on or before _____

159. **Late Payments:** If late, Buyer shall pay late fees: ☐ Yes ☐ No If "Yes", payments which are at least _____ calendar days past due

160. shall be subject to a late fee of _____ . If any balloon payment is late, then the late fee per day will be $ _____

## Figure 7.1 Purchase Contract (Page 4 of 7)

161. **Default Rate:** If payment(s) are at least 30 calendar days past due, then the principal balance shall bear interest at a default rate of **five percent (5%) or** ⬚ %
162. over the interest rate of the carryback as stated herein. Said default rate shall begin on the 31st day following the due date of the payment(s) until payment(s)
163. are brought current. Payments are first applied to accrued interest and penalties, then to principal.
164. **Credit Evaluation:** This sale ☐ is ☐ is not contingent upon Seller's approval of Buyer's credit. If applicable, Buyer shall provide to Seller a current
165. credit report from a credit reporting agency and a completed loan application on the current FNMA form within five (5) calendar days after acceptance of this
166. Contract. Disapproval of Buyer's credit requires written notice from Seller to Escrow Company within five (5) calendar days after receipt by Seller of current credit
167. report and completed loan application. Approval will not be unreasonably withheld.
168. **Due On Sale:** Loan created ☐ is ☐ is not due on sale of the Premises. If loan created herein is due on sale of the Premises, and in the event that
169. the Premises is sold, transferred or conveyed in any manner, the promissory note and deed of trust shall provide that the promissory note and deed of trust
170. become immediately due and payable.
171. **Buyer's Liability:** On certain qualified residential property, the Seller understands that under Arizona law the Buyer may have no personal liability in case
172. of a default and that the Seller's only recourse may be to look to the property for the sole and exclusive source for repayment of the debt. Buyer shall furnish
173. to Seller, at Buyer's expense, a Standard Loan Policy in the full amount of any loan carried back by Seller and secured by the real property described in
174. Lines 19-21 of this Contract. Such Standard Loan Policy shall show that Seller's lien has the priority agreed to by the parties.
175. **Taxes:** In the absence of a tax impound account, Buyer shall provide and pay for a tax service contract over the life of this loan which will provide a delin-
176. quency notice to Seller, or any successor in interest to the Seller, of any unpaid taxes.
177. **Insurance:** Buyer shall provide, maintain and deliver to Seller hazard insurance satisfactory to, and with loss payable to Seller, in at least the amount of all
178. encumbrances against the Premises. This provision shall be made a part of the language of the deed of trust.
179. **Payments Through Servicing Agent:** Payments on this loan and all prior encumbrances shall be made concurrently through a single servicing account to be
180. maintained by a duly licensed account servicing agent. Payments on this loan shall be made at least ten (10) calendar days prior to the due date of any periodic
181. payment due on any prior encumbrance. The parties hereby instruct servicing agent not to accept any payment without all other concurrent payments.

### GENERAL LOAN PROVISIONS

182. **Occupancy:** Buyer ☐ does ☐ does not intend to occupy the Premises as Buyer's primary residence.
183. **Release Of Broker:** Any loan described in this Contract will be independently investigated and evaluated by Seller and/or Buyer, who hereby acknowledge
184. that any decision to enter into any loan arrangements with any person or entity will be based solely upon such independent investigation and evaluation.
185. Buyer and Seller further hold harmless and release Broker and acknowledge that no Broker is in any way responsible for Buyer's or Seller's decisions con-
186. cerning the desirability or acceptability of any loan or any terms thereof.
187. **Changes:** Buyer shall not make any changes in the loan program or financing terms described in this Contract without the prior written consent of Seller
188. unless such changes do not adversely affect Buyer's ability to qualify for the loan, increase Seller's closing costs or delay the closing date.
189. **Return Of Earnest Money:** Unless otherwise provided herein, Buyer is entitled to a return of the earnest money, if after a diligent and good faith effort, Buyer does
190. not qualify for a loan described in this Contract. Buyer acknowledges that prepaid items paid separately from earnest money are not refundable.
191. **RESPA:** The Real Estate Settlement Procedures Act (RESPA) requires that no Seller of property that will be purchased with the assistance of a federally
192. related mortgage loan shall require, directly or indirectly, as a condition of selling the property, that title insurance covering the property be purchased by the
193. Buyer from any particular title company.

### ADDITIONAL TERMS AND CONDITIONS

194. _____
195. _____
196. _____
197. _____
198. _____
199. _____
200. _____
201. _____
202. _____
203. _____
204. _____
205. _____

206. **Escrow:** The Escrow Company shall be: _____
207. ☐ This Contract will be used as escrow instructions. ☐ Separate escrow instructions will be executed.
208. (a) If the Escrow Company is also acting as the title agency but is not the title insurer issuing the title insurance policy, the Buyer and Seller hereby request
209. the Escrow Company to deliver to the Buyer and Seller upon opening of escrow a closing protection letter from the title insurer indemnifying the Buyer and
210. Seller for any losses due to fraudulent acts or breach of escrow instructions by the Escrow Company. (b) If Seller and Buyer elect to execute escrow instruc-
211. tions to fulfill the terms hereof, they shall deliver the same to Escrow Company within fifteen (15) calendar days of the acceptance of this Contract. (c) All doc-
212. uments necessary to close this transaction shall be executed promptly by Seller and Buyer in the standard form used by Escrow Company. Escrow Company
213. is hereby instructed to modify such documents to the extent necessary to be consistent with this Contract. (d) If any conflict exists between this Contract and
214. any escrow instructions executed pursuant hereto, the provisions of this Contract shall be controlling. (e) All closing and escrow costs, unless otherwise stat-
215. ed herein, shall be allocated between Seller and Buyer in accordance with local custom and applicable laws and regulations. (f) Escrow Company is hereby
216. instructed to send to Brokers copies of all notices and communications directed to Seller or Buyer. Escrow Company shall provide to such Brokers access to
217. escrowed materials and information regarding the escrow. (g) Any documents necessary to close the escrow may be signed in counterparts, each of which
218. shall be effective as an original upon execution, and all of which together shall constitute one and the same instrument.
219. **Prorations:** Taxes, homeowners' association fees, rents, irrigation fees, and, if assumed, insurance premiums, interest on assessments, and interest on
220. encumbrances shall be prorated as of ☐ Close of Escrow ☐ Other: _____
221. **Assessments:** The amount of any assessment which is a lien as of the Close of Escrow shall be | ☐ Paid in Full by Seller | ☐ Prorated and
222. Any assessment that becomes a lien after Close of Escrow is the Buyer's responsibility. | | Assumed by Buyer
223. **IRS Reporting:** Seller agrees to comply with IRS reporting requirements. If applicable, Seller agrees to complete, sign and deliver to Escrow Company a certificate
224. indicating whether Seller is a foreign person or a non-resident alien pursuant to the Foreign Investment in Real Property Tax Act (FIRPTA).

©AAR Form 1546-830 RPC 07/94

## Figure 7.1 Purchase Contract (Page 5 of 7)

225. **Seller Property Disclosure Statement (SPDS):**
226. (a) ☐ Buyer has received, read, and approved the SPDS.
227. (b) ☐ Buyer waives review and approval of the SPDS. **(BUYERS' INITIALS ARE REQUIRED HERE TO WAIVE SPDS** _____ _____ **)**
       BUYER    BUYER
228. (c) ☐ Seller shall deliver the SPDS within five (5) calendar days after acceptance of the Contract, after which Buyer shall have five (5) calendar days after
229. receipt by Buyer to immediately terminate this Contract notwithstanding any other provisions contained herein by delivering written notice of termination to
230. either the Seller or to the Escrow Company, and in such event, Buyer is entitled to a return of the earnest money without further consent of the Seller. (AAR
231. FORM 1417, OR EQUIVALENT, SHALL SATISFY THIS REQUIREMENT.)

232. **Title and Vesting:** Escrow Company is hereby instructed to obtain and distribute to Buyer a Commitment for Title Insurance together with complete and legible
233. copies of all documents which will remain as exceptions to Buyer's policy of Title Insurance, including but not limited to Conditions, Covenants and Restrictions,
234. deed restrictions and easements. Buyer shall have five (5) calendar days after receipt of the Commitment for Title Insurance to provide written notice to Seller of
235. any of the exceptions disapproved. REFER TO LINES 283-291 FOR IMPORTANT TERMS. If thereafter the title is otherwise defective at Close of Escrow,
236. Buyer may elect, as Buyer's sole option, either to accept title subject to defects which are not cured or to cancel this Contract whereupon all money paid by
237. Buyer pursuant to this Contract shall be returned to Buyer. Seller shall convey title by general warranty deed. Buyer shall be provided at Seller's expense a
238. Standard Owner's Title Insurance Policy, or, if available, an American Land Title Association (ALTA) Residential Title Insurance Policy ("Plain Language"/"1-4
239. units") showing the title vested in Buyer as provided in Lines 5-6. Buyer may acquire extended coverage at his own additional expense.

240. **Seller's Notice of Violations:** Seller represents that Seller has no knowledge of any notice of violations of City, County, State, or Federal building, zoning,
241. fire, or health laws, codes, statutes, ordinances, regulations, or rules filed or issued regarding the Premises. If Seller receives notice of violations prior to
242. Close of Escrow, Seller shall immediately notify Buyer in writing. Buyer is allowed five (5) calendar days after receipt of notice to provide written notice to
243. Seller of any items disapproved. REFER TO LINES 283-291 FOR IMPORTANT TERMS.

244. **H.O.A./Condominium/P.U.D.:** If the Premises is located within a homeowners' association/condominium/planned unit development:

245. (a) the current regular association dues are   $ _____   ☐ monthly,   ☐ _____ ;

246. (b) Seller shall, as soon as practicable, and prior to Close of Escrow, (1) disclose in writing to Buyer any known existing or pending special assessments,
247. claims, or litigation, and (2) provide to Buyer copies of Covenants, Conditions, and Restrictions, Articles of Incorporation, bylaws, other governing docu-
248. ments, any other documents required by law, and homeowners' association approval of transfer, if applicable, and current financial statement and/or
249. budget. Buyer is allowed five (5) calendar days after receipt to provide written notice to Seller of any items reasonably disapproved.

250. REFER TO LINES 283-291 FOR IMPORTANT TERMS. Any current homeowners' assessments to be   ☐ paid in full by Seller;   ☐ assumed by Buyer

251. Transfer fees, if any, shall be paid by   ☐ Seller   ☐ Buyer   ☐ Other: _____

252. **Inspection Period (Physical, Environmental and Other Inspections):** Buyer has been advised of the benefits of obtaining independent inspec-
253. tions of the entire Premises in order to determine the condition thereof. In addition to the provisions regarding wood infestation, Buyer shall have the
254. right at Buyer's expense to select an inspector(s) to make additional inspections (including tests, surveys, and other studies) of the Premises. Buyer
255. acknowledges that more than one inspection may be required to perform the selected inspections. The inspections may include physical, environ-
256. mental and other types of inspections including, but not limited to, square footage, roof, designated flood hazard areas, structural, plumbing,
257. sewer/septic, well, heating, air conditioning, electrical and mechanical systems, built-in appliances, soil, foundation, pool/spa and related equipment,
258. cost of compliance with Swimming Pool Regulations, possible environmental hazards (such as asbestos, formaldehyde, radon gas, lead-based
259. paint, fuel or chemical storage tanks, hazardous waste, other substances, materials or products; and/or location in a federal or state Superfund area,
260. geologic conditions, location of property lines, and water/utility use restrictions and fees for services (such as garbage or fire protection). Seller shall make
261. the Premises available for all inspections. It is understood that this inspection requires that the utilities be on and the Seller is responsible for providing
262. same at his expense. Buyer shall keep the Premises free and clear of liens, shall indemnify and hold Seller harmless from all liability, claims, demands,
263. damages, and costs, and shall repair all damages arising from the inspections. Buyer shall provide Seller and Brokers, at no cost, copies of all reports
264. concerning the Premises obtained by Buyer. Buyer shall provide written notice to Seller of any items reasonably disapproved,

265. excluding cosmetic items, within **ten (10) calendar days or**   ☐ _____ **calendar days**   after acceptance of the Contract. Any repairs agreed to shall
266. be completed prior to Close of Escrow. REFER TO LINES 283-291 FOR IMPORTANT TERMS.

267. **SQUARE FOOTAGE: BUYER IS AWARE THAT ANY REFERENCE TO THE SQUARE FOOTAGE OF THE PREMISES IS APPROXIMATE. IF SQUARE**
268. **FOOTAGE IS A MATERIAL MATTER TO THE BUYER, IT MUST BE VERIFIED DURING THE INSPECTION PERIOD.**

269. **Flood Hazard Disclosure:** If the Premises is situated in an area identified as having any special flood hazards by any governmental entity including, but not limited to,
270. being designated as a special flood hazard area by the Federal Emergency Management Agency (FEMA), the Buyer's lender may require the purchase of flood haz-
271. ard insurance at the Close of Escrow or some future date. Special flood hazards may affect the ability to encumber or improve the property now or at some
272. future date. **Flood hazard designation of the Premises or cost of flood hazard insurance must be verified by Buyer during the Inspection Period.**

273. **Swimming Pool Regulations:** These Premises   ☐ do   ☐ do not   contain a swimming pool which is defined as an above or below ground swimming
274. pool or contained body of water intended for swimming, exclusive of public or semi-public swimming pools ("Swimming Pool"). Seller and Buyer acknowl-
275. edge that the State of Arizona has swimming pool barrier regulations which are outlined in the Arizona Department of Health Services Private Pool Safety
276. Notice. The parties further acknowledge that the county or municipality in which the Premises is located may have different swimming pool barrier regula-
277. tions than the state. During the Inspection Period, Buyer agrees to investigate all applicable state, county and municipal swimming pool barrier regulations
278. and, unless disapproved within the Inspection Period, agrees to comply with and pay all costs of compliance with said regulations prior to possession of
279. the Premises. If these Premises contain a Swimming Pool, BUYER ACKNOWLEDGES RECEIPT OF THE ARIZONA DEPARTMENT OF HEALTH SER-
280. VICES APPROVED PRIVATE POOL SAFETY NOTICE AS REQUIRED BY A.R.S. 36-1681 (E) AND A.D.H.S.. RULE R9-3-101.

281. **(BUYERS INITIALS ARE REQUIRED)** _____ _____
       BUYER    BUYER

282. Buyer and Seller expressly relieve and indemnify Brokers from any and all liability and responsibility for compliance with the applicable pool barrier regulations.

283. **Buyer Disapproval:** If Buyer gives written notice of disapproval of items as provided herein, Seller shall respond in writing within **five (5) calendar days or**

284. ☐ _____ **calendar days**   after receipt of such notice. Seller acknowledges that items warranted by Seller must be maintained and repaired as
285. provided in Lines 312-319. If Seller is unwilling or unable to correct additional items reasonably disapproved by Buyer, including making any repairs in a workmanlike
286. manner, then Buyer may cancel this Contract by giving written notice of cancellation to Seller within five (5) calendar days after receipt of Seller's response, or after
287. expiration of the time for Seller's response, whichever occurs first, in which case Buyer's deposit shall be returned to Buyer, without further written consent of Seller,
288. and without regard for the cancellation provisions in Lines 348-356. Notwithstanding the foregoing, if the items reasonably disapproved by the Buyer exceed ten per-
289. cent (10%) of the purchase price, the Buyer shall be entitled to cancel this Contract. **BUYER'S FAILURE TO GIVE WRITTEN NOTICE OF DISAPPROVAL OF**
290. **ITEMS OR CANCELLATION OF THIS CONTRACT WITHIN THE SPECIFIED TIME PERIODS SHALL CONCLUSIVELY BE DEEMED BUYER'S ELECTION TO**
291. **PROCEED WITH THE TRANSACTION WITHOUT CORRECTION OF ANY DISAPPROVED ITEMS WHICH SELLER HAS NOT AGREED TO CORRECT.**

©AAR Form 1546-830 RPC 07/94

# Figure 7.1 Purchase Contract (Page 6 of 7)

292. **Home Protection Plan:** Buyer and Seller are advised to investigate the various coverage options available for purchase.

293. ☐ A Home Protection Plan with the following optional coverage _____

294. at a cost not to exceed $ _____ , to be paid by ☐ Buyer, ☐ Seller, and to be issued by _____

295. ☐ Buyer and Seller elect **not** to purchase a Home Protection Plan.

296. **Wood Infestation Report:** ☐ Seller ☐ Buyer will, at his expense, place in escrow a Wood Infestation Report of all residences and buildings included in this
297. sale prepared by a qualified licensed pest control operator consistent with the rules and regulations of the Structural Pest Control Commission of the State of

298. Arizona. Seller agrees to pay up to **one percent (1%) of the purchase price or** ☐ $ _____ for costs of treatment of infestation, repair of any
299. damage caused by infestation and correction of any conditions conducive to infestation as evidenced on the Wood Infestation Report. If such costs exceed
300. this amount that the Seller agrees to pay, (1) the Buyer may immediately elect to cancel this Contract, or, (2) Seller may elect to cancel this Contract unless
301. Buyer agrees, in writing, to pay such costs in excess of those Seller agrees to pay.

302. **Sanitation and Waste Disposal Systems:** Buyer is aware and Seller warrants that the Premises is on a:

303. ☐ sewer system; ☐ septic system. Comments: _____

304. **Seller's Obligations Regarding Waste Disposal Systems:** Before Close of Escrow any septic tank on the Premises shall be inspected at Seller's
305. expense by an inspector recognized by the applicable governmental authority. Any necessary repairs shall be paid by Seller, but not to exceed **one percent**

306. **(1%) of the full purchase price or** ☐ $ _____ . If such costs exceed this amount that the Seller agrees to pay, (1) the Buyer may
307. immediately elect to cancel this Contract, or, (2) Seller may elect to cancel this Contract unless Buyer agrees, in writing, to pay such costs in excess of
308. those Seller agrees to pay. Seller shall deliver to Escrow Company, at Seller's expense, any certification and/or documentation required.

309. **Seller's Obligations Regarding Wells:** If any well is located on the Premises, Seller shall deliver to Escrow Company, before Close of Escrow, a copy of
310. the Arizona Department of Water Resources (ADWR) "Registration of Existing Wells". Escrow Company is hereby instructed to send to the ADWR a
311. "Change of Well Information". (ARS 45-593)

312. **Seller Warranties:** Seller warrants and shall maintain and repair the Premises so that at the earlier of possession or the Close of Escrow: (1) the Premises
313. shall be in substantially the same condition as on the effective date of this Contract, (2) the roof has no known leaks, (3) all heating, cooling, mechanical,
314. plumbing and electrical systems and built-in appliances will be in working condition, and (4) if the Premises has a swimming pool and/or spa, the motors, fil-
315. ter systems, cleaning systems, and heaters, if so equipped, will be in working condition. The Seller grants Buyer or Buyer's representative reasonable
316. access to conduct a final walk-through of the Premises for the purpose of satisfying Buyer that the items warranted by Seller are in working condition, and
317. that any repairs Seller agreed to make have been completed. Any personal property included herein shall be transferred in AS IS CONDITION, FREE AND
318. CLEAR OF ANY LIENS OR ENCUMBRANCES, and SELLER MAKES NO WARRANTY of any kind, express or implied (including, without limitation, ANY
319. WARRANTY OF MERCHANTABILITY).

320. **Buyer Warranties:** At the earlier of possession of the Premises or Close of Escrow, (a) Buyer warrants to Seller that he has conducted all desired independent
321. investigations and accepts the Premises, and (b) Buyer acknowledges that there will be no Seller warranty of any kind, except as stated in Lines 322-328.

322. **Warranties that Survive Closing:** Prior to the Close of Escrow, Seller warrants that payment in full will have been made for all labor, professional services,
323. materials, machinery, fixtures or tools furnished within the 120 calendar days immediately preceding the Close of Escrow in connection with the construc-
324. tion, alteration or repair of any structure on or improvement to the Premises. Seller warrants that the information on Lines 302-303 regarding connection to a
325. public sewer system, septic tank or other sanitation system is correct to the best of his knowledge. Seller warrants that he has disclosed to Buyer and
326. Brokers all material latent defects and any information concerning the Premises known to Seller, (excluding opinions of value), which materially and
327. adversely affect the consideration to be paid by Buyer. Buyer warrants that he has disclosed to Seller any information which may materially and adversely
328. affect the Buyer's ability to close escrow or complete the obligations of this Contract.

329. **Release of Brokers:** SELLER AND BUYER HEREBY EXPRESSLY RELEASE, HOLD HARMLESS AND INDEMNIFY ALL BROKERS IN THIS TRANS-
330. ACTION FROM ANY AND ALL LIABILITY AND RESPONSIBILITY REGARDING THE CONDITION, SQUARE FOOTAGE, LOT LINES OR BOUND-
331. ARIES, VALUE, RENT ROLLS, ENVIRONMENTAL PROBLEMS, SANITATION SYSTEMS, ROOF, WOOD INFESTATION AND WOOD INFESTATION
332. REPORT, COMPLIANCE WITH BUILDING CODES OR OTHER GOVERNMENTAL REGULATIONS, OR ANY OTHER MATERIAL MATTERS RELAT-
333. ING TO THE PREMISES. Neither Seller, Buyer nor any Broker shall be bound by any understanding, agreement, promise or representation, express or
334. implied, written or verbal, not specified herein.

335. **Default and Remedies:** If either party defaults in any respect on any material obligations under this Contract, the non-defaulting party may elect to be released
336. from all obligations under this Contract by cancelling this Contract as provided in Lines 348-356. The non-defaulting party may thereafter proceed against the
337. party in default upon any claim or remedy which the non-defaulting party may have in law or equity. In the case of the Seller, because it would be difficult to fix
338. actual damages in the event of Buyer's default, the amount of the earnest money may be deemed a reasonable estimate of the damages; and Seller may at
339. Seller's option retain the earnest money deposit, subject to any compensation to Brokers, as Seller's sole right to damages. In the event that the non-defaulting
340. party elects not to cancel this Contract, the non-defaulting party may proceed against the party in default for specific performance of this Contract or any of its
341. terms, in addition to any claim or remedy which the non-defaulting party may have in law or equity. In the event that either party pursues specific performance of
342. this Contract, that party does not waive the right to cancel this Contract pursuant to Lines 348-356 at any time and proceed against the defaulting party as oth-
343. erwise provided herein, or in law or equity. If Buyer or Seller files suit against the other to enforce any provision of this Contract or for damages sustained by
344. reason of its breach, all parties prevailing in such action, on trial and appeal, shall receive their reasonable attorneys' fees and costs as awarded by the court. In
345. addition, both Seller and Buyer agree to indemnify and hold harmless all Brokers against all costs and expenses that any Broker may incur or sustain in connec-
346. tion with any lawsuit arising from this Contract and will pay the same on demand unless the court grants judgment in such action against the party to be indem-
347. nified. Costs include, without limitation: attorneys' fees, expert witness fees, fees paid to investigators and court costs.

348. **Cancellation:** Except as otherwise provided herein, any party who wishes to cancel this Contract because of any breach by another party, or because escrow
349. fails to close by the agreed date, and who is not himself in breach of this Contract, except as occasioned by a breach by the other party, may cancel this Contract
350. by delivering a notice to either the breaching party or to the Escrow Company stating the nature of the breach and that this Contract shall be cancelled unless the
351. breach is cured within thirteen (13) calendar days following the delivery of the notice. If this notice is delivered to the Escrow Company, it shall contain the address
352. of the party in breach. Any notice delivered to any party must be delivered to the Brokers and the Escrow Company. Within three (3) calendar days after receipt of
353. such notice, the Escrow Company shall send the notice by mail to the party in breach at the address contained in the notice. No further notice shall be required. In
354. the event that the breach is not cured within thirteen (13) calendar days following the delivery of the notice to the party in breach or to the Escrow Company, this
355. Contract shall be cancelled; and the non-breaching party shall have all rights and remedies available at law or equity for the breach of this Contract by the breach-
356. ing party, as provided in Lines 335-347.

357. **Risk Of Loss:** If there is any loss or damage to the Premises between the date hereof and the Close of Escrow by reason of fire, vandalism, flood, earthquake or
358. act of God, the risk of loss shall be on the Seller, provided, however, that if the cost of repairing such loss or damage would exceed ten percent (10%) of the pur-
359. chase price, either Seller or Buyer may elect to cancel the Contract.

360. **Broker's Rights:** If any Broker hires an attorney to enforce the collection of the commission payable pursuant to this Contract, and is successful in collecting some
361. or all of such commission, the party(ies) responsible for paying such commission agree(s) to pay such Broker's costs including, but not limited to: attorneys' fees,
362. expert witness fees, fees paid to investigators, and court costs. The Seller and the Buyer acknowledge that the Brokers are third-party beneficiaries of this Contract.

©AAR Form 1546-830 RPC 07/94

## Figure 7.1 Purchase Contract (Page 7 of 7)

363. **Permission:** Buyer and Seller grant Brokers permission to advise the public of the sale upon execution of this Contract, and Brokers may disclose price and
364. terms herein after Close of Escrow.

365. **Attorneys' Fees:** In any action, proceeding or arbitration arising out of this Contract, the prevailing party shall be entitled to reasonable attorneys' fees and costs.

366. **Mediation:** Any dispute or claim arising out of or relating to this Contract, any alleged breach of this Contract or services provided in relation to this Contract shall
367. be submitted to mediation in accordance with the Rules and Procedures of the NATIONAL ASSOCIATION OF REALTORS® (NAR) Dispute Resolution System
368. or, if not available, another mediation provider. Disputes shall include representations made by the Buyer, Seller or any Broker or other person or entity in connec-
369. tion with the sale, purchase, financing, condition or other aspect of the Premises to which this Contract pertains, including without limitation allegations of conceal-
370. ment, misrepresentation, negligence and/or fraud. Any agreement signed by the parties pursuant to the mediation conference shall be binding. The following mat-
371. ters are excluded from mediation hereunder: (a) judicial or nonjudicial foreclosure or other action or proceeding to enforce a deed of trust, mortgage, or agreement
372. for sale; (b) an unlawful detainer action; (c) the filing or enforcement of a mechanic's lien; or (d) any matter which is within the jurisdiction of a probate court. The
373. filing of a judicial action to enable the recording of a notice of pending action, for order of attachment, receivership, injunction, or other provisional remedies, shall
374. not constitute a waiver of the obligation to mediate under this provision, nor shall it constitute a breach of the duty to mediate. All mediation costs will be paid
375. equally by the parties to the mediation, unless otherwise agreed.

376. **Entire Agreement:** This Contract, any attached exhibits and any addenda or supplements signed by the parties shall constitute the entire agreement between
377. Seller and Buyer, and shall supersede any other written or oral agreement between Seller and Buyer. This Contract can be modified only by a writing signed by
378. Seller and Buyer. A fully executed facsimile copy of the entire agreement shall be treated as an original Contract.

379. **Time of Essence:** Time is of the essence.

380. **Arizona Law:** This Contract shall be governed by Arizona law.

381. **Severability:** If a court of competent jurisdiction makes a final determination that any term or provision of this Contract is invalid or unenforceable, all other
382. terms and provisions shall remain in full force and effect, and the invalid or unenforceable term or provision shall be deemed replaced by a term or provision
383. that is valid and enforceable and comes closest to expressing the intention of the invalid term or provision.

384. **Construction of Language:** The language of this Contract shall be construed according to its fair meaning and not strictly for or against either party. Words
385. used in the masculine, feminine or neuter shall apply to either gender or the neuter, as appropriate.

386. **Compensation:** Seller and Buyer acknowledge that Brokers shall be compensated for services rendered as previously agreed by separate written agree-
387. ment(s). Any separate written agreement(s) shall be delivered to Escrow Company for payment at Close of Escrow, if not previously paid and shall consti-
388. tute an irrevocable assignment of Seller's proceeds at Close of Escrow. **COMMISSIONS PAYABLE FOR THE SALE, LEASING OR MANAGEMENT OF**
389. **PROPERTY ARE NOT SET BY ANY BOARD OR ASSOCIATION OF REALTORS®, OR MULTIPLE LISTING SERVICE, OR IN ANY MANNER OTHER**
390. **THAN BETWEEN THE BROKER AND CLIENT.**

391. **Additional Compensation:** RESPA prohibits the paying or receiving of any fee, kickback, or thing of value for the referral of any business related to set-
392. tlement or closing of a federally regulated mortgage loan, including but not limited to, any services related to the origination, processing, or funding of a
393. federally regulated mortgage loan and includes such settlement related business as termite inspections and home warranties. RESPA does not prohibit
394. fees, salaries, compensation or other payments for services actually performed. If any Broker performs any such services for a fee, Seller and Buyer con-
395. sent to the payment of this additional compensation for such services actually performed as follows:
396. _____
397. _____

398. **Time For Acceptance:** This is an offer to purchase the Premises. Unless acceptance is signed by Seller and a signed copy delivered in person, by mail, or facsimile,

399. and received by Buyer or by Broker named on lines 15-16 | by _____ , 19 _____ at _____ AM/PM, Mountain Standard Time,

400. or unless this offer to purchase has been previously withdrawn by Buyer, this offer to purchase shall be deemed withdrawn and the Buyer's earnest money
401. shall be returned.
402. The undersigned agree to purchase the Premises on the terms and conditions herein stated and acknowledge receipt of a copy hereof.

403. _____  _____
     BUYER                MO/DA/YR           BUYER                MO/DA/YR
404. _____  _____
     ADDRESS                              ADDRESS
405. _____  _____
     CITY, STATE, ZIP CODE                CITY, STATE, ZIP CODE

## ACCEPTANCE

406. **Agency Confirmation:** The following agency relationship(s) is hereby confirmed for this transaction:

407.    Listing Broker: _____
                        (PRINT FIRM NAME)
408.    Is the agent of (check one): ☐ the Seller exclusively; or   ☐ both the Buyer and Seller

409. **Subsequent Offers:** Upon acceptance of this Contract, Seller hereby waives the right to receive any subsequent offer to purchase the Premises until after
410. forfeiture by Buyer or other cancellation of this Contract.

411. **Seller Receipt of Copy:** The undersigned acknowledge receipt of a copy hereof and grant permission to Broker named on lines 15-16 to deliver
412. a copy to Buyer.

413. ☐ **Counter Offer is attached, and is incorporated herein by reference. If there is a conflict between this Contract and the Counter Offer, the**
414. **provisions of the Counter Offer shall be controlling. (NOTE: If this box is checked, Seller should sign both the Contract and the Counter Offer.)**

415. The undersigned agree to sell the Premises on the terms and conditions herein stated.

416. _____  _____
     SELLER               MO/DA/YR           SELLER               MO/DA/YR
417. _____  _____
     ADDRESS                              ADDRESS
418. _____  _____
     CITY, STATE, ZIP CODE                CITY, STATE, ZIP CODE

**For Broker Use Only:** Brokerage File/Log No. _____   Manager's Initials _____   Broker's Initials _____   Date _____
                                                                                                          MO/DA/YR

Copies of rejected offers to purchase must be kept by the broker for one year; copies of binding contracts must be kept for five years. Copies of the contracts must be kept in a transaction folder in the employing broker's principal office or licensed branch office.

Additionally, any licensee preparing a document is required to deliver a legible copy of that document to each participant as soon as practical. Copies must also be retained for the participating/employing broker's files. The licensee is responsible for preparing a sufficient number of copies to meet the requirements of the transaction.

In practice, the licensee preparing or completing the purchase contract should prepare at least three copies of the document in addition to the original (Figure 7.2). One copy is given to the purchaser when the offer is drafted; it acts as the receipt for the earnest money that the licensee accepts on behalf of the seller. Then the original and two remaining copies are presented to the seller. Upon the seller's acceptance of and signature on the offer, the licensee gives a second copy to the seller as a copy of the contract. The remaining copy is then given to the purchaser as written acceptance by the seller. The original is retained by the broker, and other required copies for lenders, escrow agents and the like are made from that original.

## Alterations to the Contract

The negotiating process in a real estate transaction involves both offers and counteroffers. If the seller wishes to make minor changes to or deletions from the purchaser's offer (thus creating a counteroffer), the licensee must have the seller and the purchaser approve such changes or deletions in writing by initialing and dating them in the margin of all copies of the contract. If the sale involves government-backed financing (either an FHA-insured loan or a VA-guaranteed loan) or if the alterations are extensive, the best practice is to complete a new contract form. Both the seller and the purchaser must sign the new contract form; the licensee should retain the original contract form as a worksheet in case of any future disagreements or misunderstandings.

## Seller Disclosures

To prevent misrepresentions in the marketing and conveyance of property, either innocent or intentional, real estate licensees are encouraging sellers to make voluntary disclosures about the condition of their property. Such disclosures protect the licensees as well as the sellers by giving the buyers information that is probably very important to their buying decision.

The Arizona Association of REALTORS® has developed the "Residential Seller's Property Disclosure Statement" (Figure 7.3) to assist in the solicitation of such information from the sellers. Although its use is required after sellers accept offers that are drafted on the "Residential Resale Real Estate Purchase Contract and Receipt for Deposit" (lines 225–231 in Figure 7.1), many licensees are obtaining this information from sellers at the time the listing on their property is taken.

**Figure 7.2 Purchase Contract Copies**

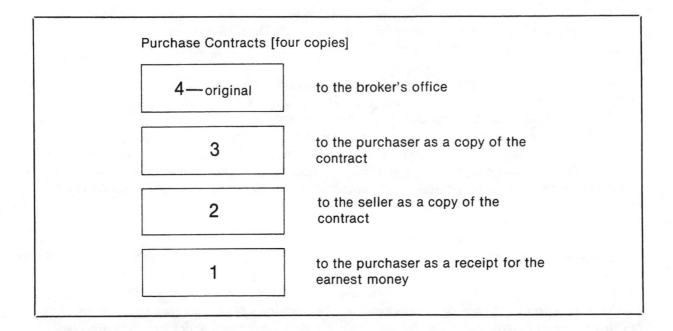

Purchase Contracts [four copies]

| | |
|---|---|
| 4—original | to the broker's office |
| 3 | to the purchaser as a copy of the contract |
| 2 | to the seller as a copy of the contract |
| 1 | to the purchaser as a receipt for the earnest money |

## BREACH OF CONTRACT

If the seller breaches the contract, the purchaser may take one of the following courses of action:

- Rescind the contract and recover the earnest money
- Sue the seller for compensatory damages
- Sue the seller for specific performance

If the purchaser breaches the contract, the seller may

- declare the contract and the earnest money forfeited,
- rescind the contract and thereby release the purchaser from any further obligations,
- sue the purchaser for compensatory damages, or
- sue the purchaser for specific performance.

Note that if the purchaser breaches the contract and the seller rescinds the contract, the seller must return any funds paid by the purchaser (such as the earnest money). The contract may contain a *liquidated damages* clause that limits the seller's damages to the earnest money deposit if the purchaser breaches.

If the purchaser breaches the contract, it is practically impossible for a seller to win a specific performance suit against a purchaser. The courts are unwilling to order a purchaser to become responsible for a property he or she does not want: the purchaser can refuse to make payments or may physically abandon or vandalize the property.

**Figure 7.3 Residential Seller's Property Disclosure Statement (SPDS)
(To Be Completed by Seller) (Page 1 of 3)**

# RESIDENTIAL
# SELLER'S PROPERTY DISCLOSURE STATEMENT (SPDS)
# (TO BE COMPLETED BY SELLER)

THE PRINTED PORTION OF THIS FORM HAS BEEN APPROVED BY THE ARIZONA ASSOCIATION OF REALTORS®. THIS IS NOT INTENDED TO BE A BINDING CONTRACT.

## MESSAGE TO THE SELLER:

Sellers are obligated by law to disclose all known material facts about the Property to the Buyer. The SPDS is designed to assist you in making this disclosure. If you know something important about the Property that is not addressed on the SPDS, add that information to the form. Prospective Buyers may rely on the information you provide in deciding whether and on what terms to buy the Property. If you don't know the answer to a question, mark "unknown".

## MESSAGE TO THE BUYER:

The information contained in the SPDS is a disclosure of the Seller's actual knowledge of the Property and not a representation of every possible defect nor a warranty of any kind. You should confirm any information you consider material to your purchase and consider obtaining a professional home inspection, which may reveal information about the Property that even the Seller did not know.

**THE FOLLOWING ARE REPRESENTATIONS OF THE SELLER(S) AND ARE NOT THE REPRESENTATIONS OF THE AGENT(S), IF ANY. THIS INFORMATION IS A DISCLOSURE AND IS NOT INTENDED TO BE PART OF ANY CONTRACT BETWEEN THE BUYER AND SELLER.**

# I. OWNERSHIP AND PROPERTY

1. THIS DISCLOSURE CONCERNS THE FOLLOWING REAL PROPERTY: _____
2. _____
3. LEGAL OWNER OF PROPERTY _____ APPROXIMATE YEAR BUILT _____
4. Owner ☐ is ☐ is not occupying property. Owner ☐ has ☐ has not occupied property in the past.
5. Property ☐ is ☐ is not rented. Property ☐ has ☐ has not been rented in the past.
6. If rented, what is the expiration date of rental agreement? _____
7. If currently vacant, how long? _____

| | YES | NO | UNKN | |
|---|---|---|---|---|
| 8. | ☐ | ☐ | ☐ | Has a rental agreement renewal or option to purchase been promised? |
| 9. | ☐ | ☐ | ☐ | Are security deposits or prepaid rents being held? By whom and how much? _____ |
| 10. | ☐ | ☐ | ☐ | Have you entered into any agreement to transfer your interest in the property in any way? Explain _____ |
| 11. | | | | _____ |
| 12. | ☐ | ☐ | ☐ | Is there a homeowners' association (HOA) governing this property? |
| 13. | ☐ | ☐ | ☐ | a. If yes, is there a fee? How much and how often? $ _____ |
| 14. | ☐ | ☐ | ☐ | b. Is there a proposed or existing homeowners' association assessment? Explain _____ |
| 15. | | | | c. Name of HOA contact _____ Telephone number: _____ |
| 16. | ☐ | ☐ | ☐ | Are there any pending or anticipated legal disputes regarding the property? Explain _____ |
| 17. | ☐ | ☐ | ☐ | Are there any liens against the property? Explain _____ |
| 18. | ☐ | ☐ | ☐ | Are there any assessments, such as paving, sewer, water or electric, regarding this property? Explain _____ |
| 19. | ☐ | ☐ | ☐ | Are there any title problems (for example, easements, use restrictions, lot line disputes, encroachments, access)? |
| 20. | | | | If yes, explain _____ |
| 21. | | | | Are the fences or walls ☐ solely owned or ☐ jointly owned? Explain _____ |
| 22. | ☐ | ☐ | ☐ | Is this property on a private road? |
| 23. | ☐ | ☐ | ☐ | If so, is there a road maintenance agreement? _____ |
| 24. | ☐ | ☐ | ☐ | Are there any zoning problems/violations/variances or conditional use permits on this property? Explain _____ |
| 25. | | | | _____ |

# II. BUILDING AND SAFETY INFORMATION

| | YES | NO | UNKN | |
|---|---|---|---|---|
| 26. | | | | **STRUCTURAL:** |
| 27. | | | | Roof type _____ Appx. age _____ |
| 28. | ☐ | ☐ | ☐ | Are there or have there ever been any roof leaks or other roof problems? Explain _____ |
| 29. | ☐ | ☐ | ☐ | Have there been any roof repairs? Explain _____ |
| 30. | | | | _____ |
| 31. | ☐ | ☐ | ☐ | Is there a roof warranty? Company name_____ Time remaining on warranty_____ |
| 32. | ☐ | ☐ | ☐ | If there is a roof warranty, is it transferable? Amount of transfer fee? _____ |
| 33. | ☐ | ☐ | ☐ | Is there a copy of the new roof warranty available? _____ |
| 34. | ☐ | ☐ | ☐ | Are there any interior wall/ceiling/door/window/floor problems? Explain _____ |
| 35. | | | | Type of floor under floor covering? _____ |
| 36. | ☐ | ☐ | ☐ | Are there any chimney or fireplace problems? Explain _____ |
| 37. | | | | a. Date chimney or fireplace last cleaned _____ |
| 38. | ☐ | ☐ | ☐ | Is the wood/coal stove in compliance with local regulations? Explain _____ |
| 39. | ☐ | ☐ | ☐ | Is there, or has there ever been, any wood infestation, termite, insect or pest problems? Explain _____ |
| 40. | | | | _____ |

©AAR Form 1616-1650 SPDS 09/95 02

SOURCE: Permission granted by Arizona Association of REALTORS®.

## Figure 7.3 Residential Seller's Property Disclosure Statement (Page 2 of 3)

| | YES | NO | UNKN | |
|---|---|---|---|---|
| 41. | ☐ | ☐ | ☐ | Is there a wood infestation or termite warranty? Company name_____ Time remaining on warranty _____ |
| 42. | ☐ | ☐ | ☐ | If there is a wood infestation or termite warranty, is it transferable? Amount of transfer fee? _____ |
| 43. | ☐ | ☐ | ☐ | Has there been any damage to the property or any structure on the property? Explain _____ |
| 44. | | | | _____ |
| 45. | | | | **HEATING & COOLING:** |
| 46. | | | | Heating: Type _____ Appx. age _____ |
| 47. | | | | Cooling: Type _____ Appx. age _____ |
| 48. | ☐ | ☐ | ☐ | Are there any unheated and/or uncooled rooms? Explain _____ |
| 49. | ☐ | ☐ | ☐ | Are there any problems in heating or cooling system(s)? Explain _____ |
| 50. | | | | _____ |
| 51. | ☐ | ☐ | ☐ | Is the property insulated? Type _____ Amount _____ |
| 52. | | | | **PLUMBING:** |
| 53. | | | | Type of plumbing pipes, such as galvanized, copper, PVC or polybutylene: _____ |
| 54. | ☐ | ☐ | ☐ | Are there any plumbing problems? Explain _____ |
| 55. | | | | _____ |
| 56. | | | | Type of hot water heater(s) _____ # of gallons _____ Appx. age _____ |
| 57. | ☐ | ☐ | ☐ | Are there any hot water problems? Explain _____ |
| 58. | ☐ | ☐ | ☐ | Is there a landscape watering system?  ☐ automatic timer  ☐ manual  ☐ both |
| 59. | ☐ | ☐ | ☐ | Are there any problems with the landscape watering system? Explain _____ |
| 60. | | | | _____ |
| 61. | ☐ | ☐ | ☐ | If applicable, are there any problems with the pool, hot tub, spa, sauna or their mechanical systems? Explain _____ |
| 62. | | | | _____ |
| 63. | | | | **ELECTRICAL:** |
| 64. | | | | Type(s) of electrical wiring (such as copper or aluminum) _____ |
| 65. | ☐ | ☐ | ☐ | Are there any electrical problems? Explain _____ |
| 66. | | | | **OTHER SYSTEMS:** |
| 67. | ☐ | ☐ | ☐ | Are there any systems/appliances that are not in good working order? Explain _____ |
| 68. | | | | |
| 69. | ☐ | ☐ | ☐ | Is there a security system and/or fire-smoke detection system? Explain _____ |
| 70. | | | | _____ |
| 71. | ☐ | ☐ | ☐ | Are there any existing leased equipment or systems? Explain _____ |
| 72. | | | | _____ |
| 73. | | | | **MISCELLANEOUS:** |
| 74. | ☐ | ☐ | ☐ | The State of Arizona and many local communities have laws and ordinances relating to swimming pool barriers on properties |
| 75. | | | | occupied by children under six (6) years of age. Is your property in compliance? Explain _____ |
| 76. | ☐ | ☐ | ☐ | Are there any building code or sanitary or fire safety code violations on this property? Explain _____ |
| 77. | | | | _____ |
| 78. | ☐ | ☐ | ☐ | Have you or others done any work on the property, such as building, plumbing, electrical or other improvements? |
| 79. | | | | Explain _____ |
| 80. | ☐ | ☐ | ☐ | a.    If work was done by others, were they licensed to perform the work? _____ |
| 81. | ☐ | ☐ | ☐ | b.    Were permits required? _____ |
| 82. | ☐ | ☐ | ☐ | c.    Were they obtained? _____ |
| 83. | ☐ | ☐ | ☐ | d.    Was work completed? Explain _____ |
| 84. | ☐ | ☐ | ☐ | Are there any obstructions to door or window openings? Explain _____ |
| 85. | | | | _____ |

# III. UTILITIES

| 86. | | | | **Do you currently receive the following services?** |
|---|---|---|---|---|
| | YES | NO | UNKN | **PROVIDER** |
| 87. | ☐ | ☐ | ☐ | 1) Electricity.................._____ |
| 88. | ☐ | ☐ | ☐ | 2) Gas .........................._____ |
| 89. | ☐ | ☐ | ☐ | 3) Cable........................_____ |
| 90. | ☐ | ☐ | ☐ | 4) Telephone................._____ |
| 91. | ☐ | ☐ | ☐ | 5) Garbage Collection .._____ |
| 92. | ☐ | ☐ | ☐ | 6) Fire .........................._____ |
| 93. | ☐ | ☐ | ☐ | 7) Irrigation..................._____ |
| 94. | ☐ | ☐ | ☐ | 8) Water ......................._____ |
| 95. | | | | Water Source: .............☐ Public  ☐ Private _____ |
| 96. | ☐ | ☐ | ☐ | Is the property served by a well? ☐ Owned or    ☐ Shared by _____ households |
| 97. | ☐ | ☐ | ☐ | Is there a maintenance agreement in effect? |
| 98. | ☐ | ☐ | ☐ | Is the well currently in use? |

©AAR Form 1616-1650 SPDS 09/95 02

## Figure 7.3 Residential Seller's Property Disclosure Statement (Page 3 of 3)

PAGE 3

| | YES | NO | UNKN | |
|---|---|---|---|---|
| 99. | ☐ | ☐ | ☐ | If not, is the well capped? |
| 100. | | | | Dept. of Water Resources Registration # _____ |
| 101. | | | | Depth _____ ; Casing size _____ ; Pumping capacity _____ Location: _____ |
| 102. | ☐ | ☐ | ☐ | Are there any water pressure problems? Explain_____ |
| 103. | | | | _____ |
| 104. | ☐ | ☐ | ☐ | Are there any drinking water problems? Explain _____ |

# IV. ENVIRONMENTAL INFORMATION

| | YES | NO | UNKN | |
|---|---|---|---|---|
| 105. | ☐ | ☐ | ☐ | Are there any soil, settlement or expansion problems? Explain _____ |
| 106. | | | | _____ |
| 107. | ☐ | ☐ | ☐ | Is any portion of the property situated on or near a sanitary landfill? _____ |
| 108. | ☐ | ☐ | ☐ | Are there any hazards or hazardous materials *on the property,* such as asbestos, dumps, pesticides, radon, lead-based paint, underground |
| 109. | | | | fuel storage tanks or leaks? Explain _____ |
| 110. | | | | |
| 111. | ☐ | ☐ | ☐ | Are there any hazards or hazardous materials *in close proximity to the property,* such as asbestos, dumps, pesticides, radon, lead-based |
| 112. | | | | paint, underground fuel storage tanks or leaks? Explain _____ |
| 113. | | | | _____ |
| 114. | ☐ | ☐ | ☐ | Is the property within an area currently of environmental concern, e.g., Superfund or wetlands area or WQARF or CERCLA sites, etc.? |
| 115. | | | | Explain _____ |
| 116. | | | | _____ |
| 117. | ☐ | ☐ | ☐ | Is the property subject to any current or proposed noises, such as airports, freeways, or rail lines? |
| 118. | | | | Explain _____ |
| 119. | ☐ | ☐ | ☐ | Is the property located within the territory in the vicinity of a military airport as defined by Arizona law (A.R.S. §2-338)? |
| 120. | ☐ | ☐ | ☐ | Are there any neighborhood odors, noises, nuisances or pollutants? Explain _____ |
| 121. | | | | _____ |
| 122. | ☐ | ☐ | ☐ | Is any portion of the property in a flood plain/way? Explain _____ |
| 123. | | | | _____ |
| 124. | ☐ | ☐ | ☐ | Has the property ever been flooded? Explain _____ |

# V. WASTE DISPOSAL

| | YES | NO | UNKN | |
|---|---|---|---|---|
| 125. | ☐ | ☐ | ☐ | Is the property connected to a sewer? |
| 126. | ☐ | ☐ | ☐ | If yes, has it been verified? Explain _____ |
| 127. | | | | **TYPE OF SEWER:** ☐ Public ☐ Private ☐ Planned and approved sewer system, but not yet connected. |
| 128. | | | | Name of Provider _____ |
| 129. | ☐ | ☐ | ☐ | On-Site Waste Disposal System: ☐ Standard septic ☐ Aerobic ☐ E-T Bed ☐ Other _____ |
| 130. | | | | Date last pumped _____ Date last inspected _____ |
| 131. | ☐ | ☐ | ☐ | Are there any sewage or waste disposal system problems? Explain _____ |
| 132. | | | | |

# VI. OTHER CONDITIONS AND FACTORS

| | YES | NO | UNKN | |
|---|---|---|---|---|
| 133. | ☐ | ☐ | ☐ | Is there any other information concerning the property which might affect the decision of a buyer to buy, or affect the value of the property, |
| 134. | | | | or affect its use by a buyer? Explain _____ |
| 135. | | | | _____ |

136. **SELLER CERTIFICATION** Seller certifies that the information contained herein is true and complete to the best of Seller's knowledge as of the date signed.
137. Seller agrees that any changes in the information contained herein will be disclosed by Seller to Buyer prior to Close of Escrow.

138. _____  _____
SELLER                                                          MO/DA/YR

139. _____  _____
SELLER                                                          MO/DA/YR

140. **BUYER'S ACKNOWLEDGEMENT OF RECEIPT** Buyer acknowledges that the information contained herein is based only on the Seller's knowledge and is not a
141. warranty of any kind. Buyer acknowledges Buyer's obligation to investigate any material facts in regards to the property to Buyer's satisfaction.
142. Buyer is encouraged to obtain a property inspection by an independent third party and to investigate home warranty protection plans. By signing below, Buyer hereby
143. acknowledges receipt of a copy of this Disclosure. Buyer's signature does not constitute approval.

144. _____  _____
BUYER                                                           MO/DA/YR

145. _____  _____
BUYER                                                           MO/DA/YR

©AAR Form 1616-1650 SPDS 09/95 02

Remember, a real estate licensee should never give legal advice to any party to a contract regarding a breach, unless that licensee is also an attorney. The rights available to the parties and any recommended courses of action are best left to legal advisers.

## HANDLING EARNEST MONEY DEPOSITS

Arizona law sets forth specific requirements for the handling of earnest money deposits and other funds entrusted to the real estate broker. Failure to account properly for trust funds is grounds for the suspension or revocation of the broker's license.

In the interest of the broker's fiduciary obligations, all funds received on behalf of others must be deposited either in a neutral escrow depository in Arizona (such as an escrow company) or in a trust account maintained in a federally insured financial institution (ARS Section 32—2151). A salesperson who receives such funds must give them promptly to the employing broker.

A broker may not deposit such funds in his or her personal account or otherwise commingle them with personal funds. However, the broker may deposit personal funds in the trust account to a maximum of $500 if this is necessary to establish the account or to maintain a minimum balance and avoid service charges. (Most banks and savings and loan associations in Arizona will allow a trust account to be established with the $500 maximum permitted by the Rules as a courtesy to real estate brokers.)

The specific provisions concerning the requirements for making trust account deposits and maintaining proper records are described in Chapter 11.

## ESCROW CLOSINGS

A large percentage of real estate sales in Arizona are closed in escrow. Standard purchase contract forms generally specify that the "seller and purchaser agree that the sale will be closed by a duly licensed escrow agent." The duties and responsibilities of the escrow agent are determined by the terms of the specific escrow agreement. Generally, he or she is responsible for assembling the necessary data to distribute any prepaid or accrued expenses to the buyer and seller; securing the assignment of mortgages and trust deeds, loan reserves and insurance policies; recording the documents that must be recorded; and delivering the documents to the respective parties. An escrow agreement of the kind widely used in Arizona, with instructions setting forth the duties of each party, is reproduced in this book (Figure 7.4).

### Agreements for Sale

A land contract is a method of purchasing and financing real estate. In Arizona, land contracts are called **agreements for sale**.

Usually, the purchaser (the **vendee**) gives the seller (the **vendor**) a down payment and agrees to pay the balance of the purchase price in regular installments, generally on a monthly basis. The vendee is entitled to the possession of the property but will not receive the deed from the vendor until all the terms of the contract have been fulfilled. Usually, this occurs when the purchase price has been paid in full.

## Figure 7.4 Escrow Instructions (Page 1 of 2)

**OLD REPUBLIC TITLE AGENCY**

3200 North Central Avenue Suite 100  •  Phoenix, AZ  •  85012  •  (602) 631-3700  •  FAX (602) 277-0674

**BUYER'S AND SELLER'S INSTRUCTIONS**

Date: _____ Escrow Officer: _____ Escrow No.: _____

These instructions to OLD REPUBLIC TITLE AGENCY  as Escrow Holder, by _____

_____ herein called Seller,

whose address is _____

Phone No. _____ and _____

_____ herein called Buyer,

whose address is _____

Phone No. _____ , are made in connection with the transfer of real property situated in _____ County,

State of Arizona, and described as follows:

| | | | SELLER | BUYER |
|---|---|---|---|---|
| Purchase price to be paid by Buyer to Seller as follows: | $ _____ | All items checked "X" or notated are the obligations which each party will pay. | | |
| | | | | |
| Earnest money to be deposited in escrow | | | | |
| _____ | $ _____ | | | |
| Balance of down payment to be deposited in escrow _____ | $ _____ | | | |
| | | Taxes | | |
| Existing loan in favor of | | Irrigation Assessments | | |
| | | Improvement Assessments | | |
| _____ | | Escrow Charges | | |
| with a principal balance remaining unpaid of approximately | $ _____ | Title Policy Insuring Owner | | |
| | | Title Policy Insuring Lender/Beneficiary | | |
| Seller pays installment due _____ and unpaid prior installments, if any. | | Recording Fees: | | |
| | | Deed | | |
| Buyer pays installment due _____ and all subsequent installments. | | Encumbrance/Deed of Trust | | |
| | | Release/Reconveyance | | |
| Existing loan in favor of | | Affidavit of Value | | |
| _____ | | Loan Status/Transfer Fee | | |
| with a principal balance remaining unpaid of approximately | $ _____ | Assumption Fees | | |
| | | | | |
| Seller pays installment due _____ and unpaid prior installments, if any. | | Account Servicing Set-up Fee | | |
| | | Account Servicing Fee | | |
| Buyer pays installment due _____ and all subsequent installments. | | Wood Infestation Report/Treatment | | |
| | | Home Warranty | | |
| Balance of | $ _____ | Homeowner's Association Transfer Fee | | |
| Evidenced by | | Irrigation Transfer Fee | | |
| Payment terms and/or additional instructions: | | Commission | | |
| | | in the amount of: | | |
| | | To: | | |

As of _____ prorate the following:

( ) Taxes (based on the most recent tax bill available)
( ) Irrigation Assessments
( ) Improvement Assessments
( ) Fire Insurance Premium, if assumed by Buyer
( ) Mortgage Insurance
( ) Homeowner's Association Dues
( ) Rents
( ) Interest on existing loan(s) based on information
    provided by lender
( ) _____

The undersigned Seller and Buyer hereby agree as follows:
( ) Credit Buyer and Debit Seller for any rental
    deposits and prepaid rents
( ) Credit Seller and Debit Buyer the amount of impounds
    if any, as disclosed by a lender's statement
( ) Buyer to provide fire insurance coverage in the
    amount of $ _____

The unpaid principal balance of any existing encumbrance is approximate; any difference shall be reflected in:

Time is of the essence.  Close of Escrow to be on _____ and thereafter unless revoked by written demand on Escrow Holder by the undersigned. Any earlier closing date requires mutual agreement of Seller and Buyer. The General Provisions are attached hereto and made a part hereof. Buyer and Seller have closing protection in the form provided in A.R.S. 6-841.02 (B).

SELLER _____    BUYER _____

  SSN _____      SSN _____

SELLER _____    BUYER _____

  SSN _____      SSN _____

RECEIVED BY:  OLD REPUBLIC TITLE AGENCY   BY: _____   DATE: _____

FTG-IS 911 11/93

SOURCE: Courtesy of Old Republic Title Insurance Agency, Inc.

# Figure 7.4 Escrow Instructions (Page 2 of 2)

**GENERAL PROVISIONS**

1. All money payable shall be paid to Escrow Holder, unless otherwise specified. Disbursement of any funds may be made by check of Escrow Holder. All funds received in this escrow shall be deposited with other escrow funds in a general escrow account or accounts of Escrow Holder with any State or National Bank, and may be transferred to any other such general escrow account or accounts. Escrow Holder shall be under no obligation to disburse any funds represented by check or draft, and no check or draft shall be payment to Escrow Holder in compliance with any of the requirements hereof until it is advised by the bank in which deposited that such check or draft has been honored. Pursuant to A.R.S. 6-834-D, the parties to this escrow waive their rights to any earnings credits or other benefits received in respect to funds deposited with Escrow Holder, unless specific instructions to the contrary are provided Escrow Holder.

2. These escrow instructions shall be of no effect unless signed by all parties and accepted by Escrow Holder. "OPENING OF ESCROW" shall mean the day these fully executed escrow instructions are delivered to and accepted by Escrow Holder. No notice, demand, declaration or amendment to these instructions shall be of any effect unless made in writing, signed by the appropriate party(ies) and presented to and accepted by Escrow Holder. These escrow instructions and any amendments shall constitute the sole and entire agreement between the Escrow Holder and the parties. Additional provisions of any purchase contract or other agreement between the parties, except as relating to the transfer of title, are not matters of concern by Escrow Holder. Furthermore, by closing hereunder the parties agree that the terms and conditions of these escrow instructions have been fully complied with, and Escrow Holder is relieved of any liability in connection therewith. It is further understood and agreed that Escrow Holder has no duty to discover or disclose any matter not expressly agreed to herein. Closed and/or cancelled escrow files shall be retained by Escrow Holder pursuant to A.R.S. 6-831 and the State of Arizona banking regulations.

3. Escrow Holder shall within 3 business days after receipt of any notice, demand, or declaration send it to the party to whom it is directed by enclosing a copy in an envelope addressed to said party at the last written address which said party shall have filed with Escrow Holder. If no written address has been filed, the copy shall be sent in care of General Delivery at the City in which the Escrow Holder is located as shown on the first page of these instructions. The copy shall be deposited in the United States mail and shall constitute notice of the contents of such instrument to the party to whom the instrument is directed as to the date of such mailing, and no further notice shall be required.

4. Escrow Holder is authorized to take any action necessary to comply with these instructions and the instructions of any lender, and to execute, utilize and prepare any and all documents which may be necessary or incidental to the carrying out of these instructions. Escrow Holder is authorized to pay from funds held, amounts necessary to procure the documents, pay charges and obligations as established by these instructions and to act upon any statement furnished by a lien holder or his agent without liability to Escrow Holder.

5. The parties designate any representative of the real estate firm(s) named on the reverse hereof, if any, as the authorized representatives for the purposes of receiving or providing any notice or documents in connection with these instructions and hereafter hold Escrow Holder harmless for any omission or misrepresentation of any material fact which may arise therefrom.

6. All prorations and/or adjustments called for in this escrow are to be made on the basis of a thirty (30) day month unless otherwise instructed in writing. In all acts relating to fire insurance, rents and rental deposits, Escrow Holder shall be fully protected in assuming that the information provided by the parties to this escrow or their agent(s) is correct, that insurance premiums have been paid, and the insurance policy is transferable. It shall be the responsibility of the Buyer to determine that the type and amount of any insurance coverage is appropriate and to increase or change fire insurance coverage, if necessary. The parties hereto hold Escrow Holder harmless with regard to the sufficiency of any fire, homeowners, or hazard insurance obtained or transferred as contemplated by this escrow.

7. Upon receipt of any conflicting instructions, Escrow Holder is no longer obligated to take any further action in connection with this escrow until further consistent instructions are received from the principals, and Escrow Holder is authorized to hold all money and instruments in this escrow until otherwise directed, either by the principals' mutual written instructions or by final order of a court of competent jurisdiction. In the event of conflicting claims to any funds or other documents, Escrow Holder has the absolute right at its election to file an action in interpleader requiring the principals to answer and litigate their several claims and rights among themselves and you are authorized to comply with the requisite interpleader statutes of the State of Arizona in this regard. Deposit of all documents and funds with the court by Escrow Holder (after deducting its charges, expenses, attorney's fees and court costs incurred in connection with such action) shall relieve Escrow Holder of all liability and responsibility.

8. Any party who wishes to cancel these escrow instructions because of any breach by another party, or because escrow fails to close by the agreed date, and who is not himself in breach of these escrow instructions, except as occasioned by a breach by the other party, may cancel these escrow instructions by delivering a notice to either the breaching party or to the Escrow Holder stating the nature of the breach and that these escrow instructions shall be cancelled unless the breach is cured within 13 days following the delivery of the notice. If this notice is delivered to the Escrow Holder, it shall contain the address of the party in breach. Any notice delivered to any party must be delivered to the Brokers and the Escrow Holder. Within three days after receipt of such notice, the Escrow Holder shall send the notice by United States mail to the party in breach at the address contained in the notice. No further notice shall be required. In the event that the breach is not cured within 13 days following the delivery of the notice to the party in breach or to the Escrow Holder, these escrow instructions shall be cancelled.

9. In the event of cancellation according to the Provisions described under Paragraph 8 above, OR BY ANY OTHER MEANS, Escrow Holder shall be entitled to retain and/or charge a cancellation fee which shall be in an amount which Escrow Holder, at its sole discretion, has determined will be sufficient to recover all costs and expenses expended or incurred by Escrow Holder prior to cancellation. Upon cancellation of these instructions, Escrow Holder shall (a) deduct from any money deposited or submit a billing for Escrow Holder's cancellation fees and any other charges; (b) pay all other money in accordance with either a delivered and accepted Cancellation Notice, Court Order or Mutual Cancellation Instructions; (c) return all documents deposited to the party who delivered them except those executed by both Seller and Buyer, which shall be retained in the file of Escrow Holder; and (d) pay any fee or commission in accordance with the signed purchase contract or other written instructions as may be applicable.

10. If Escrow Holder is the prevailing party in any action or proceeding between Escrow Holder and some or all of the parties to this escrow, Escrow Holder shall be entitled to recover all costs, expenses, and attorney's fees expended or incurred in connection therewith. If Escrow Holder is required to respond to any legal summons or proceedings not involving a breach or fault upon its part, the parties to this escrow jointly and severally agree to pay all costs, expenses, and attorney's fees expended or incurred by Escrow Holder, and the parties hereto further agree to indemnify Escrow Holder against all loss and expense in the said action or proceeding.

11. "CLOSE OF ESCROW" shall mean the day the documents are recorded. When these instructions have been complied with, Escrow Holder shall deliver by recording in the appropriate public office all necessary documents, disburse all funds, and cause to be issued the title insurance policy(ies). Delivery of documents on close of escrow, which are not required to be recorded, may be made by Escrow Holder by deposit of the same in the United States mail, addressed to the party entitled thereto, at the mailing address set forth herein. Should Escrow Holder be closed on any day of compliance with these instructions, the requirements may be met on the next succeeding day Escrow Holder is open for business.

12. Any additional services required of or performed by Escrow Holder, not inconsistent with its duties outlined herein either prior to or after close of escrow, shall be paid for by the party requesting such additional service or upon whose behalf said additional service is required.

13. If any provisions in these escrow instructions or any application thereof shall be invalid or unenforceable, the remainder of these instructions and any other application of such provision shall not be affected thereby and shall not be rendered invalid or unenforceable.

14. Escrow Holder at its election shall have the right to resign as Escrow Holder under these instructions; if this right is exercised, all funds and documents shall be returned to the party who deposited them, and thereafter Escrow Holder shall have no further duty, responsibility, or liability in connection with these escrow instructions, and purchase contract if any.

15. Any instructions necessary to close this escrow may be signed in counterpart, each of which shall be effective as an original upon execution and all of which together shall constitute one and the same instrument.

NOTE: There are matters for which Old Republic Title Agency, in any capacity, assumes no responsibility or liability. Such matters include, but are not limited to, the following: to act as legal counsel or to render legal opinion for any party; adjustment or payment of personal property taxes, utility charges or the like; possession of property; compliance with zoning, building ordinances, restrictions or any other material matters relating to the premises not specifically described in these instructions.

Agreements for sale are frequently used in three situations, although they are not limited to these situations:

1. When financing the purchase of raw or undeveloped land, because most institutional lenders will not fund loans on unimproved property
2. When the purchaser's income or credit history does not meet the standards of institutional lenders and the seller is willing to carry the contract
3. When the market interest rates are relatively high and most purchasers could not qualify for an institutional loan (many sellers will carry the contract at a less-than-market interest rate as a method of selling their property)

As the agreement for sale is primarily a financing instrument, more detail on the structuring of the contract, possession, default and forfeiture is provided in Chapter 11.

## Equitable Title

Arizona law recognizes the concept of **equitable title** (also called equitable conversion and equitable ownership), which is created under an agreement for sale.

Once an agreement of sale has been signed by the vendor and the vendee, the vendor's interest in the property converts from real property to personal property. In effect, the contract becomes—for the vendor—a negotiable instrument. The vendor has the right to receive the payments due under the contract, but is considered to own the property "in trust" for the vendee, who is the equitable owner. If the vendor dies before the contract is fulfilled, his or her personal property interest in the contract is distributed as personal property. And the contract could be sold to investors, just as a promissory note could be.

When a married couple enters into an agreement of sale to sell property that they own as community property, their interest also converts to personal property but remains as part of their community property.

The vendee acquires an equitable title in the property; his or her ownership interest includes all the rights of use and possession (the "bundle of rights"), but not the legal title to the property. Remember, the vendee does not get legal title until the agreement of sale has been fully performed. In the meantime, the vendee may possess, use, encumber and dispose of his or her interest in the property, as long as the party with whom the vendee contracts understands the limitations on the vendee's interest.

## QUESTIONS

1. According to Arizona's constitution, a real estate licensee may

   a. give legal advice.
   b. only use real estate forms drafted by his or her attorney.
   c. prevent his or her client from seeking the advice of an attorney.
   d. draft or complete any documents incidental to his or her real estate activities.

2. An option to purchase has a term of 45 days. During that 45-day period

   a. the optionor may sell the property to another, free of the option.
   b. the optionor may raise the sales price.
   c. the optionor must make sure the property is available to the optionee.
   d. the optionee may change the terms of the sale.

3. An option is a/an

   a. bilateral contract.
   b. contract with unilateral obligations.
   c. illusory contract.
   d. first right of refusal.

4. The provision in a purchase contract that provides that the purchaser will forfeit the earnest deposit if he or she fails to complete the transaction is known as

   a. compensatory damages.
   b. liquidated damages.
   c. the subordination clause.
   d. the defeasance clause.

5. A broker must keep a copy of a binding purchase contract for

   a. one year.
   b. three years.
   c. five years.
   d. six years.

6. All purchase contracts must be
   a. submitted to the commissioner for approval.
   b. reviewed and initialed by the buyer's salesperson.
   c. in writing.
   d. drafted by an attorney.

7. *A* is offering to purchase *G*'s property. While drafting the offer with *G*'s broker, *H*, *A* writes a postdated check for the earnest money deposit. As the agent for *G*, *H* should
   a. refuse to accept the offer because it involves a postdated check as earnest money.
   b. wait until the date on the check before presenting the offer to *G*.
   c. treat the postdated check as he would any other form of earnest deposit.
   d. inform *G* of the type of earnest deposit being given with the offer.

8. An earnest money deposit must be promptly

   a. deposited into a trust account or neutral escrow depository.
   b. commingled.
   c. returned to the prospective purchaser upon the seller's acceptance of the offer.
   d. submitted to the commissioner.

9. *A* sells her property to *G* under an agreement of sale. By virtue of the agreement of sale, *G* immediately acquires

   a. legal title to the property.
   b. no ownership interest to the property, only the personal property right to possess the property.
   c. equitable title.
   d. the rights to sell the land contract to an investor.

10. *G* has made a written offer to purchase *P*'s home. The offer states that *P* has five days in which to accept it. The day after *G* makes the offer and prior to *P*'s acceptance, she informs the broker that she wants to withdraw the offer. The broker should tell *G* that

    a. the offer is irrevocable and she must wait four more days.
    b. only her death would revoke the offer prior to its acceptance.
    c. she may not resubmit the offer once the five-day period has expired.
    d. she can withdraw the offer and demand the return of her earnest money.

# 8

# Transfer of Title

## DEEDS

A deed is a way in which a property owner voluntarily transfers ownership of real property. A deed usually contains warranties; thus, a grantor may have ongoing liability for promises (guarantees) made to the grantee in the deed.

### Types of Deeds Used in Arizona

Four major types of deeds are used in Arizona:

1. The general warranty deed
2. The special warranty deed
3. The bargain and sale deed
4. Special purpose deeds

Warranty deeds and bargain and sale deeds are specifically designed to transfer (alienate) a real property interest. However, special purpose deeds are designed to release an interest in, or otherwise eliminate, a possible cloud on the title to real property.

**General Warranty Deeds.** The general warranty deed (Figure 8.1) is the most frequently used deed in Arizona, as it is the conveyance document that is used for most real estate transactions. This deed contains three covenants and two warranties. These are the grantor's promises of warranty that protect the grantee's ownership interest in the property. In situations where the deed does not spell out one or more particular warranties, they may be implied by Title 33, Chapter 4, of the Arizona Revised Statutes, "Conveyances and Deeds." In fact, ARS Section 33–402 states that to convey and warrant a deed, the following wording is sufficient:

> For the consideration of . . . , I hereby convey to "X" [the grantee] the following real property [the property description] and I warrant the title against all persons whomsoever [or other words of warranty].

## Figure 8.1 General Warranty Deed

Recorded at the request of:

When recorded, mail to:

---

Order No.           **WARRANTY DEED**

For valuable consideration, receipt of which is hereby acknowledged,

do hereby convey to

the following real property situated in           County, Arizona :

SUBJECT TO current taxes, assessments, reservations in patents and all easements, rights of way, encumbrances, covenants, conditions, restrictions and all other matters affecting title as may appear of record.

The undersigned hereby warrants the title against all persons whomsoever, subject to the matters above set forth.

Dated:

_____     _____

_____     _____

STATE OF                   } ss.      This instrument was acknowledged before me

County of                        this _____ day of _____ , _____ by

_____
                                                 Notary Public

My commission will expire:

STATE OF                   } ss.      This instrument was acknowledged before me

County of                        this _____ day of _____ , _____ by

_____
                                                 Notary Public

FTGIS-980 4/93                       My commission will expire:

---

SOURCE: Courtesy of Old Republic Title Insurance Agency, Inc.

Some deed forms, however, are more specific in their wording of the warranties, stating that the grantor

> covenants to and with the grantee that he is lawfully seized in fee simple, that the premises are free from all encumbrances, that he shall warrant and forever defend the granted premises against the lawful claims and demands of all persons whomsoever.

**Special Warranty Deeds.** The special warranty deed (Figure 8.2) may also be called a "limited warranty deed." In the granting clause of the special warranty deed, the grantor conveys the property and promises to "warrant and defend against lawful claims and demands of all persons claiming by, from, through, or under the grantor." This wording limits the liability of the grantor. The grantor promises that he or she has not caused any undisclosed defects or encumbrances to be placed against the property during his or her ownership. Thus, the grantor is responsible only for claims arising from events that occurred while he or she held title to the property.

The use of a special warranty deed decreases the liability of the grantor to the grantee. However, it increases the liability of the grantee to third parties. In the absence of a title insurance policy, the grantee becomes vulnerable to any claims arising from the actions of those who owned the property prior to the grantor.

**Bargain and Sale Deeds.** This type of deed provides even less protection to the grantee than the special warranty deed. Most bargain and sale deeds offer only two implied covenants:

1. That the grantor has not previously conveyed the same estate or any part of it to any person other than the grantee
2. That at the time the deed is signed by the grantor, the estate is free from any undisclosed encumbrances

(These two covenants are implied whenever a deed contains the word "convey" or "grant," which is how a bargain and sale deed reads.)

Because of the limited protection afforded by a bargain and sale deed, most deeds used in foreclosures (for example, trustee's deeds or sheriff's deeds) and most deeds used in settling estates (for example, executor's deeds) are bargain and sale deeds. In both of these situations, the grantor wants to convey whatever interest he or she has in the property without any warranties other than the two covenants listed above.

Real estate listing contracts and purchase contracts commonly used throughout the state indicate that the seller will provide the purchaser with a warranty deed and an owner's policy of title insurance. This provision precludes the use of a bargain and sale deed in many transactions and would have to be amended should the parties decide to use a bargain and sale deed.

## After-Acquired Title

All conveyance deeds (general warranty deeds, special warranty deeds and bargain and sale deeds) are interpreted by Arizona law as transferring **after-acquired title**. After-acquired title is any interest in property obtained by a person after he or she has conveyed that property to someone else. For example, assume that at the time of conveyance, the grantor's interest in the conveyed property was defective. If the grantor perfects his or her title after the conveyance, such after-acquired title would automatically transfer to the grantee.

**Figure 8.2 Special Warranty Deed**

RECORDING REQUESTED BY:

When recorded mail to:

SPACE ABOVE THIS LINE FOR RECORDER'S USE

# SPECIAL WARRANTY DEED

For the consideration of Ten Dollars, and other valuable considerations, I or we,

do hereby convey to

the following described real property situated in _____ County, Arizona:

Subject to: Current taxes, assessments, reservations in patents and all easements, rights of way, encumbrances, liens, covenants, conditions, and restrictions as may appear of record. And the Grantor hereby binds itself and its successors to warrant and defend the title as against all acts of the Grantor herein and no other, subject to the matters above set forth.

Dated _____

_____      _____

_____      _____

STATE OF _____

COUNTY OF _____

This foregoing instrument was acknowledged before me this _____ day of _____, 19__,
by _____

My commission expires _____     _____
                                                                        **Notary Public**

STATE OF _____

COUNTY OF _____

This foregoing instrument was acknowledged before me this _____ day of _____, 19__,
by _____

My commission expires _____     _____
                                                                        **Notary Public**

SOURCE: Courtesy of Old Republic Title Insurance Agency, Inc.

## Special Purpose Deeds

Special purpose deeds are used to solve a problem. Although they may appear to act like deeds of conveyance, they are used only to release or deny a real property interest.

For example, when a developer builds the roads in a subdivision, he or she does not want to remain in the street maintenance business after all the parcels have been sold. So, after building the roads to the specifications of the jurisdiction in which the subdivision is located, the developer will surrender, or "cede," the roads to that jurisdiction with a **cession deed**.

If the developer also wants to donate land for a park or school site, he or she will give that land to the appropriate public entity specifically for that purpose with a **dedication deed**.

When an error is made in any deed—such as a misspelled name or an inaccurate legal description—the error can be corrected with a **correction deed**.

When one spouse owns separate real property and wishes to sell it, he or she conveys that separate property with a warranty deed. However, because Arizona is a community property states, and all property owned by a married person is presumed to be community property, the nonowning spouse often signs a **disclaimer deed** at the same time the owning spouse signs a warranty deed. In this way, the nonowning spouse denies in writing ever having had any interest in the separate property of the owning spouse. This prevents any future claim against that separate property by the nonowning spouse—a potential problem in the event of divorce proceedings or estate settlements. It also eliminates the possible tainting of separate property when expenses for that property (such as real estate taxes, hazard insurance premiums, etc.) have been paid for with community funds.

The most common type of special purpose deed is the **quitclaim deed** (Figure 8.4). With a quitclaim deed, the grantor "quits" any "claim" to a property. With a quitclaim deed, the grantor conveys only the interest he or she has in the property.

Quitclaim deeds contain no covenants or warranties whatsoever. Theoretically, any person can use a quitclaim deed to transfer any interest in real property. However, the interest transferred with a quitclaim deed is so unprotected that Arizona law does not consider a quitclaim deed to be a conveyance deed—a purchaser who receives a quitclaim deed as evidence of ownership is not considered to be a legitimate purchaser, and title insurance companies will not insure an ownership interest conveyed by a quitclaim deed.

Quitclaim deeds are frequently used to clear up a defect in the title to a parcel of real property (often referred to as a "cloud on title"). Therefore, quitclaim deeds are widely recognized and used throughout the real estate industry. For example, when married couples—particularly first-time buyers—purchase real property, they may receive improper advice regarding how they should hold title to the property. After escrow closes, should a couple decide to change their method of ownership, they could quitclaim their interest to a nominee ("strawman") who, in turn, would quitclaim it back to them in the desired form of ownership. In this situation, the manner of holding title can be changed.

In a divorce proceeding, one spouse may be ordered by the court to release to the other spouse his or her interest in jointly owned real property. A quitclaim deed from the releasing spouse could be used to accomplish this end.

## Figure 8.3 Disclaimer Deed

Recorded at the request of:

When recorded, mail to:

---

Order No.                                    **DISCLAIMER DEED**

WITNESSETH THIS DISCLAIMER DEED, made by

hereinafter called "the undersigned" to

hereinafter called "the spouse",

WHEREAS:

    1.   The spouse has acquired title to the following real property situated in                                    County, Arizona:

    2.   The property above described is the sole and separate property of the spouse having been purchased with the separate funds of the spouse.

    3.   The undersigned has no past or present right, title, interest, claim or lien of any kind or nature whatsoever in, to or against said property.

    4.   This instrument is executed not for the purpose of making a gift to the spouse, but solely for the purpose of clearly showing of record that the undersigned has and claims no interest in and to said property.

    NOW THEREFORE, in consideration of the premises, the undersigned does hereby disclaim, remise, release and quitclaim unto the spouse and to the heirs and assigns of said spouse forever, all right, title, interest, claim and demand which the undersigned might appear to have in and to the above described property.

Dated:                                    _____

STATE OF

                  } ss.

County of

    On this                day of                                    , before me, the undersigned officer, personally appeared

known to me to be the person whose name is subscribed to the within instrument and acknowledged that he/she  executed the same for the purpose therein contained.

In witness whereof I hereunto set my hand and official seal.

_____

Notary Public

My Commission will expire:

FTGIS - 985 4/93

---

SOURCE: Courtesy of Old Republic Title Insurance Agency, Inc.

To settle an estate, an executor or court-appointed administrator may need to have all potential claims against the estate abandoned; otherwise, the terms of the decedent's will or the laws of intestate succession might not apply. By obtaining a quitclaim deed from every potential claimant, the executor or administrator would be free to fulfill any legal obligations without fear that a claim against the estate would arise after the estate had been settled and its assets distributed.

## Joint Tenancy Deeds

When two or more owners want to take title as joint tenants with the right of survivorship, they must use a **joint tenancy deed** (Figure 8.5). The wording on the deed specifically states that the grantees take title "as joint tenants with the right of survivorship, and not as community property or as tenants in common." This complies with the "time" and "title" requirements of the four unities of joint tenancy.

Also, note that there is a designated space for the signatures of the grantees on joint tenancy deeds. Only the signature of the grantor is required to make a conveyance deed valid, and usually the grantee does not sign the deed. However, in creating a joint tenancy, the grantees must sign the deed to reaffirm their intention to take title as joint tenants. The joint tenancy is not created until all of the joint tenants have signed.

A married couple can take title to property as community property with right of survivorship and take advantage of the right of survivorship without having to hold title as joint tenants. Community property is discussed in Chapter 4.

## Acknowledgments

Acknowledgment enables deeds and other documents to be recorded. In Arizona, an acknowledgment may be taken by a notary public, a county recorder, a court clerk or a judge and certain other public officials. However, most acknowledgments are taken by notaries to meet the requirement that, before a deed of conveyance can be recorded with the county recorder, the deed first must be acknowledged by the grantor.

Anyone interested in becoming a notary public should write to the secretary of state, who appoints notaries for four-year terms.

## Affidavits of Property Value

When a conveyance deed is sent to the county recorder's office for recordation, it must be accompanied by an affidavit of property value, sometimes informally called an affidavit of value (Figure 8.6). This document, signed by the grantor and the grantee (or their representatives) and notarized, is used to monitor property values throughout the state for real estate taxation purposes. (See Chapter 6, "Real Estate Taxes and Other Liens.")

The affidavit must contain the names of the parties, the legal description of the property being transferred, the actual transfer price and any facts about the transfer that could distort the property value if they were not disclosed (such as any personal property included in the transfer, the terms of any financing used in the transaction or any familial or other relationship between the parties that could cause a less-than-market value transfer to occur).

## Figure 8.4 Quitclaim Deed

Recorded at the request of:

When recorded, mail to:

Order No.                          **QUITCLAIM DEED**

For valuable consideration, receipt of which is hereby acknowledged,

do hereby quitclaim to

the following real property situated in                      County, Arizona:

Dated:

_____          _____

_____          _____

STATE OF                          } ss.          This instrument was acknowledged before me

County of                                        this _____ day of _____, 19 _____ by

                                                 _____
                                                                        Notary Public
                                                 My commission will expire:

STATE OF                          } ss.          This instrument was acknowledged before me

County of                                        this _____ day of _____, 19 _____ by

                                                 _____
                                                                        Notary Public
                                                 My commission will expire:

FTGIS - 970  4/93

SOURCE: Courtesy of Old Republic Title Insurance Agency, Inc.

**Figure 8.5 Joint Tenancy Deed**

Recorded at the request of:

When recorded, mail to:

---

Order No.                          **JOINT TENANCY DEED**

For valuable consideration, receipt of which is hereby acknowledged, I or we,


do hereby convey to


not as tenants in common and not as community property estate, but as joint tenants with right of survivorship, the following real property situated in                                        County, Arizona:










SUBJECT TO current taxes, assessments, reservations in patents and all easements, rights of way, encumbrances, covenants, conditions, restrictions and all other matters affecting title as may appear of record.

The undersigned hereby warrants the title against all persons whomsoever, subject to the matters above set forth.

Dated:


_____          _____
                                                                                    Grantors

The Grantees by signing the acceptance below evidence their intention to acquire said premises as joint tenants with the right of survivorship, and not as community property or as tenants in common.


_____          _____
                                                                                    Grantees

STATE OF _____                      This instrument was acknowledged before me

County of _____        } ss.        this _____ day of _____, 19 ____ by


                                                           _____
                                                                                    Notary Public
                                           My commission will expire:

STATE OF _____                      This instrument was acknowledged before me

County of _____        } ss.        this _____ day of _____, 19 ____ by


                                                           _____
                                                                                    Notary Public
FTGIS - 600 4/94                           My commission will expire:

---

SOURCE: Courtesy of Old Republic Title Insurance Agency, Inc.

Once the deed is recorded, a copy of the affidavit is sent to the county assessor's office, where the value indicated by the affidavit is collated into the existing property tax records. If the property values in an area are rising—as reflected by the affidavits submitted to the county assessor—then the entire area might be revalued for tax purposes.

## Transfer Taxes

Currently, there are no documentary stamp taxes, transfer fees or other taxes on real estate conveyances in Arizona.

## ADVERSE POSSESSION

The land mass of Arizona is more than 110,000 square miles. Yet when the land owned or controlled by political subdivisions (the federal government, the state government or local government entities) is deducted, relatively little land is available for private ownership and use. Some estimates of privately owned land are as low as 11 to 13 percent of the total land mass. Therefore, each real property owner is responsible for maximizing and protecting the use of his or her property.

**Adverse possession**—a type of involuntary alienation—is based on the principle that any owner of real property must defend his or her title to that property against anyone who would take possession of it or otherwise use it without the consent of the owner. Rather than prescribe a minimum period of time during which the adverse possessor must occupy or use the property in question, the Arizona statutes on adverse possession (ARS Section 12–521 to Section 12–529) provide a maximum period of time during which the property owner has the right to take action against an adverse possessor.

Adverse possession statutes apply only to privately owned real property with a maximum size of 160 acres. To claim the title to real property, an adverse possessor must be able to prove (1) that he or she was hostile to the owner of the property (occupying or using the property without the owner's knowledge or permission) and  (2) was open and notorious in his or her possession or use (such possession or use being obvious to a third party).

Generally, the statutes provide that an action to recover the possession of real property must be brought by the owner against the adverse possessor within ten years after such adverse possession or use began. However, under certain circumstances, the statutes also provide shorter periods of time for the recovery of property held in adverse possession.

- If a person holds or uses the property in peaceable adverse possession under a recorded deed, has physically used the property and has paid the real estate taxes on the property, then any action to recover the property must be commenced within five years of the adverse user's initial possession. "Peaceable adverse possession" means that the possession of the property has been continuous and uninterrupted by an action of the owner to recover the property.
- If the property in question is a city (subdivision) lot and the person in possession claims ownership under a recorded deed and has paid the real estate taxes on the property, then an action to recover the property must be commenced within five years of the date of initial possession.
- If a person holds or uses the property in peaceable adverse possession under title or color of title, then any action to recover the property must be commenced within three years of the adverse user's initial possession. "Color of title" means a claim of ownership that appears to be valid but in fact is defective.

## Figure 8.6 Affidavit of Value

**Arizona Department of Revenue**
Division of Property Valuation & Equalization
AFFIDAVIT OF PROPERTY VALUE
DPVE Form 82162 (Rev. 4/89)

AFFIDAVIT OF PROPERTY VALUE
*SEE INSTRUCTIONS ON REVERSE*

1. ASSESSOR'S PARCEL NUMBER(S) (Primary Parcel Number)

(a) _____  _____  _____  _____
BOOK        MAP        PARCEL        SPLIT

NOTE: If the sale involves multiple parcels, how many are included?
(b) List the number of additional parcels other than
the primary parcel that are included in sale. _____
List the additional parcel numbers (up to 4) below:

(c) _____        (d) _____
(e) _____        (f) _____

2. SELLER'S NAME & ADDRESS:

_____
_____
_____

3. BUYER'S NAME & ADDRESS:

_____
_____
_____

Buyer and Seller related? Yes _____ No _____
If yes, state relationship: _____

4. ADDRESS OF PROPERTY:

_____
_____

5. MAIL TAX BILL TO: _____
_____

6. TYPE OF PROPERTY *(Check One)*:

a. ☐ Vacant Land        f. ☐ Commercial/Industrial
b. ☐ Single Fam. Residence    g. ☐ Agriculture
c. ☐ Condo/Townhouse    h. ☐ Mobile Home Affixed ☐
d. ☐ 2-4 Plex        i. ☐ Other, Specify:
e. ☐ Apartment Bldg.        _____

7. RESIDENTIAL BUYER'S INTENDED USE *(Answer if you checked, b, c, d, or h above) (Check One)*:

☐ To be occupied by owner or "family member."
☐ To be rented to someone other than "family member."

*NOTE: See reverse for definition of "family member."*

8. PARTY COMPLETING AFFIDAVIT *(Name, Address, & Phone)*

_____
_____

*(Phone)* ( ) — _____

9. FOR OFFICIAL USE ONLY *(buyer and seller leave blank)*

(a) County of Recordation: _____
(b) Docket & Page Number: _____
(c) Fee/Recording Number: _____
(d) Date of Recording: _____

Assessor/DOR Validation Codes:

(e) Assessor _____    (f) DOR _____

10. TYPE OF DEED OR INSTRUMENT *(Check One)*:

a. ☐ Warranty Deed        d. ☐ Contract or Agreement
b. ☐ Special Warranty Deed    e. ☐ Quit Claim Deed
c. ☐ Joint Tenancy Deed    f. ☐ Other _____

11. TOTAL SALE PRICE: $ _____

12. PERSONAL PROPERTY:
Did the buyer receive any personal property *(see reverse for definition)* that has a value greater than 5% of the sale price:

(a) Yes _____ No _____ . If yes, briefly describe: _____

Approximate Value: (b) $ _____

13. DATE OF SALE: _____ / _____
Month        Year

*NOTE: This is the date of the contract of sale. If you are recording title in fulfillment of a previously recorded contract, you need not complete this affidavit (see A.1 on reverse).*

14. CASH DOWN PAYMENT: $ _____

15. METHOD OF FINANCING *(check all that apply)*:

a. ☐ All Cash        b. ☐ Exchange or trade
c. ☐ Assumption of existing loan(s)    d. ☐ New loan from seller (Seller Carryback)
e. ☐ New loan(s) from financial institution:
(1) ☐ Conventional (2) ☐ VA (3) ☐ FHA
f. ☐ Other, Explain _____

16. PARTIAL INTERESTS:
Is only a partial interest (e.g., 1/3 or 1/2) being transferred?
Yes _____ No _____ If yes, explain _____

17. SOLAR ENERGY *(check all that apply)*:

a. ☐ None        b. ☐ Hot Water
c. ☐ Heating-Passive    d. ☐ Heating-Active

18. LEGAL DESCRIPTION *(attach copy if necessary)*

THE UNDERSIGNED BEING DULY SWORN, ON OATH, SAYS THAT THE FOREGOING INFORMATION IS A TRUE AND CORRECT STATEMENT OF THE FACTS PERTAINING TO THE TRANSFER OF THE ABOVE DESCRIBED PROPERTY.

_____
Signature of Seller/Agent

State of Arizona, County of _____
Subscribed and sworn to before me on this

_____ day of _____ 19 _____

Notary Public _____

Notary Expiration Date _____

_____
Signature of Buyer/Agent

State of Arizona, County of _____
Subscribed and sworn to before me on this

_____ day of _____ 19 _____

Notary Public _____

Notary Expiration Date _____

- If a person holds or uses the property for two years and claims the property by the right of possession only, such a claim will defeat any action to recover the property by a person who has no better claim.

Under adverse possession statutes, **tacking** is permitted to allow the current adverse possessor to meet the minimum statutory requirements for claiming the property. Tacking refers to the adding of successive periods of possession together. In other words, a current adverse possessor who has not possessed or used the property for the minimum time period prescribed by law can tack or add his or her possession or use to that of a prior adverse possessor. Tacking may give the current adverse possessor enough years of possession to meet the minimums established by statute and thus claim the property.

For an adverse possessor to perfect any claim to the property, he or she must file a **suit to quiet title** against the owner of the property.

## Boundary Disputes

Disputes can develop between adjacent property owners concerning their common boundary line. For example, an owner may learn that a neighbor's fence is encroaching on his or her property, and the neighbor may refuse to move the fence. In many cases, the dispute can be resolved by a written agreement between the owners or when one property owner deeds the disputed land to his or her neighbor. Arizona courts have ruled that the possession of land under mistaken ownership meets the requirements for adverse possession. If such a situation is allowed to continue, the adverse possessor will usually acquire either an easement by prescription or ownership to the strip of land by adverse possession. The existence of a fence or wall between two parcels of property does not automatically mean that the fence or wall is an official boundary between the properties. Boundary disputes can be avoided by surveying the property before any fence or wall is erected or before the property is sold.

## ALIENATION BY WILL

Alienation by will is a form of voluntary alienation: the maker of the will determines in writing how his or her property should be distributed after his or her death. Although the validity of any will can be challenged in court, the circumstances under which the court will **sequester** (set aside) or overturn a will are rare.

Title 14, Chapters 5 through 8, of the Arizona Revised Statutes sets forth the requirements for a valid will, as well as the details for the various types of wills used in Arizona and the types of property that they can transfer.

Any person who is legally competent and at least 18 years of age can make, alter or revoke a will. The provisions of a will must be prepared and the document must be signed by the maker of the will during his or her lifetime (but, of course, a will does not take effect until after the death of the maker). A will can be altered or revoked at the discretion of the maker, as the courts have generally ruled that the will that binds the estate of the decedent is the will most recently made by the decedent. Therefore, all wills and all alterations to wills should be dated by the maker when they are signed.

The most common type of will is the **formal** or **conventional will**. Usually drafted by an attorney, it must be signed by its maker (called a "testator" if a man, a "testatrix" if a woman) or signed in the maker's name by some other person on the maker's behalf and in the maker's presence. It must also be signed by at least two other persons, each of whom has witnessed either the maker's signature on the will or the signing of the will by the maker's representative. The existence and validity of a will can be proven at any time by its maker, if he or she will draft a statement to that effect and have it notarized and recorded (ARS Section 14–2504).

Another type of will is the **holographic will** (from two Greek words meaning "written in full"). To be valid, all the material provisions of the will must be in the handwriting of the maker; the will cannot be typewritten and then signed. Because of the ability of the court to verify the handwriting of the maker of a holographic will, once the will is signed and dated by its maker, it needs no further witnessing.

Both formal and holographic wills can be amended by the use of a **codicil**. The codicil must be signed and dated by the maker. Note that a codicil does not revoke a will; it only amends an existing will. To revoke a will, its maker must either replace it with another will or physically destroy the will with the intent of revoking it.

A **nuncupative** will is an oral will made in the immediate anticipation of the maker's death. It is sometimes informally referred to as a "deathbed will." Just before death, a dying person often attempts to "right things" with others by verbally changing the terms of his or her will. However, there is always the question of the dying person being lucid and rational at such a moment. Although nuncupative wills are admissible in some states, Arizona law has no provisions for the enforceability of this type of will.

Some states have recognized the validity of a **videotaped** or **audiotaped** will; Arizona has not.

Living wills were provided for by the state legislature in 1985. A **living will** is a document intended to be read not after death, but before it. This type of will does not transfer any property; in fact, it does not even address property ownership. Sometimes referred to in conjunction with the terms "death with dignity" and "euthanasia," it is used by an individual to request that, should he or she become terminally incapacitated by injury or illness, no life-sustaining procedures be used to artificially prolong life. A living will typically requests that the individual be given only the medication, food and fluids necessary to alleviate as much pain as possible for the duration of his or her lifetime.

Details on the living will, including recommended wording and a sample declaration, can be found in ARS Sections 36–3201 to 36–3211.

## ALIENATION BY DESCENT

Descent comes into play when a decedent dies without leaving a valid will. When a person dies without a will, he or she is said to have died **intestate**. The law presumes that an intestate decedent consciously chose not to make a will, chose to marry or not to marry, chose to have children or not to have children, etc. Therefore, as the courses of action taken by the decedent were the result of conscious decisions, the transfer of the decedent's property by descent is considered voluntary.

Under ARS Section 14–2101 and subsequent sections of the Arizona Revised Statutes, the law addresses the transfer of property owned by a person who died intestate. These laws (called the **laws of intestate succession**) distribute the decedent's property among surviving family members.

According to ARS Section 14–2102, if the decedent is survived only by a spouse or by a spouse and children ("issue") of that marital relationship, then all of the decedent's separate property and the decedent's one-half interest in any community property automatically passes to the surviving spouse.

(The surviving spouse already has a one-half interest in any community property; therefore, after the death of the decedent, the survivor would own all the former community property in severalty.)

If the decedent is survived by a spouse and children, one or more of whom are not from that marital relationship (such as children by a previous marriage), then the surviving spouse receives only one-half of the decedent's separate property and none of the decedent's one-half interest in any community property. Any part of the intestate estate not passing to the surviving spouse under ARS Section 14–2102 (or the entire intestate estate, if there is no surviving spouse) passes as follows:

- To the child or children of the decedent equally (or to the descendants of any deceased children of the decedent)
- If there are no surviving children of the decedent, then to the decedent's parent or parents equally
- If there are no surviving children or parents of the decedent, then to the child or children of both of the decedent's parents equally (the decedent's brothers and sisters), or to the child or children of either of the decedent's parents equally (the decedent's half-brothers and half-sisters)
- If there are no surviving children, parents or siblings of the decedent, but the decedent is survived by one or more grandparents or the child or children of grandparents (the decedent's aunts and uncles), then one half of the decedent's estate passes to the paternal grandparent or grandparents equally, or to their child or children equally if both of the paternal grandparents are deceased; the remaining one-half of the decedent's estate passes to the maternal grandparent or grandparents equally, or to their child or children equally if both of the maternal grandparents are deceased. If there are no surviving grandparents or children of grandparents on either the paternal side or the maternal side, then the entire estate passes to the relatives on the other side in the same manner as the original one-half.

For the purposes of intestate succession, ARS Section 14–2104 states that any person who fails to survive the decedent for at least 120 hours (five days) is considered to have died before the decedent, and the decedent's heirs are determined accordingly.

Any intestate estate is divided into as many equal shares as there are heirs in the closest degree of kinship to the decedent. The descendants of a deceased heir take their share of the estate **per stirpes** (by representation) and divide that heir's share equally among themselves.

A spouse may waive his or her intestate rights in the property owned by the other spouse. This may be done either before marriage (with an antenuptial or prenuptial agreement) or after marriage (with a separate contract). However, this waiver does not affect any rights the spouse may have in any community property at the death of the other spouse.

**Figure 8.7 Alienation Reference Chart**

1.  **Alienation**

    A.   Voluntary Alienation
         1.   Sale
         2.   Gift
    B.   Involuntary Alienation
         1.   Foreclosure
         2.   Adverse Possession
         3.   Eminent Domain
         4.   Escheat
    C.   Alienation by Will
    D.   Alienation by Descent

2.  **Alienation by Will**

    A    Testator [man]
         Testatrix [woman]    makes a will [is testate] and appoints an    Executor [man]
                                                                           Executrix [woman]

3.  **Alienation by Descent**

    One with no will is intestate and the probate court appoints an    Administrator [man]
                                                                       Administratrix [woman]

## QUESTIONS

1.  Upon the execution of a judgment lien, the deed given at the sale is a/an

    a.   warranty deed.
    b.   sheriff's deed.
    c.   disclaimer deed.
    d.   executor's deed.

2.  Which of the following wills would be least enforceable in court?

    a.   A conventional will
    b.   A living will
    c.   A nuncupative will
    d.   A holographic will

3.  Adverse possession statutes require all of the following for a legitimate claim *except*

    a.   open and notorious use.
    b.   hostility use.
    c.   uninterrupted use.
    d.   payment of the real estate taxes.

4.  All of the following acts would modify or invalidate a will *except* the

    a.   drafting of a codicil.
    b.   death of the testator.
    c.   destruction of the will.
    d.   drafting of another will.

5.  When a recorded deed is challenged in court, the party with the weakest position is a/an

    a.  person with a prior unrecorded deed who is not in possession.
    b.  person in possession with a prior unrecorded deed.
    c.  tenant in possession with nine months left on a lease.
    d.  unpaid painter who is half-finished at the time of the sale.

6.  Personal property given in a will is referred to as a

    a.  devise.
    b.  demise.
    c.  legacy.
    d.  bequest.

7.  The type of deed that limits a grantor's liability only to the grantor's ownership is a/an

    a.  bargain and sale deed.
    b.  administrator's deed.
    c.  special warranty deed.
    d.  executor's deed.

8.  *C* is selling his small office building. He wants to convey title to the property but also wants to limit his liability in the conveyance as severely as possible. Which of the following deeds would *C* use to accomplish this?

    a.  A disclaimer deed
    b.  A quitclaim deed
    c.  A dedication deed
    d.  A bargain and sale deed

9.  *E* purchased *G*'s residence, but *E* inadvertently recorded his deed in the wrong county. Which of the following statements is true regarding this situation?

    a.  A new deed will have to be issued to *E* and properly recorded.
    b.  Though improper, *E*'s recording still gives constructive notice.
    c.  *E* has valid title to the property in spite of the error, even against future claims that are properly recorded.
    d.  Between *G* and *E*, *E* has valid title to the property.

10. *M* purchased a duplex from *R*. Shortly thereafter, a representative from an air-conditioning contractor called *M* to complain that his company had not been paid for a new air conditioning unit that was installed only days before the property closed escrow and *M* received her deed. *M* could hold *R* liable for the cost of the work under which of the following covenants in the deed?

    a.  The covenant of seisin
    b.  The covenant of further assurance
    c.  The covenant against encumbrances
    d.  The covenant of quiet enjoyment

# 9
# Title Records

## RECORDING DOCUMENTS

According to Arizona law, all documents affecting the title to real property should—not must—be recorded. A document must be in English, and it must be acknowledged (proved and certified) to be eligible for recording. Then it must be delivered to the county recorder's office for the county in which the property is located. In addition, when a deed is submitted for recording, it must be accompanied by an affidavit of property value (as discussed in Chapter 8). A separate recording fee must be paid for each document to be recorded, including the affidavit of value.

Under the concept of caveat emptor ("let the buyer beware"), a potential purchaser of real property is responsible for having both actual knowledge and constructive knowledge of the property to be purchased. **Actual knowledge** is based on actual notice: the purchaser must physically inspect the property to his or her satisfaction. Actual knowledge also includes the purchaser's being aware of any documents, activities or events that could affect the ownership or value of the property.

**Constructive knowledge** is based on **constructive notice**: the purchaser is charged with knowing what is contained in all recorded documents that affect the property. Recording a document gives the world at large constructive notice of that document: the county recorder's records are the most commonly used source of public information regarding real property ownership. (Note that recording also establishes the priority of lien rights.)

There are other sources of public information (such as the Bureau of Vital Statistics) that maintain information on births, deaths, marriages and divorces. These sources also give constructive notice to the extent that information obtained from them can be used to eliminate clouds on title. For example, if a grantor disputes a transfer of ownership by claiming to have been a minor when he or she signed the conveyance deed, the county recorder would have a copy of the deed, but the Bureau of Vital Statistics would have a copy of the grantor's birth certificate. Was the grantor a minor at the time of conveyance? These two documents from two separate public sources would allow the legitimacy of the conveyance to be verified or denied.

Unrecorded documents—including deeds—are valid between the parties to the transaction (ARS Section 33–412, paragraph B). However, they are not binding on subsequent purchasers who would have no constructive notice of the documents (ARS Section 33–412, paragraph A). The importance of recording a deed is reinforced by an Arizona statute that provides that the rights of a prior purchaser who failed to record the deed or take possession of the property are terminated in favor of a subsequent purchaser from the same grantor (ARS Section 33–411, paragraph A).

Under Arizona's recording statutes, the county recorder is required to maintain separate books for the recording of conveyance deeds and the recording of mortgages and trust deeds. Deeds are indexed under the names of the grantor and the grantee. Mortgages and trust deeds are indexed under the names of the borrower (mortgagor or trustor) and the lender (mortgagee or beneficiary).

To assist the county recorder in maintaining accurate records, Arizona real estate law requires that all new subdivisions be surveyed and the resultant plat maps be recorded, so that all future legal descriptions can be made by reference to the lot and block numbers indicated on the plat maps.

## UNRECORDED INTERESTS

As stated above, caveat emptor charges a potential purchaser with both the inspection of the property and the search of the public record. A person claiming an interest in real property can give notice of the interest merely by being in possession of the property. For example, a purchaser who has not recorded the deed can take possession of the property and thus give actual notice of his or her interest. (This is not to suggest that the deed should remain unrecorded!) Should another person want to purchase the property from the original seller, an inspection of the property would reveal who is in possession of it, as well as other potential unrecorded interests (such as an easement that is being used, an encroachment on the property by a neighbor's wall or fence, or evidence of recent construction on the property that would indicate the possibility of an unrecorded mechanic's lien).

Although a search of the public record would show the original seller as the owner of the property, the courts would rule that a subsequent purchaser could have been able to determine by physical inspection that someone other than the seller was in possession of the property. This should have raised the question of who legally owned the property and had the right to transfer the title. Consequently, under caveat emptor, the subsequent purchaser would have no valid claim to the property or any interest in it. The purchaser would be limited to civil recourse against the seller, should he or she believe that fraud had been committed by the seller.

## TITLE EVIDENCE

In most residential real estate transactions in Arizona, the seller is obligated to provide the purchaser with a "good and sufficient conveyance" and a policy of title insurance protecting the purchaser's interest in the property. The term "good and sufficient conveyance" is a common reference to a warranty deed, usually a general warranty deed. The title insurance policy is not required by law; it is merely a well-established custom in real estate transactions—so well-established that almost all purchase contracts obligate the seller to provide the purchaser with a title insurance policy.

In some types of transactions, the parties to the contract prefer to use an abstract of title and attorney's opinion rather than title insurance. This is acceptable under Arizona law. However, most abstracts are valuable only for their historical significance—no financial protection is afforded to the purchaser should a claim against the title develop—therefore, title insurance is the preferred method of protecting title.

## Title Insurance

Unlike other types of insurance companies, which base their rates on statistical data (such as actuarial tables), title insurance companies base their exposure to risk on publicly available documents. The greater the number of documents affecting a property that a title insurance company can trace and verify, the less likely that the company will ultimately have to pay a claim against a policy it issued.

Therefore, every title insurance company either owns or shares a complete title plant (the documents division of the company). Each title plant contains a complete title history of every parcel of land located in each county in which that company has an office. The company will insure a title only as far back as the records on that property can be documented. So, to avoid potential claims against policies and to maintain documentation as accurately as possible, the company attempts to trace the history of each parcel from the current date back to the original government patent.

When a title insurance policy is ordered, a professional researcher (sometimes called a title examiner) will research the documents in the title plant to determine the ownership history of the subject property. The title examiner will also research any other documents that could affect ownership, such as mortgage liens, trust deed liens, mechanic's liens, homesteads, easements and the like. The results of that title search will then be used to issue a preliminary title report. The preliminary title report contains a list of all of the current encumbrances that affect the ownership rights in the subject property. At the close of the transaction, a title insurance policy will be issued based on the data contained in the preliminary title report. If the title insurance company has previously issued a policy on the subject property, a complete title search might not be necessary. The company may simply choose to bring the previously compiled ownership history current.

## Types of Policies

Several types of title insurance policies are issued throughout Arizona, depending on the type of interest to be insured (that is, whether the interest is an owner's, a lender's, or a lessee's). Each of these forms has been standardized by the American Title Association (ATA). The two most commonly used forms are the form insuring the owner's interest and the form insuring the lender's interest.

An **owner's policy** insures a purchaser's title interest and is based on information found in the public record. The premium for the title insurance policy, which is based on the purchase price of the property, is usually paid by the seller; the purchaser is named as the insured party. The condition of the title is insured as of the date of the policy, which is usually the date escrow closes. As with most policies, the owner's policy insures against losses due to forged documents; improperly drafted, signed or delivered deeds or other documents; and documents signed by incompetent parties. It also insures against previous legal proceedings to establish title that later prove to be defective; unknown or undiscovered heirs of a deceased former owner who now claim an interest in the property; and spouses of former owners who claim that they did not join in the signing of a conveyance for property held as community property.

The owner's policy does not insure against those items that are listed as exceptions, including:

- defects in the title known by the owner (regardless of whether they are disclosed to the title insurance company);
- unrecorded easements;
- mechanics' liens and other liens, claims or rights not shown in the public record;
- rights of parties in possession (adverse possessors) not indicated in the public record;

- encroachments;
- factors that would be disclosed by an accurate survey and physical inspection of the property; and
- any government restrictions, such as building codes, zoning ordinances and condemnation under eminent domain.

A **lender's policy** (sometimes referred to as an extended coverage, broad form or ATA policy) typically provides a more extended coverage than the owner's policy. The premium for the lender's policy, which is based on the amount of the new financing, is paid by the purchaser (the borrower), and the lender is named as the insured party. Although the purchaser may have an insured interest in the property through an owner's policy, lenders are generally reluctant to fund a loan when a potential claim against the property's title could jeopardize the lender's security interest in the property. By requiring a lender's policy as part of the loan package, the lender tries to eliminate the possibility of funding an uncollectible loan.

A lender's policy insures the condition of the mortgage or trust deed loan for the lender, including the lien priority of the loan. The policy provides coverage against matters of public record, plus it protects against matters that can be determined through a physical inspection of the property. Thus, the lender is protected against claims that might result from unrecorded easements, unrecorded liens, parties in possession or encroachments.

When both an owner's policy and lender's policy are required, they can often be ordered together and prepared from the same title search. Title insurance companies commonly discount the lender's policy when it is purchased at the same time as an owner's policy.

Title insurance companies also provide detailed information to various parties in special situations, including

- foreclosure reports that specify the condition of the title, list the requirements necessary to complete the foreclosure action and name the appropriate parties to be notified of the foreclosure (for example, lienholders with claims subordinate to that of the foreclosing lienholder;
- deed in lieu of foreclosure reports, which identify the liens that must be released when the lender is negotiating to purchase a defaulting borrower's equity in the subject property; and
- limited realty reports, which concern only the owner of record of the property and list any outstanding encumbrances against the property.

## Fees

Each title insurance company charges various rates depending on the type of real property interest to be insured, the type of coverage to be provided and the type of client using the company's services (such as property owners, lenders, subdividers or developers). The fees to be charged are established by each company, which must file its rate schedule with the Arizona Department of Insurance (which regulates all insurance companies doing business within the state). These rates vary from company to company and are periodically revised.

Under the provisions of the **Real Estate Settlement Procedures Act** (RESPA), sellers are usually prohibited from requiring the use of a particular title insurer. The choice is typically the buyers.

## BUSINESS SALES

No matter how large or how small they are, businesses use real property. And when a business is sold, the property or the lease to the real property used in connection with the business may be included as a part of the sale. For this reason, any person who sells or negotiates the sale of businesses for others for a fee is generally required to have a real estate license, either as a broker operating independently or as a salesperson working for a broker.

Chapter 7 discusses many of the considerations involved in utilizing real estate purchase contracts. When a transaction includes the sale of trade fixtures and personal property (such as inventory) as well as an interest in real property, an additional agreement should be completed by the seller and the purchaser. Although items of personal property may be listed in a standard purchase contract, they are not included in the deed granting title to the real property. Therefore, when a business sale closes, a **bill of sale** should be prepared by the escrow officer and signed by the seller in addition to the deed. A bill of sale transfers the title to all of the personal property included in the sale, such as trade fixtures, machinery and equipment and inventory.

### Uniform Commercial Code

The Uniform Commercial Code (UCC) has been adopted in Arizona with some modifications. The section of the UCC most applicable to the real estate industry is Title 47, Chapter 6, "Bulk Sales" (ARS Section 47–6101 through Section 47–6110). A "bulk sale" or "bulk transfer" is defined as

> any transfer in bulk and not in the ordinary course of the transferor's business of the major part of the materials, supplies, merchandise, or other inventory (ARS Section 47–6102, paragraph A).

The regulations involving bulk transfers are written to protect both the creditors of an existing business and the purchaser of that business. Creditors may be subjected to fraud by a business owner who sells the business (including the trade fixtures and inventory) and then disappears, leaving the creditors unpaid. When this occurs, the creditors cannot demand payment from the purchaser of the business unless it can be proved that the purchaser had actual knowledge of the fraud. A business purchaser may also be the victim of a seller's fraud if the purchaser buys personal property from the seller that was on consignment or lease and was not actually owned by the seller.

To prevent these types of frauds from occurring in the sale of a business, the purchaser should require the seller to sign a **bulk sale affidavit**. The affidavit is a sworn statement identifying any liens or unpaid bills that might become liens against the trade fixtures, machinery and equipment and inventory to be included in the sale. The affidavit also identifies any creditors of the business, including their addresses and the amounts owed to them. It becomes the responsibility of the purchaser to notify each creditor (by certified or registered mail) of the pending sale at least ten days before the scheduled closing of the sale. The purchaser of a business who fails to obtain a bulk sale affidavit from the seller or fails to give the creditors the appropriate notice of the pending sale can be held responsible for all unpaid bills even though the seller was paid for the full value of the personal property involved.

The purchaser must keep the affidavit for at least six months after the sale closes and must allow the affidavit to be inspected by the seller's creditors during that time period. After the six-month period has expired, no action may be brought to repossess any of the property transferred in the sale.

## QUESTIONS

1. An owner's title insurance policy will protect against losses from all of the following *except*

   a. unknown or undiscovered heirs of a deceased former owner.
   b. defective legal proceedings used to establish title.
   c. forged or improperly drawn deeds and other documents.
   d. encroachments, unrecorded easements and mechanics' liens.

2. A search of the public records will always disclose the existence of a

   a. judgment lien.
   b. homestead.
   c. mortgage.
   d. trust deed.

3. The legal process used to clear a title is called a/an

   a. quitclaim deed.
   b. quiet title action.
   c. action in equity.
   d. action in personam.

4. *M* purchased property from *S* as an investment. He did not record his deed, nor did he occupy the property. *S* also sold the property to *R* two weeks later. *R* promptly recorded his deed and moved onto the property. According to Arizona law

   a. *M* has title to the property.
   b. *R* has title to the property.
   c. Neither *M* nor *R* has title to the property.
   d. *M* has title to the property, subject to a lien in favor of *R*.

5. *J* filed a judgment against *W* and thus obtained a lien on *W*'s property for the amount of the judgment. Later, *W* negotiates the sale of her property to *B*. *B* is considered to have knowledge of the judgment lien by virtue of the doctrine of

   a. constructive notice.
   b. actual notice.
   c. recording notice.
   d. the bulk sales act.

6. The recording of a document that transfers or encumbers real property has all of the following effects *except*

   a. creating the presumption of delivery.
   b. preventing the creation of any prior liens.
   c. giving notice of the contents of the documents.
   d. giving priority over subsequently recorded documents.

7. The *H*s are purchasing a small hardware store from *B*. *B* is planning to retire in North Dakota after the sale is closed. The *H*s do not want to be held liable for any of the debts that *B* may have incurred while he owned the business. Which of the following would be the best way for the *H*s to protect themselves?

   a. Obtain a list of *B*'s creditors from the local credit bureau and provide in the contract that *B* must pay them from the proceeds of the sale.
   b. Have *B* sign an affidavit that he will pay all creditors from the sale and that the *H*s will be released from all liability for *B*'s debts.
   c. Obtain *B*'s new address in North Dakota and refer any creditors who show up after the sale directly to *B* for their funds.
   d. Have *B* sign a bulk sales affidavit listing his creditors and then notify those creditors of the impending sale.

8.  *M* is interested in purchasing a large parcel of property from *T*. *T* does not live on the property. *M* could determine all of the following facts by a physical inspection of *T*'s property *except*

    a.  a family, without *T*'s knowledge, is living in an abandoned house on the property.
    b.  the local bank holds three different mortgage loans against the property.
    c.  the phone company has an easement across the property for poles and wires.
    d.  a neighbor's fence is actually erected three feet inside *T*'s property line.

9.  While searching the documents at the county recorder's office, *B* discovered a trust deed recorded against her property prior to her purchasing it. All of the following statements concerning this situation are true *except* she

    a.  purchased the property and took over the seller's existing financing.
    b.  can have the trust deed released by recording a reconveyance deed from the trustee.
    c.  may be responsible for making the payments on the note secured by the trust deed.
    d.  can ignore the trust deed as it must have been recorded against the property in error.

10. *T* sold his "Wash 'n' Dry" franchise to the *S*s, who purchased the business as a retirement investment. In compliance with the Uniform Commercial Code requirements, *T* provided the *S*s with a list of his creditors prior to the sale, and the *S*s properly notified each of the creditors on the list. However, *J*, who supplied *T* with coat hangers and was notified of the sale, was unable to attend the closing to receive the money *T* owed him. Which of the following statements regarding *J*'s situation is true?

    a.  He will now have to contact *T* directly to receive his funds.
    b.  The *S*s will be holding his funds in escrow pending his picking them up.
    c.  He has lost all rights as one of *T*'s creditors now that the sale is closed.
    d.  He will have to sue both *T* and the *S*s to collect the funds due to him.

# 10
# Real Estate License Laws

Real estate activities in Arizona are subject to the provisions of the Arizona Real Estate Code and the Commissioner's Rules. The code appears as Title 32, Chapter 20, of the Arizona Revised Statutes. It contains ten articles:

1. Real Estate Department
2. Licensing
3. Regulation
3.1 Property Management
4. Sale of Subdivided Lands
5. Real Estate Recovery Fund
6. Organization and Regulation of Cemeteries
7. Sale of Unsubdivided Lands
9. Real Estate Time-Shares
10. Membership Camping

The Commissioner's Rules, as authorized by statute, allow the Real Estate Commissioner to develop and implement regulations that interpret, clarify and expand the code.

The Commissioner's Rules have the same force and effect as law. Therefore, a real estate licensee is subject to two sets of regulations when practicing his or her profession: the code and the rules.

The code and the rules have been reproduced in one concise book available from the Arizona Department of Real Estate. All licensees should have a copy of this book either in their possession or available to them through their real estate office. The summary of the code and the rules in this chapter is intended to acquaint the reader with their general provisions. The sections addressing subdivisions and unsubdivided lands are addressed in Chapter 14.


## WHO MUST BE LICENSED?

All states currently require those offering real estate services in expectation of compensation to have a real estate license. According to Arizona Revised Statutes Section 32–2122, it is unlawful for any person to act as a real estate broker or salesperson without first obtaining a license from the commissioner. Any broker or salesperson who initiates a suit to recover a commission for performing a regulated real estate activity must first be able to prove that he or she was properly licensed at the time the claim arose (ARS Section 32–2152).

According to the Real Estate Code (ARS Section 32–2101) a **real estate broker** means a person, other than a salesperson, who, for another and for compensation

- sells, exchanges, purchases, rents or leases real estate or time-share intervals;
- offers to sell, exchange, purchase, rent or lease real estate or time-share intervals;
- negotiates or offers, attempts or agrees to negotiate the sale, exchange, purchase, rental or leasing of real estate or time-share intervals;
- lists, offers, attempts or agrees to list real estate or time-share intervals;
- auctions or offers, attempts or agrees to auction real estate or time-share intervals;
- buys, sells, offers to buy or sell or otherwise deals in options on real estate or time-share intervals or improvements thereon;
- collects or offers, attempts or agrees to collect rent for the use of real estate or time-share intervals;
- advertises or holds himself or herself out as being engaged in the business of buying, selling, exchanging, renting or leasing real estate or time-share intervals or counseling or advising thereon;
- assists or directs in the procuring of prospects, calculated to result in the sale, exchange, leasing or rental of real estate or time-share intervals;
- assists or directs in the negotiation of any transaction calculated or intended to result in the sale, exchange, leasing or rental of real estate or time-share intervals;
- incident to the sale of real estate, negotiates or offers, attempts or agrees to negotiate a loan secured or to be secured by a mortgage or other encumbrance upon or transfer of real estate or time-share interval subject to the provisions of Subsection C of Section 32-2155. The provisions of this subdivision do not apply to mortgage brokers as defined in and subject to the provisions of Title 6, Chapter 9, Article 1;
- engages in the business of assisting or offering to assist another in filing an application for the purchase or lease of, or in locating or entering upon, lands owned by the state or federal government;
- claims, demands, charges, receives, collects or contracts for the collection of an advance fee in connection with any employment enumerated in this section, including employment undertaken to promote the sale or lease of real property by advance fee listing, by furnishing rental information to a prospective tenant for a fee paid by such prospective tenant, by advertisement or by any other offering to sell, lease, exchange or rent real property or selling kits connected therewith. This shall not include the activities of any communications media of general circulation or coverage not primarily engaged in the advertisement of real estate or any other specific communications media that are specifically exempt;
- engages in any of the foregoing activities for the sale or lease of other than real property if a real property sale or lease is a part of, contingent on or ancillary to the transaction; or
- performs any of the foregoing acts as an employee of, or in behalf of, the owner of real estate or interests therein or improvements affixed thereon, for compensation.

A corporation, limited liability company or partnership may obtain a real estate broker's license, as each is legally considered a person.

**Real estate salesperson** means a natural person, a professional limited liability company or a professional corporation engaged by or on behalf of a licensed real estate broker, or by or on behalf of a limited liability company, partnership or corporation that is licensed as a real estate broker to perform any act or participate in any transaction in a manner included in the definition of real estate broker subject to the provisions of Subsection C of Section 32–2155.

## Exceptions to the Licensing Requirement

According to ARS Section 32–2121, the licensing provisions of the Arizona Real Estate Code do not apply to the following:

- A natural person, a corporation through its officers, a partnership through its partners, or a limited liability company through its members or managers that deals in his or its own property, including cemetery property and membership camping contracts, and that does not receive special compensation for the transaction (including property management fees or consulting fees for the property management services performed)
- A person holding a valid power of attorney that is being used for a specific purpose in an isolated transaction and not as a method of conducting a real estate business
- An attorney at law in the performance of his or her duties as an attorney at law
- A receiver, trustee in bankruptcy or other person acting under a court order
- A trustee selling under a deed of trust
- Natural persons who are acting as residential leasing agents or managers of residential rental property, who are performing residential leasing activities on residential income property at no more than one location during the period of the agent's or manager's regular work day, and who are employed by the owner or the owner's licensed management agent to perform the duties customarily associated with such employment. A leasing agent may, however, receive a limited performance-based bonus.  For purposes of this paragraph, "residential leasing agents or managers" means natural persons employed by the owner or the owner's licensed management agent whose normal duties and responsibilities include any one or a combination of the following:
    a. Preparing and presenting to any person a residential lease, application or renewal or any amendment of the lease
    b. Collecting or receiving a security deposit, a rental payment or any related payment for delivery to and made payable to a property, a property manager or owner or the location
    c. Showing a residential rental unit to any prospective tenant
    d. Executing residential leases or rental agreements for condominium units
    e. Acting on behalf of the owner or the owner's licensed management agent to deliver notice pursuant to Title 12, Chapter 8 and Title 33, Chapters 10 and 11
- Any officer or employee of a governmental agency in the conduct of his or her official duties
- One natural person acting as a property manager for no more than one nonresidential income property who is employed by the owner or the owner's licensed management agent to perform the duties customarily associated with such employment
- Natural persons, in the employ of a designated broker, who perform clerical, bookkeeping, accounting and other administrative and support duties; who are not engaged in any other acts requiring a real estate license; and whose employment is not conditioned on or designed to perform duties otherwise requiring a license
- Communications media or their representatives who are primarily engaged in advertising real estate and who perform no other acts requiring a real estate license, if
    a. they do not compile or represent that they compile information about specific prospective purchasers or tenants except general information, such as demographic and marketing information,
    b. they do not make representations to prospective real property sellers or landlords, or their representatives, concerning specific prospective purchasers or tenants or specific sales or leasing leads,
    c. the fee charged for advertising is based solely on the advertising services provided,
    d. the advertisements provide for direct contact between the seller or landlord and the prospective buyers or tenants, or for contact through a licensed real estate broker or

property management firm. The communications media or their representatives cannot act as intermediaries or assist in any intermediary action between prospective parties to a real estate transaction.

Note that these licensing requirements apply to the sales of cemetery property and membership camping contracts except for the sales by a natural person, who is not engaged in the business of selling cemetery property or membership camping contracts, acting with reference to property he or she owns in his or her own name. In addition, nursing and life care institutions, and certain other nonprofit charitable   project-based residential housing corporations, may conduct property management activities without obtaining a real estate broker's license.

## Penalties (ARS Section 32–2154)

A person, corporation, limited liability company or partnership who acts as a broker or salesperson or who advertises in a manner that indicates that he or she is a broker but who is not properly licensed is guilty of a Class 6 Felony. A Class 6 Felony is punishable by fine, imprisonment or both.

## ADMINISTRATION OF THE REAL ESTATE CODE (ARS Section 32–2107, paragraph A)

The Real Estate Code is administered and enforced by the Arizona Department of Real Estate under the direction of the Real Estate Commissioner.

## Real Estate Commissioner (ARS Section 32–2106 through Section 32–2108)

The commissioner is appointed by the governor and serves at the pleasure of the governor for an unspecified time. A candidate for the position of commissioner must have at least five years of experience in real estate, title insurance, banking or mortgage brokerage as well as three years of administrative experience. In addition, he or she must not be acting as a real estate licensee or have any financial involvement with any real-estate-related enterprise at the time of accepting the appointment as commissioner, except through a trust over which he or she has no control.

The commissioner may employ any staff personnel necessary to administer the department and carry out the provisions of the code. The duties of the commissioner include

- publishing educational material that is helpful and proper for the guidance and assistance of both real estate licensees and the general public;
- prescribing such rules as he or she may determine are necessary to carry out the provisions of the Real Estate Code; and
- upon the receipt of a verified written complaint, or upon his or her own motions, investigating the actions of any licensee and taking appropriate disciplinary actions based on the results of his or her findings.

## Real Estate Advisory Board (ARS Section 32–2104 through Section 32–2105)

The commissioner is aided in his or her administration of the Real Estate Code by the **Real Estate Advisory Board**. The Real Estate Advisory Board is composed of seven members who are appointed by the governor to advise the commissioner and make recommendations regarding the code, the real estate industry and the best interests of the general public. Each board member serves a six-year term of office. The terms are staggered so that two members' terms expire in each odd-numbered year and three members' terms expire in every third odd-numbered year.

The membership of the Real Estate Advisory Board must include the following:

- Two members who have been active real estate brokers for at least five years prior to their appointments
- Two members who are primarily engaged in subdividing property in Arizona
- Three members appointed from the general public who are not related to any Arizona real estate licensee

Only one member can be appointed from any one county.

Each year the board selects a chairman from among its members. Board members receive no compensation for their services, but they are reimbursed for their actual expenses in connection with board functions (the board must meet at least quarterly to transact its business). In addition, the board must present to the governor an annual evaluation of the department activities and the commissioner's performance.

## Attorney General (ARS Section 32–2111)

The commissioner is advised on all legal matters by the attorney general.

## LICENSING PROCEDURES

Three sets of requirements must be met before a person can obtain a real estate license in Arizona: general requirements, educational requirements and examination requirements.

## General Requirements (ARS Section 32–2123 through Section 32–2125 and Other Sections)

**Salesperson License.** When applying for an original real estate salesperson license, the applicant must

- be at least 18 years of age;
- not have had a real estate license denied within one year preceding the date of the application (pursuant to ARS Section 32–2153);
- not have had a real estate license revoked within two years preceding the date of the application (pursuant to ARS Section 32–2153);
- submit evidence that the applicant has completed and passed an examination on a real estate course of at least 90 hours that was prescribed and approved by the commissioner;
- submit certification of having passed the Arizona Real Estate Salesperson Licensing Examination;
- submit a completed fingerprint card (this form is available through the department);
- submit any additional information that the commissioner may require to determine the good moral character of the applicant, such as prior criminal records, background information, an

affidavit that the applicant has had participation or an interest in a land development company that has filed or is subject to a petition under any chapter of the Federal Bankruptcy Act, etc.; and

- pay the appropriate fees to the department.

**Broker License.** At the time of applying for an original real estate broker, cemetery broker or membership camping broker license, the applicant must

- be at least 18 years of age;
- be legally in the United States;
- have at least three years of actual experience as a real estate salesperson or broker during the five years immediately preceding the date of the application;
- not have had a real estate license denied within one year preceding the date of the application (pursuant to ARS Section 32–2153);
- not have had a real estate license revoked within two years preceding the date of the application (pursuant to ARS Section 32–2153);
- submit evidence that the applicant has completed and passed examinations on real estate courses of at least 90 hours that were prescribed and approved by the commissioner;
- submit certification of having passed the Arizona Real Estate Broker Licensing Examination;
- submit a completed fingerprint card;
- submit any additional information that the commissioner may require to determine the good moral character of the applicant, such as prior criminal records, background information, an affidavit that the applicant has had participation or an interest in a land development company that has filed or is subject to a petition under any chapter of the Federal Bankruptcy Act, etc.; and
- pay the appropriate fees to the department.

Although the statutes require a broker license applicant to be at least 18 years of age, the experience requirements means that virtually all broker license applicants will be at least 21 years of age. No state or Canadian province will issue a real estate license to anyone who is younger than 18 years of age; therefore, broker license applicants will be at least 21 years of age by the time they meet the three-year experience requirement and apply for their broker licenses.

Within 90 days of the issuance of a salesperson or broker license, additional education requirements must be met. Salespersons must complete a mandatory six-hour-minimum continuing education course on **contract writing** (per Rule R4–28–401.E). The purpose of this course is to familiarize licensees with the practical aspects of completing various types of real estate contracts (specifically, listing contracts, purchase contracts and leases). Brokers must attend a **Broker Audit Clinic**, which is offered free of charge by the Arizona Department of Real Estate. Brokers must then continue to take a Broker Audit Clinic once every four years.

**Corporation, Limited Liability Company or Partnership (ARS Section 32–2125).** A corporation, limited liability company or partnership that applies for a real estate broker's license must designate one of its officers, members, managers or partners to act as the broker of record, or **designated broker**, for that entity. The designated broker must meet all of the requirements that any other broker license applicant would, unless that individual already has a valid broker's license.

The designated broker represents the corporation, limited liability company or partnership in its real estate activities and is therefore responsible for the management of those activities, including the supervision of all sales personnel.

The corporation's, limited liability company's or partnership's license is in effect only as long as the designated broker is associated with that entity. If, for any reason, the association is terminated, the entity's license becomes inactive. In this situation, the corporation or partnership must cease all brokerage activities until a qualified officer or partner completes and files the appropriate forms with the commissioner to become the newly designated broker for the entity.

A real estate broker may employ professional corporations or professional limited liability companies that are licensed as salespersons or associate brokers. The license of such a company ends with the death of a shareholder.

## Educational Requirements (ARS Section 32–2124 and Rule R4–28–401)

Before applying to take the state licensing examination, the license applicant must have completed the appropriate educational requirement. The courses offered to meet the educational requirement can be taken at a private real estate school, as long as the courses have received the prior approval of the commissioner. Courses may also be taken at a community college or a university.

Each course must include a comprehensive final examination, which the applicant must pass to receive credit for having taken the course. Once the course is completed, the instructor or other school official will sign and stamp an Education Certificate, which is used as evidence of completion of the course. The applicant will present the certificate when taking the state licensing examination.

The requirement for both a salesperson and a broker license applicant is the completion of a 90-hour course. The salesperson applicant course is on real estate principles and practices; the broker applicant's education requirement can be met by completing a similar 90-hour course or by completing two of the 45-hour courses from the list of four topics approved by the commissioner at a college or university:

1. Real estate law
2. Real estate finance
3. Real estate appraisal
4. Real estate office management

The prelicense courses offered for salesperson license applicants cannot be used to meet the educational requirement for broker license applicants. Nonresident licensees who apply for an Arizona real estate license must complete 27 hours of Arizona-specific prelicensure education prior to taking the real estate examination.

## Examination Requirements (ARS Section 32–2124 and Rule R4–28–402 and Other Sections)

License applicants are required to pass a state licensing examination on topics relevant to the practice of real estate, cemeteries or membership camping, depending on which license is sought. Each real estate license applicant is tested to determine whether he or she has an appropriate knowledge and understanding of

- the English language, including reading, writing and spelling;
- the arithmetical calculations common to the practice of real estate;
- the principles of real estate conveyances;
- the general purposes and legal effects of contracts, including listing contracts, purchase contracts and deposit receipts, deeds, mortgages, trust deeds, land contracts, leases, property

management agreements, security agreements and bills of sale, and any other areas the commissioner deems necessary and proper;

- the obligations between principals and agents (fiduciary relationships), the principles of the practice of real estate and business opportunity sales, and the canons of business ethics; and
- the Arizona Real Estate Code and the Commissioner's Rules.

Obviously, the examination for a broker's license will be more exacting and of a broader scope than the examination for a salesperson's license.

Applicants for cemetery or membership camping licenses are tested on material appropriate to their industry.

The commissioner has the option of either having the department write and administer the licensing examinations or having the state contract with a professional testing service on behalf of the department. Currently, the licensing examinations for both salespersons and brokers are administered via electronic testing by Assessment Systems Incorporated (ASI) of Bala Cynwyd, Pennsylvania.

**Examination Waived.** An applicant for a real estate salesperson or broker license who currently holds an equivalent license in another state may be exempt from taking the national portion of the real estate examination if the applicant can demonstrate that

- he or she took an ASI exam in another state within the last ten years;
- he or she was licensed after taking that exam; and
- he or she is currently licensed.

Applicants must obtain these items: a duplicate score report from ASI showing the state where they were tested and the date of the test, a license history from the state where they were licensed after the test, and if applicable a license history from the state they are currently licensed in. These must be presented to the test center manager when the candidate requests that the general portion of the test be waived.

## License Application

**General Requirements.** License applications are to be in writing and signed by the applicant. A broker or salesperson application must include

- the legal name, residence address and social security number of the applicant;
- the name and place of business of the applicant's present employer, if any;
- whether the applicant has ever been convicted of a felony, and if so, information about the felony;
- whether the applicant has ever been refused any occupational license in any state or whether any occupational license has been suspended or revoked in any state; and
- the name of any business entity that is or ever has been licensed in which the applicant exercised control.

In addition, a broker applicant's application must include

- the name under which the business is to be conducted and
- the location and mailing address of the applicant's place of business.

**Fingerprints.** When applying for an original salesperson or broker license, the application must be accompanied by a fingerprint card, the form of which is specified by the commissioner. The applicant's fingerprints may be taken either by a local law enforcement agency or by a private company.

**Fees (ARS Section 32–2132 and Rule R4–28–301).** The Department is authorized to charge fees for both obtaining and maintaining real estate licenses. Because of the frequency with which these fees change, check with the Department of Real Estate for current fees.

Every applicant for a real estate and cemetery license must also pay a fee into the Real Estate Recovery Fund. The required fee for the recovery fund is $10 for original salesperson license applicants and $20 for original broker license applicants. Licensees are also required to make additional payments into the fund in years when the balance of the fund falls below $600,000. In such years, renewing salespersons must pay $10 each into the fund, and renewing brokers must pay $20 each into the fund. (This is in addition to the moneys collected by the department from original license applicants.) The Real Estate Recovery Fund is discussed later in this chapter.

All moneys collected by the department (except for payments into the recovery fund) are periodically deposited in the state general fund.

## Licenses (ARS Section 32–2125.01 Through Section 32–2127 and Rules R4–28–301 Through R4–28–305)

**License Issued.** A new real estate licensee is authorized to engage in the activities of a salesperson or broker according to the Arizona Real Estate Code and the Commissioner's Rules. An original license is issued for a period of two years, up to and including the last day of the month in which the license was originally granted.

Both a salesperson and a broker license will be mailed to the broker's business address, except in the case of an inactive salesperson's license, which is kept by the commissioner. An **inactive license** is a license that has been returned to the commissioner and is being held by the commissioner on an inactive status during the current license period.

**Confidentiality (ARS Section 32-2125.03).** If a licensee reasonably believes he or she faces a risk of personal danger or harassment, the licensee may request that his or her home address and telephone number not be disclosed. The Department may not disclose a licensee's social security number to any person other that a court or government agency.

**License Denied.** The commissioner can refuse to issue a license when it appears that the applicant either is guilty of certain illegal activities or has not shown that he or she is a person of honesty, truthfulness and good reputation.

In addition, the commissioner can refuse to issue a license to any entity that desires to operate under the same name or under a similar name as a current licensee, if the commissioner determines that the situation would be detrimental to the public interest.

**Temporary Broker's License (ARS Section 32–2133).** Under certain circumstances, the commissioner can issue a temporary broker's license to an otherwise qualified individual who has not taken the broker licensing examination. Temporary licenses may be issued to the following persons:

- The surviving spouse, next of kin, executor or administrator of a deceased licensed broker — valid for a maximum period of 15 months

- The spouse, next of kin, employee, legal guardian or conservator of a licensed broker who is disabled by sickness, injury or insanity — valid for a maximum period of 90 days

Only one temporary broker's license can be issued to an individual within any 12-month period. A temporary broker has the same powers and obligations that he or she would have under a permanent license.

**Entity Licenses.** Entities that engage in real estate activities, such as a partnership or professional corporation, now have a separate license, which may expire on a different date than the broker running the entity. There is a separate entity renewal form that is available from the department.

**License Renewal.** Unless subsequently suspended or revoked, every original real estate license issued in Arizona is valid for two years; it expires two years after issuance on the last day of the month in which it was originally issued. Prior to the expiration of a license, it may be renewed by a licensee who submits to the department

- the appropriate renewal form,
- the appropriate renewal fee and
- proof that he or she has attended the required number of classroom hours of continuing education.

Licensees who missed their renewal deadline have a one-year grace period for late renewal.

Arizona Revised Statutes Section 32–2130, paragraph A, specifies that, during any biennial licensing period, a licensee must attend 24 classroom hours of real estate oriented continuing education courses prescribed and approved by the commissioner. At least three hours must be devoted to each of the following topics:

- Arizona real estate law
- The Commissioner's Rules
- Agency law
- Contract law
- Fair housing issues
- Environmental issues

Note that cemetery brokers and membership camping brokers are exempt from this continuing education requirement.

Licensees holding either a salesperson's license or a broker's license can receive continuing education credit for attending courses approved by the commissioner on such non-real-estate-oriented topics as motivation, sales techniques, sales management, time management and the like; these are referred to as "self-improvement" topics. Credit for attendance at such courses is limited to a maximum of 3 hours of the 24 hours required in any biennial licensing period.

Licensees holding an original broker's license can use their mandatory attendance at the Broker Audit Clinic for three hours of continuing education credit.

Licensees holding an original salesperson's license can use their mandatory attendance at the Contract Writing course for at least six hours of continuing education credit.

Note that the Arizona Department of Real Estate will not renew the license of a person who has been convicted of a felony offense and who is currently incarcerated for the conviction, paroled, under community supervision or who is on probation as a result of the conviction. (Licensees must give ten-days' notice when they are convicted of a felony or when an adverse judgment relating to real estate is entered against them.)

## GENERAL OPERATION OF A REAL ESTATE BUSINESS

### Place of Business

Every licensed broker must maintain a definite place of business; this is usually the address given on the broker's license application. The licenses of all salespersons and associate brokers who work for the employing broker must be available for inspection at the broker's office. The broker's license must be prominently displayed at the broker's office. The broker must place a sign at the entrance to his or her business that is visible to all who enter the premises. In addition, the sign must indicate the broker's name, the name under which he or she is conducting business (if it is different from the broker's given name) and the fact that he or she is a real estate broker, cemetery broker or membership camping broker. The broker must not display any business name at the location indicated on the broker's license except the name under which he or she is licensed.

A broker must notify the commissioner in writing of any change in his or her business location. Upon receipt of the appropriate forms and fees, the commissioner will then issue a new license for the broker's new location for the unexpired portion of that license term. (All the licenses of the affiliated licensees must also be reissued with the new address.) When changing business locations, it is the broker's responsibility to remove the sign from his or her former location. This must be done immediately upon cessation of business activity at that location.

### Branch Offices (ARS Section 32–2127 and Rule R4–28–301)

A broker must obtain an additional license for each branch office he or she maintains. A branch office license is issued in the same name as the broker's principal office license. The branch office license must be posted at the branch office in a manner similar to the posting of the principal office license. And a sign that conforms to the same requirements given for the principal office sign must be posted at the entrance, including the additional designation of "branch office."

The principal office is under the management of the employing broker. Any branch office must be under the management of either a salesperson or a broker who is directly responsible to the employing broker.

If a designated broker is unable to act for a period of 24 hours, he or she may designate a licensee or another designated broker to act in his or her behalf. The designation must be in writing and must be kept on file for a period of a least one year. This designation shall not exceed 30-day's duration and may authorize the designee to perform all the normal designated broker's duties, except that a salesperson cannot be authorized to hire or fire licensees. A written designation is required for each temporary absence. The written designation does not need to be submitted to the department unless the designated broker must sign a form that is sent to the department. In this case, the written designation is attached to the form.

## Termination of Employment (ARS Section 32–2128)

The license of any licensee other than the employing broker must remain with that broker for the license to be active. Should a licensee leave the broker's employ, the broker must return the license to the department.

## Reinstatement of License (ARS Section 32–2131)

During a license period, the commissioner can reinstate any license that was canceled but not suspended or revoked upon receiving an application and the appropriate fee from the licensee.

## Professional Conduct (Rules R4–28–1101 Through R4–28–1102)

In general, it is the licensee's responsibility to protect the public against fraud and to assist the department in regulating real estate activities. The licensee must guard against inaccuracies in all representations made to clients and to customers. Under the law, a misstatement or misrepresentation—including failure to disclose zoning ordinances, deed restrictions and other conditions affecting the use of a property—constitutes fraud. In the case of a misrepresentation by a licensee, the purchaser may justifiably refuse to complete the transaction and the seller may be able to refuse to pay any commission due.

As an agent or a subagent, a licensee has a fiduciary obligation to the principal. However, he or she must deal fairly with all parties to a transaction. In addition, the licensee must never discourage any party to a transaction from seeking competent legal advice.

A licensee cannot accept any compensation from both parties to a transaction without first obtaining the written permission of both parties. If the licensee is selling a property that he or she owns or holds an interest in, this fact must be disclosed to the purchaser. (This is often referred to as "making your position clear.") Likewise, if the licensee is purchasing a property or acquiring an interest in a property, he or she must disclose this fact to the seller. These types of disclosures, while customarily made throughout the marketing and negotiating processes, must be made in writing on the purchase contract between the licensee and the other party.

The licensee must perform the activities for which he or she was employed as promptly and efficiently as possible. The licensee must not allow any controversy between himself or herself and another licensee to jeopardize, delay or interfere in any manner with the activities to be performed on behalf of a client. Any intentional or negligent delay on the part of the licensee could be cause for the suspension or revocation of his or her license.

When a property is listed exclusively with one broker, all negotiations for such property must be made through that listing broker, unless the seller waives this requirement in writing and no representative of the listing broker is available for at least 24 hours. Also, a broker may not accept any profit or compensation from a real estate transaction on behalf of his or her client without the client's written permission.

## Care and Handling of Funds (ARS Section 32–2151)

Unless otherwise provided in writing by all parties to a transaction, a broker who accepts funds in connection with a real estate transaction must deposit such funds in one of two places: either into a trust fund account that the broker maintains through his or her office specifically for client funds, or into a neutral escrow depository in Arizona. (Note that under certain conditions, a trust fund account can be placed in a federally insured financial institution outside of Arizona.) The neutral escrow depository can be a title insurance company, a lending institution, an attorney or some other authorized person or entity. In a transaction in which the broker or a member of his or her family or company has a seller's or purchaser's interest in the property, the earnest money should be deposited into a neutral escrow to avoid any possibility of the appearance of commingling.

A broker cannot allow any advance payment of funds belonging to others to be deposited into the broker's personal account or to be commingled with any personal funds. However, when establishing a trust fund account, the broker may deposit a maximum of $500 to keep the account open or to avoid service charges for an insufficient minimum balance.

Every deposit into the broker's trust fund account must be made with a deposit slip that identifies the depository, the amount of the deposit and the names of the parties to the transaction. When depositing funds into an escrow account, the broker should obtain a receipt containing the same information. In addition, the broker must retain a complete record in his or her office of all funds received in connection with real estate transactions, including the following information:

- The person or persons from whom the funds were received
- The amount of funds received
- The date of the receipt
- The place of deposit
- The date of deposit
- The final disposition of the funds after the transaction has been closed

Any funds entrusted to a broker may be used only for the transaction for which they were provided. All cash, checks or other items of value received by a licensee in connection with a real estate transaction must be placed in the care of the employing broker as soon as possible.

## Record Keeping (ARS Section 32–2151.01)

A broker is required to keep records of all real estate transactions handled directly or indirectly through his or her office, including

- listing contracts,
- purchase contracts and earnest money receipts, and
- closing statements, showing all receipts, disbursements and adjustments (including evidence of their delivery).

All transactions must be numbered consecutively in the broker's records. Those records must be kept in the broker's principal office or in the branch office of their origination. Records of any transaction must be kept by the broker for at least five years from the termination date of the transaction. (If a property was listed but did not sell, the documents must be kept for one year from the expiration of the listing—including any rejected offers.) The records must be kept open for inspection by the commissioner or his or her representative at all reasonable times.

## Documents

Article XXVI of the Arizona Constitution, an amendment passed in late 1962, authorizes real estate licensees to draft or complete any document relative to a real estate transaction, as long as the licensee is representing one or both of the parties to the transaction and he or she does not charge a separate fee for providing this service. However, the provisions of Article XXVI do not automatically endow a licensee with the competence required to adequately draft or complete the necessary documents. Proficiency in real estate contracts and contract law is essential, and it is always wise for a licensee to recommend that the parties seek legal advice from their attorneys.

In preparing any real estate document, the licensee is responsible for making enough copies of the document so that each party will have one. (For example, purchase contracts are usually prepared in sets of four, as noted in Chapter 7.) Once a document has been signed by the parties, the licensee must—as soon as reasonably practical—deliver a legible copy of the document to each party.

The designated broker (the employing broker in the case of a corporation, limited liability company or partnership) is responsible for reviewing all documents through his or her office within five business days after the document is signed. (A licensee managing a branch office may be given the right to approve documents on behalf of the broker with the broker's written permission.) The broker is required to review the contract for form and content—that is, to be sure that the document is properly drafted or completed. The broker must place his or her initials and the date of review on the document as evidence of his or her review and approval.

A licensee must not knowingly prepare or cause to be processed any document that contains misleading or inaccurate information, such as purchase prices or statements of income; to do so can be grounds for disciplinary action.

**Listing Contracts.** Every real estate listing contract must be in writing in clear and unambiguous language, contain all the material terms of the agreement (such as the price at which the property is to be offered), be signed by the appropriate parties and contain dates of inception and termination. A listing must automatically terminate as of its expiration date; it cannot require the seller to notify the broker in order to cancel the listing. In addition, a listing contract is a contract for the broker's personal and professional services, and as such, it cannot be assigned to another broker without the written consent of the client.

A licensee must not procure or attempt to procure a listing contract on a property that is already subject to an existing exclusive listing contract (this activity is sometimes called "contract raiding") unless the seller is informed in writing that the creation of additional listing contracts on the property could expose the seller to a liability for additional commissions. Contract raiding is both unprofessional and unethical.

**Property Management Contracts.** Every property management contract must be in writing, contain all the material terms of the agreement, be signed by the appropriate parties and contain dates of inception and termination. It must also provide for

- the disposition of all monies collected by the licensee,
- the frequency of status reports to be sent to the client and
- the amount of funds to be set aside or expended for improvements or repairs or other expenses incurred on behalf of the client and the extent of the licensee's authority to order such improvements or repairs.

Property management agreements must have cancellation provisions that are mutually agreed upon. Like listing agreements, property management agreements cannot be assigned without the express written consent of the client.

**Purchase Contracts.** Every offer to purchase real property and every purchase contract must be in writing. The form of the earnest money deposit—cash, check, promissory note, etc.—must be specifically stated in the receipt for the deposit.

A licensee is obligated to submit promptly to his or her client all offers to purchase the property, regardless of their sources. Should a licensee receive one offer on the property, it should be submitted promptly (through the listing agent) for the client's consideration. Should a licensee receive multiple offers within a reasonably close time frame, they should all be presented to the client at the same time. The licensee is required to explain to the client the benefits and the potential liabilities of each offer and to give sound, unbiased advice as the client requests it.

**Closing Statements.** After the closing of escrow of every real estate transaction in which the broker participated as an agent, he or she is responsible for seeing that complete detailed closing statements are delivered to the seller. Such statements must include an accounting of all funds received and disbursed by the broker. Common practice holds that the escrow agent will deliver the closing statements to the parties; however, this does not relieve the broker of his or her liability according to the Commissioner's Rules (Rules R4–28–801 through R4–28–802). Brokers representing buyers should also deliver closing statements to the buyers.

## Advertising and Promotional Practices (Rules R4–28–501 Through R4–28–504)

The Commissioner's Rules on advertising are quite broad: for these purposes, advertising includes all print and broadcast media, including radio and television commercials, newspapers, magazines, circulars, business cards and stationery.

"High-powered" selling and promotional activities by licensees will not be tolerated by the Real Estate Commissioner. Any licensee utilizing such practices will be subject to the surveillance of the Arizona Department of Real Estate, and the continuance of such prohibited practices may result in a loss of license. Furthermore, a licensee cannot solicit, sell or offer to sell any real property by offering free lots or by conducting lotteries or contests in order to influence a purchaser or prospective purchaser of the property being marketed. Note that new laws allow the use of some contests and lotteries in the sale of subdivision properties. (See Chapter 14.)

Any offer of a "free" gift or item made in connection with a sales promotion must be without conditions. Furthermore, any gift or item offered (even if not labeled "free") must be clearly described, including the approximate retail value, and any costs or conditions associated with the receipt of the item must be clearly disclosed before anyone participates in the offer. Any offer of reduced-price or free travel, accommodations, meals or entertainment cannot be described as "awards" or "prizes" or similar phrases; and any costs, limitations or restriction must be fully disclosed.

Many people receive solicitations mailed by development companies, indicating that they will receive a specified gift if they visit the development, sit through a sales presentation and take a tour of the property. This type of marketing is permitted because the receipt of the gift is not contingent on the purchase of the property; any qualified person who receives the solicitation can receive the gift merely by complying with the terms of the solicitation.

A licensee cannot advertise a property or offer it for sale or lease without the written permission of the owner or the owner's representative. In addition, a licensee may place a sign on the property offering it for sale, rent, lease or exchange only with the written consent of the owner. Any sign so placed must be removed immediately upon the owner's request.

A licensee cannot advertise in a manner that indicates that the offer is being made by an individual who is not engaged in the real estate business. This type of advertisement is referred to as a "blind ad," and it is misleading and deceptive to the public. Advertisements that give only a post office box number, street address or telephone number are also prohibited.

All advertising done by a broker and the licensees he or she employs must be done in the name of the employing broker; if possible, all such advertising should be done under the employing broker's direct supervision. A licensee cannot advertise in his or her name only; the name of the employing broker must be included in the advertisement and must appear in a manner that is conspicuous and designed to attract the attention of the reader. The exception to this requirement is advertising done by a franchiser to promote the franchise name, but that does not refer to any specific property (this type of advertising is referred to as **institutional advertising**).

Copies of new advertising used in connection with the offering of subdivided lands (Article 4 of the Arizona Real Estate Code), unsubdivided lands (Article 7), time-shares (Article 9), condominiums and cooperatives must be submitted to the department within 21 days of the first usage. Such advertising must meet the disclosure requirements dictated by the department, such as the estimated dates for the completion of construction, the progress of construction according to pictorial representations, the size and volume of standing bodies of water on the property, and so on.

## Stigmatized Properties (ARS Section 32–2156)

Under new laws, no criminal, civil or administrative action can be brought against a property seller or lessor or a broker working on behalf of a buyer, seller or lessor for failing to disclose that the property is or has been

- the site of a natural death, suicide or homicide or any other felony crime; or
- owned or occupied by a person exposed to the HIV virus or diagnosed as having AIDS or any other disease that is not known to be transmitted through common occupancy of real estate.

The failure to disclose any of these facts cannot be used as grounds to terminate or rescind any real property transaction.

## Compensation and Commissions (ARS Section 32–2163 and Rule R4–28–701)

It is unlawful for any real estate broker to employ or compensate, either directly or indirectly, any person for performing any regulated activity if that person is not an active licensee in the employ of that broker or is not another real estate broker. Furthermore, any licensee—broker or salesperson—cannot pay or give a commission, gift, certificate, coupon or any other valuable consideration to an unlicensed person. Therefore, "bird dog fees," "finder's fees" and the like are strictly prohibited. However, a broker licensed in Arizona can share commissions with brokers licensed in other states.

Any licensee involved in a transaction must disclose to all parties to that transaction the identity of any other person receiving a portion of the commission. However, the payment or sharing of any compensation with an unlicensed individual is still prohibited.

## SUSPENSION OR REVOCATION OF A LICENSE

### Grounds for Suspension or Revocation (ARS Section 32–2153)

The commissioner can suspend or revoke a license or deny the issuance or the renewal of a license if it appears that the licensee or applicant has committed any of the following acts while engaged in regulated real estate activities within the preceding five years:

- Made any substantial misrepresentation or false promises
- Acted for more than one party in a transaction without the knowledge and consent of all parties to that transaction
- Disregarded or violated any of the provisions of the license law or rules of the commission
- Knowingly authorized, directed, connived or aided in the publication, advertisement, distribution or circulation of any material false statement or representation concerning his or her business or any land, cemetery property, subdivision or membership campground or camping contract offered for sale in Arizona or in any other state
- Willfully used the term "real estate broker" or "cemetery broker" without being properly licensed
- Employed any unlicensed salesperson
- Accepted compensation as a salesperson for performing regulated real estate activities from any person other than the employing broker under whom he or she was licensed
- Represented or attempted to represent a broker other than the employing broker under whom he or she was licensed without the express knowledge and consent of the employing broker
- Failed, within a reasonable time, to account for or to remit any monies or to give to the rightful owner any documents or other valuable property belonging to others that had come into his or her possession; or issued an appraisal report on real property or cemetery property in which he or she held an interest, unless the nature and extent of such an interest was fully disclosed in the report
- Paid or received any rebate, profit, compensation or commission in violation of the Arizona Real Estate Code
- Induced any party to a contract to break the contract for the purpose of substituting a new contract with the same or a different principal, if such a substitution was motivated by the personal gain of the licensee
- Placed a sign on any property offering it for sale or for rent without the specific written authority of the owner or the owner's authorized agent
- Solicited, sold, or offered for sale any real property by offering "free lots" or any other inducement of a speculative nature involving a game of chance or risk or conducting lotteries or contests
- Failed to pay to the commissioner promptly, and before the time specified, the biennial renewal fee
- Failed to keep an escrow account, trust account or other record of funds deposited with him or her in conjunction with any real estate transaction
- Commingled the money or property of the principal with his or her own
- Failed or refused upon demand to produce any document, book or record in his or her possession concerning any real estate or cemetery property transacted by him or her for inspection by the Real Estate Commissioner or the commissioner's representative
- Failed to maintain a complete record of each real estate transaction covered by the Arizona Real Estate Code
- Violated the Federal Fair Housing Law, the Arizona Civil Rights Act or any local ordinance of a similar nature

- Tendered to the buyer a wood infestation report in connection with the transfer of residential real property or an interest in residential real property knowing that wood infestation exists or that the wood infestation report was inaccurate or false as of the date of the tender or that an inspection was not done in conjunction with the preparation of the wood infestation report
- As a licensed broker, failed to exercise reasonable supervision over the activities of salespersons, associate brokers or others under his or her employ or failed to exercise reasonable supervision and control over the activities for which a real estate license is required of a corporation or partnership on behalf of which he or she acts as designated broker
- Demonstrated negligence in the performance of any act for which a real estate license is required
- Sold or leased property to a buyer or lessee that was not the property represented to the buyer or lessee
- Demonstrated a lack of mental competence necessary to reasonably accomplish the responsibilities and duties of a licensee
- Violated any federal or state law, regulation or rule that relates to real estate or securities or that involves forgery, theft, extortion, fraud, substantial misrepresentation, dishonest dealings or violence against another person or intentional failure to deal fairly with any party to a transaction that materially and adversely affected the transaction
- Violated any condition or term of a commissioner's order

The commissioner can also suspend or revoke a license or deny the issuance or the renewal of a license, if it appears that the licensee or applicant has

- procured or attempted to procure a real estate license through fraud, misrepresentation or deceit, or filed a license application that was false or misleading;
- been convicted of a felony in a court of competent jurisdiction in Arizona or in any other state at any time, either prior to applying for a license or after obtaining a license;
- made any substantial misrepresentation;
- made any false promises of a character likely to influence persuade or induce;
- been guilty of any conduct that constitutes fraud or dishonest dealing;
- engaged in the business of a real estate, cemetery or membership camping broker or salesperson without being properly licensed;
- not shown that he or she is a person of honesty, truthfulness or good reputation.

Rule R4–28–301 requires a real estate licensee to notify the commissioner within ten days of any adverse decision of a court of competent jurisdiction rendered as the result of a civil suit or judgment in which the licensee appeared as the defendant and in which the subject matter involved a real estate transaction to which the licensee was a party. Any misdemeanor or felony conviction must also be reported within ten days.

## Procedure  (ARS Section 32–2157 and Rules R4–28–1301 through R4–28–1306)

Before suspending, revoking or denying the renewal of a license, the commissioner must notify the licensee in writing of the charges filed against him or her and give the accused licensee an opportunity to be heard, either in person or through an attorney. A copy of the complaint and a notice of the date and time of the hearing must be either personally served on the accused licensee or sent to him or her by registered or certified mail to the last known address of the licensee according to the records of the department. Within ten days of such service, the licensee must file a verified answer to the complaint with the commissioner.

If the commissioner determines that the public health, safety or welfare requires immediate action, he or she can order a summary suspension of the license of the accused, pending formal proceedings for a license revocation.

The lapsing or suspension of a license, either by an operation of law or by an order of the commissioner or a court, does not terminate the commissioner's authority to proceed with an investigation of—or legal or disciplinary proceedings against—a licensee. Such circumstances also do not terminate the commissioner's authority to suspend, revoke or deny the renewal of a license.

### Hearing (ARS Section 32–2158 through 32–2159 and Rules R4–28–1307 through R4–28–1312)

After notifying the accused licensee of the complaint and receiving a verified answer, the commissioner must hold a hearing on the matter. The commissioner has the power to subpoena witnesses and accept testimony taken by deposition. Any party to the hearing has the right to request that the commissioner subpoena witnesses. A decision by the commissioner may be appealed to the Superior Court of Maricopa County.

### Corporations and Partnerships (ARS Section 32–2160)

The commissioner can suspend or revoke the license of an officer of a corporation or a partner of a partnership without actually revoking the entity's license.

### Prosecution of Licensees (ARS Section 32–2160)

For any violation of the Arizona Real Estate Code, the commissioner can file a formal complaint against a licensee in a court of competent jurisdiction. The commissioner, his or her deputies, assistants and attorney can also assist in the prosecution of the licensee, which is brought by the county attorney in the county in which the violation occurred. In addition, the commissioner can request that the attorney general or the county attorney apply to the superior court of the appropriate county for an injunction restraining the licensee from engaging in whatever activity it was that appeared to violate the Arizona Real Estate Code.

### Penalties (ARS Section 32–2154 and Section 32–2161)

Any unlicensed person found guilty of acting as a broker or a salesperson without being properly licensed, or of implying via advertising that he or she was a broker, is guilty of a Class 6 Felony, which can result in fine, imprisonment or both.

In addition, any person connected with a publication or promotional material that contains false or fraudulent statements or misrepresentations, and any person who in any way violates any of the provisions of the Arizona Real Estate Code or the Commissioner's Rules, can be found guilty of a Class 6 Felony. If that person is a licensee, his or her license can be suspended or revoked, in addition to the individual being subjected to a fine, imprisonment or both.

While the Arizona Department of Real Estate receives thousands of complaints each year, most of the complaints are not justifiable or are beyond the jurisdiction of the department, such as complaints between licensees concerning the sharing of a commission. (Note that the commissioner may also initiate investigations on his or her own.) However, when the commissioner believes the situation warrants a hearing, the licensee who is accused of the violation is often headed toward a license suspension and fine at best, and criminal prosecution at worst. The commissioner and the department take very seriously their responsibility to protect the public and to regulate the industry.

## REAL ESTATE RECOVERY FUND (ARS Section 32–2186 Through Section 32–2193.01)

When a licensee violates the Arizona Real Estate Code or the Commissioner's Rules, members of the public may be financially harmed. The Real Estate Recovery Fund was established to provide a means of compensating these injured persons. Every applicant for an original real estate license must make a one-time payment into the fund as described earlier in this chapter. Original salesperson license applicants pay $10 each, and original broker license applicants pay $20 each. In years during which the balance of the fund falls below $600,000, renewing licensees will also make additional payments into the fund ($10 when renewing a salesperson's license, and $20 when renewing a broker's license).

Note that a licensee who acts as a principal or an agent in a real estate transaction has no protection afforded to him or her by the fund; the licensee is bound to act in a legal and ethical manner and therefore cannot initiate a claim against the fund.

### Recovery from the Fund (ARS Section 32–2188)

The maximum claim that can be paid from the Real Estate Recovery Fund is $20,000 per transaction, regardless of the number of aggrieved persons involved or the number of parcels of real estate involved. The aggregate that will be paid from the fund on behalf of any one licensee is $40,000.

Any aggrieved person who desires to collect a claim from the fund must first initiate a suit to obtain a judgment against the licensee. Such an action must be started within five years of the incident on which the claim will be based. In addition, the aggrieved person must notify the Real Estate Commissioner in writing by certified mail or return receipt requested at the time the suit is filed. The commissioner has the right to intervene in the suit and defend the actions of the licensee in court.

If the aggrieved person prevails in any court of competent jurisdiction, he or she will obtain a valid judgment against the licensee. Once all proceedings—including reviews and appeals—are concluded, the aggrieved person can file a verified claim in the court in which the judgment was entered. He or she must then give the commissioner and the judgment debtor (the licensee) written notice before applying to have the court direct payment of the judgment from the fund. The court must hold a hearing on the matter as soon as possible, unless the judgment debtor fails to respond to the application, in which case the commissioner can order payment from the fund.

If a hearing does take place, the aggrieved person must be able to show that he or she has obtained a proper judgment against the licensee and has complied with all of the requirements concerning the fund. He or she must also show that all possible legal steps have been taken to collect the judgment from the licensee, that reasonable inquiries and searches into the licensee's assets have been made and that the licensee does not have enough assets to satisfy the entire award of the judgment. If the aggrieved person has recovered any funds from the licensee in an out-of-court settlement, the court must be so informed. In addition, the aggrieved person must prove that he or she is not the licensee's spouse nor a representative of the licensee's spouse.

If the court is satisfied that the aggrieved person has truthfully complied with all of the appropriate requirements, it will direct the commissioner to make payment against the judgment from the fund.

### Automatic Termination (ARS Section 32–2188, Paragraph F)

Whenever the commissioner is directed by a court to pay money from the fund, the license of the salesperson or broker against whom the claim was made is automatically revoked. The revoked license can not be reinstated until the licensee has repaid to the fund the entire principal amount expended, plus interest at the rate of 6 percent per year. A payment from the fund creates a nondischargeable debt: bankruptcy will not relieve the individual of the obligation to repay the fund with interest.

### Subrogation (ARS Section 32–2192)

Once the commissioner has paid a claim from the fund to an aggrieved person, the commissioner acquires all rights to the claim of the aggrieved person. With this subrogation, the commissioner can deposit into the fund any monies collected from the former licensee, both principal and interest.

### Waiver of Rights (ARS Section 32–2193)

Any aggrieved person who fails to comply with all of the requirements concerning a claim against the Real Estate Recovery Fund loses his or her right to collect from the fund.

### False Statement (ARS Section 32–2190)

Any person who files any document with the commissioner, in connection with a claim against the fund, that is false or contains misstatements is guilty of a Class 2 misdemeanor.

### CEMETERIES  (ARS Section 32–2194 Through Section 32–2194.30)

Article 6 of the Arizona Real Estate Code provides for the licensing and regulation of cemetery brokers, cemetery salespersons and cemetery properties and services.

**Cemetery broker** means a person other than a real estate broker or real estate salesperson who, for another and for compensation, engages in any of the following activities regarding cemetery property or interment services:

- Sells, leases or exchanges such property or services for another or on his or her own account
- Offers to purchase, sell, lease or exchange such property or services for another or on his or her own account
- Negotiates the sale, purchase, lease or exchange of any such property or services
- Negotiates the sale, purchase, lease or exchange, or lists or solicits or negotiates a loan on or the leasing of any such property or services

A corporation or partnership can also obtain a cemetery broker's license.

**Cemetery salesperson** means a natural person or a corporation, other than a real estate broker or real estate salesperson, engaged by or on behalf of a licensed broker, or by or on behalf of a corporation that is licensed as a cemetery salesperson, to perform any act or transaction included in the definition of cemetery broker.

There is much confusion concerning dual licensing. Can one person hold both a real estate license and a cemetery license? The answer is yes. One person can hold both types of licenses; however, unusual situations can occur. A person holding both a real estate broker's license and a cemetery broker's license can employ salespersons licensed in either or both of those regulated areas. A person holding a real estate broker's license and a cemetery salesperson's license (or vice versa) can operate a brokerage business in the realm of his or her broker's license but will have to activate the salesperson's license with a cemetery broker. A person holding a real estate salesperson's license and a cemetery salesperson's license would best be employed by a broker holding licenses in both areas; however, some salesperson licensees have two employing brokers: one with whom their real estate license is activated and one with whom their cemetery license is activated.

Cemetery or cemetery property includes all of the following:

- A burial park for earth interments
- A mausoleum for crypt or vault interments
- A crematory, or a crematory and columbarium, for cinerary interments
- A cemetery plot, including interment rights, mausoleum crypts, niches and burial spaces

The requirements for a cemetery license were discussed earlier in the chapter.

Cemetery properties must receive the approval of the commissioner before they can be sold or offered for sale. (The filing and disclosure requirements for cemetery properties are very similar to those required for subdivisions and unsubdivided lands, as discussed in Chapter 14.) Exempted from such regulation are cemeteries operated by religious organizations and churches, cemeteries operated by fraternal organizations (not exceeding ten acres in size) and cemeteries owned and operated by political subdivisions such as cities and towns.

## QUESTIONS

1. A real estate licensee who is an officer in a corporation and acts as the principal broker for that entity is called the

   a. employing broker.
   b. associate broker.
   c. designated broker.
   d. corporation broker.

2. A real estate broker must maintain records of all transactions in his or her office for a period of

   a. three years from the inception of a transaction.
   b. three years from the termination of a transaction.
   c. five years from the inception of a transaction.
   d. five years from the termination of a transaction.

3. The members of the Real Estate Advisory Board are appointed by the

   a. commissioner.
   b. governor.
   c. secretary of state.
   d. attorney general.

4. The maximum amount to be paid from the Real Estate Recovery Fund is

   a. $10,000 per licensee.
   b. $15,000 per licensee.
   c. $20,000 per transaction.
   d. $30,000 per transaction.

5. The composition of the Real Estate Advisory Board is

   a. two brokers, three subdividers and two public members.
   b. two brokers, two subdividers and three public members.
   c. three brokers, two subdividers and two public members.
   d. three brokers, two subdividers and three public members.

6. Document preparation by real estate licensees is authorized by

   a. Article XXVI of the Arizona Constitution.
   b. the Arizona Supreme Court.
   c. the Arizona Real Estate Code.
   d. the Commissioner's Rules.

7. The statute of limitations for claims against the Real Estate Recovery Fund is

   a. one year.
   b. two years.
   c. three years.
   d. five years.

8. A real estate license must be renewed on or before the

   a. first day of the month of issuance every year.
   b. first day of the month of issuance every two years.
   c. last day of the month of issuance every year.
   d. last day of the month of issuance every two years.

9. A real estate salesperson's license

   a. must be carried by the licensee at all times.
   b. may be carried by the licensee at his or her discretion.
   c. is mailed to the licensee's residence address.
   d. is mailed to the licensee's business address.

10. Before placing a sign on property offering it for sale, the licensee must have

    a. an exclusive right to sell listing.
    b. any type of exclusive listing agreement.
    c. the written permission of the owner.
    d. the verbal permission of the owner.

11. Whenever the commissioner is required to satisfy a claim against a licensee with a payment from the Real Estate Recovery Fund, the

    a. licensee can continue engaging in real estate activities under the direct supervision of the commissioner.
    b. licensee's license is revoked, and the licensee must repay the amount expended plus interest to the fund before his or her license can be reinstated.
    c. commissioner can collect additional damages by forcing the sale of any property belonging to the licensee.
    d. licensee must pay twice the normal amount for the one-time fee for the fund at every renewal.

12. Broker *B* had a formal complaint filed against him for unethical real estate practices. His license had been temporarily suspended by the Real Estate Commissioner, but it has since been revoked. As a result of the revocation, which of the following courses of action is available to *B*'s salesperson licensees?

    a. They can close their transactions as quickly as possible.
    b. They can close their transactions but must cancel their listings.
    c. They can activate their licenses with other real estate brokers.
    d. They can continue to operate as before under a temporary broker's license.

13. All of the following are required of a real estate salesperson *except* to

    a. complete at least 24 hours of continuing education for every license renewal period.
    b. disclose his or her position as a licensee when purchasing or selling property on his or her own behalf.
    c. accept a position as the branch manager for the employing broker at the broker's branch office.
    d. obtain all listings taken in the name of the employing broker in writing.

14. The Real Estate Commissioner is responsible for all of the following *except*

    a. writing or arranging the writing of a real estate licensing examination.
    b. prescribing such rules as he or she determines are necessary to carry out the provisions of the Arizona Real Estate Code.
    c. meeting quarterly with the members of the Real Estate Advisory Board.
    d. investigating the actions of licensees and taking appropriate action based on his or her findings.

15. Salesperson *H* accepted a $500 earnest money check with a purchase offer from the *B*s on property owned by the *R*s. Which of the following is *H*'s best course of action?

    a. Deposit the check into his trust account.
    b. Deposit the check into his employing broker's trust account.
    c. Cash the check and turn the funds over to his employing broker.
    d. Turn the check over to his employing broker with the offer.

16. All of the following situations could be cause for the licensee's license to be suspended or revoked by the commissioner *except*

    a. Broker *K* acted for both the seller and the purchaser in a transaction after receiving written permission from both of them.
    b. Broker *W* employed his wife as a real estate salesperson while she was studying to take her state licensing examination.
    c. Salesperson *M*, who sold a property for the *S*s, received a commission bonus from them for a "job well done."
    d. Salesperson *D* had been found guilty by the superior court of driving while intoxicated.

17. *H*, who was unlicensed, represented himself as a broker in a real estate transaction between the *M*s and the *C*s. Upon hearing of *H*'s activities, the Real Estate Commissioner can initiate action against him which can result in *H*'s

    a. fine.
    b. imprisonment.
    c. fine and/or imprisonment.
    d. fine, imprisonment and loss of license.

18. Which of the following must have a real estate broker's license to transact business?

    a. *S*, who owns a six-unit apartment and personally manages the building, collects rent and shows apartments to prospective tenants
    b. *A*, who negotiates the sale of entire businesses, including their stock, machinery, equipment and buildings
    c. *D*, the superintendent of a large apartment complex, who shows apartments to prospective tenants as part of his regular duties.
    d. *S*, who has a special power of attorney from her father to sell and convey a residence that he owns.

19. Salesperson *K* is unhappy with the terms of her current employment and has decided to change brokers. Before *K* can start selling for her future employer,

    a. her current broker must send *K*'s license to the Department of Real Estate, and the license must be activated with her future employer.
    b. her current broker must notify the commissioner in writing of the change.
    c. *K* must notify the commissioner in writing of the change in her employment.
    d. her current broker must return *K*'s license to her and she must activate it with her future broker.

20. Broker *A* took a listing on a small office complex owned by *F*. As the property is in exceptional condition and produces a steady income, *A* has decided to purchase it for himself as an investment. To comply with the Commissioner's Rules, *A* must

    a. resign as *F*'s agent and propose his offer only after *F* has retained another broker.
    b. have a third party purchase the property on his behalf.
    c. file a notice of the intended purchase with the Department of Real Estate.
    d. disclose his position and obtain *F*'s approval.

# 11
# Real Estate Financing

Arizona law authorizes the use of both mortgages and trust deeds (deeds of trust) to hypothecate real estate as security for a debt and to create a voluntary lien on the subject property. In Arizona, the trust deed is the preferred type of security instrument.

With regard to mortgage and trust deed loans, Arizona is a **lien theory** state. This means that a mortgage or deed of trust gives a lender a lien on the property rather than a title interest in the property. The law also provides that mortgages and trust deeds are not conveyances. Upon default, the owner of the mortgage or trust deed cannot recover the property without a foreclosure action. Trust deeds are foreclosed nonjudicially.

## PROMISSORY NOTES

The promissory note is one of the two instruments signed by the borrower in connection with a mortgage or trust deed loan. A promissory note is referred to as a **negotiable instrument**, that is, a written promise to pay a specific sum of money. An instrument is negotiable when its holder (the person to whom the money is to be paid) may negotiate, assign or transfer his or her right to the payment to a third party. This may be accomplished by signing the instrument over to the third party or, in some cases, by merely delivering the instrument to the third party. The new owner of the note is known as the **holder in due course**, as he or she is entitled to receive whatever rights were held by the original owner of the note. Other examples of negotiable instruments are checks and bank drafts.

To be negotiable, an instrument (such as a promissory note) must fulfill the requirements established by the Uniform Commercial Code (UCC). To be negotiable, the instrument must

- be in writing,
- be made payable from one person to another,
- be signed by the maker (the one who agrees to pay the money) and
- contain an unconditional promise to pay a sum of money either at a specific future date or on the demand of the holder of the instrument.

In addition, the instrument must be made payable either to a specific, named person ("to order") or to the person who has physical possession of the instrument ("to bearer"). Instruments that are payable "to order" are transferred by the endorsement of the holder. Instruments that are payable "to bearer" may be transferred by physical delivery.

A promissory note used with a mortgage or trust deed loan must always be payable to the mortgagee named in the mortgage or to the beneficiary named in the trust deed.

## Types of Notes

Generally, three types of promissory notes are used with mortgages and trust deeds. A **straight note** calls for periodic payments of interest only, with the principal to be paid at the end of the loan term. An **installment note** calls for a set periodic payment of the principal, plus an additional amount for the interest due on the unpaid principal balance. An **amortized note**, the most commonly used note, requires a set periodic payment that is first applied to the interest due on the principal balance, with the remainder of the payment being used to reduce that principal balance.

## MORTGAGES

In Arizona, a mortgage is similar to an ordinary deed, but includes a **defeasance clause** that states, "To be void upon (the) condition that I pay . . . " and other pertinent provisions. A mortgage is a contract and therefore must include all of the elements of a contract as described in Chapter 7.

## Recording a Mortgage

When a loan is secured using real estate as the collateral, the borrower signs two documents. The promissory note is the evidence of the debt created by the borrower (the "mortgagor"), and the mortgage is the security for the note. If it is necessary for the lender (the "mortgagee") to foreclose, the basis for the foreclosure suit is the specific set of rights granted to the mortgagee in the mortgage.

The mortgage must be in writing, signed by all parties and acknowledged before an authorized official (usually a notary public). In addition, the mortgage should be recorded in the county in which the property is located to give constructive notice of the mortgagor's obligation and to establish the priority of the mortgagee's lien. (In Arizona, lien priorities are determined according to the date and time of recordation, except for a mechanic's lien, which takes priority from the date the first work was performed. One exception to this rule is a mortgage that has been subordinated by agreement.)

While the law does not require a mortgage to be recorded to be valid, the mortgagee will naturally want to protect his or her security interest in the property by recording the mortgage. An unrecorded mortgage is still valid between the parties, but it does not protect the rights of the parties against subsequent purchasers or lenders who do not have actual notice of the mortgage.

The recorded lien continues in effect until the note is paid off or until the lien is foreclosed, released by a court order or barred by the statute of limitations. Although payment of the note terminates the lien, the county records should be updated by recording a **satisfaction piece** (also known as a satisfaction of mortgage or a satisfaction of lien).

## Assignment of the Mortgage

A mortgage may be assigned from one mortgagee (lender) to another. The assignment must be in writing, signed, acknowledged and recorded. In addition, the note must be endorsed by the mortgagee and delivered to the new owner along with the mortgage.

## Release of the Mortgage

When a real estate loan secured by a mortgage has been completely repaid, the mortgage may be released in one of two ways. A notation acknowledging the release (or satisfaction) may be written in the margin of the recorded mortgage document and signed by the mortgagee in the presence of the county recorder. The more common method of releasing a mortgage is recording a separate satisfaction piece, which is signed by the mortgagee and states that the mortgage loan has been paid, satisfied or discharged. If a mortgagee fails to discharge a mortgage lien within 60 days after the mortgage is satisfied, a title insurer may prepare, execute and record a satisfaction piece for a reasonable fee.

## Foreclosure of the Mortgage—The Sheriff's Sale

If the mortgagor defaults (that is, fails to pay off the loan as agreed or violates some other provision of the mortgage contract), the mortgagee can file a foreclosure suit. In the suit, the mortgagee requests a sheriff's sale of the security property to satisfy the outstanding debt. Usually, a title search of the property is made so all those who have a possible interest in the property or who might be adversely affected by the foreclosure are notified and given an opportunity to protect their interests. Junior mortgages and other junior liens are usually eliminated by a mortgagee's foreclosure action.

A **lis pendens** (notice of pending litigation) is filed with the county recorder, and all parties are served with a summons and complaint. The foreclosure action is the result of a breach of contract by the mortgagor; and unless there are mitigating circumstances, the court will find in favor of the plaintiff mortgagee and issue a judgment to that effect. Then the court issues a **writ of execution** authorizing the county sheriff to sell the property. The sale must be advertised at least once each week for four consecutive weeks in a newspaper of general circulation in the county where the property is located, after which the sheriff's sale can be held. The successful purchaser at a mortgage foreclosure sale receives a "certificate of sale" from the county sheriff.

## Redemption Procedures

**Equity of Redemption.** Arizona law provides for the common law concept of **equity of redemption** (or equitable redemption). Equitable redemption permits a defaulted mortgagor to redeem the property up until the time of the sheriff's sale. The mortgagor may redeem the property during this period if he or she pays the entire amount of the debt awarded by the court in the foreclosure suit, plus whatever interest and costs have been incurred by the mortgagee in the foreclosure.

**Statutory Redemption.** In addition to the right of equitable redemption, Arizona law provides for a statutory redemption period, which takes place after a sheriff's sale. In Arizona, the statutory redemption period is six months. During this period, the mortgagor may redeem the property by making a lump-sum payment through the court to the purchaser of the certificate of sale. That payment must include the price for which the certificate of sale was purchased, plus interest at the annual rate of 10 percent, prorated for the period of time between the sale and the redemption. The redeeming mortgagormust also repay the purchaser for any taxes and assessments that the purchaser has paid; a reasonable sum for any insurance premiums, maintenance and repairs the purchaser has paid; and interest on the entire amount. If the mortgagor redeems the property, all subordinate liens against the property that were released by the foreclosure action are reinstated as of the date of the foreclosure sale.

If the defaulted mortgagor does not redeem the property within the six-month statutory period, junior creditors or lienholders may redeem the property. The creditor holding the lien with the highest priority after the foreclosed mortgage may redeem the property within five days of the expiration of the six-month period. At the expiration of the first five-day period, the creditor having the lien of the next-highest priority may redeem within five days, and so on, until all junior lienholders have been given an opportunity to redeem the property.

A creditor redeeming the property must pay the purchaser of the certificate of sale the amount for which the certificate was purchased; he or she must also pay off any superior liens against the property. Any subordinate creditor who wants to redeem the property must record and serve upon the county sheriff a written statement of his or her intentions to do so. This statement must be recorded and served within six months after the sheriff's sale.

If neither the defaulted mortgagor nor any of the mortgagor's creditors redeem the property, the purchaser of the certificate of sale will receive the sheriff's deed to the property and thus become the legal owner.

## Deficiency Judgments

A mortgagee may be entitled to obtain a deficiency judgment—a personal judgment against the defaulted mortgagor—if the foreclosure sale does not produce sufficient funds to pay the loan balance and the expenses of the foreclosure. Under Arizona mortgage law, defaulting mortgagors who cause the mortgagee to "lose" money under a mortgage foreclosure may be held personally liable for such an amount. However, there is one major exception to this general rule. If the mortgage was to secure the purchase of residential property (property that is two-and-one-half acres or less and is used for a one-family or two-family dwelling), the mortgagee cannot obtain a deficiency judgment against the mortgagor. The exception is federally insured or guaranteed mortgage loans. Remember, federal law supersedes state statutes.

## TRUST DEEDS

In Arizona, trust deeds have almost exclusively replaced mortgages as the lender's choice of security instruments. Because of the greatly reduced time and expense of trust deed foreclosures compared to mortgage foreclosure, lenders—particularly those whose funds come from outside the state—prefer to use trust deeds.

The Arizona Trust Deed Act (ARS Section 33–801 through Section 33–821) has been in effect since August 1971. A trust deed is a three-party instrument involving the borrower (the "trustor"), the lender (the "beneficiary") and the third party (the "trustee," who represents the beneficiary). The trustee is given a "limited power of sale" (sometimes referred to as "bare" title or "naked" title), and it allows the trustee to sell the property on behalf of the beneficiary in the event of default.

As stated earlier, a trust deed does not convey the title to the property to the trustee; it merely gives the beneficiary a lien on the property, which may be foreclosed through a trustee's sale.

The law provides that the trustee and the beneficiary must be two different persons or entities. Arizona Revised Statutes Section 33–803 lists the necessary qualifications for a trustee. Generally, any of the following may serve as a trustee under a trust deed in Arizona:

- An Arizona real estate broker
- An attorney who belongs to the Arizona State Bar
- An insurance agent licensed in Arizona
- A bank, savings and loan association, trust company or other financial institution authorized to transact business under Arizona or federal law
- An insurance company or escrow company authorized to transact business under Arizona law

Most first trust deeds are made out to title insurance companies or to affiliated firms of financial institutions. Most junior trust deeds are typically in the name of a selected title insurance company.

## Use of the Trust Deed

In creating a trust deed loan, the trustor signs a trust deed and a promissory note. These are then held by the beneficiary until the debt is completely repaid, the trust deed is assigned or the trustor defaults under the terms of the note. The trustee does not have to be an active participant in the security transaction until there is a default or until the debt is repaid and the trustee must convey the bare or naked title back to the trustor. In either case, the beneficiary must request the trustee's services in writing.

In the event of a default, the trustee has the authority to foreclose the property and sell it without court proceedings under the power-of-sale clause (this is referred to as a "nonjudicial foreclosure"). The power of sale clause is the principal reason for the popularity of trust deeds as security instruments.

## Recording a Trust Deed

Recording a trust deed is similar to recording a mortgage in that the document is recorded in the county in which the property is located. This is done to protect the lender's interest in the property and to establish the priority of the trust deed lien. Even though an unrecorded trust deed is still valid between the parties, it will not protect the parties against the claims of subsequent purchasers of either the property or the trust deed and note.

The recorded trust deed lien continues in effect until the note is paid off or until the lien is foreclosed, released by a court order or barred by the statute of limitations. Although payment of the note terminates the effect of the lien, the trustee is responsible for the delivery of a deed of reconveyance to the trustor, which will cancel the trust deed lien when recorded. The trustor is responsible for recording the deed of reconveyance.

## Assignment of the Trust Deed

To assign a trust deed to a third party, the beneficiary must complete an "Assignment of Trust Deed by Beneficiary," which is signed, acknowledged and recorded. Then the assigned trust deed and note are delivered to the third party. Recording the assignment form with the county recorder is sufficient notice to the trustee of its existence.

Occasionally there are circumstances under which a trustee must be replaced. For example, when the trust deed is assigned by the original beneficiary, the third party receiving the trust deed may want a new trustee. In these situations, the holder of the trust deed must inform the original trustee of his or her intention to replace that trustee. The new trustee must be informed of and consent to the replacement in writing.

## Release of the Trust Deed

When a loan secured by a trust deed has been completely repaid, the beneficiary completes a "Request for Full Reconveyance" form (which is located on the reverse side of the trust deed). He or she must then deliver the trust deed to the trustee, together with the promissory note (which is generally marked "paid in full") and any other papers (such as a fire insurance policy) that must be returned to the trustor. After receiving the written request, the trustee signs and delivers a trustee's "Deed of Reconveyance" to the trustor, which conveys the bare or naked title back to the trustor. The deed of reconveyance should be acknowledged and recorded to clear the title to the property and cancel the trust deed lien.

## Foreclosure of the Trust Deed—The Trustee's Sale

If the trustor defaults on the trust deed, the beneficiary sends a written request to the trustee asking the trustee to institute foreclosure proceedings. The trustee must advertise the sale of the property at least once each week for four consecutive weeks, as well as schedule the date, time and location of the trustee's sale. To exercise the power of sale contained in the trust deed, the trustee must sign and record a "Beneficiary's Notice of Default and Election to Sell." The Notice of Default identifies the specific trust deed involved, states that there has been a breach of contract (the promissory note), declares the entire debt due and payable and stipulates the date, time and location of the trustee's sale.

After recording the Notice of Default, the trustee must mail a Notice of Sale to all those who have a possible interest in the property or who might be adversely affected by the foreclosure. The Notice of Sale must be personally served on the occupants of the property (whether they are the owners or tenants) or posted on the property at least 90 days before the sale. The four-week advertising requirement must also be met during this 90-day period.

At the trustee's sale, the trustee auctions off the property to the highest bidder, who receives a trustee's deed. Once the successful bidder has received the trustee's deed, he or she becomes the legal owner of the property; and all rights to the property held by the defaulting trustor are terminated.

## Reinstatement Procedures

**Rights of Reinstatement.** Under the Arizona Trust Deed Act, a trustor or a subordinate creditor may reinstate the trust deed at any time between the default and the trustee's sale. This is accomplished by paying the amount of the delinquency, the beneficiary's expenses associated with the default plus any trustee's fees and attorney's fees incurred as a result of the default (the fees for the trustee and any attorney may not exceed $250 or one-half of one percent of the entire unpaid principal sum—whichever is greater—for each party); and the fees charged for services rendered by one party cannot duplicate or include the fees charged for services rendered by the other party. Although there can be no equitable relief after the trustee's sale, the 90-day waiting period that must elapse between the Notice of Sale and the sale itself serves as the trustor's opportunity to reinstate the trust deed by bringing himself or herself "current" in terms of any financial obligations to the beneficiary.

The purpose of the reinstatement provisions of trust deed law is to allow a defaulted trustor the opportunity to correct (without the loss of his or her property) any minor problems that may occur, such as a late payment due to postal service problems or a misunderstanding about the amounts required for impound accounts. Thus, the trustor is less likely to lose his or her property due to error if the property's financing is secured by a trust deed.

**Statutory Redemption.** There is no statutory redemption period for property sold at a trustee's sale in Arizona.

## Judicial Foreclosure

In the event of a default, the beneficiary has an alternative to the trustee's sale: judicial foreclosure. Should the beneficiary believe it beneficial to sue the trustor in court for breach of contract (to avoid the loss of deficiency judgment rights, for example), he or she may follow the procedures of a court-ordered foreclosure and sheriff's sale as prescribed for mortgage foreclosure.

## Deficiency Judgments

As with mortgages, Arizona law prohibits deficiency judgments in a trustee's sale of a property that is a single-family residence or duplex on two-and-one-half acres or less.

## DEED IN LIEU OF FORECLOSURE

A defaulting mortgagor or trustor often wants only to "get out from under" the debt against a property that was financed. In such a situation, the borrower may give a **deed in lieu of foreclosure** to the lender. This type of deed states that the conveyance is being made because the borrower is in default, cannot make his or her payments and wants the debt to be discharged.

With a deed in lieu of foreclosure, the borrower conveys only his or her interest in the property, but there are benefits for both the borrower and the lender. Although the borrower must forfeit his or her equity in the property when giving a deed in lieu of foreclosure, the deed is less injurious to the borrower's credit rating than a completed foreclosure would be, and there is no possibility of a deficiency judgment. The lender will receive the property more quickly than through a foreclosure action, and there are no redemption or reinstatement periods. Thus, the property can be placed on the market more quickly with a price favorable to the lender.

However, a lender is not obligated to accept a deed in lieu of foreclosure. If it would be disadvantageous to accept the deed, the lender can refuse the deed and proceed with the appropriate foreclosure action against the borrower.

## "CASH TO LOAN" SITUATIONS

Often, a purchaser wants to "buy out" a seller's equity position in a property and take title with the existing financing in place. Such transactions are often referred to as "cash to mortgage" transactions, although—with the predominant use of trust deeds in Arizona—a more accurate phrase would be "cash to loan."

Three situations can arise in a cash to loan transaction, based on the relative degrees of liability for the existing financing that the seller is willing to retain and the purchaser is willing to accept. It is imperative that a licensee involved in such a transaction correctly word the proposed financing arrangements in the purchase contract. The licensee is also obligated to inform and explain to all of the parties their rights, obligations and liabilities regarding the existing financing.

With the written permission of the original lender, a property may be sold "subject to" existing financing; and the seller remains totally liable for the payment of the loan balance even though the purchaser owns the property. In this situation, the purchaser does not have to qualify with the lender for the balance of the loan. While this may appear financially risky for the seller, the risk depends upon the amount of cash taken by the seller for his or her equity and the relationship of the balance of the loan to the market value of the property.

If the purchaser "assumes" the existing financing, the wording in the purchase contract should refer to the purchaser "assuming and agreeing to pay" the loan balance. In this situation, the purchaser will have to qualify with the lender to assume the loan balance and thus become primarily liable for the payment of the loan. The liability of the seller is reduced to a secondary position, and the seller would be liable only for any deficiency judgment that might result from a foreclosure action by the lender.

If the seller wants to be totally released from any liability for the existing financing, an "assumption with novation" may be arranged. As previously noted, a purchaser would have to qualify with the lender to assume the loan balance and primary liability for its payment. The novation part of this arrangement occurs when the lender gives the seller a written release of liability (a novation certificate) from the loan assumed by the purchaser. The advantage of the novation is that the seller can obtain new financing on another property without having to qualify for two loan payments, as would occur with the "subject to" financing and possibly the assumption without a novation situation.

## PURCHASE MONEY FINANCING

Sometimes a purchaser does not have adequate funds to buy out the seller's equity position in the property. In this situation, the purchaser can ask the seller to extend credit to the purchaser in an amount equal to the difference between the seller's equity and the purchaser's available cash. This extension of credit is referred to as **purchase money financing**, a **seller carryback** or a **soft money loan**.

The parties can use either a note and a mortgage, or a note and a trust deed, or an agreement for sale to secure the amount of credit extended. The documents used will depend on many factors, such as the risk perceived by the seller in extending credit, the amount of the credit, the terms of the credit, the foreclosure rights of the seller, the seller's immediate need for cash and the seller's desire to sell the loan to an investor.

Should the seller need to foreclose, he or she would use the foreclosure procedures appropriate for the type of documents used to secure the credit. However, because purchase money financing does not involve the transfer of cash that an institutional loan would, the seller is not entitled to any deficiency judgment; at best, the seller could only recover the property from the purchaser.

## AGREEMENTS FOR SALE

The agreement for sale (also called a contract for deed, contract for sale, installment contract, installment sales contract or land contract) is the third alternative for financing the purchase of real property in addition to trust deeds and mortgages. Under an agreement for sale, the seller (the vendor) extends credit to the purchaser (the vendee) to facilitate the sale of the property. The vendee is entitled to possess the property while making regular installment payments to the vendor, but the vendee will not receive the deed from the vendor until the terms of the contract have been fulfilled.

### Making an Agreement for Sale

In drafting an agreement for sale, a licensee should provide for a number of factors. As in a real estate purchase contract, the purchase price and the method by which it will be paid must be specifically stated. If the property being sold on an agreement for sale is encumbered by an existing mortgage or trust deed loan, the contract should state this information, identify in detail the encumbrance that the property is subject to and—most importantly—specify whether the vendor or the vendee must make the underlying loan payments while the agreement for sale is in effect. (Existing loans that affect property being sold on an agreement for sale are often referred to as "underlying encumbrances.")

A similar situation arises when the property being sold under an agreement for sale is subject to an existing agreement for sale under which the vendor owes money. In this situation, the new agreement for sale should describe the interest in the property that the vendor is selling (the equitable ownership). It should identify in detail the existing agreement for sale, the parties to that contract, its date and term and the balance still unpaid. The new agreement for sale should also specify whether the vendor or the vendee must make the payments on the underlying agreement for sale.

### Possession

In the absence of an agreement to the contrary, the right to possess property generally follows the legal title (the deed). However, under an agreement for sale, the deed will not be given to the vendee for a number of years, yet the vendee expects to use the property during that time. Therefore, any agreement for sale should include provisions for the vendor's delivery of possession to the vendee, as well as a definite possession date.

### Judgment Against the Vendee

In general, the vendee under an agreement for sale who has a judgment recorded against his or her property can assign the agreement for sale interest to a creditor without having the judgment become a lien against that property. This applies in all situations except when the lien is a federal tax lien. Such a lien affects all ownership interests, whether they are outright interests in real property or equitable interests under an agreement for sale.

## Default by the Vendee

In some states, when the vendee under an agreement for sale misses even a single payment, the vendor automatically has the right to terminate the contract, repossess the property, and keep all of the funds he or she has received under the contract. This is known as **strict forfeiture**. However, the concept of equitable title as adopted by Arizona precludes such an event. As the equitable owner of the property, a vendee is protected by law, and the vendor must take legal action against the vendee to recover the equitable ownership rights.

In the event of a default, the vendor generally has the right to initiate a suit either to foreclose on the agreement for sale or to sue the vendee directly to obtain a personal judgment against him or her. However, most agreement for sales in Arizona include some type of forfeiture clause, which provides that the vendor can declare the vendee's interest in the property forfeited if there is a default in the payments. The defaulted vendee will be granted a statutory period of time during which he or she can cure the default and reinstate the contract, based on the percentage of the total contract price already paid by the vendee.

Some agreement for sale forms contain a clause that provides that the vendor's only remedy in a default is to institute judicial foreclosure proceedings, but this is not a common occurrence.

## Forfeiture by the Vendee

Arizona Revised Statutes Sections 33–741 through 33–749 provide specific details on the remedies available to a vendor under a defaulted agreement for sale. Should the vendor file a foreclosure suit, the court will issue an **interlocutory** (temporary) **decree**, which states the amount of money owed and gives the vendee a specified period of time in which to pay that amount. If the vendee fails to pay within the specified time period, the court will issue a final decree in favor of the vendor that forecloses all of the vendee's interest in the property. Because the foreclosure of an agreement for sale is an action in equity (it concerns the equitable title held by the vendee), the defaulted vendee does not receive the benefit of any statutory redemption or reinstatement period.

Most agreement for sales written in Arizona contain a forfeiture clause, which gives the vendor the right of a nonjudicial foreclosure against the vendee. **Forfeiture** is the preferred method of foreclosure because of the minimized time and expense involved compared to a judicial foreclosure. The forfeiture clause allows the vendor to declare the defaulted vendee's interest in the property forfeited, thus terminating the contract and permitting the vendor to retain all payments made by the vendee. The vendor must then wait the statutory time period to institute the forfeiture action. This time period is based on the percentage of the contract price that the vendee has paid. In effect, this waiting period creates a type of reinstatement period during which the defaulted vendee can reinstate the contract by making it current and thus cure the default. This is accomplished by paying all past due amounts and any penalties provided for in the contract.

The statutory waiting periods are as follows:

- If the vendee has paid less than 20 percent of the contract, the reinstatement period is 30 days.
- If the vendee has paid at least 20 percent but less than 30 percent of the contract, the reinstatement period is 60 days.
- If the vendee has paid at least 30 percent but less than 50 percent of the contract, the reinstatement period is 120 days.

- If the vendee has paid at least 50 percent of the contract, the reinstatement period is nine months.

For the purpose of computing the percentage of the purchase price that the vendee has paid under the contract, the following amounts may be added together:

- The down payments paid to the vendor
- The principal payments made to the vendor under the contract
- The principal payments paid to lienholders on the property, the principal portion of which constitutes a portion of the purchase price as stated in the contract

After the expiration of the appropriate reinstatement period, the vendor or the vendor's agent must record a "Notice of Election to Forfeit" with the county recorder in the county in which the property is located. A copy of the notice must also be mailed to or personally served on both the defaulted vendee and any other party with a secured interest in the property that is subordinate to the interest of the vendee; this must occur at least 20 days prior to the effective date of the forfeiture. During that 20-day period, the vendee or any other party can cure the default by paying the amount of the delinquency due (as specified in the contract) plus any penalties as provided for in the contract. In this regard, the reinstatement of an agreement for sale is similar to the reinstatement of a trust deed; the borrower can cure the default merely by paying any past-due amounts, plus whatever penalties and expenses are called for in the contract. If the default on the agreement for sale is cured, the vendor must record a "Notice of Reinstatement" with the county recorder, which will cancel the "Notice of Election to Forfeit."

If the defaulted vendee or other party does not cure the default within the 20-day period, the vendor or the vendor's agent must record an "Affidavit of Completion of Forfeiture." Once the affidavit is recorded, the vendee's interest in the property under the contract is terminated, and all equitable ownership rights revert to the vendor.

## LEGAL RATE OF INTEREST

Sometimes a situation occurs when an obligation to pay interest is created but no specific rate is agreed to by the parties, such as a contract where the interest rate has been inadvertently omitted or a judgment lien issued by the court. In such situations, Arizona law applies the legal rate of interest, which is currently 10 percent simple interest.

## SOURCES OF REAL ESTATE FINANCING

Prior to 1981, most institutional lenders—savings and loan associations (sometimes called thrifts), mutual savings banks, commercial banks, mortgage bankers and insurance companies—preferred to lend their funds to specific segments of the real estate industry. This market segmentation was based on both numerous federal and state regulations and long-established business relationships.

But in 1982, two major events at the federal level hastened the deregulation and restructuring of the real estate lending industry. The first of these was the 1982 decision of the U.S. Supreme Court in the case of *Fidelity Federal Savings and Loan Association* [of California] v. *de la Cuesta*. The Supreme Court held that the regulations promulgated by the Federal Home Loan Bank Board superseded any state regulations regarding real estate loans made by a federally chartered savings and loan association. In effect, this decision empowered all federally chartered savings and loan associations to enforce the due-on-sale clauses in their real estate loans for purely economic reasons. This caused federally chartered commercial banks and state-chartered lending institutions to demand parity in regard to their due-on-sale clauses. As a result, the second major event occurred: the Garn-St. Germain Depository Institutions Act, signed by President Reagan on October 15, 1982. This legislation provided for a gradual phasing out of the statutory differences among various federally regulated lending institutions. In keeping with both the spirit and the letter of the law, the Federal Home Loan Bank Board and the Federal Reserve Board began deregulating their savings and loan associations and commercial banks, respectively. At the same time, the Arizona Banking Department initiated legislation to deregulate its entities so that they could remain competitive with federally chartered institutions.

One result of the deregulation of financial institutions is the "savings and loan bailout," which cost the federal government billions of dollars. Another result is the gradual disappearance of the major differences between the lending practices of the various financial institutions.

## Savings and Loan Associations

Arizona has had both federally chartered and state-chartered savings and loan associations. State-chartered associations may be mutually owned or they may be organized as corporations, issuing and selling stock and paying dividends.

Arizona statutes require that all state-chartered associations belong to the Office of Thrift Supervision (OTS); thus, they are regulated by both the OTS and the Arizona Banking Department. Arizona also requires all state-chartered associations to participate in the Savings Association Insurance Fund (SAIF), which insures individual accounts to a maximum of $100,000.

In Arizona, the assets of many failed savings and loans have been purchased by commercial banks, primarily those doing business on an interstate basis. Although there are still many existing statutes that regulate savings and loan associations in Arizona, the Financial Institutions Reform, Recovery and Enforcement Act (FIRREA) has superseded most of these regulations nationally and transferred such regulation authority almost exclusively to the OTS and the Resolution Trust Corporation.

## Mutual Savings Banks

Counterparts to the savings and loan associations are the mutual savings banks. These depositor-owned institutions, which operate similarly to savings and loan associations, are located primarily in the northeastern United States. They are active participants in the residential real estate lending markets in their regions, although they may lend on nonresidential properties as well.

## Commercial Banks

Because of the deregulation of the banking industry, the lessening role of savings and loan associations in real estate lending, and the advent of interstate banking in Arizona, many commercial banks have active real estate loan departments or separate subsidiaries created specifically for such lending activities.

Both federally chartered and state-chartered banks operate in Arizona. Federally chartered banks must belong to the Federal Reserve System (FRS) and are regulated by the Federal Reserve Board (FRB). They must also participate in the Bank Insurance Fund (BIF) program, which insures deposits in bank accounts to a maximum of $100,000.

State-chartered banks are not required by the Arizona Banking Department to belong to the FRS; they are allowed to evaluate the relative costs and merits of FRS membership and join only if they decide it would be beneficial for them. However, state-chartered banks are required to participate in the BIF insurance program.

## Mortgage Bankers

**Mortgage bankers** (sometimes called mortgage banking companies) act primarily as loan correspondents; that is, they originate real estate loans with funds provided by other entities (such as insurance companies, pension funds, and individual investors) and then continue as the liaison between the lenders and the borrowers by servicing the loans that they originated.

Usually organized as a stock corporation, the mortgage banker is involved in all types of real estate lending activities. Each mortgage banker generally works with a specific group of investors, seeking borrowers for the investors' funds. When a real estate loan is originated, the mortgage banker is compensated by the borrower with the loan origination fee, usually one percent of the amount of money borrowed. After the origination of the loan, the mortgage banker will continue to work for the investor-lender by servicing the loan. Loan servicing involves activities such as receiving and accounting for principal and interest payments; establishing impound (escrow) accounts for real estate tax payments, hazard insurance premiums and mortgage insurance premiums; making tax payments and renewing insurance policies when they are due; handling defaults; and initiating and managing foreclosures. The mortgage banker is paid a separate fee for these services by the investor-lender.

Some mortgage bankers have sufficient funds of their own to make real estate loans that may later be sold to investors, with the mortgage banker receiving fees for servicing such loans.

Sometimes the mortgage banker will work with the promoters of a real estate project, seeking investors to provide funding for the project. The mortgage banker is capable of managing not only the flow of funds required by such a project but also the paperwork generated in the process. Some mortgage banking companies have special departments specifically for real estate development, which can take a project through the development process from planning and acquisition, to meeting the appropriate governmental requirements, to construction management, to the marketing and financing of the individual interests that might result from the project's completion.

For many years, Arizona had no real distinction between mortgage bankers and mortgage brokers, although their functions in the lending industry were not related. Mortgage bankers were known for their ability to service loans. However, Arizona Revised Statutes Sections 6–941 through 6–985, which became effective in 1987, now provide specific requirements for the licensing and operation of a mortgage banking enterprise.

## Mortgage Brokers

**Mortgage brokers** are individuals who are licensed to act as financial intermediaries, in that they bring borrowers and lenders together for a fee. They locate potential borrowers, process the preliminary loan applications and submit the applications to potential lenders for final approval. Frequently, they work with or for mortgage bankers in their activities. Mortgage brokers are compensated for their work by the loan origination fees (or a percentage of such fees) that they receive from the borrowers.

Mortgage brokers are now specifically licensed by Arizona Revised Statutes Sections 6–901 through 6–910, which became effective in 1987. However, many mortgage brokers are also real estate brokers who offer financing services in addition to their real estate brokerage activities. Arizona Revised Statutes Section 32–2155, paragraph C, indicates that a real estate licensee can collect both a fee for negotiating a real estate loan and a real estate commission in the same transaction, provided that

- the licensee is also licensed as a mortgage broker or mortgage banker or is an employee, officer or partner of the mortgage broker/mortgage banker entity,
- the licensee discloses to all parties compensating him or her that two separate fees are being paid for the two separate activities involved in the transaction, and
- the compensation does not violate any other state or federal law.

## Insurance Companies and Pension Funds

Insurance companies amass large sums of money from the premiums paid by their policy holders. Pension funds accumulate large sums of money from both corporate and individual contributions to retirement plans. While some of these funds are held in reserve to cover operating expenses and pay insurance claims and retirement benefits, a good portion of these funds is invested in profit-earning enterprises, such as long-term real estate loans.

Insurance companies and pension funds rely heavily on actuarial statistics to determine the likelihood of their paying claims and benefits. Because of the long-term nature of their liabilities, they prefer to balance these liabilities with long-term assets such as real estate loans on commercial, industrial and agricultural properties. They also invest in residential real estate loans by purchasing large blocks of FHA-insured and VA-guaranteed loans and other mortgage-backed securities (MBS) from the participants in the secondary mortgage market.

Insurance companies and pension funds will usually work through loan correspondents such as mortgage banking companies, although they will sometimes place their own representatives directly into areas with active real estate lending markets. In some situations they lend directly to borrowers, usually for the high-dollar long-time projects in which they can create a participation loan and earn not only the interest on the loan but also a percentage of the profits generated by the project. During the 1960s, large shopping centers were the favorite investments of insurance companies and pension funds, although pension fund involvement at that time was much less than it is today. In the 1970s, the preferred investments were large commercial projects, such as office buildings and industrial parks. The 1980s found the insurance companies and pension funds attempting to purchase farmland at the greatly reduced prices dictated by the marketplace. However, many states were concerned about the extinction of the "family farm" at the expense of corporate farming and, as a result, have enacted noncorporate-farming laws, which limit corporate farm ownership and management to family owned corporations. Arizona currently has no prohibition against the ownership or management of agricultural property by insurance companies or pension funds.

Because of the great amount of money that they control, insurance companies and pension funds are an important source of funds for nonresidential real estate loans. And because of their working through mortgage bankers—which are not as stringently regulated as commercial banks and savings and loan associations—these funds are put to productive use more quickly than they would be if the insurance companies and pension funds were to lend only through their own representatives.

## Endowed Institutions

Organizations that have been classified as tax-exempt by the Internal Revenue Service under Section 503 of the Internal Revenue Code often invest some of the contributions that they receive in real estate loans. Churches, charities, educational institutions, cultural associations, medical research groups and the like are permitted to invest their funds in profitable enterprises, as long as the organizations use those profits for the promotion of the goals for which they were established (such as providing religious education and services or finding a cure for a disease). These funds are usually invested through mortgage bankers, and sometimes the funds are earmarked for loans to borrowers with particular characteristics, such as a borrower from a minority group, a borrower with a certain religious affiliation or a borrower with a particular disease. Such loans are often called "ethical loans" within the industry because of the unique requirements placed on them by the organizations that provide their funds.

## Individuals

Individual investors and other private lenders supply an important source of funds for real estate loans, particularly for junior (second and third) loans. The arrangements are usually made through a mortgage banker or mortgage broker, although some individual investors prefer to make their loans directly to the borrowers. And while some investors have their loans serviced by a mortgage banker, others prefer to service the loans themselves.

The majority of loans made by individual investors are for smaller properties, usually single-family residences through fourplexes. Because there are no standardized lending practices for individuals and no statutory regulations as there are for financial institutions, many of these loans involve high-risk borrowers or types of property that would be unacceptable to institutional lenders. The individual investor is able to make the loan at an interest rate that is commensurate with the risk involved, even though he or she does not have the financial stability or diversity of risk that an institutional lender would.

## QUESTIONS

1. After a mortgage is recorded, who is the legal owner of the property?

    a. The mortgagor
    b. The mortgagee
    c. The trustor
    d. The beneficiary

2. Promising real property as collateral for a loan without giving up the possession of the property is known as

    a. pledging.
    b. hypothecating.
    c. nonamortizing.
    d. substitution.

3. When a purchaser closes escrow on a property that was bought subject to the existing financing, the

    a. purchaser assumes all liability for the repayment of the loan.
    b. seller is released from all liability except for a deficiency judgment.
    c. purchaser assumes no liability for the repayment of the loan.
    d. seller is released from all liability including a deficiency judgment.

4. A deed of reconveyance is used to

    a. cancel a mortgage lien in the public records.
    b. convey title to a trustee to hold in trust.
    c. cancel a trust deed lien in the public records.
    d. convey title to a trustor to hold in trust.

5. *F* has a trust deed loan on his residence from a commercial bank. According to the terms of *F*'s trust deed and note, the bank could initiate foreclosure proceedings against him for any of the following *except* failure to

    a. pay the loan interest as it comes due.
    b. obtain the bank's permission before renting the property.
    c. keep the property tax payments current.
    d. renew the property hazard insurance policy as appropriate.

6. *O* is losing his property through foreclosure for not keeping his loan payments current. All of the following are viable alternatives for *O* to consider *except*

    a. ask his lender to accept a deed in lieu of foreclosure to stop the foreclosure action and protect his credit rating.
    b. list his property with a local real estate broker and attempt to sell the property before the foreclosure is complete.
    c. attempt to lease the property on a long-term basis and use the rent payments to bring his loan current.
    d. try to refinance the property with his lender and use the cash from his equity to provide for future loan payments.

7. *W* obtained a deed of trust loan from a savings and loan association to purchase her single-family home, which is located on a city lot. She defaulted on the loan, and her lender foreclosed. She owed $130,000. The property sold at a foreclosure sale for $125,000. Which of the following statements is true?

   a. *W* has six months in which to redeem her property.
   b. The lender can get a deficiency judgment against *W*.
   c. The purchaser at the foreclosure sale will get a deed in lieu of foreclosure.
   d. All *W*'s rights in the property terminated when the property was sold at the foreclosure sale.

8. *S* is negotiating with *L* to purchase *L*'s property. *S* is willing to pay *L* her asking price of $107,500 if she will accept 15 percent of the price as downpayment and carry the balance on the following terms: quarterly principal payments of $1,745 and interest on the balance at 9 percent until the loan is paid. What type of financing is *S* trying to obtain?

   a. Term financing
   b. Balloon financing
   c. Nonamortizing financing
   d. Installment financing

9. *S* is purchasing ten acres of undeveloped land from *P* on an agreement for sale. She paid $135,000 for the property, giving *P* $24,000 in cash at the signing of the contract two years ago. Since that time she has made two annual interest payments of $9,400 each. If she now defaults on the contract, how long will *P* have to wait before initiating foreclosure proceedings against her?

   a. 30 days.
   b. 60 days.
   c. 120 days.
   d. 9 months.

10. *C* defaulted on his deed of trust loan. He has the right to reinstate the loan up until the day of the trustee's sale by paying

   a. the entire loan balance.
   b. only the past due amounts.
   c. all past due amounts, plus interest and expenses.
   d. nothing, because *C* has no right to reinstate the loan.

# 12
# Leases

In Arizona, a freehold estate is an "estate of indefinite duration," theoretically running forever or at least for the unknown lifetime of an individual. A leasehold estate is an "estate of definite duration," one in which a real property owner transfers the rights of possession and quiet enjoyment to another in exchange for some consideration.

Leasehold estates are considered to be personal property. Personal property of a tangible nature—such as automobiles, furniture and livestock—is called **chattel** (the Old English word from which we derive the word "cattle"). However, a personal property interest in real property (such as a leasehold estate) is intangible; it cannot be seen or touched. This type of personal property interest is referred to as **chattel real.**

There are four types of leasehold estates. The first type, an **estate for years,** is characterized by a definite term and a stated expiration date. No notice is required to terminate this type of estate. As a general rule, if the landlord sells the property, the purchaser is obligated to honor the terms of any leases in effect at the time of the sale. If the landlord or the tenant dies during the term of the lease, the heirs of the decedent are obligated to honor the terms of the lease, although the heirs would probably attempt to mitigate their obligations under the lease.

The second type of leasehold estate is an estate from period to period, commonly called a **periodic estate.** The lessee's rights continue from year-to-year or month-to-month or week-to-week or for some stipulated time period. At the end of each period, the lease automatically renews itself. If the lease's recurring period is at least one month in duration, the lessor or the lessee can terminate the lease by giving the other party at least 30-days' written notice. If the lease's recurring period is less than one month in duration (such as a week-to-week lease), the lease can be terminated with ten-day's written notice (ARS Section 33–1375).

The third type of leasehold estate is an **estate at will.** With this type of leasehold estate, the lessor-lessee relationship is informal and usually created by the oral consent of the lessor. (An estate at will is frequently compared to a license for the property's use.) An estate at will can be terminated by giving verbal notice to the lessee and allowing the lessee a reasonable time to vacate the premises.

The fourth leasehold estate is an **estate at sufferance,** which occurs when a lessee originally obtained possession of a property legally but who is remaining on the premises illegally. An estate at sufferance exists without the consent of the lessor. A lessee who stays on a property once his or her lease has expired (a holdover tenant), an owner who refuses to vacate a property lost through foreclosure and an owner who stays in property taken under eminent domain are all examples of tenants at sufferance. No notice is required to terminate this tenancy; the lessor normally institutes an eviction action to repossess the property.

## Essentials of a Valid Lease

A lease is a contract between the lessor (the landlord) and the lessee (the tenant) and, like any other contract, should include all of the terms and conditions of the agreement.

Under the Arizona Statute of Frauds (ARS Section 44–101), leases for more than one year must be in writing and signed by the lessor and the lessee to be enforceable. A lease for less than one year does not need to be in writing to be enforceable; a lease for exactly one year does not need to be in writing unless it will take effect at some time after its execution. Of course, it is advisable for the protection of both parties that all leases be in writing, regardless of the lease term.

A lease must specify the amount of rent or other consideration (such as labor contributed by a tenant), the dates of payment and the place of payment. Unless stated otherwise, rent is payable in advance at the beginning of each rent-paying term.

It is usually not necessary to record a short-term lease. However, long-term leases (leases with terms of five years or longer) are often acknowledged and recorded by the tenant to protect his or her interest against a subsequent purchaser or lender who might not have actual knowledge of the lease.

## Options

**Renewal Options.** Options are sometimes included in a lease. An option to renew a lease allows the tenant to renew or extend the lease for another term when the original lease expires. Under the clause, the tenant is given a definite period of time prior in which to notify the landlord of his or her decision to exercise the option and renew the lease. Typically, the tenant is given the right to renew a lease only once.

Some leases provide for automatic renewal or extension. In this situation, the tenant must notify the landlord if he or she does not desire to renew the lease.

**Options to Buy.** Some leases grant the lessee an option to purchase the leased property. The purchase price is usually stated in the option clause in some manner—either as a specific price or as a formula that can be used to calculate the purchase price when the option is exercised. Sometimes, the clause may simply require the parties to negotiate a sales price when the option is exercised. Options to purchase are frequently included in ground leases (where the tenant leases unimproved property and then builds a structure on it).

An option to purchase should not be confused with a lease/purchase. With a lease/purchase, the tenant leases property that he or she has agreed to purchase for a specified price at a future date. Lease/purchases may be arranged for tax and investment reasons, and are often used to give a purchaser time to acquire the funds necessary to close a purchase transaction.

## ARIZONA RESIDENTIAL LANDLORD AND TENANT ACT

In 1972, the Uniform Residential Landlord and Tenant Act was drafted to simplify the rights and obligations of parties to residential property leases. In 1973, Arizona became the first state to adopt the uniform act. Since then, many states have adopted either some or all of the provisions of the uniform act.

The Arizona Residential Landlord and Tenant Act addresses only residential leasing situations. The act does not affect Arizona's original landlord and tenant statutes, which still apply to nonresidential leasehold interests.

### The Scope of the Landlord and Tenant Act (ARS Section 33–1308)

The provisions of the act apply to all residential leases except

- residence at a public or private institution, if the residence is incidental to detention or the provision of medical, educational, counseling or religious services;
- occupancy of a residential property sold on a land contract, if the occupant is the purchaser or a successor to the purchaser's interest;
- occupancy by a member of a fraternal or social organization in a structure operated for the benefit of the organization;
- transient occupancy in a hotel, motel or recreational lodge;
- occupancy by an employee of a lessor as a manager or custodian whose right to occupancy is conditional upon employment on the premises;
- occupancy by an owner of a condominium unit or a holder of a proprietary lease in a cooperative; and
- occupancy in or the operation of public housing as authorized, provided or conducted under Arizona or federal law.

### Discrimination Against Persons with Children (ARS Section 33–1317)

Anyone who knowingly refuses to rent or lease a residential dwelling unit to a person because that person has children is guilty of a petty offense under Arizona law (such a refusal would also be in violation of the Arizona Fair Housing Act and the Federal Fair Housing Act). The same holds true for anyone who advertises restrictions against children in connection with the renting or leasing of residential property. Civil penalties can include actual damages, three times the monthly rent, court costs and attorneys' fees.

Note that it is also a violation of the act to rent or lease property to families with children if that property—or the subdivision in which it is located—has a valid deed restriction or meets the requirements for housing for older persons. Furthermore, no one can be forced to rent or lease property to families with children if it would violate any previously published reasonable occupancy standards that address health and safety considerations, including a ratio of the number of occupants to the size of the unit.

### Security Deposits (ARS Section 33–1321)

The act places restrictions on the amount of security deposit a landlord can require. A security deposit (including prepaid rent) can be no greater than one-and-one-half times a month's rent. A landlord can require additional deposits for such items as cleaning, redecorating and pets as long as the purpose for the deposits is stated in writing. Any deposit that is not designated as nonrefundable will automatically be considered refundable.

When a lease expires, a landlord can apply the security deposit against all unpaid rent and other charges stated in the lease and/or damages caused to the property. In order to do so, however, the damages must be itemized on a written notice that must be given to the tenant within 14 days (excluding weekends and holidays) after the expiration of the lease. Any remaining amounts must be returned to the tenant within that same 14-day period. If the deposit (or what is left of the deposit) is not returned within the 14-day period, the lessee may seek damages equal to the amount due, plus an amount that is equal to twice the amount of deposit wrongfully withheld.

## Disclosures (ARS Section 33–1322)

On or before the beginning of a leasehold estate, the landlord or his or her representative must disclose to the tenant in writing the name and address of both the person authorized to manage the premises and the person who will represent the landlord for the purposes of the service of process and the receipt of notices and demands. This information must be kept current.

If the lease is in writing, each party must receive a properly signed copy of the lease. The lease contract must be entirely filled in (there can be no blank spaces), or the party responsible for the blank space can be deemed a breach of the contract. For those moving into leased premises or entering into a new lease after January 1, 1996, the landlord must furnish the tenant with

- a signed copy of the lease,
- a move-in form (used to specify existing damage to the premises) and
- written notice that the tenant may be present at the move-out inspection. (NOTE: if the landlord has reason to fear the tenant, the landlord does not have to arrange for a joint move-out inspection.)

These documents must be given to the tenant when he or she moves into the premises. Furthermore, at or before the tenancy begins, the landlord must inform the tenant, in writing, that a free copy of the Arizona Residential Landlord and Tenant Act is available from the Arizona Secretary of State's office.

## Rules and Regulations (ARS Section 33–1342)

A landlord can establish reasonable, equitable and understandable rules and regulations concerning use and occupancy of the property as long as they

- promote the convenience, safety or welfare of the tenants, preserve the property, or make a fair distribution of services and facilities;
- are reasonably related to their purpose;
- apply to all tenants in a fair manner;
- are sufficiently explicit to enable the tenants to understand and comply with them;
- are not for the purpose of evading the landlord's legal obligations; and
- the tenant has notice of them when he or she enters into the lease agreement.

If a rule is adopted after a lease has been entered into, it becomes enforceable only after the tenant's 30-day notice of the rule, and it does not result in a substantial modification of the original contract.

If state, county, or municipal entities change their rules affecting existing rental agreements, the landlord may immediately change the terms of the rental agreement to bring them into compliance with the law. The landlord must then notify the tenant in writing that the agreement has been changed and explain the changes and the effective date.

## Landlord's Obligations (ARS Section 33–1324)

Under the Landlord Tenant Act, a landlord is responsible for providing safe, habitable premises to his or her tenants. The landlord must comply with all applicable building and housing codes that affect the property. He or she is responsible for maintaining the common areas and for keeping all electrical, plumbing, heating, air-conditioning and other major systems in good operating condition. The landlord must also provide adequate waste and trash receptacles and arrange for waste and trash removal. Running water and reasonable amounts of hot water must be available to each tenant, and the landlord must make all the repairs necessary to keep the premises in a fit and habitable condition.

The landlord and the tenant can arrange to share some of these obligations, including repairs, maintenance, alterations and remodeling. All agreements must be in writing and properly signed, with each party receiving a sign copy of the document. However, no such agreement will be enforceable against the tenant if it was negotiated by the landlord for the purpose of avoiding his or her obligations to the tenant.

Sometimes, a landlord purchases utility services in bulk for distribution throughout the property and charges the tenants for those services. This situation is common when the property is master metered—there is only one service entrance to and one meter for the property, and the distribution system for such service is located entirely on the property. When a property is master metered, the aggregate amounts charged to the tenants cannot exceed the total amount paid by the landlord for those services. Water, electricity, natural gas and cable television are the most common master-metered services.

If the landlord sells the property, he or she is usually relieved of all liability for anything occurring after the sale, except in the instance of gross negligence. However, the sale of the property does not terminate the landlord's liability to account for all the deposits held on behalf of the tenants; the landlord either transfers them to the purchaser or refunds them to the tenants according to the terms of the lease and sale documents.

## Tenant's Obligations (ARS Section 33–1341)

A tenant must comply with all applicable building and housing codes that affect the property. He or she is responsible for maintaining the leased premises so that they are as clean and safe as the condition of the property permits, including properly disposing of trash and waste generated on the leased premises. The lessee must use all utility systems (such as water, heating and air-conditioning) and elevators in a reasonable manner and keep all plumbing fixtures as clean as their use permits.

The tenant and any of the tenant's guests must conduct themselves so as not to disturb the peaceful enjoyment of the property by the other tenants. This includes providing adequate supervision and cleanup for children and pets.

Occasionally, a tenant may make improvements to the leased premises without the written consent of the lessor, for example, the installation of special plumbing fixtures (such as shower heads and water purifiers), built-in bookshelves, hanging lamps and ceiling fans, and special wiring for telephone and cable television service. These additions often become the real property of the landlord and the lessee may not have the right to remove them. For the protection of both parties, the lease (or a separate agreement) should provide for

- what items a tenant can install,
- what type of installation is allowed by the tenant,
- when and how such items are to be removed by the lessee,
- the ownership of any questionable items and
- how repairs must be made when an item is removed and who must pay for them..

## Landlord's Right to Enter (ARS Section 33–1343 and Section 33–1376)

Normally, a tenant is given exclusive possession of the leased premises. However, under the act, a landlord is given the right to enter the leased premises during reasonable hours to inspect the unit, make necessary or agreed repairs or alterations, supply or maintain services or show the unit to workmen or to actual or prospective lessees, purchasers or lenders. The landlord must give the tenant 48 hours' notice of his intent to enter.

In emergency situations, the landlord can enter the premises without notice or permission.

If a tenant refuses to allow lawful entry, the landlord can either obtain an injunction to force access or terminate the lease. In either situation, the landlord can recover any actual damages caused by the tenant's refusal.

Note that a landlord cannot use this right to enter to harass the tenant. If the landlord makes an unlawful entry or a lawful entry in an unreasonable manner, or if he or she makes repeated demands for entry that have the effect of harassing the tenant, the tenant can either obtain an injunction to stop the activity or terminate the lease. In either situation, the tenant can recover any actual damages caused by the landlord's action or damages in the amount of one month's rent, whichever is greater.

## Tenant's Remedies for the Landlord's Noncompliance
## (ARS Section 33–1361, Section 33–1362 and Section 33–1364)

**General Noncompliance.** If a landlord significantly fails to meet his or her obligations under the act (particularly those regarding habitability), the tenant can give the landlord a written notice of breach of lease that (1) identifies the acts and omissions that constitute the breach and (2) states that, unless the landlord corrects the breach within ten days of the receipt of the notice, the lease will terminate in ten days.

If the landlord's noncompliance materially affects the health and safety of the tenant, the lease can be terminated in five days if the breach is not corrected by the landlord within five days of the receipt of the notice.

In addition to terminating the lease, the tenant can sue for damages, obtain a refund of any security deposit held by the landlord and obtain an injunction against the landlord directing him or her to correct the breach.

If the landlord corrects the conditions that caused the breach of the lease prior to the date specified in the notice or if the conditions were caused by the deliberate or negligent acts or omissions of the tenant or the tenant's family or guests, the lease will not terminate.

**Failure to Provide Services.** If the landlord fails, either deliberately or negligently, to supply water, gas or electrical services, reasonable amounts of hot water, heating, air-conditioning or other services specified in the lease, the tenant can give the lessor a written notice of breach of lease and then either

- acquire the services not provided and deduct their cost from the rent due;
- recover damages based on the reduced value of the leased premises while the services were not being provided; or
- procure reasonable substitute housing during the period of the landlord's noncompliance.

In the first instance, if the failure to provide the services is caused by the landlord's failure to pay his or her utility bill, and there are no individual meters for each tenant, the tenant (or all the tenants) can arrange with the utility company to pay the landlord's bill (after written notice to the landlord of the tenant's intent to do so). The tenant(s) may then deduct from the amount of rent owed the amount of the payment made to the utility company on the landlord's behalf.

In the third instance listed above, the tenant is excused from paying rent until the landlord provides the necessary services.

Again, the tenant's rights are waived if the failure to provide services is the result of the intentional or negligent acts of the tenant or the tenant's family or guests. (ARS Section 33–1363)

**Failure to Deliver Possession.** If a landlord fails to deliver physical possession of the leased premises, the tenant can either

- terminate the lease with a minimum five-day written notice, and recover any security deposit held by the lessor; or
- sue for the possession of the leased premises.

In the second situation, the tenant does not have to pay rent under the lease terms until he or she receives physical possession of the premises.

Occasionally, a landlord technically delivers possession, but the premises are unusable in their present condition or the landlord fails to provide agreed services. In that situation, the landlord is said to have "constructively" prevented the delivery of physical possession. When that occurs, the tenant can pursue one of the courses available for the failure to deliver services.

If a landlord willfully fails to deliver physical possession of the leased premises, the tenant may be able to recover damages equal to two months' rent or twice the actual damages sustained, whichever is greater.

## Self-Help for Minor Defects (ARS Section 33–1363)

If the landlord fails to properly maintain the property and the reasonable cost of such maintenance is equal to one-half of one month's rent or $300 (whichever is greater), the tenant can either

- recover damages or
- notify the lessor in writing of his or her intention to correct the unacceptable conditions at the landlord's expense.

If the landlord fails to correct the conditions within ten days of the receipt of the notice—or as soon after the receipt as an emergency situation might require—the tenant can employ a licensed contractor to correct the conditions and make the appropriate repairs, submit an itemized statement of costs and a waiver of lien to the landlord and deduct the cost of the repairs from the rent due (note that the cost of the repairs cannot exceed one-half of one month's rent or $300, whichever is greater).

Again, the tenant's rights are waived if maintenance problems are the result of the intentional or negligent acts of the tenant or the tenant's family or guests.

### Remedies for Tenant's Noncompliance (ARS Section 33–1368)

**General Noncompliance.** If the tenant significantly fails to meet his or her obligations to properly maintain the property and to act in such a way as to not interfere with other tenants' quiet enjoyment, the landlord can give the tenant a written notice of breach of lease that

- identifies the acts and omissions that constitute the breach, and
- states that, unless the lessee corrects the breach within ten days of the receipt of the notice, the lease will terminate in ten days.

If the tenant's noncompliance materially affects the health and safety of the landlord or the other tenants, the lease can be terminated in five days if the breach is not corrected within five days of the receipt of the notice.

If the tenant does correct the breach within the specified period of time, the lease will remain in effect. However, if there is another act of noncompliance of the same or a similar nature within the remainder of the term of the lease, the landlord can institute a special detainer action (which is necessary to remove the tenant from the premises) ten days after giving the lessee a written notice of the second instance of such noncompliance (ARS Section 33–1377).

**Material and Irreparable Noncompliance.** If the tenant's breach is both material and irreparable (such as the discharge of a firearm on the property, street gang activity, illegal drug activity or the infliction of serious bodily harm), the landlord can terminate the lease immediately—on written notice to the tenant—and may institute a special detainer action.

**Failure to Pay Rent.** If the tenant fails to pay the rent when it becomes due, the landlord can give the tenant a written notice of breach of lease stating that, unless the past-due rent and any reasonable late charge specified in the lease are paid within five days, the lease will terminate at the end of the fifth day. If the rent has not been paid by the end of the five-day period, the landlord can institute a special detainer action. Once the special detainer action is filed, the lease can be reinstated if the tenant pays the past-due rent, late charges, and any court costs and attorneys fees incurred by the landlord in connection with the breach. After a judgment has been entered in a special detainer action in favor of the landlord, reinstatement of the rental agreement is in the sole discretion of the landlord.

In addition to the remedies listed above, a landlord can recover all reasonable damages resulting from the tenant's noncompliance, including reasonable attorney's fees and all quantifiable damages caused by the tenant to the exterior of the unit. The landlord can also discontinue utility services that he or she has provided to the tenant on the day after the day on which a writ of restitution or a writ of execution is executed, as long as any disconnection is performed by a representative of the utility whose service is being disconnected.

A landlord is not required to accept a partial rent payment. If a landlord does accept a partial payment of rent, he or she still has the right to proceed against the tenant as long as the tenant agrees in writing to the terms and conditions of the continuation of the tenancy. If the tenant then breaches this "partial payment" agreement, the landlord may terminate the tenancy without additional notice.

## Abandonment

Abandonment is defined as an absence from the leased premises for at least seven days without notice to the landlord, when the rent is at least ten days past due.

If a tenant abandons the leased premises, the landlord must send the tenant a notice of abandonment by certified mail with a return receipt requested and post the notice of abandonment in a conspicuous place on the property for five days. If the tenant has not left any personal property behind, the landlord can simply reclaim and relet the premises five days after the notice of abandonment has been both mailed and posted. The tenant's security deposit is considered forfeited and the landlord may apply it to any accrued rent and other costs that may have been caused by the abandonment. If the landlord does not make a reasonable attempt to relet the unit, the lease is considered terminated as of the date of the landlord's knowledge of the abandonment (for purposes of calculating any damages owed to the landlord).

The landlord can remove any personal property left by the tenant in the unit, but the landlord must hold it for at least ten days after the landlord's declaration of abandonment. Unless the tenant notifies the landlord of his or her intention to reclaim the personal property (which must be done before the expiration of the ten-day holding period), the landlord can sell the personal property (or otherwise dispose of it as provided for in the lease) and apply the proceeds of the sale to any past-due rent (ARS Section 33–1370). Any excess funds must be mailed to the tenant at the tenant's last known address.

## Fire or Casualty Damage (ARS Section 33–1366)

If the leased premises are so severely damaged or destroyed by fire or casualty that their use is substantially impaired, the tenant can do one of the following:

- Immediately vacate the premises and notify the landlord in writing within 14 days of his or her intention to terminate the lease (in this situation, the lease terminates when the tenant vacates the premises)
- If continued occupancy is lawful, vacate any part of the premises that was rendered unusable by fire or casualty (in this situation, the tenant's obligation for rent is reduced in proportion to the part of the premises that is still usable)

If the tenant chooses to terminate the lease, he or she is entitled to any security deposit held on his or her behalf by the landlord. If the tenant chooses to remain on the premises and prorate the rent, the proration must begin on the effective date of the reduced use of the premises.

## Landlord's Retaliation (ARS Section 33–1381)

A landlord may not retaliate against a tenant by increasing rent, decreasing services or threatening a detainer action merely because the lessee has

- filed a complaint against the landlord with any appropriate governmental agency,
- filed a complaint with the landlord for failure to maintain fit premises or
- organized or joined a tenant's union or similar organization.

## SUIT FOR POSSESSION

A suit for possession is used when a tenant retains possession of the leased premises after the expiration of the lease. The landlord brings a suit for possession when he or she wants to evict the tenant.

## Forcible Entry and Detainer (ARS Section 12–1171 Through Section 12–1183)

Forcible entry and detainer, which are both instances of wrongful possession of property, are based on the concepts of trespass and theft. For example, if a landlord intrudes onto leased premises during the term of a lease without the consent of the tenant, the landlord is guilty of trespass—the landlord is depriving the tenant of the rights of possession and quiet enjoyment. And if the landlord cannot relet leased premises after the expiration of a lease because the tenant refuses to vacate the premises, the tenant is guilty of theft—the tenant is depriving the landlord of the rights to the income from the property.

**Forcible entry** is an entering onto property against the will of the person who is legally entitled to possess a property. It includes any unlawful entry, with or without physical force, including the entry of a landlord into premises held by a tenant at will or a tenant at sufferance.

**Forcible detainer** is the possession of real property by one who is not legally entitled to such possession. It includes any unlawful possession, with or without physical force, including possession by

- a tenant at sufferance who refuses to vacate the premises;
- a tenant at will who refuses to vacate the premises;
- a lessee under a periodic estate of month-to-month or a shorter duration who refuses to vacate the premises;
- a lessee who refuses to vacate the premises after receiving a written demand for possession from the lessor;
- a lessee or anyone who has made a forcible entry into leased premises (or anyone who succeeds one who has made a forcible entry) who refuses to vacate the premises for five days after receiving a written demand for possession; and
- anyone who has lost the lawful right of possession because of a foreclosure or forfeiture who refuses to vacate the property.

Although forcible detainer is usually associated with a tenant refusing to vacate premises after the expiration of a lease, it can also be committed by a landlord who "locks out" a tenant who is legally entitled to the possession of a property.

### Special Detainer Actions (ARS Section 33–1377)

A landlord recovers the possession of property by filing a special detainer action. This action begins when a party files a written complaint under oath with a justice of the peace or the clerk of the superior court. The complaint must specify the property in question and the details of the rights that entitle the plaintiff to lawful possession. The defendant in the complaint must appear in court to answer the complaint within three to six days after the summons and complaint has been served, mailed or posted (there can be different time requirements depending on the method(s) of notification to the defendant).

A jury trial is optional. The plaintiff can request a jury trial when the summons and complaint is issued, or the defendant can request one when he or she responds to the complaint. A justice court jury consists of 6 jurors, and a superior court jury consists of 12 jurors.

If the defendant (tenant) is found guilty, the court will issue a writ of restitution in favor of the plaintiff (landlord). The plaintiff can recover possession of the premises in question, plus attorneys' fees and court costs, plus all past-due rent. If the defendant is found not guilty, the court will issue a writ of restitution in favor of the defendant, and he or she can recover possession, fees, costs and rent.

Title 12, Chapter 8, of the Arizona Revised Statutes (ARS Section 12–1171 et al.) addresses all special actions and proceedings relating to property. However, ARS Section 33–1377, which concerns special detainer actions, is incorporated into the Arizona Residential Landlord and Tenant Act. Because of the technical differences between the two sections of law, the reader is advised to obtain competent legal counsel, particularly with respect to when and how each section should be used and to the rights of the parties involved under each section.

## ARIZONA MOBILE HOME PARKS RESIDENTIAL LANDLORD AND TENANT ACT

Title 33, Chapter 11, of the Arizona Revised Statutes contains the Arizona Mobile Home Parks Residential Landlord and Tenant Act, which is similar in design and intent to the Arizona Residential Landlord and Tenant Act (Title 33, Chapter 10). However, this chapter was enacted to address the overlap of real property rights and personal property rights found in mobile home parks but not found in permanent residential structures. Because of the nature of mobile home parks and their leasehold interests, no attempt to explain the act can be made in this text.

Anyone desiring a copy of either the Arizona Residential Landlord and Tenant Act or the Arizona Mobile Home Parks Residential Landlord and Tenant Act should call or write to the Arizona Secretary of State's Office.

## QUESTIONS

1. An oral lease for nine months starting in six months would be

   a. void.
   b. voidable.
   c. unilateral.
   d. unenforceable.

2. If there is noncompliance with a lease by either party and the breach materially affects the health and safety of the other residents, what is the minimum time permitted before the lease is considered to be terminated?

   a. Five days.
   b. Seven days.
   c. Ten days.
   d. Fifteen days.

3. Under the Arizona Residential Landlord and Tenant Act, which of the following rules would be unenforceable should it be instituted by the landlord?

   a. A requirement that the tenants cannot park their boat trailers in the covered parking area
   b. A requirement that the tenants must call at least one week in advance to schedule the cleaning of their carpet
   c. A requirement that the swimming pool area must be closed by 11:00 P.M.
   d. A requirement that the tenants cannot use the elevators after 11:00 P.M.

4. For reasons unknown, landlord *G* has disconnected the utilities to tenant *D*'s apartment. All of the following remedies are available to *D except*

   a. take action to acquire the services and deduct their cost from the rent she owes *G*.
   b. unilaterally rescind the lease and demand the return of any security deposits held for her by *G*.
   c. sue for and recover damages based on the reduced value of the unit while the utilities were shut off.
   d. obtain reasonable substitute housing during the period of *G*'s noncompliance with the lease.

5. The Arizona Residential Landlord and Tenant Act would apply to which of the following situations?

   a. *S*, a sophomore marketing major, is living in a dormitory at Arizona State University.
   b. The *F*s, residents of Iowa, are spending their winter months at the Hohokam Lodge Apartments in Tucson.
   c. *H*, a Loyal Bison, is living at the Loyal Bison Retirement Home in Show Low.
   d. *T*, a roadie for the Grateful Dead, is spending two months at the Little America Hotel in Flagstaff.

6.  *B*'s lease calls for monthly rental payment of $470. The lease contains no expiration date. *B* is being transferred by her employer to another state and she must move. How much advance notice must she give to her landlord to terminate her lease?

    a.  Five days.
    b.  Ten days.
    c.  Twenty days
    d.  Thirty days.

7.  *V* operates a bookstore in a shopping center. He has a five-year lease for the premises that includes an automatic renewal clause for an additional five years. If *V* desires to continue occupying the premises at the end of the first five-year term, he should

    a.  notify the lessor of his decision at least 90 days before the original expiration date.
    b.  simply retain possession of the premises as the renewal of the lease is automatic.
    c.  together with the lessor, sign a new lease for another five-year term.
    d.  record a memorandum of lease renewal with the county recorder.

8.  The *J*s have leased their cabin in the mountains to *M* for June, July and August. *M*'s interest in the property is an estate

    a.  at will.
    b.  for years.
    c.  at sufferance.
    d.  from month-to-month.

9.  *C* rented an apartment from *M* for a one-year term, with *C* paying rent on the first of each month. During the term of the lease, *C* built some bookshelves into the living room walls, added a vanity cabinet in the bathroom and built his microwave oven into an open cabinet in the kitchen. His lease did not address these activities. In this situation, which of the following statements applies?

    a.  *C* can take his bookshelves, vanity and microwave with him when his lease expires.
    b.  *C* can take his microwave with him, but he must leave the bookshelves and vanity.
    c.  *C* has installed trade fixtures in his unit for use only during the term of his lease.
    d.  *M* probably became the owner of the improvements *C* made as soon as they were installed.

10. *H*'s lease expired two weeks ago, and since then she has refused to surrender her apartment to her landlords, the *B*s. The *B*s are preparing to file suit against *H* for forcible detainer. All of the following statements regarding the suit are correct *except*

    a.  to begin the suit, the *B*s must file a complaint against *H*.
    b.  *H* must appear and answer the *B*'s complaint within ten days.
    c.  if *H* is found guilty, a writ of restitution will be issued in favor of the *B*s.
    d.  if *H* is not found guilty, a writ of restitution will be issued in favor of *H*.

# 13
# Appraisal

The principles of appraisal and the methods of appraising real property are uniform throughout the country. Who can perform appraisals and the **requirements for licensing and certification**, however, differ from state to state. Title XI of FIRREA (enacted in 1989) requires real estate appraisals made in connection with federally related transactions be performed by state-licensed or state-certified appraisers. It is the responsibility of each state to adopt its own laws regarding the minimum standards for licensure and certification. These standards must meet the minimum criteria established by the **Appraiser Qualifications Board** of **The Appraisal Foundation** in Washington, D.C. (The Appraiser Foundation is a national body authorized by Congress and composed of representatives of professional appraisal associations and related organizations and users of appraisal services.)

## ARIZONA APPRAISAL LICENSURE AND CERTIFICATION REQUIREMENTS

Arizona law provides for three types of appraisal licenses or certificates: (1) the licensed real property appraiser; (2) the certified residential real property appraiser; and (3) the certified general real property appraiser. The various education, experience and examination requirements for each are as follows:

**Licensed real property appraiser** applies to the appraisal of noncomplex one- to four-unit residential properties with a transaction value of less than $1 million.

- Education requirements include a minimum of 75 classroom hours of courses in subjects related to real estate appraisal, including at least 15 hours on the Uniform Standards of Professional Appraisal Practice. All courses must be completed before the state licensing examination can be taken.
- Experience requirements include a minimum of 2,000 hours of documentable appraisal experience.
- Examination requirements include successful completion of the Appraiser Qualifications Board—endorsed Uniform State Licensing/Certification Examination or its equivalent.

**Certified residential real property appraiser** applies to the appraisal of one- to four-unit residential properties without regard to the complexity or value of the property.

- Education requirements include a minimum of 120 classroom hours of courses in subjects related to real estate appraisal, including at least 15 hours on the Uniform Standards of Professional Appraisal Practice. Educational hours used to meet the requirements for licensure can also be used to meet the requirements for residential certification. All courses must be completed before the state certification examination can be taken.

- Experience requirements include a minimum of 2,000 hours of documentable appraisal experience acquired over a minimum period of 24 months.
- Examination requirements include successful completion of the Appraiser Qualifications Board-Endorsed Uniform State Licensing/Certification Examination or its equivalent.

**Certified general real property appraiser** applies to the appraiser of all types of real property interests.

- Education requirements include a minimum of 165 classroom hours of courses in subjects related to real estate appraisal, including at least 15 hours on the Uniform Standards of Professional Appraisal Practice. Education hours used to meet the requirements for licensure or residential certification can also be used to meet the requirements for general certification. All courses must be completed before the state certification examination can be taken.
- Experience requirements include a minimum of 2,000 hours of documentable appraisal experience acquired over a minimum period of 24 months. At least half of the experience cited must be nonresidential appraisal work.
- Examination requirements include successful completion of the Appraiser Qualifications Board-Endorsed Uniform State Licensing/Certification Examination or its equivalent.

## CONTINUING EDUCATION

Appraisal licenses and certificates are issued for two-year periods (biennial licensure). To renew a license or certificate, an appraiser must submit proof of at least 20 hours of continuing education at each renewal.

For more information about appraisal licensure and certification, please contact

Arizona Board of Appraisal
1400 West Washington Street, Suite 360
Phoenix, AZ 85007
(602) 542–1539

# 14

# Property Development and Subdivision

The Arizona laws that regulate the subdividing and sale of land within the state are contained in the Real Estate Code (Title 32, Chapter 20, of the Arizona Revised Statutes). These laws were enacted to eliminate many undesirable and potentially dishonest practices that had become common, at one time, in the development and sale of unimproved land.

A **subdivision**, or **subdivided lands**, are defined as improved or unimproved land divided or proposed to be divided for the purpose of sale or lease into six or more lots or parcels that are less than 36 acres each in size. (The definition of subdivisions includes both condominiums and cooperatives but generally does not include the leasing of improvements for commercial, industrial or agricultural purposes.) **Unsubdivided lands** are defined as land divided or proposed to be divided for the purpose of sale or lease into six or more lots or parcels that are at least 36 acres but less than 160 acres each (ARS Section 32–2101).

Subdivided lands are regulated under Article 4 of the code (ARS Section 32–2181 through Section 32–2185.09). Unsubdivided lands are regulated under Article 7 of the code (ARS Section 32–2195.01 through Section 32–2195.10).

The following discussion is designed to acquaint the reader with the major provisions of these articles, but is not intended as a complete reference. Details of the technical requirements for subdividing property can be obtained directly from the Subdivisions Section of the Arizona Department of Real Estate.

## SUBDIVIDED LANDS (Article 4)

### Notice (ARS Section 32–2181, Paragraph A)

Before offering subdivided lands for sale or lease, the owner, agent or subdivider must notify the commissioner in writing of his or her intention. This is done by sending the commissioner a "Notice of Intention." Copies of the "Subdivided Lands Questionnaire," which can be used as a working checklist to complete the Notice of Intention, are available from the subdivisions section of the department. The Notice of Intention must include the following:

- The name and address of the owner or owners. If any ownership interest is held by a legal entity such as a corporation, partnership or trust, then anyone holding a minimum ten percent interest in such an entity must be identified along with the amount of his or her interest
- The name and address of the subdivider
- The legal description and area of the land
- A statement of the condition of the title to the property that identifies all encumbrances that affect the property, and the conditions under which a purchaser can acquire clear title to a lot under the developer's blanket encumbrance
- The terms and conditions on which the land is intended to be disposed, including copies of any documents to be used (such as purchase contracts, deeds, leases and assignments) and other such information that is to be presented to a prospective purchaser or lessee
- A properly recorded subdivision map of the property
- A comprehensive statement describing the land on and the locality in which the subdivision is located
- A statement of the provisions that have been made for permanent access and provisions, if any, for health-department-approved sewage and solid waste collection and disposal and public utilities
- A statement of the location of the nearest public elementary and high schools available for attendance by any school-age children who would be residing on the subdivided property
- A statement of the use or uses for which the proposed subdivision will be offered
- A statement of the provisions, if any, limiting the use or occupancy of the parcels of the subdivision, along with copies of any restrictive covenants affecting all or part of the subdivision
- The name and business address of the Arizona real estate broker selling or leasing parcels in the subdivision, if applicable
- A statement of the approximate amount of any indebtedness that is a lien on all or part of the subdivision and that was incurred to pay for the construction of any off-site or on-site improvements or any community or recreational facilities
- A statement or reasonable estimate, if applicable, of the amount of any indebtedness that has been or is proposed to be incurred by an existing or proposed special taxing or assessment district, within the boundaries of which all or part of the subdivision is located, and that is to pay for the construction or installation of any improvements or community or recreational facilities for the subdivision, and which amounts are to be obtained by ad valorem tax or special assessment against all or part of the subdivision
- A statement of the approximate amount of annual taxes, special assessments and fees to be paid by the purchaser of a parcel for the proposed annual maintenance of any common facilities within the subdivision
- A statement of the provisions for easements for permanent access for irrigation water, if applicable
- A statement of assurances for the installation of off-site improvements, such as roads and utilities, and the approval of the political subdivision having such authority
- A statement of the nature of any improvements to be installed by the developer, the estimated schedule for their completion or installation and the estimated costs relative to such improvements that will be borne by the purchaser of a parcel in the subdivision
- A statement of the availability of sewage disposal facilities and other public utilities in the subdivision, the estimated schedule for their completion or installation and the estimated costs relative to such facilities and utilities that will be borne by the purchaser of a parcel in the subdivision
- A statement as to whether all or part of the subdivision is located in an open range or area in which livestock may roam at large under state law, and what provisions, if any, have been made for the fencing of the subdivision to preclude livestock from roaming within the subdivided lands

- If the subdivider is a subsidiary corporation, a statement identifying the parent corporation and any of the following in which the parent or any of its subsidiaries are, or have been within the previous five years, involved:
  a.  Any subdivision in the state of Arizona
  b.  Any subdivision, wherever located, for which registration is required pursuant to the Federal Interstate Land Sales Full Disclosure Act
  c.  Any subdivision, wherever located, that would have been required to register pursuant to the Federal Interstate Land Sales Full Disclosure Act, but for the exemption for subdivisions whose parcels are all 20 acres or more in size
- A statement identifying all other subdivisions specified in the previous paragraph in which any of the following are, or have been within the previous five years, directly or indirectly involved:
  a.  The holder of any ownership interest in the land
  b.  The subdivider
  c.  Any principal or officer in the holder or the subdivider
- Such other information and such other documents and certifications as the commissioner may reasonably require

If the subdivision is within a groundwater active management area, a copy of the "Certificate of Assured Water Supply" issued by the director of the Arizona Department of Water Resources must accompany the Notice of Intention, unless the subdivision is located within an area designated as having an assured water supply by the department or is exempt from such a requirement, or if the subdivider has submitted a certificate of assured water supply to a city, town or county prior to approval of the plat by the city, town or county and this has been noted on the face of the plat (ARS Section 32–2181, paragraph C).

## Exceptions (ARS Section 32–2181, Paragraph E)

There are some instances in which the provisions of the Subdivision Act does not apply, including when the fractional interests

- are at least 36 acres each in size;
- are the result of a foreclosure sale, a sale by a trustee selling under a deed of trust or the grant of a deed in lieu of foreclosure;
- are created by a valid court order or decree or by any operation of law;
- consist of any interests, permits, claims or rights in any oil, gas or mineral leases and are regulated as securities by the federal or state government;
- are registered as securities under federal or state law; or
- are exempted by a special order of the commissioner when it has been satisfactorily shown that compliance with the requirements of the act is not essential to the protection of the public interest.

## Exemptions (ARS Section 21–2181.02)

The following situations are also exempt from the requirements of the act:

- The sale or lease in bulk of six or more lots or parcels to one buyer in one transaction
- The sale or lease of lots or parcels of 160 acres or more

The following situations are exempt from the **filing requirements** of the act:

- The sale or lease of lots or parcels that are zoned and restricted to commercial or industrial uses
- The sale or lease of lots or parcels located in a subdivision by a subdivider if
  a. a public report has been issued on the subdivision lots or parcels;
  b. the subdivision meets all the other requirements of the act;
  c. the sale or lease of the lots or parcels meets all other requirements of the act;
  d. the lots or parcels are included on a recorded subdivision plat that is approved by a municipal or county government;
  e. the construction of all improvements (other than a residence to be built) are complete, paid for and free of any blanket encumbrance;
  f. if the improvements are not complete, their completion is assured according to the provisions of the act;
  g. there have been no material changes to the information set forth in the previous public report;
  h. no owner of 10 percent or more, subdivider, director, partner, agent, officer or developer of the subdivision has been convicted of a felony involving violence or fraud, has had a civil judgment awarded in a case involving fraud, or had a business or professional license denied, suspended or revoked;
  i. the sale of the subdivided lands violates no laws or ordinances;
  j. the subdivider provides all buyers with copies of the most recent public report before those buyers enter into a purchase contract;
  k. the subdivider has provided to the buyer or lessee a signed statement that the subdivider has reviewed and is in compliance with the terms of the exemption provisions in the act;
  l. before any sale or lease, the subdivider has notified the commissioner of the subdivider's intent to sell or lease lots or parcels pursuant to this paragraph. The notice must include:
     1. the name, address, and telephone number of the subdivider;
     2. the name, address and telephone number of any real estate broker retained by the subdivider to help sell or lease lots;
     3. the name and location of the subdivision;
     4. the most recent subdivision public report reference number on the lots; and
     5. the completion status of subdivision improvements;
- The conveyance to a person who previously conveyed the lot to a home builder for the purpose of constructing a dwelling for the person

The commissioner can also establish exemptions from certain subdivision requirements, depending on the circumstances under which the property is to be divided or transferred.

Note that Commissioner's Rule R4–28–1201, paragraph A, stipulates that if two or more contiguous parcels are acquired by the same owner, they will be considered to be a single parcel for the purposes of the subdivision laws. However, parcels on two sides of a barrier will be considered noncontiguous if the barrier was not created by the owner and the parcels cannot be reunited.

## Water Disclosures (ARS Section 32–2181, Paragraph F)

As previously indicated, subdivided property located in a groundwater active management area is required to have either a "Certificate of Assured Water Supply" from the Arizona Department of Water Resources or the approval of the commissioner that there is a political subdivision or a private water provider that can deliver adequate supplies of water to the subdivision. However, if the subdivision is outside of a groundwater active management area and there is either an inadequate supply of water to meet the needs of the subdivision as projected by the developer or no water available to the subdivision, then all promotional materials and contracts relative to the sale or lease of such property must indicate such facts as represented by the report from the director of the Arizona Department of Water Resources.

## Subdivision Examination and Fees (ARS Section 32–2182)

The Notice of Intention must be accompanied by a filing fee. Also, before a subdivision can be marketed, it must first be inspected by the commissioner or his or her representative. The subdivider is responsible for reimbursing the department for the actual costs of travel, food and lodging incurred by the individual who is sent to perform the subdivision inspection.

## Public Report (Rules R4–28–803 Through R4–28–804)

Unless there are grounds for denial, the commissioner will issue a public report to the subdivider authorizing the sale or lease of parcels in the approved subdivision. The report must contain substantially the same information as the Notice of Intention. The purpose of the public report is to inform any prospective purchaser or lessee about the property and to answer in advance questions that would commonly be asked of the subdivider. The subdivider is responsible for reproducing the report and providing a copy of it to every prospective purchaser or lessee. (The subdivider must get a receipt in exchange for the report.) A copy of the report must be given to every purchaser or lessee before he or she signs any contracts relative to the subdivided property (ARS Section 32–2183). Any sale or lease without the issuance and provision of the public report is voidable by the purchaser or lessee for three years (ARS Section 32–2183, paragraph E).

Unless the commissioner waives the requirement, no subdivision will be approved without a provision for permanent access to each parcel by conventional motor vehicle (ARS Section 32–2185.02). The sale of landlocked property is illegal on the part of the seller, and the transaction is voidable by the purchaser.

The commissioner can suspend, revoke or deny issuance of a public report for any of the following reasons:

- The owner, agent or subdivider has failed to comply with the appropriate provisions of the act and the Commissioner's Rules regarding subdivided lands.
- The sale or lease of the parcels would constitute misrepresentation, deceit or fraud.
- There is an inability to deliver title or any other interest contracted for.
- There is an inability to demonstrate to the commissioner that adequate financial or other arrangements have been made for the provision of the off-site improvements included in the offering.
- There is a failure to show that the parcels can be used for the purpose for which they are being offered.
- The owner, agent, subdivider, officer, director, partner, trust beneficiary or anyone holding a minimum 10 percent interest in any legal entity involved with the subdivision has
  a. been convicted of a crime involving fraud or a crime relating to a real estate transaction;
  b. been permanently or temporarily barred from engaging in any real estate activities;
  c. had an order entered against him or her by a real estate or securities regulatory agency;
  d. had an adverse judgment entered against him or her involving fraud or dishonesty in the conduct of any real estate transaction; or
  e. disregarded or violated any provision of the Real Estate Code.

- There is a procurement or an attempt to procure a public report by misrepresentation, deceit or fraud, or there is a false or misleading application for such a report.
- If applicable, there is a failure to file the appropriate condominium documents with the commissioner.
- There is a failure of any blanket encumbrance on the subdivision property to include provisions that would allow a lot or parcel purchaser to acquire clear title.
- There is a failure to demonstrate permanent access to the lots or parcels.
- The use of the lots presents an unreasonable health risk.

Any applicant objecting to the denial of a public report has 30 days in which to file a request for a hearing with the commissioner.

## Lot Reservations (ARS Section 32–2101)

Under certain conditions, a deposit can be accepted by a subdivider from a prospective purchaser as a lot reservation prior to the issuance of the public report. A **lot reservation** is defined as an expression of interest by a prospective purchaser in buying at some future date a subdivided or unsubdivided lot, unit or parcel. Subsequent affirmative action must be taken by the prospective purchaser to create a contractual obligation to purchase. In other words, a lot reservation does not obligate the prospective purchaser to actually buy the property.

A deposit on a lot reservation prior to the issuance of a public report can only be accepted if the following requirements are met:

- Before accepting any lot reservation, the prospective seller shall mail or deliver written notice of the seller's intention to accept lot reservations to the department. The notice must include
  a.  the name, address and telephone number of the seller;
  b.  the name, address and telephone number of any real estate broker involved in promoting lot reservations;
  c.  the name and location of the project; and
  d.  the form to be used for accepting lot reservations.
- The reservation deposit for a single lot or parcel may not exceed $5,000.
- Within one business day after the acceptance of a lot reservation, the deposit must be delivered to an escrow agent, who must deposit it into an escrow account; the deposit must remain in the escrow account until the lot reservation terminates or a purchase contract is entered into.
- Within 15 calendar days of the receipt of the public report, the prospective purchaser must receive a copy of the public report and a copy of the proposed purchase contract. The prospective buyer and seller then have seven business days in which to enter into a purchase contract. If no contract is entered into during that seven-day period, the lot reservation automatically terminates.
- A prospective buyer may cancel a lot reservation at any time by delivering written notice to the seller.
- Within five business days after a lot reservation has been terminated for any reason, the seller must return to the buyer all reservation deposits, including any interest earned on the deposit.
- A prospective buyer may not transfer rights under a lot reservation without the prior written consent of the seller.
- If the application for a public report is denied, the seller must notify all the prospective purchasers of the denial and return all deposits to them.
- All required notices must be in writing and either hand-delivered or sent by certified mail, return receipt requested.

- Each lot reservation form must contain the following statement:

> The State Real Estate Department has not inspected or approved this project and no public report has yet been issued for the project. No offer to sell may be made and no offer to purchase may be accepted before issuance of a public report for the project (ARS 32–8181.03).

## Marketing Subdivided Lands

Although the laws regulating the sale of subdivided lands are part of the Real Estate Code, a subdivider must be a licensed real estate broker only if he or she actually sells or leases the parcels. Subdividers often employ a broker to act as the subdivider's agent and to sell or lease the parcels. The laws and rules discussed in Chapter 10, "Real Estate License Laws," regarding advertising, promotional practices and sales tactics apply in the marketing of subdivided lands.

## Advertising and Promotional Activities (ARS Section 32–2183.01 and Rules R4–28–502 Through R4–28–504)

Within ten days after a request from the commissioner, a subdivider must provide the commissioner copies of all advertising and promotional materials to be used in connection with the marketing of the subdivision. No advertising or promotional material or oral statement made by any representative of the subdivider to the public may contain

- any untrue statement of material fact or any omission of material fact that would make such a statement misleading in light of the circumstances under which the statement was made;
- any statement or representation that the parcels are offered without risk or that loss is impossible;
- any statement, representation or pictorial presentation of proposed improvements or nonexistent scenes without a clear indication that the improvements are merely proposed and such scenes do not, in fact, exist; or
- any statement or representation that the parcels are suitable as homesites or building sites unless
    a. potable water is available from a political subdivision or a private water provider, and either an individual sewage (septic) system will operate on the parcel or a sewer system is available from a political subdivision, or
    b. any facts to the contrary are clearly and conspicuously incorporated into all advertising and promotional materials.

All advertising and sales literature must be consistent with the information contained in the notice of intention and the public report. Subdividers must keep copies of all advertising materials available for review by the commissioner for three years after their last use.

Unless the offer of a gift made in connection with a sales promotion is without conditions, terms such as "free" and "no obligation" may not be used to describe the offered item. Any gift must be clearly described, along with its approximate retail value; and any costs or conditions associated with the gift must be disclosed.

Offers of travel, accommodations, meals or entertainment at no cost or reduced cost in connection with a sales promotion cannot be described as "awards" or "prizes" or by words of similar implication. Any costs or conditions associated with such items must be disclosed.

Any offer or inducement to purchase that is presented as restricted in quantity or time must stipulate a numerical quantity or specific time.

A subdivider may hold a drawing or contest to encourage prospects to visit a subdivision if the following requirements are met:

- There is a current public report in effect for the subdivision.
- The subdivision is not the subject of an ongoing investigation by the department.
- The details of the drawing or contest are submitted to the department for review and approval prior to holding the drawing or contest.
- The drawing or contest is limited in time, scope and geographic location.
- The material terms of the drawing or contest are fully disclosed in writing to participants.
- No fee is charged to any participant.
- No participant must attend a sales presentation or take a tour as a condition of participation
- The subdivider is in compliance with all other applicable laws involving drawings or contests.
- The subdivider is responsible for the conduct of any drawing or contest.

Advertising and promotional materials that characterize a subdivision as a "retirement community" or "adult community" or a community in which only adults will be allowed to reside will be permitted only if a valid restrictive covenant addressing such residency has been appropriately drafted and properly recorded. Of course, the provisions of the Federal Fair Housing Act and Arizona Fair Housing Act must be met.

The commissioner maintains final approval on all advertising and promotional materials used in connection with the marketing of subdivided lands. In addition to the previously mentioned items, he or she can require disclosure and approval of references to monthly payments, financing costs, interest rates, private facilities, bodies of water, distances to communities and urban areas and similar items that could materially influence the decisions or prospective purchasers and lessees.

## Contract Disclosures (ARS Section 32–2185.06 and Rules R4–28–803 Through R4–28–804)

All contract forms for the purchase or lease of subdivided lands from an owner, agent or subdivider must clearly and conspicuously disclose the nature of the document, the purchaser's or lessee's right to receive a copy of the commissioner's public report and, if applicable, the purchaser's rights of rescission for an unimproved parcel. Contracts omitting these disclosures are unenforceable against the purchaser.

## Sale of Lots (ARS Section 32–2183, Paragraph C)

It is unlawful for a subdivider to sell any subdivision lot unless one of the following occurs:

- All of the proposed improvements have been completed.
- The completion of all proposed improvements is assured by financial arrangements.
- The municipal or county government agrees to prohibit occupancy and the subdivider agrees not to close escrow for lots in the subdivision until all proposed improvements have been completed.
- The municipal or county government enters into an assurance agreement with a trustee not to convey lots until the proposed improvements are completed, if the improvements can be used

and maintained separately from the improvements required for the entire subdivision. The agreement must be properly recorded.

## Sale of Unimproved Parcels (ARS Section 32–2185.01)

In the sale of unimproved parcels in a subdivision, the owner, agent or subdivider must follow one of three procedures for other-than-cash transactions. These rules are specifically designed to protect the purchasers of unimproved property.

First, the owner, agent or subdivider can sell the parcel by providing its financing. The seller must sign and deliver to the purchaser a conveyance deed transferring marketable title, subject only to those exceptions to which the purchaser has agreed in writing. The seller can then take back a purchase money mortgage or trust deed for any unpaid balance of the purchase price. The seller must then record the deed and the mortgage or trust deed within 60 days after their being signed by the seller and the purchaser.

Second, the sale can be completed through an escrow agent. The purchase contract must be signed by the seller and the purchaser, recorded and deposited with the escrow agent within 60 days of its being signed. The seller must also give the escrow agent the preliminary title report, a conveyance deed transferring marketable title and any other documents required by the escrow agent, including those necessary to release the parcel being sold from any blanket encumbrance against the subdivision. The conveyance deed and, if applicable, the releasing documents must be recorded by the escrow agent within 60 days after the purchaser has fulfilled all of his or her obligations under the terms of the purchase contract, including payment to the escrow agent of the purchase price.

Third, the sale can be completed through a trustee. As with a sale through an escrow agent, the purchase contract must be signed, recorded and deposited with—in this instance—the trustee within 60 days after the signing of the contract. The seller must sign, record and deliver to the trustee a deed in trust conveying title to the trustee. He or she must also give the trustee a trust agreement and any documents necessary to release the parcel being sold from any blanket encumbrance against the subdivision. Under the terms of the trust agreement, the trustee must sign, record and deliver to the purchaser a conveyance deed transferring marketable title and, if applicable, any releasing documents, within 60 days after the purchaser has fulfilled his or her obligations under the terms of the purchase contract, including payment to the trustee of the purchase price.

## Purchaser's Inspection and Rescission Rights (ARS Section 32–2185.01, Paragraph D and Paragraph E, and Rules R4–28–803 Through R4–28–804)

To protect a prospective purchaser against inaccurate statements and high-pressure sales tactics, and to provide a "cooling off" period, the legislature determined that all contracts for the sale of unimproved parcels in a subdivision can be unilaterally rescinded without cause by the purchaser of the parcel. The rescission period varies, depending on whether the purchaser inspected the property. If the purchaser of the unimproved parcel did not inspect the parcel prior to signing the purchase contract, he or she has six months in which to rescind the contract. If the purchaser did inspect the parcel prior to signing the purchase contract (and signed an affidavit to that effect), he or she has seven days in which to rescind the contract. (The commissioner can require that the purchaser's affidavits be submitted to the Arizona Department of Real Estate by the subdivider.)

To rescind a purchase contract, the purchaser must send or deliver to the owner, agent or subdivider a written notice of rescission by midnight of the last day of the rescission period. Once the notice has been tendered, the purchaser is entitled to a full and immediate refund of all monies paid under the contract, including any down payment and any subsequent installment payments.

## Enforcement (ARS Section 32–2183 and Rules R4–28–1301 Through R4–28–1312)

Once a subdivision has been approved and offered for sale or lease, the commissioner can take action to enforce the law regardless of whether he or she has received a formal complaint. If there is sufficient evidence to the commissioner that the owner, agent or subdivider has violated the Real Estate Code or the Commissioner's Rules, has engaged in any fraudulent practices or has deviated from the provisions specified in the public report, the commissioner can investigate the subdivision and examine its books and records.

In addition to such an investigation, if the commissioner believes that he or she has satisfactory evidence that the law has been violated or anyone associated with the subdivision has been involved in questionable activities or convicted of a felony as previously discussed, he or she can take certain actions to stop the sale or lease of the subdivided parcels.

First, the commissioner must notify the accused party of the charges being brought against him or her and provide that party with an opportunity to be heard. (The procedure is the same as that specified for a real estate licensee who faces the suspension or revocation of his or her license.) The commissioner can also issue a summary suspension of the public report, thus stopping the sale or lease of the subdivided lands until the scheduled hearing is held.

After the hearing, the commissioner can issue further orders and place additional restrictions on the subdivision to protect the public and assure compliance with the law. He or she can also bring suit against any persons associated with the subdivision to prevent them from continuing to violate the law or engage in activities similar to those that caused the initial investigation by the commissioner.

In addition, if it appears that any person is engaging in unlawful activities in the sale of subdivided lands and has made arrangements to conceal his or her assets or leave the state, the commissioner can apply to the superior court to have a receiver appointed to take responsibility for that person's assets.

## Violation

Anyone who knowingly violates any of the provisions of the laws or Commissioner's Rules regarding subdivided lands, including misstating or omitting any material fact in or filing a falsified Notice of Intention, is guilty of a Class 5 Felony, and may be assessed (after a hearing by the commissioner) with a civil penalty up to $1,000 per infraction.

In any civil suit brought against a subdivider for fraudulent activities, the purchaser can generally hold the subdivider liable for an amount of money reflecting the difference between the purchase price of the land plus the cost of any improvements and the value of the property at the time the suit is filed. In addition, the purchaser is entitled to recover court costs and attorneys' fees as set by the court.

## UNSUBDIVIDED LANDS (Article 7)

As stated earlier, unsubdivided lands are defined as land divided or proposed to be divided for the purpose of sale or lease into six or more lots or parcels that are at least 36 acres but less than 160 acres each (ARS 32–2101). The creation of six or more parcels that are at least 160 acres each would be an unregulated activity.

While subdivided lands under Article 4 are usually marketed as potential homesites, unsubdivided lands under Article 7 are marketed primarily as recreational properties. Therefore, some of the regulations under Article 7 are less stringent than those under Article 4. However, there are a great number of similarities between the provisions of both Article 4 and Article 7. For example, the process for filing a Notice of Intention and receiving a public report are virtually identical (however, less information is required for the Notice of Intention for unsubdivided lands and there are fewer grounds for denying a public report).

There is a filing fee for unsubdivided lands. The restrictions for advertising and promotional materials are similar for unsubdivided land, except that a subdivider must submit copies of all advertising and promotional materials to the commissioner at least 21 days prior to their use. The requirements for contract disclosures, the sale of unimproved unsubdivided lands, and rescission rights are the same; and enforcement procedures and penalties are very similar.

## MUNICIPAL REGULATION OF SUBDIVISIONS AND UNSUBDIVIDED LANDS

Under Arizona law, the legislative body of every municipality in the state is responsible for regulating all land within its boundaries, including subdivisions and unsubdivided lands. These municipal legislative bodies must comply with both the applicable state statutes and the provisions of certain state agencies, such as the Arizona Departments of Transportation, Health Services and Water Resources. In certain areas, the municipality must enact ordinances requiring procedures and standards for subdivisions and unsubdivided lands. In addition, the municipality can enact ordinances requiring that land within the area be set aside for schools, parks, police and fire stations and community recreational areas.

Subdivisions and unsubdivided lands that are located outside municipal boundaries fall under the jurisdiction of the local County Board of Supervisors. Each board has the same authority as is granted to a municipal legislative body. However, the Real Estate Commissioner has jurisdiction over any violations of the Arizona Real Estate Code and the Commissioner's Rules as they relate to subdivisions and unsubdivided lands; the commissioner's authority cannot be superseded by any other regulatory agency or political subdivision, regardless of its jurisdiction.

## SUBDIVISION RECOVERY FUND

In 1993, the Subdivision Recovery Fund was merged into the Real Estate Recovery Fund. Now, all claims involving subdivisions and unsubdivided lands where a real estate licensee is involved are handled through the Real Estate Recovery Fund. See Chapter 10, "Real Estate License Laws," for a complete discussion of the Real Estate Recovery Fund.

## REAL ESTATE TIME-SHARES (Article 9)

Time-sharing is a form of subdividing, as it involves the creation of **time-share estates** (which are the rights of occupancy coupled with real property interests) or **time-share uses** (which are the contractual rights of occupancy with no real property interests). As such, time-sharing is regulated by Article 9 of the Arizona Real Estate Code (ARS Section 32–2197 through Section 32–2197.17).

Time-share laws specifically regulate the creation of and the sale or lease of time-share subdivisions, which are defined as 12 or more time-share estates or uses having terms of five years or more, or having terms of less than five years if they include renewal options. (Only time-share uses for nonresidential structures are exempt from this definition.)

Many similarities exist between the requirements for time-share projects and the requirements for subdivisions and unsubdivided lands, including the filing of a Notice of Intention and the subsequent issuance of a public report by the commissioner. However, some of the peculiar requirements for a time-share Notice of Intention include

- a comprehensive statement of the time-share program;
- a complete disclosure of all of the projected or actual operating costs of the time-share project;
- a statement of how any dwelling units will be assessed for the purposes of real estate taxation;
- a recorded declaration of dedication for the project (specified under ARS Section 32–2197.04) and any other documents related to the creation, operation and management of the time-share project (including the management agreement with the developer and whether the developer will be bonded or insured);
- a statement regarding the ownership of personal property within the project and how such property's use will be assured to a purchaser or lessee;
- if the project is located in the United States but outside of Arizona, evidence that the project meets all of the legal requirements set by the state in which it is located; and
- if the project is located outside of the United States, evidence that the project meets all of the legal requirements set by the country in which it is located.

The Notice of Intention must be accompanied by a filing fee of $20 per interval unit, up to a maximum fee of $1,000 (ARS Section 32–2197.05).

If a time-share interest is leased or sold before the issuance of a Public Report, the sale or lease is voidable by the purchaser or lessee within five years of the date of the signing of any contract (ARS Section 32–2197.07).

Any contract to purchase or lease a time-share interest can be rescinded by the purchaser or lessee without cause by sending or delivering a written notice of rescission to the owner by midnight of the seventh day following the day on which the contract was signed. Once the notice has been tendered, the purchaser or lessee is entitled to a full and immediate refund of all monies paid under the contrac (ARS Section 32–2197.02).

Time-shares are also discussed in Chapter 4.

## MEMBERSHIP CAMPING (Title 33, Chapter 14, Arizona Revised Statutes)

Arizona Revised Statutes Sections 33–1601 through 33–1619 regulate membership camping in Arizona, a concept under which a person can purchase the right or license to use the camping and recreational facilities promoted by a membership camping operator. There is no real property interest carried by such a membership; the purchaser has only the right to use the facilities provided by the operator.

The land on which the rights to use will be sold can either be owned or be leased by the operator; many operators own a few acres in fee and lease the remainder of the land needed for their operations from private individuals or the Bureau of Land Management. However, the duration of any membership contract to be sold cannot exceed the time period for which the operator has an interest in the land. Some are sold for as little as one year; others are sold for the lifetime of the purchaser.

In general, the original purchaser of a membership camping contract cannot "rent" or "lend" the membership rights to someone else. The operator would be legitimately concerned about one person purchasing the membership and then letting his or her acquaintances use the membership rights. The operator would also be concerned about a group of people purchasing one membership for their collective use. (Membership use by the immediate members of a family is usually not prohibited.)

Membership contracts can be sold by their purchasers. But two major considerations are (1) competition in the form of representatives selling memberships on behalf of the operator and (2) the existence of an after-market for such membership contracts.

The major concern of the commissioner is the financial stability of the operator. He or she must be able to prove not only that the proper interests exist in the land and facilities in which the memberships are to be sold; he or she must also be able to prove that the project has sufficient financial strength to be able to provide the land and facilities and to honor the membership rights for the duration of all contracts that are to be sold.

Because of the unique nature of membership camping organizations and their resultant regulation by the Arizona Department of Real Estate, no attempt will be made in this text to discuss the statutory requirements governing them. Details of the technical requirements for membership camping operations can be obtained directly from the Subdivisions Section of the Department.

## QUESTIONS

1. To close the sale of unimproved land for other than cash, a conveyance deed must be given by the owner, agent or subdivider to the purchaser, the trustee or the

   a. escrow agent.
   b. mortgagee.
   c. beneficiary.
   d. seller.

2. The maximum filing fee for a Notice of Intention for a time-share project is

   a. $500.
   b. $1,000.
   c. $2,000.
   d. $5,000.

3. For a subdivision to receive a formal exemption from the requirements of Article 4, all of the following requirements would have to be met *except*

   a. all of the parcels within the subdivision would have to be improved.
   b. there must be adequate recreational facilities to serve the parcels.
   c. there must be adequate sewage facilities to serve the parcels.
   d. there must be adequate water service to serve the parcels.

4. The purchaser of unimproved property has rights of rescission based upon whether he or she has seen the property. In the event that the property was purchased without having been previously inspected by the purchaser, the maximum rescission time after the signing of the contract is

   a. seven days.
   b. six months.
   c. one year.
   d. three years.

5. All of the following statements regarding the sale of subdivided or unsubdivided lands would be permitted under the provisions of the Arizona Real Estate Code *except*

   a. "This is one of the nicest parcels we have available."
   b. "You couldn't do much better than to buy this real estate."
   c. "This is about as close to the recreation area as you can get."
   d. "You really can't lose anything by buying this property."

6. The creation of 11 equally sized parcels from a 400-acre parcel would be regulated under

   a. Article 4, "Subdivided Lands."
   b. Article 7, "Unsubdivided Lands."
   c. Article 9, "Real Estate Time-Shares."
   d. None of the above—it would not be regulated.

7. The maximum rescission period for the purchaser of a time-share interest is

   a. seven days.
   b. six months.
   c. one year.
   d. five years.

8. A personal right to use would be most commonly associated with

   a. unsubdivided lands.
   b. membership camping.
   c. a time-share.
   d. a condominium.

9. The greatest distinction between subdivided property and undivided property is in the

   a. requirement for the commissioner's public report.
   b. rescission right for unimproved parcels.
   c. requirement for permanent access.
   d. size of the resulting parcels.

10. The real estate commissioner can suspend, revoke or deny the issuance of a public report for any of the following reasons *except*

    a. there is an inability to deliver marketable title.
    b. there is fraud or deceit in the procurement of the public report.
    c. the subdivider has been convicted of fraud or dishonesty.
    d. the subdivider does not hold a valid real estate broker license.

# Fair Housing and Ethical Practices

Real estate licensees must be familiar with Arizona's laws on fair housing. The Arizona Fair Housing Law can be found in Title 41, Chapter 9, Article 7.

## PROHIBITED ACTIVITIES

Just like the Federal Fair Housing Law, Arizona law prohibits a variety of activities when they are based on race, color, religion, sex, handicap, familial status or national origin. These activities include the following:

- Refusing to sell or rent or negotiate to sell or rent a dwelling or making a dwelling unavailable
- Discriminating against any person in the terms, conditions or privileges of the sale or rental of a dwelling, or in providing services or facilities in connection with the sale or rental of a dwelling
- Making, printing or publishing, or causing to be made, printed or published any notice, statement or advertisement with respect to the sale or rental of a dwelling that indicates any preference, limitation or discrimination
- Representing to any person that a dwelling is not available for inspection for sale or rental if the dwelling is available for inspection
- Inducing or attempting to induce a person to sell or rent a dwelling by representations regarding the entry or prospective entry into a neighborhood of a person belonging to a protected class
- Making or purchasing loans or providing other financial assistance either to purchase, construct, improve, repair or maintain a dwelling, or to secure residential real estate;
- Selling, brokering, or appraising real property
- Denying, restricting or modifying any person's access to or membership or participation in a multiple-listing service, real estate brokers' organization or other service, organization, or facility relating to the business of selling or renting dwellings.

As you can see, this list of prohibited activities includes just about any activity a real estate licensee would be likely to engage in in the normal course of business. Thus, it is important for licensees to be on constant guard against any intentional or accidental discriminatory behavior.

Note that a person may not coerce, intimidate, threaten or interfere with any person who is exercising his or her rights under the fair housing laws.

## Familial Status

Arizona laws include special provisions in its fair housing law to define familial status. As defined in Arizona law, familiar status includes all persons who are

- pregnant;
- living with a minor, when that person either is the parent or legal custodian of the minor, or has the written permission of the minor's parent or legal custodian to live with that minor; or
- in the process of obtaining legal custody of a minor.

## Handicap

Special provisions of Arizona's fair housing law relate to discrimination based on handicap. A **handicap** is defined as a mental or physical impairment that substantially limits at least one major life activity. A handicap does not include current illegal use of or addiction to any controlled substance. For example, someone who is blind, confined to a wheelchair, or suffering from a mental illness would be considered handicapped. Someone who is currently addicted to crack cocaine would not be. Note that this state definition of handicap coincides with the federal definition of *disabled*.

A person may not discriminate in any manner in the sale or rental of housing, or in the provision of services or facilities in connection with a dwelling because of the handicap of

- the buyer or renter;
- a person residing in or intending to reside in that dwelling after it is sold, rented or made available; or
- a person associated with that buyer or renter.

For example, an apartment manager could not refuse to rent an apartment to someone because he uses a seeing eye dog, has a girlfriend who is confined to a wheelchair or has a mother who is schizophrenic.

For the purpose of this requirement, discrimination refers to

- a refusal to permit reasonable modifications of existing premises if the modifications may be necessary to afford the handicapped person full enjoyment of the premises. In the case of a renter, a landlord may require the renter to agree to restore the interior of the premises to the condition that existed before the modifications (reasonable wear and tear excepted);
- a refusal to make reasonable accommodations in rules, policies, practices or services if the accommodations may be necessary to afford the handicapped person equal opportunity to use and enjoy a dwelling; and
- in connection with the design and construction of new covered multifamily dwellings, a failure to design and construct those dwellings in a manner that includes all of the following:
  a. Public-use and common-use areas that are readily accessible to the handicapped person
  b. Doors designed to allow passage using a wheelchair
  c. An accessible route into and through the dwelling
  d. Light switches, electrical outlets, thermostats, and other controls in accessible locations
  e. Reinforcements in bathroom walls to allow later installation of grab bars
  f. Usable kitchens and bathrooms so that an individual in a wheelchair can maneuver about the space

Note that a dwelling does not have to be made available to an handicapped individual when his or her tenancy would constitute a direct threat to the health or safety of other individuals or when that tenancy would result in substantial physical damage to the property of others. For example, an apartment owner may not have to rent an apartment to someone who is mentally ill, when that mental illness has caused that person to be arrested for assaulting next-door neighbors.

## EXEMPTIONS

There are several exemptions from the provisions of Arizona's fair housing law. These exemptions are similar to the exemptions from the Federal Fair Housing Law. The exemptions include

- the sale or rental of a single-family house sold or rented by an owner if
  a. the owner does not own or have an interest in more than three single-family houses at any one time;
  b. the house was sold or rented without the use of a real estate licensee or discriminatory advertisement; and
  c. the owner enters into only one sale or rental transaction in a 24-month period if the owner was not the most recent resident of the house at the time of the sale or rental;
- the sale or rental of rooms or units in a dwelling containing living quarters occupied or intended to be occupied by no more than four families if the owner maintains and occupies one of the living quarters as his or her residence;
- a religious organization that gives preference to or limits the sale, rental or occupancy of dwellings it owns or operates for other than a commercial purpose to persons of the same religion;
- a private club that is not open to the public that gives preference to or provides incidental lodging for a noncommercial purpose to its members; or
- housing for older persons that is specifically designed and operated to assist elderly persons under a federal or state program or that is intended for, and solely occupied by, at least one person 55 years of age or older.

Note that Arizona's fair housing law does not prohibit a person from discriminating against a person who has been convicted under federal or state law of illegal drug activities, nor does it prohibit an appraiser from taking into consideration factors other than race, color, religion, sex, handicap, familial status or national origin. Furthermore, the fair housing law does not affect reasonable local or state restrictions on the maximum number of occupants permitted to occupy a dwelling or a restriction relating to health or safety standards. Thus, if local ordinances limit the number of occupants of a two-bedroom apartment to four, a landlord could exclude a family of six without fear of being accused of discriminating on the basis of familial status.

## ENFORCEMENT

Any aggrieved person may file a complaint with the attorney general alleging discriminatory housing practices within one year of the event. The attorney general must investigate all complaints received, which must be in writing, under oath and in the proper form. (The attorney general may also investigate alleged discriminatory practices on his or her own initiative.) When the complaint is filed, the attorney general notifies the complainant that the complaint has been received, advises the complainant of the various forums available and notifies the respondent that a complaint has been filed against him or her. The notice sent to the respondent identifies the alleged discriminatory practice, advises him or her of all procedural rights and obligations and includes a copy of the original complaint.

Within ten days after receipt of the notice from the attorney general, the respondent must file an answer to the complaint, in writing, under oath and in the prescribed form.

If, after investigation, the attorney general determines that there is reasonable cause to believe that a discriminatory housing practice has occurred, he or she must try to effectuate a conciliation agreement between the parties. If no conciliation agreement can be reached, the attorney general must file a civil action in superior court. If the attorney general determines that the complaint was unfounded, he or she must promptly dismiss the complaint and give written notice of the dismissal to the parties.

An aggrieved party may also file a civil action in superior court no later than two years after the incident occurred. The filing of an civil action does not affect the attorney general's duty to investigate and make a determination on a complaint that has been filed. (However, if the attorney general succeeds in effecting a conciliation agreement during the complaint process, the aggrieved party may not file a civil suit with regard to that discriminatory housing practice.) If the court finds in favor of the plaintiff, it may award

- actual and punitive damages;
- reasonable attorney fees;
- court costs; and
- a permanent or temporary injunction or restraining order enjoining the defendant from engaging in the discriminatory practice or ordering appropriate affirmative action.

If the attorney general has reason to believe that a person has engaged in a pattern or practice of discriminatory behavior or that a person has been denied a right to fair housing that raises an issue of general public importance, the attorney general may file a civil action in superior court for appropriate relief. Under these circumstances, the court may

- award punitive relief, including an injunction, restraining order or other order necessary to assure the full enjoyment of the rights to fair housing;
- award other appropriate relief, including monetary damages, reasonable attorney fees, and court costs; or
- assess a civil penalty against the respondent in an amount not to exceed $50,000 for a first violation or $100,000 for a subsequent violation.

## QUESTIONS

1. Under Arizona law, familial status includes those

   a. living alone.
   b. living with a dependent senior citizen.
   c. who are pregnant.
   d. living with the teenage runaway friend of an adult child.

2. While real estate licensees may not discriminate in the brokering of dwellings, they may legally discriminate

   a. in the arrangement of purchase loans.
   b. against those convicted of illegal drug activity.
   c. in real estate advertisements.
   d. in the membership requirements of their professional associations.

3. Which of the following would not be considered handicapped under Arizona law?

   a. A person currently addicted to heroin
   b. A person with a multiple personality disorder who cannot hold down a full-time job
   c. A blind person
   d. A person with post-traumatic stress disorder

4. All of the following are subject to the provisions of the Arizona fair housing laws *except*

   a. *J*, the owner of a duplex, who is renting out one unit while living in the other.
   b. Country University, in renting out units in an apartment complex it owns and operates for profit.
   c. *M*, who owns four single-family homes, in renting out one of those homes.
   d. *W*, when obtaining listings by advising prospects of the entry of a protected class of people into the neighborhood.

5. *H* owns and manages an apartment building. He only rents to those who have no children. *B*, one of his tenants, reports his discriminatory practices to the attorney general. *H* then threatens *B* with eviction.

   a. *B* should move out immediately, as *H* is within his rights.
   b. *B* should report *H*'s threats to the attorney general, as they are a violation of the fair housing law.
   c. *B* could file a civil suit against *H*, but then the attorney general would be relieved of any duty to investigate *H*'s activities.
   d. *B* should do nothing and hope for the best.

6. *S* rents an apartment unit to *A*, a handicapped person. *A* alters the unit to accommodate her blindness. *S*

   a. can require *A* to pay a penalty for making alterations in the unit.
   b. can require *A* to restore the unit to its original condition (except for normal wear and tear).
   c. can report *A* to the attorney general for misuse of property.
   d. does not have to rent any more units to handicapped persons as renting one unit to *A* satisfies the requirements of the fair housing law.

7. *M* owns a ten-unit apartment building. He dislikes animals and firmly enforces his no-pet rule. *H*, a prospective tenant, has a girlfriend who uses a seeing-eye dog. *H*'s girlfriend is likely to visit the apartment frequently. *M* knows that he cannot keep *H*'s girlfriend from bringing the dog into the apartment building, so he simply refuses to rent the apartment to *H*.

   a. *M* has not violated any provision of the fair housing law, since *H* is not a disabled person.
   b. *M*'s' actions come within an exemption to the fair housing law.
   c. *M* has violated the fair housing law, because he has discriminated against *H* because of a handicapped person associated with *H*.
   d. *M* is within his rights as long as he does not use a broker to rent the unit.

8. *S* feels she has been unlawfully discriminated against when she was refused an apartment. *S* feels that her application was rejected because she is eight months pregnant. *S* has how long to file a complaint with the attorney general?

   a. Three months
   b. Six months
   c. One year
   d. Two years

9  A certain real estate licensee habitually refuses to take listings from Native Americans. The attorney general

   a. must wait until someone files a written complaint before investigating.
   b. may file an action in superior court, based on the pattern of discriminatory actions.
   c. must get the real estate licensee to admit to the behavior before beginning an investigation into the matter.
   d. can revoke the licensee's real estate license.

10. *S* has been an appraiser for 30 years. He firmly believes that homes in minority neighborhoods are less valuable than comparable homes in all-white neighborhoods. *S* is asked to appraise a home in a minority neighborhood and, as usual, he reduces its value by 20 percent because of the racial makeup of the neighborhood.

   a. *S* has not violated Arizona's fair housing laws because location is a legitimate factor to consider when preparing an appraisal.
   b. *S* has violated Arizona's fair housing laws by considering race in determining the appraised value of the home.
   c. *S* is not subject to Arizona's fair housing laws because he is not a real estate licensee.
   d. *S* has violated Arizona's fair housing laws, but is only subject to a reprimand by the attorney general, as no one has filed a complaint against him.

# 16

# Closing the Real Estate Transaction/Closing Problem

## CLOSING THE TRANSACTION

In many states, real estate transactions are closed by attorneys, lending institutions and even the brokers themselves. However, most real estate transactions in Arizona are closed by an escrow company, usually one that is also licensed as a title insurance company. This eliminates the unnecessary time and expense that would be incurred by the seller and the purchaser if the escrow service was to be performed by one company and the title insurance policy was to be provided by another.

## Escrow Closings

Separate escrow instructions that govern the closing process may have to be drafted by the parties to a real estate transaction, depending on the region in which the property is located. For example, in Maricopa County it is customary for the seller and the purchaser to sign the purchase contract and then later draft a separate set of escrow instructions. Both parties to the transaction and the escrow agent sign this document. These escrow instructions act as the employment contract between the parties and the escrow agent. In Pima County it is common for the purchase contract to serve as the escrow instructions; one document creates both the obligations between the seller and the purchaser and the subsequent obligations between the parties and the escrow agent. It is important to remember, however, that when a separate set of escrow instructions is used and there is a conflict between the content of the escrow instructions and the contents of the purchase contract, the purchase contract becomes the prima facie evidence of the original intent of the seller and the purchaser. (Sample escrow instructions are shown in Chapter 7.)

## Escrow Agents

Arizona Revised Statutes Sections 6–801 through 6–860 regulate the activities of escrow agents throughout the state. Escrow agents hold funds and prepare and hold documents for others, so they fall under the jurisdiction (and supervision) of the Arizona Banking Department.

The licensing requirements for an escrow agent include an application fee, a $100,000 corporate surety bond in favor of the state and an annual renewal fee for the principal office of the company and for each branch office. Escrow agents must also maintain a special trust account for depositing their clients' funds.

Certain persons are exempt from the licensing requirements for escrow agents, including

- financial institutions that are otherwise regulated by the superintendent of banks, even though escrow activities might be a regular part of their business activities.;
- attorneys licensed to practice law in Arizona who are not actively engaged in the escrow business;
- trustees acting under deeds of trust;
- persons acting as executors, administrators, bankruptcy trustees or attorneys-in-fact;
- persons acting under an order of the court; and
- real estate brokers.

Although brokers in Arizona can close transactions in which they assume the role of a "neutral third party" for the seller and the purchaser, most prefer not to act in such a capacity because

- the concept of neutrality prevents them from closing a transaction in which they have any interest (a commission qualifies as an interest);
- they cannot charge for their escrow services (Article XXVI of the Arizona Constitution prohibits such a fee, and the broker would need to be licensed as an escrow agent to collect one); and
- a professional escrow agent can handle a closing more efficiently and less expensively than a full-time broker can.

## Broker's Responsibilities

Commissioner's Rule R4–28–802 stipulates that the broker in any transaction must give the seller a detailed statement showing the receipts and disbursements handled by the broker, as well as copies of any other documents relative to the transaction that are requested by the seller. The broker must keep copies of these documents in his or her file, including evidence of the seller's receipt. (A sample closing statement is reproduced in this chapter as Figure 16.1.)

In addition, ARS Section 32–2151.01 requires the broker to "keep records of all real estate transactions handled by or through him" or her for at least five years from the closing date of the transaction. This would include copies of the closing statements prepared by the escrow agent.

If the broker anticipates having an escrow agent close the transaction, he or she should be prepared to deliver a copy of the purchase contract and the earnest money to the escrow agent in order to open the escrow. Some brokers do not maintain separate trust accounts for clients' funds, and in such instances, they usually have the earnest money check made payable directly to the escrow agent. The broker also is responsible for reviewing the closing statements prior to closing to be sure that the prorations are correct and every item has been properly accounted for.

## Title Evidence

As discussed in Chapter 9, most transactions in Arizona require the seller to furnish a title insurance policy and a warranty deed to the purchaser as evidence that the title being transferred is marketable. Although an abstract and legal opinion might be used occasionally, this is not a common occurrence.

The owner's title insurance policy, which insures the purchaser's interest, is customarily paid for by the seller. If the lender requires a lender's policy as a condition of funding a purchase loan, the cost of that policy becomes the purchaser's expense.

## Figure 16.1 Sample Closing Statement (Page 1 of 3)

A. **Settlement Statement**

**OLD REPUBLIC TITLE AGENCY**

U.S. Department of Housing
and Urban Development

OMB No. 2502-0265

**B. TYPE OF LOAN**

| 1. ☐ FHA | 2. ☐ FmHA | 3. ☐ Conv. Unins. | 6. File Number | 7. Loan Number | 8. Mortgage Insurance Case Number |
|---|---|---|---|---|---|
| 4. ☐ VA | 5. ☐ Conv. Ins. | | | | |

C. **NOTE:** This form is furnished to give you a statement of actual settlement costs. Amounts paid to and by the settlement agent are shown. Items marked "(p.o.c.)" were paid outside the closing; they are shown here for informational purposes and are not included in the totals.

| D. Name and Address of Borrower | E. Name and Address of Seller | F. Name and Address of Lender |
|---|---|---|
| | | |

| G. Property Location | H. Settlement Agent |
|---|---|
| | Place of Settlement |

I. Settlement Date

| J. SUMMARY OF BORROWER'S TRANSACTION | | K. SUMMARY OF SELLER'S TRANSACTION | |
|---|---|---|---|
| **100. GROSS AMOUNT DUE FROM BORROWER** | | **400. GROSS AMOUNT DUE TO SELLER** | |
| 101. Contract sales price | | 401. Contract sales price | |
| 102. Personal property | | 402. Personal property | |
| 103. Settlement charges to borrower (line 1400) | | 403. | |
| 104. | | 404. | |
| 105. | | 405. | |
| | | | |
| **Adjustments for items paid by seller in advance** | | **Adjustments for items paid by seller in advance** | |
| 106. City/town taxes              to | | 406. City/town taxes              to | |
| 107. County taxes                 to | | 407. County taxes                 to | |
| 108. Assessments                  to | | 408. Assessments                  to | |
| 109. | | 409. | |
| 110. | | 410. | |
| 111. | | 411. | |
| 112. | | 412. | |
| 113. | | 413. | |
| 114. | | 414. | |
| **120. GROSS AMOUNT DUE FROM BORROWER** | | **420. GROSS AMOUNT DUE TO SELLER** | |
| **200. AMOUNTS PAID BY OR IN BEHALF OF BORROWER** | | **500. REDUCTIONS IN AMOUNT DUE TO SELLER** | |
| 201. Deposit or earnest money | | 501. Excess deposit (see instructions) | |
| 202. Principal amount of new loan(s) | | 502. Settlement charges to seller (line 1400) | |
| 203. Existing loan(s) taken subject to | | 503. Existing loan(s) taken subject to | |
| 204. | | 504. Payoff of first mortgage loan | |
| 205. | | 505. Payoff of second mortgage loan | |
| 206. | | 506. | |
| 207. | | 507. | |
| 208. | | 508. | |
| 209. | | 509. | |
| | | | |
| **Adjustments for items unpaid by seller** | | **Adjustments for items unpaid by seller** | |
| 210. City/town taxes              to | | 510. City/town taxes              to | |
| 211. County taxes                 to | | 511. County taxes                 to | |
| 212. Assessments                  to | | 512. Assessments                  to | |
| 213. | | 513. | |
| 214. | | 514. | |
| 215. | | 515. | |
| 216. | | 516. | |
| 217. | | 517. | |
| 218. | | 518. | |
| 219. | | 519. | |
| **220. TOTAL PAID BY/FOR BORROWER** | | **520. TOTAL REDUCTION AMOUNT DUE SELLER** | |
| **300. CASH AT SETTLEMENT FROM/TO BORROWER** | | **600. CASH AT SETTLEMENT TO/FROM SELLER** | |
| 301. Gross amount due from borrower (line 120) | | 601. Gross amount due to seller (line 420) | |
| 302. Less amounts paid by/for borrower (line 220) | ( ) | 602. Less reductions in amount due seller (line 520) | ( ) |
| **303. CASH** ☐ FROM ☐ TO BORROWER | | **603. CASH** ☐ TO ☐ FROM SELLER | |

HUD—1 (3-86)
RESPA, HB 4305.2

FTGIS-40 9/91

SOURCE: Courtesy of Old Republic Title Insurance Agency, Inc.

# Figure 16.1 Sample Closing Statement (Page 2 of 3)

| L. SETTLEMENT CHARGES | | Paid From Borrower's Funds At Settlement | Paid From Seller's Funds At Settlement |
|---|---|---|---|
| 700. Total sales/broker's commission based on price $    @    % = | | | |
| Division of commission (line 700) as follows: | | | |
| 701. $    to | | | |
| 702. $    to | | | |
| 703. Commission disbursed at settlement | | | |
| 704. | | | |
| **800. ITEMS PAYABLE IN CONNECTION WITH LOAN** | | | |
| 801. Loan Origination Fee | | | |
| 802. Loan Discount | | | |
| 803. Appraisal Fee | | | |
| 804. Credit Report | | | |
| 805. Lender's Inspection Fee | | | |
| 806. Mortgage Insurance Application Fee to | | | |
| 807. Assumption Fee | | | |
| 808. | | | |
| 809. | | | |
| 810. | | | |
| 811. | | | |
| **900. ITEMS REQUIRED BY LENDER TO BE PAID IN ADVANCE** | | | |
| 901. Interest from    to    @ $    /day | | | |
| 902. Mortgage insurance premium for    mo. to | | | |
| 903. Hazard insurance premium for    yrs. to | | | |
| 904. Flood insurance premium for    yrs. to | | | |
| 905. | | | |
| **1000. RESERVES DEPOSITED WITH LENDER** | | | |
| 1001. Hazard insurance    mo. @ $    /mo. | | | |
| 1002. Mortgage insurance    mo. @ $    /mo. | | | |
| 1003. City property taxes    mo. @ $    /mo. | | | |
| 1004. County property taxes    mo. @ $    /mo. | | | |
| 1005. Annual assessments    mo. @ $    /mo. | | | |
| 1006.    mo. @ $    /mo. | | | |
| 1007.    mo. @ $    /mo. | | | |
| 1008.    mo. @ $    /mo. | | | |
| **1100. TITLE CHARGES** | | | |
| 1101. Settlement or closing fee    to | | | |
| 1102. Abstract or title search    to | | | |
| 1103. Title examination    to | | | |
| 1104. Title insurance binder    to | | | |
| 1105. Document preparation    to | | | |
| 1106. Notary fees    to | | | |
| 1107. Attorney's fees    to | | | |
| (includes above items numbers:) | | | |
| 1108. Title insurance    to | | | |
| (includes above items numbers:) | | | |
| 1109. Lender's coverage    $ | | | |
| 1110. Owner's coverage    $ | | | |
| 1111. | | | |
| 1112. | | | |
| 1113. | | | |
| 1114. | | | |
| **1200. GOVERNMENT RECORDING AND TRANSFER CHARGES** | | | |
| 1201. Recording fees: Deed $    Mortgage $    Releases $ | | | |
| 1202. City/county tax/stamps:    Deed $    Mortgage $ | | | |
| 1203. State tax/stamps:    Deed $    Mortgage $ | | | |
| 1204. | | | |
| 1205. | | | |
| **1300. ADDITIONAL SETTLEMENT CHARGES** | | | |
| 1301. Survey    to | | | |
| 1302. Pest inspection    to | | | |
| 1303. | | | |
| 1304. | | | |
| 1305. | | | |
| 1306. | | | |
| 1307. | | | |
| 1308. | | | |
| 1309. | | | |
| 1310. | | | |
| **1400. TOTAL SETTLEMENT CHARGES** (enter on lines 103, Section J and 502, Section K) | | | |

FTGIS-3056A 9/91

## Figure 16.1 Sample Closing Statement (Page 3 of 3)

Addendum to HUD-1
Settlement Statement

NOTICE TO ALL PARTIES: If information is obtained which indicates that the source of the borrower's financial contribution is other than from the borrower or other than stated by the lender in its closing instructions, the settlement agent is to obtain written instructions from the lender before proceeding with settlement.

Certification of Buyer in an FHA-Insured Loan Transaction

I certify that I have no knowledge of any loans that have been or will be made to me (us) or loans that have been or will be assumed by me (us) for purposes of financing this transaction, other than those described in the sales contract dated _____ . I certify that I (we) have not been paid or reimbursed for any of the cash downpayment. I certify that I (we) have not and will not receive any payment or reimbursement for any of my (our) closing costs which have not been previously disclosed in the sales contract (including addenda) and/or my application for mortgage insurance submitted to my (our) mortgage lender.

_____     _____

_____     _____

Borrowers/Buyers                                         _____
                                                                                          Date

Certification of Seller in an FHA-Insured Loan Transaction

I certify that I have no knowledge of any loans that have been or will be made to the borrower(s), or loans that have been or will be assumed by the borrower(s) for purposes of financing this transaction, other than those described in the sales contract dated _____ (including addenda). I further certify that I have not and will not pay or reimburse the borrower(s) for any part of the cash downpayment. I further certify that I have not and will not pay or reimburse the borrower(s) for any part of the borrower's closing costs which have not been previously disclosed in the sales contract (including any addenda).

_____     _____

_____     _____

Sellers                                                            _____
                                                                                          Date

Certification of Settlement Agent in an FHA-Insured Loan Transaction

To the best of my knowledge, the HUD-1 Settlement Statement which I have prepared is a true and accurate account of the funds which were (i) received, or (ii) paid outside closing, and the funds received have been or will be disbursed by the undersigned as part of the settlement of this transaction. I further certify that I have obtained the above certifications which were executed by the borrower(s) and seller(s) as indicated.

_____

Settlement Agent                                           _____
                                                                                          Date

[The certifications contained herein may be obtained from the respective parties at different times or may be obtained on separate addenda.]

WARNING: It is a crime to knowingly make false statements to the United States on this or any other similar form. Penalties upon conviction can include a fine and imprisonment. For details, see: Title 18 U.S. Code Sections 1001 and 1010.

FTGIS-42 9/91

In Arizona, a title insurance policy is issued as of the date of the close of escrow. There is no gap between the date the policy is issued and closing.

## Real Estate Settlement Procedures Act (RESPA)

The Real Estate Settlement Procedures Act requires the disclosure of all of the settlement costs in the closings of transactions that involve "federally related" real estate loans. Copies of the "Uniform Settlement Statement" (HUD Form 1) must be prepared by the lender and given to the purchaser (the borrower) and the seller. Customarily, this is handled through the escrow agent.

## CLOSING PROBLEM

Complete the listing contract, purchase contract and closing statement at the end of this chapter, using the facts given in the following description of a real estate transaction.

On July 5, 1996, Janet DeWinter, a salesperson for Newhouse Realty Company at 123 Broadway, Tempe, Arizona, and a member of the local multiple-listing service, secured a 90-day exclusive right to sell listing from George and Martha Cellars on their residence at 1234 East Coppertown Drive, Tempe, Arizona.

The Cellars' home is a ranch-style slump block house with a shake roof. It was built in 1985 on a 100' by 120' lot. The legal description of the property is Lot 13, Block B of the Paradise Sands Subdivision, according to the plat map recorded in Maricopa County. The county assessor's tax parcel number is 198–76–543.

The house measures 2,296 square feet, including a sunken living room (20' × 14'), dining area (14' × 12'), family room (20' × 14'), kitchen (14' × 12'), master bedroom (18' × 16'), two smaller bedrooms (14' × 12' each), master bathroom (12' × 8') and two smaller bathrooms (9' × 6' each). Each of the three bedrooms has adequate closet space. The laundry room (10' × 8') and the storage room (14' × 6') are both accessible from the inside of the house. The dining area overlooks a covered patio (16' × 12'), and there is a five-foot-high block wall completely enclosing the rear yard. There is a double carport (24' × 20') at the side of the house.

The kitchen appliances include a built-in range and oven combination, dishwasher and garbage disposal. The floors are covered with wall-to-wall carpeting, except in the kitchen, bathrooms, laundry room and storage room. There is a Rheem forced-air gas furnace for heat and a five-ton Westinghouse refrigeration unit for cooling. The insulation factors in the house are unknown.

Electricity is provided by Arizona Public Service, and Southwest Gas Corporation supplies natural gas to the property. Water is provided by the City of Tempe.

The Cellars have decided to take their draperies when they move into their new home. However, they will leave the carpeting, as well as the General Electric refrigerator (model GS-5760), the Maytag washing machine (model MRF-18026) and the Hotpoint electric drier (model HP-714-B).

DeWinter has listed the house for $155,000 and negotiated a 6 percent commission based on the actual selling price.

Mountain Valley Bank holds a trust deed on the property with an unpaid loan balance of $114,600 after the July 1 payment is made. The loan number is 987,654. Interest on the fixed rate loan is 11 percent, and the monthly payments of $1,143.60 are applied first to the interest due, and then to the outstanding principal balance. In addition, the Cellars are paying $150 per month into their impound account: $100 for estimated real estate taxes and $50 for property insurance premiums. The lender has indicated that this loan can be assumed by a qualified purchaser.

The real estate taxes for 1996 have not yet been billed but are estimated to be $1,200 based on the 1995 tax bill. There are no outstanding assessments against the property.

Arrangements to show the property must be made through Newhouse Realty at 555–5297.

On August 15, DeWinter obtained an offer on the Cellars' property from Jay and Linda Binder of 314 Home Street, Tucson, Arizona. The Binders offered $150,000 for the property, based on their assumption of the Cellars' loan and an additional $35,400 in cash. The Binders have agreed to reimburse the Cellars at the closing for the money in the impound account, which will be $1,617.50 as of the closing date.

The offer was accompanied by an earnest money check for $2,500, which will be deposited with the escrow agent, and the purchasers have agreed to increase the deposit to $7,500 upon the sellers' acceptance. Possession is to be given to the Binders at the close of escrow, which is to be no later than September 8, 1996. The Cellars accepted the offer from the Binders on August 17.

The expenses for closing this transaction include the following:

| | |
|---|---|
| Title insurance policy | $760 |
| Escrow service fee | $350 |
| Termite inspection report (seller's expense) | $48 |
| Loan transfer fee (customarily divided between the seller and the purchaser) | $50 |
| Premium for a new hazard insurance policy | $300 |
| Recording fee for the deed | $6 |
| Affidavit of property value | $2 |

In completing the prorations necessary to fill in the closing statement, note that in Arizona expenses attributable to the day of closing date belong to the purchaser. For example, if the sale is closed on March 19, a proration from January 1 to the day of closing would be two months and 18 days.

Compute all prorations on the basis of a 30-day month. Carry proration computations out to three decimal places and round off when the computation is complete. Check your solution with the one given in the Answer Key.

Type **ER**

Legal I.D.

## EXCLUSIVE RIGHT TO SELL/RENT
### (LISTING CONTRACT LEGAL LANGUAGE)

**THIS IS INTENDED TO BE A LEGALLY BINDING CONTRACT. NO REPRESENTATION IS MADE AS TO THE LEGAL VALIDITY OR ADEQUACY OF ANY PROVISION OR THE TAX CONSEQUENCES THEREOF. IF YOU DESIRE LEGAL OR TAX ADVICE, CONSULT YOUR ATTORNEY OR TAX ADVISOR.**

1. **EXCLUSIVE RIGHT TO SELL AND RENT.** In consideration of the acceptance by the undersigned licensed Arizona real estate broker ("Broker") of the terms of this Listing Contract ("Listing") and Broker's promise to endeavor to effect a ☐ sale or rental ☐ sale ☐ rental of the property described below ("Property"). I or we, as owner(s) ("Owner"), employ and grant Broker the exclusive and irrevocable right commencing on _____, 19____, and expiring at 11:59 p.m. _____, 19____, to sell, rent, exchange, or option the Property described in Paragraph 2.

2. **THE PROPERTY.** For purposes of this Listing, the "Property" means the real property in _____ County, Arizona described below, plus all fixtures and improvements thereon, all appurtenances incident thereto and all personal property described in Paragraphs 4 and 9.

   Street Address _____ City/Town _____

   Legal Description _____

3. **PRICE.** The listing price shall be:    Sale: $ _____

   Rental: $ _____ per month, plus all applicable lease or rental (transaction privilege) taxes to be paid as described in the Owner's Profile Sheet ("Data Entry Form"), or such other price and terms as are accepted by Owner.

4. **FIXTURES AND PERSONAL PROPERTY.** The Property includes personal property and excludes leased equipment as described in the Data Entry Form. Except as provided in the Data Entry Form, the Property also includes all of the following existing fixtures or personal property: storage sheds; heating and cooling equipment; built-in appliances; attached light fixtures and ceiling fans; window and door screens; sun screens; storm windows and doors; towel, curtain and drapery rods; draperies and other window coverings; attached carpeting; attached fireplace equipment; pool and spa equipment (including any mechanical or other cleaning systems); garage door openers and controls; attached TV antennas (excluding satellite dishes); attached plant watering, fire suppression and misting systems; water treatment systems; smoke detectors and fire warning systems; security systems and fences.

5. **ACCESS AND LOCKBOX.** Owner ☐ does ☐ does not authorize Broker to install and use, on the Property, a lockbox containing a key to the Property. Owner acknowledges that a lockbox and any other keys left with or available to Broker will permit access to the Property by Broker or any other broker, with or without potential purchasers or tenants ("Prospects"), even when Owner and occupant are absent. If the Property is occupied by someone other than Owner, Owner will provide to Broker the occupant's written permission for the installation of the lockbox and the publication and dissemination of the occupant's name and telephone number. Owner acknowledges that neither the Arizona Regional Multiple Listing Service ("ARMLS"), nor any Board or Association of REALTORS®, nor any broker, is insuring Owner or occupant against theft, loss or vandalism resulting from any such access. Owner is responsible for obtaining appropriate insurance.

6. **AGENCY RELATIONSHIPS.**

   a. Owner understands that Broker is Owner's agent with respect to this Listing. Owner understands that a Prospect may also wish to be represented by Broker in connection with the purchase or rental of the Property. In that event, Broker would be serving as the agent for both Owner and the Prospect. Since Owner does not wish to limit the range of Prospects at this time, Owner agrees to work with Broker to resolve any potential agency conflicts that may arise.

   b. Owner initially authorizes Broker to cooperate with other brokers ☐ in any manner whatsoever ☐ as subagents only ☐ without offering subagency . This election does not relieve Broker of his obligation to present all offers except as provided in Paragraph 28.

7. **COMPENSATION TO BROKER.** Owner agrees to compensate Broker as follows:

   a. **RETAINER.** Broker acknowledges receipt of a non-refundable retainer fee of _____ payable to Broker for initial consultation, research and other services.

   b. **COMMISSIONS.** If Broker produces a ready, willing and able purchaser or tenant in accordance with this Listing, or if a sale, rental, option or exchange of the Property is made by Owner or through any other agent, or otherwise, during the term of this exclusive listing, for services rendered, Owner agrees to pay Broker a commission of

   Sale: _____

   Rental: _____

   With respect to any holdovers or renewals of rental, regardless of whether this Listing has expired, Owner agrees to pay a commission of _____ The amount of the sale or rental commission shall be due and payable to Broker if, without the consent of Broker, the Property is withdrawn from this Listing, otherwise withdrawn from sale or rental or rented, transferred, or conveyed by Owner.

c. **PURCHASE BY TENANT.** If during the terms of any rental of the Property, including any renewals or holdovers, or within [ ] days after its termination, any tenant, or his heirs, executors, or assigns shall buy the Property from Owner, the sale commission described in Paragraph 7(b) shall be deemed earned by and payable to Broker.

d. **AFTER EXPIRATION.** After the expiration of this Listing, the same commissions, as appropriate, shall be payable if a sale, rental, exchange, or option is made by Owner to any person to whom the Property has been shown or with whom Owner or any broker has negotiated concerning the Property during the term of this Listing (1) within [ ] days after the expiration of this Listing, unless the Property has been listed on an exclusive basis with another broker, or (2) during the pendency, including the closing, of any purchase contract or escrow relating to the Property that was executed or opened during the term of this Listing, or (3) as contemplated by Paragraph 7(c).

e. **FAILURE TO COMPLETE.** If completion of a sale or rental is prevented by default of Owner, or with the consent of Owner, the entire sale or rental commission, as appropriate, shall be paid to Broker by Owner. If any earnest deposit is forfeited for any other reason, Owner shall pay a brokerage fee equal to the lesser of one-half of the earnest deposit or the full amount of the commission.

f. **PAYMENT FROM ESCROW OR RENT.** Owner instructs the escrow company, if any, to pay all such compensation to Broker in cash as a condition to closing or upon cancellation of the escrow, and to the extent necessary, irrevocably assigns to Broker all money payable to Owner at the closing or cancellation of the escrow. Broker is authorized to deduct compensation from any rent or other monies received on behalf of Owner.

g. **OTHER BROKERS.** Owner authorizes Broker to divide all such compensation with other brokers in any manner acceptable to Broker.

h. **NO LIMITATION.** Nothing in this Listing shall be construed as limiting applicable provisions of law relating to when commissions are earned or payable.

8. **HOME PROTECTION PLAN.** Owner acknowledges that home protection plans are available and that such plans may provide additional protection and benefits to Owner and any purchaser of the Property. Owner ☐ does ☐ does not agree to provide at his expense a home protection plan for the purchaser that will be effective at the close of escrow.

9. **ADDITIONAL TERMS.** _____

_____

_____

10. THE TERMS AND CONDITIONS ON THE REVERSE SIDE HEREOF PLUS ALL INFORMATION ON THE DATA ENTRY FORM ARE INCORPORATED HEREIN BY REFERENCE. COMMISSIONS PAYABLE FOR THE SALE, RENTAL OR MANAGEMENT OF PROPERTY ARE NOT SET BY ANY BOARD OR ASSOCIATION OF REALTORS' OR MULTIPLE LISTING SERVICE OR IN ANY MANNER OTHER THAN BY NEGOTIATION BETWEEN THE BROKER AND THE CLIENT. BY SIGNING BELOW, OWNER ACKNOWLEDGES THAT HE HAS READ, UNDERSTANDS AND ACCEPTS ALL TERMS AND PROVISIONS CONTAINED HEREIN AND THAT HE HAS RECEIVED A COPY OF THIS LISTING.

Print Name of Owner _____ Print Name of Owner _____

Street _____ City/Town _____ State _____ Zip _____

Phone _____ Fax Phone _____

Owner's Signature _____ Mo/Da/Yr _____ Owner's Signature _____ Mo/Da/Yr _____

11. In consideration of Owner's representations and promises in this Listing, Broker agrees to endeavor to effect a sale, rental, exchange, or option in accordance with this Listing and further agrees to provide this Listing for publication by a local Board or Association of REALTORS' and dissemination to the users of ARMLS.

Firm Name (Broker) _____ Office Phone _____

By: _____ Fax Phone _____

Agent's Signature _____ Date _____

Copyright February 1993 by Arizona Regional Multiple Listing Service, Inc. For Use with Data Entry Forms 1, 2, 3,

For Broker's office use only:

Broker's File/Lot No.: _____ Manager's Initials: _____ Broker's Initials: _____ Date: _____

**OWNER**

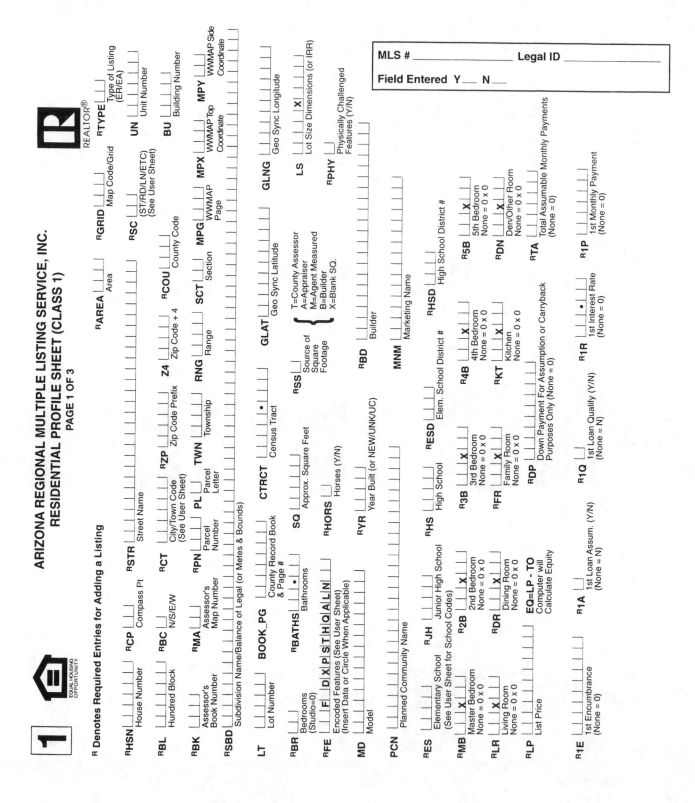

R2E — 2nd Encumbrance (None = 0)

R2A — 2nd Loan Assum. (Y/N) (None = N)

R2Q — 2nd Loan Qualify (Y/N) (None = N)

R2R — 2nd Interest Rate (None = 0)

R2P — 2nd Monthly Payment (None = 0)

R3E — 3rd/All Encumbrances (None = 0)

R3A — 3rd Loan Assum. (Y/N) (None = N)

R3Q — 3rd Loan Qualify (Y/N) (None = N)

R3R — 3rd Interest Rate (None = 0)

R3P — 3rd Monthly Payment (None = 0)

TO = 1E + 2E + 3E — Computer will Calculate Total Encumbrances

TP — |P|I|T|I|M|F| Monthly Payment Includes (Circle Where Applicable)

RTX — Taxes

RTY — Tax Year

WK — Week Available (Timeshares)

RHOA — Homeowner's Association (Y/N)

RHO — Homeowner's Association Fee None = 0

HF — Paid  M = Monthly  Q = Quarterly  S = Semi-Annually  A = Annually

RPD — Pad Fee None = 0

PF — Paid  M = Monthly  Q = Quarterly  S = Semi-Annually  A = Annually

RLL — Land Lease Fee None = 0

LF — Paid  M = Monthly  Q = Quarterly  S = Semi-Annually  A = Annually

RTN — Occupant  V = Vacant  O = Owner  T = Tenant  I = Interim Occ.

RON — Owner/Occupant Name

OT — Owner/Occupant Phone

RSBA — Subagents (Y/N)

RCS — Comp. to Subagent

RBB — Buyer Broker (Y/N)

RCB — Comp. to Buyer Broker

XC — Other Compensation

RVCOM — Variable Commission (Y/N)

RLO — List Office Code

OPH2 — Office Other Phone Number

OFAX — Office Fax Phone Number

RLA1 — Agent 1 Code

List Agent Name

RLD — List Date

REXP — Expire Date

HP1 — Agent 1 Home Phone

MB1 — Agent 1 Mobile Phone

PAG1 — Agent 1 Pager Phone

LA2 — Agent 2 Code

HP2 — Agent 2 Home Phone

MB2 — Agent 2 Mobile Phone

PAG2 — Agent 2 Pager Phone

The undersigned Owner acknowledges and reaffirms that this Profile Sheet is an integral part of the Listing Contract between Owner and Broker, that all information in the Profile Sheet is true, correct and complete, that the Owner will promptly notify Broker if there is any material change in such information during the term of this Listing and that Owner will indemnify other persons for inaccuracies in such information as further provided in the Listing Contract. If there is a conflict between the Listing Contract and this Profile Sheet, the terms of this Profile Sheet shall prevail. Owner agrees to indemnify and hold Broker, all Boards or Associations of REALTORS®, ARMLS and all other brokers harmless against any and all claims, liability, damage or loss arising from any misrepresentation or breach of warranty by Owner in this Listing, any incorrect information supplied by Owner and any facts concerning the Property not disclosed by Owner, including without limitation, any facts known to Owner relating to adverse conditions or latent defects.

_____     _____
OWNER SIGNATURE                                                        DATE

The undersigned Broker represents and warrants that the information in and manner of execution of this Profile Sheet and the related Listing Contract comply in all respects with the Rules and Regulations of ARMLS and the Broker's Board or Association of REALTORS®.

_____     _____
BROKER SIGNATURE                                                       DATE

## CLASS 1 - PAGE 2 OF 3

**(FEATURES: For Adding a Listing, underline the proper feature selections. (R) denotes required entries for Adding a Listing. All required Features must be entered for a new listing.)**

**RDTYP** Dwelling Type

A. Single Family-Detached (SF DET)
B. Patio Home (PATIO)
C. Townhouse (TOWNHS)
D. Apartment Style (APT)
E. Gemini/Twin Home (GEMINI)
F. Mobile Home (MOBILE)
G. Manufactured Housing (MNFACT)

**ROWNS** Ownership

A. Fee Simple (FEE)
B. Leasehold (LEASE)
C. Condominium (CONDO)
D. Timeshare (TSHAR)
E. Co-Operative (COOP)

**RARCH** Architecture

A. Single Level (SNGL)
B. Multi-Level (MULT)
C. Ranch (RNCH)
D. Territorial (TERR)
E. Spanish (SPAN)
F. Contemporary (CONT)
G. Other (See Remarks) (OTHR)

**BSTY** Building Style

A. 2-3-4 Plex (234P)
B. Clustered (CLUST)
C. String (STRNG)
D. High-Rise (HRISE)

**RAPSF** Approx. Sq. Ft. Range

A. <1,000 (<1,000)
B. 1,001-1,200 (1,001,1,200)
C. 1,201-1,400 (1,201-1,400)
D. 1,401-1,600 (1,401-1,600)
E. 1,601-1,800 (1,601-1,800)
F. 1,801-2,000 (1,801-2,000)
G. 2,001-2,250 (2,001-2,250)
H. 2,251-2,500 (2,251-2,500)
I. 2,501-2,750 (2,501-2,750)
J. 2,751-3,000 (2,751-3,000)
K. 3,001-3,500 (3,001-3,500)
L. 3,501-4,000 (3,501-4,000)
M. 4,001-4,500 (4,001-4,500)
N. 4,501-5,000 (4,501-5,000)
O. 5,001 + (5,001 +)

**CPOL** Pool - Community

A. Community Pool (PL)
B. Community Pool - Heated (PLH)
C. Community Spa (SP)
D. Community Spa - Heated (SPH)

**RDIN** Dining Area

A. Formal (FORML)
B. Eat-In Kitchen (EATIN)
C. Breakfast Room (BRKRM)
D. Dining in Living/Great Room (LR/GR)
E. Dining in Family Room (FAM)
F. Breakfast Bar (BRKBR)
G. Other Dining (See Remarks) (OTHR)

**RKFEA** Kitchen Features

A. Range/Oven (RG&OV)
B. Dishwasher (DISH)
C. Disposal (DSPL)
D. Microwave (MICRO)
E. Compactor (CMPAC)
F. Refrigerator (REFRG)
G. Pantry (PNTRY)
H. Kitchen Island (ISLND)
I. None (NONE)
J. Other (See Remarks) (OTHR)

**RLNDRY** Laundry

A. Washer Included (WASHER)
B. Dryer Included (DRYER)
C. Stacked Washer/Dryer Included (STACKD)
D. Washer/Dryer Hook-Up Only (HOOKUP)
E. Inside Laundry (I-LND)
F. Community Laundry (C-LND)
G. Laundry in Garage (G-LND)
H. Coin-Op Laundry (COINOP)
I. None (NONE)
J. Other (See Remarks) (OTHR)

**RPRK** Parking

A. 1 Car Garage (1G)
B. 2 Car Garage (2G)
C. 3 Car Garage (3G)
D. 4+ Car Garage (4+G)
E. 1 Car Carport (1C)
F. 2+ Car Carport (2+C)
G. Detached (DETACH)
H. Slab (SLAB)
I. Assigned Parking (ASSN)
J. Unassigned Parking (UNASN)
K. Side Vehicle Entry (SIDE)
L. Rear Vehicle Entry (REAR)
M. RV Parking (RVPKG)
N. RV Gate (RVGATE)
O. Electric Door Opener(s) (ELEOPN)
P. Separate Storage Area(s) (SEPSTG)
Q. Other (See Remarks) (OTHR)

**RCNST** Construction

A. Block (BLOCK)
B. Frame - Wood (FRMWD)
C. Frame - Metal (FRMMT)
D. Brick (BRICK)
E. Slump Block (SL-BLK)
F. Adobe (ADOBE)
G. Other (See Remarks) (OTHR)

**RFNSH** Construction - Finish

A. Painted (PAINT)
B. Stucco (STUCCO)
C. Brick Trim/Veneer (BKTRIM)
D. Stone (STONE)
E. Siding (SIDING)
F. Other (See Remarks) (OTHR)

**CSTA** Construction - Status

A. To-Be-Built (BEBULT)
B. Under Construction (UNCNST)
C. Completed Spec Home (SPECHM)

## RROOF  Roofing

A. Comp-Shingle (COMP)
B. Built-Up (BLT-UP)
C. All Tile (TILE)
D. Partial Tile (P-TILE)
E. Rock (ROCK)
F. Shake (SHAKE)
G. Concrete (CONCRT)
H. Foam (FOAM)
I. Rolled (ROLLED)
J. Metal (METAL)
K. Other (See Remarks) (OTHR)

## RCOOL  Cooling

A. Refrigeration (REF)
B. Evaporative (EVAP)
C. Both Refrig & Evap (BOTH)
D. Window/Wall Unit (W/W)
E. No Cooling (NONE)

## RHEAT  Heating

A. Electric Heat (ELEC)
B. Gas Heat (GAS)
C. Wall/Floor Heat (WFLR)
D. No Heat (NONE)
E. Other (See Remarks) (OTHR)

## EGY  Energy Features

A. Solar Hot Water (S-HWTR)
B. Sunscreen(s) (SUNSCR)
C. Ceiling Fan(s) (C-FAN)
D. Multi-Pane Windows (MLTPAN)
E. Load Controller (LDCONT)
F. Multi-Zones (M-ZONE)

## RUTIL  Utilities

A. APS (APS)
B. SRP (SRP)
C. SW Gas (SW GAS)
D. City Electric (C-ELE)
E. City Gas (C-GAS)
F. Other Electric (O-ELE)
G. Other Gas (O-GAS)
H. Butane/Propane (BUTANE)
I. Other (See Remarks) (OTHR)

## RWTR  Water

A. City Water (C-WT)
B. Private Water Comany (P-WT)
C. Well - Privately Owned (WLPO)
D. Well - Shared (WLSH)
E. Hauled (HAUL)
F. Water Softener (Owned) (WS-O)
G. Water Softener (Leased) WS-L)
H. Irrigation (IRR)
I. Drinking Water Filtering System (FILT)

## RFEA  Features

A. Fix-Up (FIXUP)
B. Remodeled (See Remarks) (REMODL)
C. Skylight(s) (SKYLIT)
D. Vaulted Ceiling(s) (VAULTD)
E. Central Vacuum (CNTVAC)
F. Wet Bar(s) (WETBAR)
G. Intercom (INTCOM)
H. Roller Shields (ROLLSH)
I. Fire Sprinklers (FIRESP)
J. Elevator (ELEVTR)
K. Security System (Owned) (SECOWN)
L. Security System (Leased) (SECLSD)
M. Cable TV Available (CABLE)
N. Furnished (See Remarks) (FURNSH)
O. None (NONE)
P. Other (See Remarks) (OTHR)

## RMS  Other Rooms

A. Family Room (FAMRM)
B. Great Room (GRTRM)
C. Library/Den (LB/DN)
D. Basement (BSMNT)
E. Game/Rec Room (GAME)
F. Arizona Room/Lanai (AZ RM)
G. Loft (LOFT)
H. Guest Qtrs-Sep Entrance (GSTQTR)
I. Exercise/Sauna Room (SAUNA)
J. Separate Workshop (SEPWK)
K. Clubhouse (CLUBHS)

## RXFEA  Exterior Features

A. Separate Guest House (GSTHSE)
B. Tennis Court(s) (TENNIS)
C. Handball/Racquetball Court(s) (HNDRAC)
D. Sport Court(s) (SPORT)
E. Patio (PATIO)
F. Covered Patio(s) (CPATIO)
G. Balcony/Deck(s) (BAL/DCK)
H. Gazebo/Ramada (GAZRAM)
I. Storage Shed(s) (STGSHD)
J. Circular Drive (CIRDRV)
K. Private Street(s) (PVT ST)
L. Private Yard(s)/Courtyard(s) (PVTYRD)
M. Yard Watering System-Front (WTRFRT)
N. Yard Watering System-Back (WTRBCK)
O. Children's Play Area (KIDPLY)
P. None (NONE)
Q. Other (See Remarks) (OTHR)

## MH  Mobile Home Features

A. Single Wide (SINGL)
B. Multi Wide (MULTI)
C. Built after 1976 (1976+)
D. In Subdivision (INSUB)
E. Affidavit of Fixture (AFFID)
F. Mobile Home - 5+ Acres (5+ AC)
G. Mobile Home - Waterline Hookup (WTRHU)
H. Mobile Home - Financing Available (FINAV)

## RMBTH  Master Bathroom

A. 3/4 Bath Master Bedroom (3/4 MSTR)
B. Full Bath Master Bedroom (FULL MSTR)
C. Separate Shower and Tub (SEP SH/TB)
D. Double Sinks (2 SINKS)
E. 2 Master Baths (2 MST BTH)
F. Tub with Jets (TUBJET)
G. Bidet (BIDET)
H. None (NONE)

## BED  Additional Bedroom Information

A. Master Bedroom Split (MSPLT)
B. Other Bedroom Split (OSPLT)
C. 2 Master Bedrooms (2MBR)
D. Master Bedroom Upstairs (MBRUP)
E. Master Bedroom Downstairs (MBRDN)
F. Master Bedroom Sitting Room (MBSIT)
G. Separate Bedroom Exit (EXIT)
H. Master Bedroom Walk-In Closet (MWLKN)
I. Other Bedroom Walk-In Closet (OWLKN)

## RFP  Fireplace

A. 1 Fireplace (1)
B. 2 Fireplaces (2)
C. 3+ Fireplaces (3+)
D. Fireplace in Family Room (FM)
E. Fireplace in Living Room (LR)
F. Fireplace in Master Bedroom (MB)
G. Two Way Fireplace (2W)
H. Gas Fireplace (GS)
I. Freestanding Fireplace (FS)
J. Exterior Fireplace (EX)
K. Firepit (PT)
L. No Fireplace (NO)
M. Other (See Remarks) (OT)

## RPPOL  Pool - Private

A. Pool-Private (PVT)
B. Fenced Pool (FNC)
C. Diving Pool (DIV)
D. Heated Pool (HTD)
E. Play Pool (PLY)
F. Lap Pool (LAP)
G. Above Ground Pool (AGD)
H. No Pool (NO)

## RPSPA  Spa - Private

A. Spa Private (SPA)
B. Above Ground Spa (AGS)
C. Spa-Heated (SPH)
D. None (NO)

**Owner acknowledges receipt of copy of this page,**
**which constitutes Page 2 of 3 Pages.**

Owner's Initials (    )

Broker's Initials (    )

# CLASS 1 - PAGE 3 OF 3

(FEATURES: For Adding a Listing, underline the proper feature selections. (R) denotes required entries for Adding a Listing. All required Features must be entered for a new listing.)

**RSWR Sewer**
A. Sewer - Public (PUBL)
B. Sewer - Private (PRIV)
C. Sewer - Available (AVAL)
D. Sewer in and Connected (SCON)
E. Septic (SEPT)
F. Septic in and Connected (SPIN)
G. No Sewer/Septic (NONE)
H. Other (See Remarks) (OTHR)

**SERV Services**
A. City Service (CIT)
B. County Services (COU)
C. Other (See Remarks) (OTHR)

**RFNC Fencing**
A. Block (BLOK)
B. Wood (WOOD)
C. Chain Link (LINK)
D. Concrete Panel (CONC)
E. Wire (See Remarks) (WIRE)
F. Partial (PART)
G. None (NONE)
H. Other (See Remarks) (OTHR)

**PROP Property Description**
A. Borders Preserve/Public Land (PUBLD)
B. Waterfront Lot (WFRNT)
C. Lake Subdivision (LAKE)
D. Golf Course Lot (GLFLT)
E. Golf Course Subdivision (GLFSB)
F. Hillside Lot (HILSD)
G. Cul-De-Sac Lot (CDSAC)
H. Corner Lot (CORNR)
I. Desert Front (DSFRT)
J. Desert Back (DSBCK)
K. Historic District (HDIST)
L. City Light View(s) (CTYVW)
M. Mountain View(s) (MTNVW)
N. Gated Community (GATED)
O. Guarded Entry (GUARD)
P. North/South Exposure (N/S)
Q. Alley (ALLEY)
R. Street(s) Not Paved (NOPAV)
S. Adjacent to Wash (WASH)
T. Borders Common Area (BDCOM)

**RSHOW Show Instructions**
A. Alarm Activated (ALRM)
B. Call Lister (LSTR)
C. Special Instr/Pets (CLO) (PETS)
D. Call Occupant (OCC)
E. Subagent-Use Lockbox (LBSA)
F. Buyer Broker-Use Lockbox (LBBB)
G. Lockbox-Occupied (LBOC)
H. Lockbox-Vacant (LBVA)
I. Lockbox - Not ARMLS (LBNA)
J. Vacant (VAC)
K. KILO or Courtesy Key (KILO)
L. Key at Guard Gate (KAGG)
M. Tenants Rights (TRGT)

**RPOS Possession**
A. By Agreement (AGREE)
B. Close of Escrow (COE)
C. Close of Escrow +2 days (COE+2)
D. Tenants Rights (T/RGT)

**USTY Unit Style**
A. All on One Level (1LVL)
B. Two Levels (2LVL)
C. Three or More Levels (3+LVL)
D. No Common Walls (NCMWAL)
E. One Common Wall (1CMWAL)
F. Two Common Walls (2CMWAL)
G. Three Common Walls (3CMWAL)
H. Neighbors Above (NABOVE)
I. Neighbors Below (NBELOW)
J. End Unit (END)
K. Poolside (PLSIDE)
L. Ground Level (GLVL)

**RFEES Association Fees Include**
A. Exterior Maintenance of Unit (EXTU)
B. Roof Maintenance - Partial (ROFP)
C. Roof Mainenance - Full (ROFF)
D. Blanket Insurance Policy (INSR)
E. Water (WTR)
F. Sewer (SWR)
G. Garbage Collection (GRBG)
H. Pest Control (PEST)
I. Air Conditioning/Heating (ACHT)
J. Electric (ELEC)
K. Gas (GAS)
L. Cable or Satellite TV (CBTV)
M. Front Yard Maintenance (FYRD)
N. Common Area Maintenance (CAM)
O. Street Maintenance (STMT)
P. No Fee (NONE)
Q. Other (See Remarks) (OTHR)

**RLN1 Existing 1st Loan**
A. FHA (FHA)
B. VA (VA)
C. Conventional (CONV)
D. Farm Home (FMHA)
E. Private (PRIV)
F. Wrap (WRAP)
G. Treat as Free and Clear (F&C)
H. Other (See Remarks) (OTHR)

**TRM1 Existing 1st Loan Terms**
A. Assume - No Quality (NOQUAL)
B. Assume - Quality (ASSM-Q)
C. Non Assumable (NOASUM)
D. Balloon/Call Provision (BALOON)
E. No Prepay Penalty (NOPRE)
F. Interest Only (INTONL)
G. Financial Information Subject to Verification (VERIFY)
H. All Assumable Existing Encumberances-No Qualify (ALLNQ)
I. Not Applicable (N/A)

**TYP1 Existing 1st Loan Type**
A. Fixed (FIX)
B. Adjustable/Graduated (ADJ)
C. Not Applicable (N/A)

**TRMO Existing Other Loan Terms**
A. Interest Only (INTO)
B. Balloon - Call Provision (BALL)
C. Other (See Remarks) (OTHR)
D. Not Applicable (N/A)

**MISC Miscellaneous**
A. Retirement Only (RETIRE)
B. Owner/Agent (OWN/AGT)
C. Court Approval Required (COURT APP)
D. Lender/Corp Approval Required (LENDR APP)
E. REO Property (REO PROP)
F. Exclusions (See Remarks) (EXCLUSION)
G. Flood Plain (FLOOD PLN)
H. Home Warranty (HOME WTY)
I. Have 1st Right/Accepting Backups (1RGHT/BU)

**HRSE**   Horses

A.   Corral (CORL)
B.   Stall (STAL)
C.   Barn (BARN)
D.   Tack Room (TACK)
E.   Arena (ARNA)
F.   Auto Water (AWTR)
G.   Hot Walker (WLKR)
H.   Commercial Breed (CBRD)
I.   Commercial Board (CBOA)
J.   Bridle Path Access (BPTH)
K.   Other (See Remarks) (OTHR)

**LTSZ**   Lot Size

A.   1-7,500 (1-7,500)
B.   7,501-10,000 (7,501-10,000)
C.   10,001-12,500 (10,001-12,500)
D.   12,501-15,000 (12,501-15,000)
E.   15,001-18,000 (15,001-18,000)
F.   18,001-24,000 (18,001-24,000)
G.   24,001-35,000 (24,001-35,000)
H.   35,001-43,559 (35,001-43,559)
I.   1 to 1.9 Acres (1 TO 1.9 AC)
J.   2 to 4.9 Acres (2 TO 4.9 AC)
K.   5 to 9.9 Acres (5 TO 9.9 AC)
L.   10 + Acres (10+ AC)

**RREST**   Association Restrictions

A.   Pets OK (See Remarks) (PETS OK)
B.   No Trucks, Trailers, or Boats (NO TRK)
C.   Separate RV Parking (SEP RV)
D.   HOA Approval of Buyer Required (HOA BYR)
E.   None (NONE)
F.   Other (See Remarks) (OTHR)

**RINFO**   Associaton Information

A.   FHA Approved Project (FHAOK)
B.   VA Approved Project (VAOK)
C.   Special Assessment Pending (SPASMPD)
D.   Professionally Managed (PRO-MGD)
E.   Self Managed (SLF-MGD)
F.   Not Managed (NOT-MGD)
G.   Club, Membership Optional (CLUB)
H.   None (NONE)
I.   Other (See Remarks) (OTHR)

**RNFIN**   New Financing

A.   Cash (CASH)
B.   CTL (CTL)
C.   VA (VA)
D.   FHA (FHA)
E.   Conventional (CONV)

F.   Farm Home (FMHA)
G.   Buy Down Subsidy (BUYD)
H.   Seller to Approve Points (SAPP)
I.   No Carry (NCAR)
J.   Seller May Carry (MCAR)
K.   Wraparound (WRAP)
L.   Lease Option (LSOP)
M.   Lease Purchase (LSPU)
N.   Also For Rent (RENT)
O.   Equity Share (EQSH)
P.   Exchange (EXCH)

**RDISC**   Disclosures

A.   Seller Disclosure Available (SPDS)
B.   Super Fund/WQARF/DOD Area (SFND)
C.   Agency Disclosure Required (AGCY)
D.   Special Assessment District (SAD)
E.   None (NONE)

**PHO**   Photo Code

A.   Take Photo (TAKE)
B.   Photo Submitted (SUBM)
C.   Sketch Submitted (SKTC)
D.   No Photo Requested (NON)
E.   Extra Photos/Sketches Submitted (EXTR)

**EXM:** ⌐‾‾‾‾¬
         For Office Use Only

**DIRECTIONS: Enter up to 159 Characters Maximum (including spaces and punctuation) to detail directions to the property.**

XST
Cross Street

DIR1 (Line 1)

DIR2 (Line 2)

**REMARKS: 560 Characters Maximum (including spaces and puntuation) to specify any additional information.**

RM1 (Line 1)

RM2 (Line 2)

RM3 (Line 3)

RM4 (Line 4)

RM5 (Line 5)

RM6 (Line 6)

RM7 (Line 7)

Owner acknowledges receipt of copy of this page, which constitutes Page 3 of 3 Pages.   Owner's Initials ( _____ )   Broker's Initials ( _____ )

# RESIDENTIAL RESALE REAL ESTATE
# PURCHASE CONTRACT AND RECEIPT FOR DEPOSIT

THE PRINTED PORTION OF THIS CONTRACT HAS BEEN APPROVED BY THE ARIZONA ASSOCIATION OF REALTORS™. THIS IS INTENDED TO BE A BINDING CONTRACT. NO REPRESENTATION IS MADE AS TO THE LEGAL VALIDITY OR ADEQUACY OF ANY PROVISION OR THE TAX CONSEQUENCES THEREOF. IF YOU DESIRE LEGAL, TAX OR OTHER PROFESSIONAL ADVICE, CONSULT YOUR ATTORNEY, TAX ADVISOR OR PROFESSIONAL CONSULTANT.

## RECEIPT

1. **Received From:** _____ ("Buyer")

2. **Agency Confirmation:** Broker named on Line 16 is the agent of (check one):

3. ☐ the Buyer exclusively; or   ☐ the Seller exclusively; or   ☐ both the Buyer and Seller

4. **Title:** The manner of taking title may have significant legal and tax consequences. Therefore, please consult your legal or tax advisor if you have any questions.

5. Buyer will take title as:   ☐ Determined before Close of Escrow   ☐ Community Property   ☐ Joint Tenants with Right of Survivorship

6. ☐ Sole and Separate Property   ☐ Tenants in Common   ☐ Other: _____

7. **Earnest Money:** Earnest money shall be held by Broker until offer is accepted. Upon acceptance, Broker is authorized to deposit the earnest money with
8. any Escrow Company to which the check is payable. If the check is payable to Broker, Broker may deposit the check in Broker's trust account or endorse
9. the check without recourse and deposit it with a duly licensed Escrow Company. Buyer agrees that, if Buyer breaches this Contract, any earnest money is
10. subject to forfeiture. All earnest money is subject to collection. In the event any check for earnest money is dishonored for any reason, at Seller's option,
11. Seller shall be immediately released from all obligations under this Contract notwithstanding any provisions contained herein. Unless otherwise provided
12. herein, all earnest money is considered to be part of the purchase price for the Premises described below.

13. a. | Amount of     b. | Form of   ☐ Personal Check     c. | Deposited   ☐ Broker's Trust Account
14. Deposit $ _____     Earnest Money:  ☐ Other: _____     With:   ☐ Escrow Company: _____

15. **Received By:** _____
   (PRINT SALESPERSON'S NAME)                (SALESPERSON'S SIGNATURE)          MO/DA/YR

16. _____
   (PRINT NAME OF FIRM)

## OFFER

17. **Property Description and Offer:** Buyer agrees to purchase the real property and all fixtures and improvements thereon and appurtenances incident there-
18. to, plus personal property described below (collectively the "Premises").

19. Premises Address: _____   Assessor's #: _____
20. City: _____   County: _____   AZ, Zip Code: _____
21. Legal Description: _____

22. **Fixtures and Personal Property:** All existing fixtures attached to the Premises: including storage sheds, electrical, plumbing, heating and cooling equip-
23. ment; built-in appliances; light fixtures; ceiling fans; window and door screens, sun screens; solar systems; storm windows and doors, shutters, awnings;
24. water-misting systems; fire detection/suppression systems; towel, curtain and drapery rods; draperies and other window coverings; attached floor coverings;
25. air cooler(s) and/or conditioner(s); attached fireplace equipment; wood-burning stoves; pool and spa equipment (including any mechanical or other cleaning
26. systems if owned by Seller); garage door openers and controls; security systems and/or alarms (if owned by Seller); timers; mailbox; attached TV
27. antennas (excluding satellite dishes); and all existing landscaping, including trees, cacti and shrubs shall be left upon and included with the Premises.

28. **Additional Existing Personal Property Included:** _____
29. _____
30. **Fixtures and Leased Equipment NOT Included:** _____

31. **Addenda Incorporated:**   ☐ AAR Addendum   ☐ Other _____

32. $ _____   **Full Purchase Price**, payable as follows:
33. $ _____   Earnest money as indicated above. _____
34. $ _____
35. $ _____
36. _____
37. _____
38. _____
39. _____
40. _____
41. _____
42. _____
43. _____
44. _____

45. **Closing Date:** Seller and Buyer will comply with all terms and conditions of this Contract and close escrow on [ _____ ] . Any earlier closing
   MO/DA/YR
46. date requires mutual agreement of Seller and Buyer. Seller and Buyer hereby agree that the Close of Escrow shall be defined as recordation of the docu-
47. ments. If escrow does not close by such date, this Contract is subject to cancellation as provided in Lines 348-356.

48. **Possession and Keys:** Possession and occupancy shall be delivered to Buyer **at Close of Escrow, or** ☐ _____
49. _____
50. Seller shall provide keys and/or means to operate all locks, mailbox, security system/ alarms, and access to all common area facilities.

51. **IF THIS IS AN ALL CASH SALE, GO TO LINE 194.**

©AAR Form 1546-830 RPC 07/94

# FINANCING OPTIONS

52. **This sale is contingent upon Buyer qualifying for a new first loan.**

53. **Loan Amount:** $ _____  **Term of Loan:** _____

54. **Type Of Loan:** ☐ Conventional Fixed Rate   ☐ Conventional Adjustable Rate   ☐ Other _____

55. **Interest Rate:** Interest rate shall not exceed _____ % as an annual rate for a fixed rate loan or an initial rate for an adjustable rate loan.

56. Buyer agrees to establish the interest rate and "points" by separate written agreement with the lender at the time of the loan application.

57. **Loan Application:** Buyer agrees to file a substantially complete loan application within five (5) calendar days after the acceptance of this Contract and to

58. promptly supply all documentation required by the lender. Buyer agrees to pay such fees as required by the lender.

59. **Conditional Loan Approval:** Within **fifteen (15) calendar days or** ☐ _____ **calendar days** after acceptance of this Contract, Buyer must place in

60. escrow a written conditional (preliminary) loan approval from the lender based on a completed loan application and preliminary credit report. If such condi-

61. tional (preliminary) loan approval is not received within the time specified, then Seller may give Buyer a five (5) calendar day written notice to perform. If

62. Buyer does not deliver to Escrow Company written conditional (preliminary) loan approval within said five (5) calendar days, then this Contract shall be

63. deemed cancelled and all earnest money shall be released to Buyer without further written consent of the parties and without regard to cancellation provi-

64. sions provided for elsewhere in this Contract. Buyer instructs lender to send copies of such approval to Brokers and Seller. Buyer authorizes the lender to

65. provide loan status updates to Brokers.

66. **Loan Costs:** Private Mortgage Insurance is required for certain types of loans. The cost will be paid by Buyer at the Close of Escrow in a manner acceptable to

67. lender. The following may be paid by either party:

68. **Discount points paid by:**          **Discount points shall not exceed:** _____

69. ☐ Buyer  ☐ Seller  ☐ _____                                    _____ total points. (does not include origination fee)

| | Buyer | Seller | | Buyer | Seller |
|---|---|---|---|---|---|
| 70. | | | | | |
| 71. A.L.T.A. Lender Title Insurance Policy | ☐ | ☐ | Loan Origination Fee (Not to exceed ____ % of loan amount) | ☐ | ☐ |
| 72. Escrow Fees | ☐ | ☐ | | | |
| 73. Appraisal Fee | ☐ | ☐ | ☐...Paid by Buyer and | ☐.....Paid by Seller and | |
| 74. | | | reimbursed by Seller at closing | reimbursed by Buyer at closing | |

75. Any additional costs not otherwise agreed upon by Seller shall be paid by Buyer.

76. **Appraisal:** This sale is contingent upon an appraisal of the Premises by an appraiser acceptable to the lender for **at least the sales price or**

77. ☐ _____ . The party responsible for paying for the appraisal shall do so within **five (5) calendar days of**

78. **Contract acceptance or** ☐ _____ Buyer and Seller acknowledge that the appraisal is an opinion

79. of value for lending purposes only, and may be different from the full purchase price.

## NEW FHA FIRST LOAN OR VA FIRST LOAN

80. **This sale is contingent upon Buyer qualifying for a new FHA or VA first loan:**

81. **Loan Amount:** $ _____ (excluding MIP, or Funding Fee)   **Term of Loan:** _____

82. **Type Of Loan:** ☐ FHA          ☐ VA

83. **FHA Mortgage Insurance Premium (MIP) or VA Funding Fee:** Amount $ _____ To be financed by Buyer which will increase the loan

84. amount to: $ _____ , or to be paid by Buyer in cash at Close of Escrow.

85. **Interest Rate:** Interest rate shall not exceed _____ % as an annual rate for a fixed rate loan or an initial rate for an adjustable rate loan.

86. Buyer agrees to establish the interest rate and "points" by separate written agreement with the lender at the time of the loan application.

87. **Loan Application:** Buyer agrees to file a substantially complete loan application within five (5) calendar days after the acceptance of this Contract and to

88. promptly supply all documentation required by the lender. Buyer agrees to pay such fees as required by the lender.

89. **Conditional Loan Approval:** Within **fifteen (15) calendar days or** ☐ _____ **calendar days** after acceptance of this Contract, Buyer must place in

90. escrow a written conditional (preliminary) loan approval from the lender based on a completed loan application and preliminary credit report. If such condi-

91. tional (preliminary) loan approval is not received within the time specified, then Seller may give Buyer a five (5) calendar day written notice to perform. If

92. Buyer does not deliver to Escrow Company written conditional (preliminary) loan approval within said five (5) calendar days, then this Contract shall be

93. deemed cancelled and all earnest money shall be released to Buyer without further written consent of the parties and without regard to cancellation provi-

94. sions provided for elsewhere in this Contract. Buyer instructs lender to send copies of such approval to Brokers and Seller. Buyer authorizes the lender to

95. provide loan status updates to Brokers.

96. **Loan Costs:** When maximizing the Buyer's loan amount under FHA "acquisition method," the Buyer's new loan amount **may** be reduced and additional

97. cash required at closing from the Buyer if the Seller pays for any of the items on Lines 98-105. The following may be paid by either party:

98. **Discount points paid by:**          **Discount points shall not exceed:** _____

99. ☐ Buyer  ☐ Seller  ☐ _____                                    _____ total points. (does not include origination fee)

| | Buyer | Seller | | Buyer | Seller |
|---|---|---|---|---|---|
| 100. | | | | | |
| 101. A.L.T.A. Lender Title Insurance Policy | ☐ | ☐ | Loan Origination Fee | ☐ | ☐ |
| 102. Credit Report | ☐ | ☐ | Recording to Vest Title in Buyer | ☐ | ☐ |
| 103. Escrow Fees (V.A. - All by Seller) | ☐ | ☐ | | | |
| 104. Appraisal Fee | ☐ | ☐ | ☐...Paid by Buyer and | ☐.....Paid by Seller and | |
| 105. | | | reimbursed by Seller at closing | reimbursed by Buyer at closing | |

106. **Mandatory Costs:** FHA regulations require the Buyer to pay for the following items: Reserves (impounds) for property taxes and hazard insurance, plus adjusted

107. interest. Both FHA and VA require that the Seller must pay for the following fees, if applicable: assignment, flood certification, recordings to clear title, bringdown

108. endorsement, document preparation, photo/inspection, tax service and warehousing. In addition, VA requires the Seller to pay all escrow fees.

109. Any additional costs not otherwise agreed upon by Seller shall be paid by Buyer.

110. **Appraisal:** The party responsible for paying for the appraisal shall do so within **five (5) calendar days or** ☐ _____ **calendar days** of Contract
111. acceptance. Buyer and Seller acknowledge that the appraisal is an opinion of value for lending purposes only, and may be different from
112. the full purchase price.
113. **VA Amendatory Clause:** It is expressly agreed that notwithstanding any other provision of this Contract, the Purchaser shall not incur any penalty by forfei-
114. ture of earnest money or otherwise be obligated to complete the purchase of the property described herein if the Contract purchase price or costs exceeds
115. the reasonable value of the property established by the Veterans Administration. The Purchaser shall, however, have the privilege and option of proceeding
116. with the consummation of this Contract without regard to the amount of the reasonable value established by the Veterans Administration.
117. **FHA Amendatory Clause:** It is expressly agreed that notwithstanding any other provisions of this Contract, the purchaser shall not be obligated to complete
118. the purchase of the property described herein or to incur any penalty by forfeiture of earnest money deposits or otherwise unless the purchaser has been
119. given in accordance with HUD/FHA or VA requirements a written statement by the Federal Housing Commissioner, Veterans Administration, or a Direct

120. Endorsement lender setting forth the appraised value of the property of not less than $ _____ .The purchaser shall have the
121. privilege and option of proceeding with consummation of the contract without regard to the amount of the appraised valuation. The appraised valuation is
122. arrived at to determine the maximum mortgage the Department of Housing and Urban Development will insure. HUD does not warrant the value nor the
123. condition of the property. The purchaser should satisfy himself/herself that the price and condition of the property are acceptable.
124. **Notice To Buyer:** If the residence was constructed prior to 1978, the U.S. Department of Housing and Urban Development requires that the Buyer receive
125. and sign a copy of "Notice to Purchasers of Housing Constructed Prior to 1978" before signing any purchase contract contingent upon FHA financing. The
126. notice explains potential risks if the residence contains lead-based paint.

## ASSUMPTION OF EXISTING FIRST LOAN

127. **Buyer agrees to assume the existing loan(s) and pay all payments subsequent to Close of Escrow.**
128. **Assumption:** This sale ☐ is   ☐ is not contingent upon the Buyer qualifying for assumption of the existing first loan.
129. **Release of Seller's Liability:** This sale ☐ is   ☐ is not contingent upon Seller being released by lender from liability for loan being assumed. If
130. Seller is not released from liability, Seller acknowledges that there may be continuing liability in the event of a Buyer default.

131. **Type Of Loan:** ☐ Conventional   ☐ VA   ☐ FHA _____   ☐ Other _____

132. **Current Interest Rate:** [_____]   **Current Payment Amount:**
133. ☐ Fixed   ☐ Adjustable _____ %   $ _____ ☐ PITI   ☐ PI   ☐ Other _____

134. **Loan Balance:** $ _____
135. The balance of any encumbrance being assumed is approximate. Any difference shall be reflected in the:
136. ☐ Cash Down Payment   ☐ Seller Carryback   ☐ Other: _____

137. **Impounds:** Buyer shall   ☐ reimburse Seller for any impounds transferred to Buyer or ☐ _____

138. **Loan Transfer and Assumption Fees:** To be paid by   ☐ Buyer   ☐ Seller   ☐ _____ [All other lender charges shall be paid by Buyer.]
139. If more than one loan is being assumed, go to Additional Terms and Conditions (Lines 194-205).
140. **Credit Evaluation:** This sale ☐ is   ☐ is not contingent upon Seller's approval of Buyer's credit. If applicable, Buyer shall provide to Seller a current
141. credit report from a credit reporting agency and a completed loan application on the current FNMA form within five (5) calendar days after acceptance of this
142. Contract. Disapproval of Buyer's credit requires written notice from Seller to Escrow Company within five (5) calendar days after receipt by Seller of current
143. credit report and completed loan application. Approval will not be unreasonably withheld. Escrow Company is directed to record a Notice of Request for
144. Sale on behalf of the Seller and at Seller's expense.
145. **Lender Requirements:** Buyer and Seller agree to cooperate fully with lender and supply the necessary documentation to complete the assumption.
146. **Mortgage Insurance:** The loan amount assumed may include mortgage insurance, which Buyer also assumes and agrees to pay exclusive of life insurance.

## SELLER CARRYBACK FINANCING

147. **A portion of the purchase price shall be financed by the Seller and paid by the Buyer as follows, with the first payment due** [_____] .
   MO/DA/YR

148. **Loan Amount:** $ _____   as adjusted, if necessary, pursuant to lines 134-136.

149. **Priority Of Loan:** ☐ First   ☐ Second   ☐ _____

150. **Type Of Financing Instrument:** Buyer shall execute a promissory note and deed of trust in favor of Seller and record the deed of trust against the Premises.

151. **Interest Rate:** The unpaid balance shall bear interest at the rate of _____ % per year,   beginning at the Close of Escrow.

152. **Payment Intervals:** ☐ Monthly   ☐ Quarterly   ☐ Semi-annually   ☐ Annually   ☐ Other _____

153. **Collection Fees:** Collection setup fees and servicing costs shall be paid by   ☐ Buyer   ☐ Seller   ☐ _____

154. Collection account to be handled by _____

155. **Payment Amount:** $ _____ , or more, including the above stated interest.
156. If an adjustment in the loan amount is necessary pursuant to line 148, parties agree to adjust the:   ☐ Payment amount   ☐ Term

157. **Loan Term:** ☐ Amortizing over _____ years   ☐ If balloon payment, principal balance due on or before _____
158. ☐ Interest-only payments, with principal balance due on or before _____

159. **Late Payments:** If late, Buyer shall pay late fees:   ☐ Yes   ☐ No   If "Yes", payments which are at least _____ calendar days past due

160. shall be subject to a late fee of _____ . If any balloon payment is late, then the late fee per day will be $ _____ .

161. **Default Rate:** If payment(s) are at least 30 calendar days past due, then the principal balance shall bear interest at a default rate of **five percent (5%) or** ☐_____ %
162. over the interest rate of the carryback as stated herein. Said default rate shall begin on the 31st day following the due date of the payment(s) until payment(s)
163. are brought current. Payments are first applied to accrued interest and penalties, then to principal.
164. **Credit Evaluation:** This sale ☐ is ☐ is not contingent upon Seller's approval of Buyer's credit. If applicable, Buyer shall provide to Seller a current
165. credit report from a credit reporting agency and a completed loan application on the current FNMA form within five (5) calendar days after acceptance of this
166. Contract. Disapproval of Buyer's credit requires written notice from Seller to Escrow Company within five (5) calendar days after receipt by Seller of current credit
167. report and completed loan application. Approval will not be unreasonably withheld.
168. **Due On Sale:** Loan created ☐ is ☐ is not due on sale of the Premises. If loan created herein is due on sale of the Premises, and in the event that
169. the Premises is sold, transferred or conveyed in any manner, the promissory note and deed of trust shall provide that the promissory note and deed of trust
170. become immediately due and payable.
171. **Buyer's Liability:** On certain qualified residential property, the Seller understands that under Arizona law the Buyer may have no personal liability in case
172. of a default and that the Seller's only recourse may be to look to the property for the sole and exclusive source for repayment of the debt. Buyer shall furnish
173. to Seller, at Buyer's expense, a Standard Loan Policy in the full amount of any loan carried back by Seller and secured by the real property described in
174. Lines 19-21 of this Contract. Such Standard Loan Policy shall show that Seller's lien has the priority agreed to by the parties.
175. **Taxes:** In the absence of a tax impound account, Buyer shall provide and pay for a tax service contract over the life of this loan which will provide a delin-
176. quency notice to Seller, or any successor in interest to the Seller, of any unpaid taxes.
177. **Insurance:** Buyer shall provide, maintain and deliver to Seller hazard insurance satisfactory to, and with loss payable to Seller, in at least the amount of all
178. encumbrances against the Premises. This provision shall be made a part of the language of the deed of trust.
179. **Payments Through Servicing Agent:** Payments on this loan and all prior encumbrances shall be made concurrently through a single servicing account to be
180. maintained by a duly licensed account servicing agent. Payments on this loan shall be made at least ten (10) calendar days prior to the due date of any periodic
181. payment due on any prior encumbrance. The parties hereby instruct servicing agent not to accept any payment without all other concurrent payments.

## GENERAL LOAN PROVISIONS

182. **Occupancy:** Buyer ☐ does ☐ does not intend to occupy the Premises as Buyer's primary residence.
183. **Release Of Broker:** Any loan described in this Contract will be independently investigated and evaluated by Seller and/or Buyer, who hereby acknowledge
184. that any decision to enter into any loan arrangements with any person or entity will be based solely upon such independent investigation and evaluation.
185. Buyer and Seller further hold harmless and release Broker and acknowledge that no Broker is in any way responsible for Buyer's or Seller's decisions con-
186. cerning the desirability or acceptability of any loan or any terms thereof.
187. **Changes:** Buyer shall not make any changes in the loan program or financing terms described in this Contract without the prior written consent of Seller
188. unless such changes do not adversely affect Buyer's ability to qualify for the loan, increase Seller's closing costs or delay the closing date.
189. **Return Of Earnest Money:** Unless otherwise provided herein, Buyer is entitled to a return of the earnest money, if after a diligent and good faith effort, Buyer does
190. not qualify for a loan described in this Contract. Buyer acknowledges that prepaid items paid separately from earnest money are not refundable.
191. **RESPA:** The Real Estate Settlement Procedures Act (RESPA) requires that no Seller of property that will be purchased with the assistance of a federally
192. related mortgage loan shall require, directly or indirectly, as a condition of selling the property, that title insurance covering the property be purchased by the
193. Buyer from any particular title company.

# ADDITIONAL TERMS AND CONDITIONS

194. _____
195. _____
196. _____
197. _____
198. _____
199. _____
200. _____
201. _____
202. _____
203. _____
204. _____
205. _____

206. **Escrow:** The Escrow Company shall be: _____
207. ☐ This Contract will be used as escrow instructions. ☐ Separate escrow instructions will be executed.
208. (a) If the Escrow Company is also acting as the title agency but is not the title insurer issuing the title insurance policy, the Buyer and Seller hereby request
209. the Escrow Company to deliver to the Buyer and Seller upon opening of escrow a closing protection letter from the title insurer indemnifying the Buyer and
210. Seller for any losses due to fraudulent acts or breach of escrow instructions by the Escrow Company. (b) If Seller and Buyer elect to execute escrow instruc-
211. tions to fulfill the terms hereof, they shall deliver the same to Escrow Company within fifteen (15) calendar days of the acceptance of this Contract. (c) All doc-
212. uments necessary to close this transaction shall be executed promptly by Seller and Buyer in the standard form used by Escrow Company. Escrow Company
213. is hereby instructed to modify such documents to the extent necessary to be consistent with this Contract. (d) If any conflict exists between this Contract and
214. any escrow instructions executed pursuant hereto, the provisions of this Contract shall be controlling. (e) All closing and escrow costs, unless otherwise stat-
215. ed herein, shall be allocated between Seller and Buyer in accordance with local custom and applicable laws and regulations. (f) Escrow Company is hereby
216. instructed to send to Brokers copies of all notices and communications directed to Seller or Buyer. Escrow Company shall provide to such Brokers access to
217. escrowed materials and information regarding the escrow. (g) Any documents necessary to close the escrow may be signed in counterparts, each of which
218. shall be effective as an original upon execution, and all of which together shall constitute one and the same instrument.
219. **Prorations:** Taxes, homeowners' association fees, rents, irrigation fees, and, if assumed, insurance premiums, interest on assessments, and interest on
220. encumbrances shall be prorated as of ☐ Close of Escrow ☐ Other: _____

221. **Assessments:** The amount of any assessment which is a lien as of the Close of Escrow shall be ☐ Paid in Full by Seller ☐ Prorated and
222. Any assessment that becomes a lien after Close of Escrow is the Buyer's responsibility. Assumed by Buyer
223. **IRS Reporting:** Seller agrees to comply with IRS reporting requirements. If applicable, Seller agrees to complete, sign and deliver to Escrow Company a certificate
224. indicating whether Seller is a foreign person or a non-resident alien pursuant to the Foreign Investment in Real Property Tax Act (FIRPTA).

©AAR Form 1546-830 RPC 07/94

225. **Seller Property Disclosure Statement (SPDS):**
226. (a) ☐ Buyer has received, read, and approved the SPDS.
227. (b) ☐ Buyer waives review and approval of the SPDS. **(BUYERS' INITIALS ARE REQUIRED HERE TO WAIVE SPDS** _____ _____ )
                                                                                        BUYER        BUYER
228. (c) ☐ Seller shall deliver the SPDS within five (5) calendar days after acceptance of the Contract, after which Buyer shall have five (5) calendar days after
229. receipt by Buyer to immediately terminate this Contract notwithstanding any other provisions contained herein by delivering written notice of termination to
230. either the Seller or to the Escrow Company, and in such event, Buyer is entitled to a return of the earnest money without further consent of the Seller. (AAR
231. FORM 1417, OR EQUIVALENT, SHALL SATISFY THIS REQUIREMENT.)

232. **Title and Vesting:** Escrow Company is hereby instructed to obtain and distribute to Buyer a Commitment for Title Insurance together with complete and legible
233. copies of all documents which will remain as exceptions to Buyer's policy of Title Insurance, including but not limited to Conditions, Covenants and Restrictions,
234. deed restrictions and easements. Buyer shall have five (5) calendar days after receipt of the Commitment for Title Insurance to provide written notice to Seller of
235. any of the exceptions disapproved. REFER TO LINES 283-291 FOR IMPORTANT TERMS. If thereafter the title is otherwise defective at Close of Escrow,
236. Buyer may elect, as Buyer's sole option, either to accept title subject to defects which are not cured or to cancel this Contract whereupon all money paid by
237. Buyer pursuant to this Contract shall be returned to Buyer. Seller shall convey title by general warranty deed. Buyer shall be provided at Seller's expense a
238. Standard Owner's Title Insurance Policy, or, if available, an American Land Title Association (ALTA) Residential Title Insurance Policy ("Plain Language"/"1-4
239. units") showing the title vested in Buyer as provided in Lines 5-6. Buyer may acquire extended coverage at his own additional expense.

240. **Seller's Notice of Violations:** Seller represents that Seller has no knowledge of any notice of violations of City, County, State, or Federal building, zoning,
241. fire, or health laws, codes, statutes, ordinances, regulations, or rules filed or issued regarding the Premises. If Seller receives notice of violations prior to
242. Close of Escrow, Seller shall immediately notify Buyer in writing. Buyer is allowed five (5) calendar days after receipt of notice to provide written notice to
243. Seller of any items disapproved. REFER TO LINES 283-291 FOR IMPORTANT TERMS.

244. **H.O.A./Condominium/P.U.D.:** If the Premises is located within a homeowners' association/condominium/planned unit development:
245. (a) the current regular association dues are  $ _____   ☐ monthly,  ☐ _____ ;
246. (b) Seller shall, as soon as practicable, and prior to Close of Escrow, (1) disclose in writing to Buyer any known existing or pending special assessments,
247. claims, or litigation, and (2) provide to Buyer copies of Covenants, Conditions, and Restrictions, Articles of Incorporation, bylaws, other governing docu-
248. ments, any other documents required by law, and homeowners' association approval of transfer, if applicable, and current financial statement and/or
249. budget. Buyer is allowed five (5) calendar days after receipt to provide written notice to Seller of any items reasonably disapproved.
250. REFER TO LINES 283-291 FOR IMPORTANT TERMS. Any current homeowners' assessments to be   ☐ paid in full by Seller;   ☐ assumed by Buyer
251. Transfer fees, if any, shall be paid by   ☐ Seller   ☐ Buyer   ☐ Other: _____

252. **Inspection Period (Physical, Environmental and Other Inspections):** Buyer has been advised of the benefits of obtaining independent inspec-
253. tions of the entire Premises in order to determine the condition thereof. In addition to the provisions regarding wood infestation, Buyer shall have the
254. right at Buyer's expense to select an inspector(s) to make additional inspections (including tests, surveys, and other studies) of the Premises. Buyer
255. acknowledges that more than one inspection may be required to perform the selected inspections. The inspections may include physical, environ-
256. mental and other types of inspections including, but not limited to, square footage, roof, designated flood hazard areas, structural, plumbing,
257. sewer/septic, well, heating, air conditioning, electrical and mechanical systems, built-in appliances, soil, foundation, pool/spa and related equipment,
258. cost of compliance with Swimming Pool Regulations, possible environmental hazards (such as asbestos, formaldehyde, radon gas, lead-based
259. paint, fuel or chemical storage tanks, hazardous waste, other substances, materials or products; and/or location in a federal or state Superfund area,
260. geologic conditions, location of property lines, and water/utility use restrictions and fees for services (such as garbage or fire protection). Seller shall make
261. the Premises available for all inspections. It is understood that this inspection requires that the utilities be on and the Seller is responsible for providing
262. same at his expense. Buyer shall keep the Premises free and clear of liens, shall indemnify and hold Seller harmless from all liability, claims, demands,
263. damages, and costs, and shall repair all damages arising from the inspections. Buyer shall provide Seller and Brokers, at no cost, copies of all reports
264. concerning the Premises obtained by Buyer. Buyer shall provide written notice to Seller of any items reasonably disapproved,
265. excluding cosmetic items, within **ten (10) calendar days or** ☐ _____ **calendar days** after acceptance of the Contract. Any repairs agreed to shall
266. be completed prior to Close of Escrow. REFER TO LINES 283-291 FOR IMPORTANT TERMS.

267. **SQUARE FOOTAGE: BUYER IS AWARE THAT ANY REFERENCE TO THE SQUARE FOOTAGE OF THE PREMISES IS APPROXIMATE. IF SQUARE**
268. **FOOTAGE IS A MATERIAL MATTER TO THE BUYER, IT MUST BE VERIFIED DURING THE INSPECTION PERIOD.**

269. **Flood Hazard Disclosure:** If the Premises is situated in an area identified as having any special flood hazards by any governmental entity including, but not limited to,
270. being designated as a special flood hazard area by the Federal Emergency Management Agency (FEMA), the Buyer's lender may require the purchase of flood haz-
271. ard insurance at the Close of Escrow or some future date. Special flood hazards may affect the ability to encumber or improve the property now or at some
272. future date. **Flood hazard designation of the Premises or cost of flood hazard insurance must be verified by Buyer during the Inspection Period.**

273. **Swimming Pool Regulations:** These Premises ☐ do ☐ do not contain a swimming pool which is defined as an above or below ground swimming
274. pool or contained body of water intended for swimming, exclusive of public or semi-public swimming pools ("Swimming Pool"). Seller and Buyer acknowl-
275. edge that the State of Arizona has swimming pool barrier regulations which are outlined in the Arizona Department of Health Services Private Pool Safety
276. Notice. The parties further acknowledge that the county or municipality in which the Premises is located may have different swimming pool barrier regula-
277. tions than the state. During the Inspection Period, Buyer agrees to investigate all applicable state, county and municipal swimming pool barrier regulations
278. and, unless disapproved within the Inspection Period, agrees to comply with and pay all costs of compliance with said regulations prior to possession of
279. the Premises. If these Premises contain a Swimming Pool, BUYER ACKNOWLEDGES RECEIPT OF THE ARIZONA DEPARTMENT OF HEALTH SER-
280. VICES APPROVED PRIVATE POOL SAFETY NOTICE AS REQUIRED BY A.R.S. 36-1681 (E) AND A.D.H.S.. RULE R9-3-101.

281. **(BUYERS INITIALS ARE REQUIRED)** _____ _____
                                             BUYER       BUYER
282. Buyer and Seller expressly relieve and indemnify Brokers from any and all liability and responsibility for compliance with the applicable pool barrier regulations.

283. **Buyer Disapproval:** If Buyer gives written notice of disapproval of items as provided herein, Seller shall respond in writing within **five (5) calendar days or**
284. ☐ _____ **calendar days** after receipt of such notice. Seller acknowledges that items warranted by Seller must be maintained and repaired as
285. provided in Lines 312-319. If Seller is unwilling or unable to correct additional items reasonably disapproved by Buyer, including making any repairs in a workmanlike
286. manner, then Buyer may cancel this Contract by giving written notice of cancellation to Seller within five (5) calendar days after receipt of Seller's response, or after
287. expiration of the time for Seller's response, whichever occurs first, in which case Buyer's deposit shall be returned to Buyer, without further written consent of Seller,
288. and without regard to the cancellation provisions in Lines 348-356. Notwithstanding the foregoing, if the items reasonably disapproved by the Buyer exceed ten per-
289. cent (10%) of the purchase price, the Buyer shall be entitled to cancel this Contract. **BUYER'S FAILURE TO GIVE WRITTEN NOTICE OF DISAPPROVAL OF**
290. **ITEMS OR CANCELLATION OF THIS CONTRACT WITHIN THE SPECIFIED TIME PERIODS SHALL CONCLUSIVELY BE DEEMED BUYER'S ELECTION TO**
291. **PROCEED WITH THE TRANSACTION WITHOUT CORRECTION OF ANY DISAPPROVED ITEMS WHICH SELLER HAS NOT AGREED TO CORRECT.**

292. **Home Protection Plan:** Buyer and Seller are advised to investigate the various coverage options available for purchase.

293. ☐ A Home Protection Plan with the following optional coverage _____ ,

294. at a cost not to exceed $ _____ , to be paid by ☐ Buyer, ☐ Seller, and to be issued by _____

295. ☐ Buyer and Seller elect **not** to purchase a Home Protection Plan.

296. **Wood Infestation Report:** ☐ Seller ☐ Buyer will, at his expense, place in escrow a Wood Infestation Report of all residences and buildings included in this
297. sale prepared by a qualified licensed pest control operator consistent with the rules and regulations of the Structural Pest Control Commission of the State of

298. Arizona. Seller agrees to pay up to **one percent (1%) of the purchase price or** ☐ $ _____ for costs of treatment of infestation, repair of any
299. damage caused by infestation and correction of any conditions conducive to infestation as evidenced on the Wood Infestation Report. If such costs exceed
300. this amount that the Seller agrees to pay, (1) the Buyer may immediately elect to cancel this Contract, or, (2) Seller may elect to cancel this Contract unless
301. Buyer agrees, in writing, to pay such costs in excess of those Seller agrees to pay.

302. **Sanitation and Waste Disposal Systems:** Buyer is aware and Seller warrants that the Premises is on a:
303. ☐ sewer system; ☐ septic system. Comments: _____

304. **Seller's Obligations Regarding Waste Disposal Systems:** Before Close of Escrow any septic tank on the Premises shall be inspected at Seller's
305. expense by an inspector recognized by the applicable governmental authority. Any necessary repairs shall be paid by Seller, but not to exceed **one percent**

306. **(1%) of the full purchase price or** ☐ $ _____ . If such costs exceed this amount that the Seller agrees to pay, (1) the Buyer may
307. immediately elect to cancel this Contract, or, (2) Seller may elect to cancel this Contract unless Buyer agrees, in writing, to pay such costs in excess of
308. those Seller agrees to pay. Seller shall deliver to Escrow Company, at Seller's expense, any certification and/or documentation required.

309. **Seller's Obligations Regarding Wells:** If any well is located on the Premises, Seller shall deliver to Escrow Company, before Close of Escrow, a copy of
310. the Arizona Department of Water Resources (ADWR) "Registration of Existing Wells". Escrow Company is hereby instructed to send to the ADWR a
311. "Change of Well Information". (ARS 45-593)

312. **Seller Warranties:** Seller warrants and shall maintain and repair the Premises so that at the earlier of possession or the Close of Escrow: (1) the Premises
313. shall be in substantially the same condition as on the effective date of this Contract, (2) the roof has no known leaks, (3) all heating, cooling, mechanical,
314. plumbing and electrical systems and built-in appliances will be in working condition, and (4) if the Premises has a swimming pool and/or spa, the motors, fil-
315. ter systems, cleaning systems, and heaters, if so equipped, will be in working condition. The Seller grants Buyer or Buyer's representative reasonable
316. access to conduct a final walk-through of the Premises for the purpose of satisfying Buyer that the items warranted by Seller are in working condition- and
317. that any repairs Seller agreed to make have been completed. Any personal property included herein shall be transferred in AS IS CONDITION, FREE AND
318. CLEAR OF ANY LIENS OR ENCUMBRANCES, and SELLER MAKES NO WARRANTY of any kind, express or implied (including, without limitation, ANY
319. WARRANTY OF MERCHANTABILITY).

320. **Buyer Warranties:** At the earlier of possession of the Premises or Close of Escrow, (a) Buyer warrants to Seller that he has conducted all desired independent
321. investigations and accepts the Premises, and (b) Buyer acknowledges that there will be no Seller warranty of any kind, except as stated in Lines 322-328.

322. **Warranties that Survive Closing:** Prior to the Close of Escrow, Seller warrants that payment in full will have been made for all labor, professional services,
323. materials, machinery, fixtures or tools furnished within the 120 calendar days immediately preceding the Close of Escrow in connection with the construc-
324. tion, alteration or repair of any structure on or improvement to the Premises. Seller warrants that the information on Lines 302-303 regarding connection to a
325. public sewer system, septic tank or other sanitation system is correct to the best of his knowledge. Seller warrants that he has disclosed to Buyer and
326. Brokers all material latent defects and any information concerning the Premises known to Seller, (excluding opinions of value), which materially and
327. adversely affect the consideration to be paid by Buyer. Buyer warrants that he has disclosed to Seller any information which may materially and adversely
328. affect the Buyer's ability to close escrow or complete the obligations of this Contract.

329. **Release of Brokers:** SELLER AND BUYER HEREBY EXPRESSLY RELEASE, HOLD HARMLESS AND INDEMNIFY ALL BROKERS IN THIS TRANS-
330. ACTION FROM ANY AND ALL LIABILITY AND RESPONSIBILITY REGARDING THE CONDITION, SQUARE FOOTAGE, LOT LINES OR BOUND-
331. ARIES, VALUE, RENT ROLLS, ENVIRONMENTAL PROBLEMS, SANITATION SYSTEMS, ROOF, WOOD INFESTATION AND WOOD INFESTATION
332. REPORT, COMPLIANCE WITH BUILDING CODES OR OTHER GOVERNMENTAL REGULATIONS, OR ANY OTHER MATERIAL MATTERS RELAT-
333. ING TO THE PREMISES. Neither Seller, Buyer nor any Broker shall be bound by any understanding, agreement, promise or representation, express or
334. implied, written or verbal, not specified herein.

335. **Default and Remedies:** If either party defaults in any respect on any material obligations under this Contract, the non-defaulting party may elect to be released
336. from all obligations under this Contract by cancelling this Contract as provided in Lines 348-356. The non-defaulting party may thereafter proceed against the
337. party in default upon any claim or remedy which the non-defaulting party may have in law or equity. In the case of the Seller, because it would be difficult to fix
338. actual damages in the event of Buyer's default, the amount of the earnest money may be deemed a reasonable estimate of the damages; and Seller may at
339. Seller's option retain the earnest money deposit, subject to any compensation to Brokers, as Seller's sole right to damages. In the event that the non-defaulting
340. party elects not to cancel this Contract, the non-defaulting party may proceed against the party in default for specific performance of this Contract or any of its
341. terms, in addition to any claim or remedy which the non-defaulting party may have in law or equity. In the event that either party pursues specific performance of
342. this Contract, that party does not waive the right to cancel this Contract pursuant to Lines 348-356 at any time and proceed against the defaulting party as oth-
343. erwise provided herein, or in law or equity. If Buyer or Seller files suit against the other to enforce any provision of this Contract or for damages sustained by
344. reason of its breach, all parties prevailing in such action, on trial and appeal, shall receive their reasonable attorneys' fees and costs as awarded by the court. In
345. addition, both Seller and Buyer agree to indemnify and hold harmless all Brokers against all costs and expenses that any Broker may incur or sustain in connec-
346. tion with any lawsuit arising from this Contract and will pay the same on demand unless the court grants judgment in such action against the party to be indem-
347. nified. Costs shall include, without limitation: attorneys' fees, expert witness fees, fees paid to investigators and court costs.

348. **Cancellation:** Except as otherwise provided herein, any party who wishes to cancel this Contract because of any breach by another party, or because escrow
349. fails to close by the agreed date, and who is not himself in breach of this Contract, except as occasioned by a breach by the other party, may cancel this Contract
350. by delivering a notice to either the breaching party or to the Escrow Company stating the nature of the breach and that this Contract shall be cancelled unless the
351. breach is cured within thirteen (13) calendar days following the delivery of the notice. If this notice is delivered to the Escrow Company, it shall contain the address
352. of the party in breach. Any notice delivered to any party must be delivered to the Brokers and the Escrow Company. Within three (3) calendar days after receipt of
353. such notice, the Escrow Company shall send the notice by mail to the party in breach at the address contained in the notice. No further notice shall be required. In
354. the event that the breach is not cured within thirteen (13) calendar days following the delivery of the notice to the party in breach or to the Escrow Company. this
355. Contract shall be cancelled; and the non-breaching party shall have all rights and remedies available at law or equity for the breach of this Contract by the breach-
356. ing party, as provided in Lines 335-347.

357. **Risk Of Loss:** If there is any loss or damage to the Premises between the date hereof and the Close of Escrow by reason of fire, vandalism, flood, earthquake or
358. act of God, the risk of loss shall be on the Seller, provided, however, that if the cost of repairing such loss or damage would exceed ten percent (10%) of the pur-
359. chase price, either Seller or Buyer may elect to cancel the Contract.

360. **Broker's Rights:** If any Broker hires an attorney to enforce the collection of the commission payable pursuant to this Contract, and is successful in collecting some
361. or all of such commission, the party(ies) responsible for paying such commission agree(s) to pay such Broker's costs including, but not limited to: attorneys' fees,
362. expert witness fees, fees paid to investigators, and court costs. The Seller and the Buyer acknowledge that the Brokers are third-party beneficiaries of this Contract.

363. **Permission:** Buyer and Seller grant Brokers permission to advise the public of the sale upon execution of this Contract, and Brokers may disclose price and
364. terms herein after Close of Escrow.

365. **Attorneys' Fees:** In any action, proceeding or arbitration arising out of this Contract, the prevailing party shall be entitled to reasonable attorneys' fees and costs.

366. **Mediation:** Any dispute or claim arising out of or relating to this Contract, any alleged breach of this Contract or services provided in relation to this Contract shall
367. be submitted to mediation in accordance with the Rules and Procedures of the NATIONAL ASSOCIATION OF REALTORS® (NAR) Dispute Resolution System
368. or, if not available, another mediation provider. Disputes shall include representations made by the Buyer, Seller or any Broker or other person or entity in connec-
369. tion with the sale, purchase, financing, condition or other aspect of the Premises to which this Contract pertains, including without limitation allegations of conceal-
370. ment, misrepresentation, negligence and/or fraud. Any agreement signed by the parties pursuant to the mediation conference shall be binding. The following mat-
371. ters are excluded from mediation hereunder: (a) judicial or nonjudicial foreclosure or other action or proceeding to enforce a deed of trust, mortgage, or agreement
372. for sale; (b) an unlawful detainer action; (c) the filing or enforcement of a mechanic's lien; or (d) any matter which is within the jurisdiction of a probate court. The
373. filing of a judicial action to enable the recording of a notice of pending action, for order of attachment, receivership, injunction, or other provisional remedies, shall
374. not constitute a waiver of the obligation to mediate under this provision, nor shall it constitute a breach of the duty to mediate. All mediation costs will be paid
375. equally by the parties to the mediation, unless otherwise agreed.

376. **Entire Agreement:** This Contract, any attached exhibits and any addenda or supplements signed by the parties shall constitute the entire agreement between
377. Seller and Buyer, and shall supersede any other written or oral agreement between Seller and Buyer. This Contract can be modified only by a writing signed by
378. Seller and Buyer. A fully executed facsimile copy of the entire agreement shall be treated as an original Contract.

379. **Time of Essence:** Time is of the essence.

380. **Arizona Law:** This Contract shall be governed by Arizona law.

381. **Severability:** If a court of competent jurisdiction makes a final determination that any term or provision of this Contract is invalid or unenforceable, all other
382. terms and provisions shall remain in full force and effect, and the invalid or unenforceable term or provision shall be deemed replaced by a term or provision
383. that is valid and enforceable and comes closest to expressing the intention of the invalid term or provision.

384. **Construction of Language:** The language of this Contract shall be construed according to its fair meaning and not strictly for or against either party. Words
385. used in the masculine, feminine or neuter shall apply to either gender or the neuter, as appropriate.

386. **Compensation:** Seller and Buyer acknowledge that Brokers shall be compensated for services rendered as previously agreed by separate written agree-
387. ment(s). Any separate written agreement(s) shall be delivered to Escrow Company for payment at Close of Escrow, if not previously paid and shall consti-
388. tute an irrevocable assignment of Seller's proceeds at Close of Escrow. **COMMISSIONS PAYABLE FOR THE SALE, LEASING OR MANAGEMENT OF**
389. **PROPERTY ARE NOT SET BY ANY BOARD OR ASSOCIATION OF REALTORS®, OR MULTIPLE LISTING SERVICE, OR IN ANY MANNER OTHER**
390. **THAN BETWEEN THE BROKER AND CLIENT.**

391. **Additional Compensation:** RESPA prohibits the paying or receiving of any fee, kickback, or thing of value for the referral of any business related to set-
392. tlement or closing of a federally regulated mortgage loan, including but not limited to, any services related to the origination, processing, or funding of a
393. federally regulated mortgage loan and includes such settlement related business as termite inspections and home warranties. RESPA does not prohibit
394. fees, salaries, compensation or other payments for services actually performed. If any Broker performs any such services for a fee, Seller and Buyer con-
395. sent to the payment of this additional compensation for such services actually performed as follows:
396. _____
397. _____

398. **Time For Acceptance:** This is an offer to purchase the Premises. Unless acceptance is signed by Seller and a signed copy delivered in person, by mail, or facsimile,

399. and received by Buyer or by Broker named on lines 15-16   by _____ , 19 _____ at _____ AM/PM, Mountain Standard Time,

400. or unless this offer to purchase has been previously withdrawn by Buyer, this offer to purchase shall be deemed withdrawn and the Buyer's earnest money
401. shall be returned.
402. The undersigned agree to purchase the Premises on the terms and conditions herein stated and acknowledge receipt of a copy hereof.

403. BUYER _____ MO/DA/YR       BUYER _____ MO/DA/YR
404. ADDRESS _____       ADDRESS _____
405. CITY, STATE, ZIP CODE _____       CITY, STATE, ZIP CODE _____

# ACCEPTANCE

406. **Agency Confirmation:** The following agency relationship(s) is hereby confirmed for this transaction:

407. Listing Broker: _____
(PRINT FIRM NAME)

408. Is the agent of (check one): ☐ the Seller exclusively; or   ☐ both the Buyer and Seller

409. **Subsequent Offers:** Upon acceptance of this Contract, Seller hereby waives the right to receive any subsequent offer to purchase the Premises until after
410. forfeiture by Buyer or other cancellation of this Contract.

411. **Seller Receipt of Copy:** The undersigned acknowledge receipt of a copy hereof and grant permission to Broker named on lines 15-16 to deliver
412. **a copy to Buyer.**

413. ☐ **Counter Offer is attached, and is incorporated herein by reference. If there is a conflict between this Contract and the Counter Offer, the**
414. **provisions of the Counter Offer shall be controlling. (NOTE: If this box is checked, Seller should sign both the Contract and the Counter Offer.)**

415. The undersigned agree to sell the Premises on the terms and conditions herein stated.

416. SELLER _____ MO/DA/YR       SELLER _____ MO/DA/YR
417. ADDRESS _____       ADDRESS _____
418. CITY, STATE, ZIP CODE _____       CITY, STATE, ZIP CODE _____

**For Broker Use Only:** Brokerage File/Log No. _____ Manager's Initials _____ Broker's Initials _____ Date _____
MO/DA/YR

A. **Settlement Statement**

**OLD REPUBLIC TITLE AGENCY**

U.S. Department of Housing
and Urban Development

OMB No. 2502-0265

**B. TYPE OF LOAN**

| | | | |
|---|---|---|---|
| 1. ☐ FHA | 2. ☐ FmHA | 3. ☐ Conv. Unins. | 6. File Number |
| 4. ☐ VA | 5. ☐ Conv. Ins. | | 7. Loan Number |
| | | | 8. Mortgage Insurance Case Number |

C. **NOTE:** This form is furnished to give you a statement of actual settlement costs. Amounts paid to and by the settlement agent are shown. Items marked "(p.o.c.)" were paid outside the closing; they are shown here for informational purposes and are not included in the totals.

| D. Name and Address of Borrower | E. Name and Address of Seller | F. Name and Address of Lender |
|---|---|---|
| | | |

| G. Property Location | H. Settlement Agent |
|---|---|
| | Place of Settlement |
| | I. Settlement Date |

| J. SUMMARY OF BORROWER'S TRANSACTION | | K. SUMMARY OF SELLER'S TRANSACTION | |
|---|---|---|---|
| **100. GROSS AMOUNT DUE FROM BORROWER** | | **400. GROSS AMOUNT DUE TO SELLER** | |
| 101. Contract sales price | | 401. Contract sales price | |
| 102. Personal property | | 402. Personal property | |
| 103. Settlement charges to borrower (line 1400) | | 403. | |
| 104. | | 404. | |
| 105. | | 405. | |
| | | | |
| **Adjustments for items paid by seller in advance** | | **Adjustments for items paid by seller in advance** | |
| 106. City/town taxes to | | 406. City/town taxes to | |
| 107. County taxes to | | 407. County taxes to | |
| 108. Assessments to | | 408. Assessments to | |
| 109. | | 409. | |
| 110. | | 410. | |
| 111. | | 411. | |
| 112. | | 412. | |
| 113. | | 413. | |
| 114. | | 414. | |
| **120. GROSS AMOUNT DUE FROM BORROWER** | | **420. GROSS AMOUNT DUE TO SELLER** | |
| **200. AMOUNTS PAID BY OR IN BEHALF OF BORROWER** | | **500. REDUCTIONS IN AMOUNT DUE TO SELLER** | |
| 201. Deposit or earnest money | | 501. Excess deposit (see instructions) | |
| 202. Principal amount of new loan(s) | | 502. Settlement charges to seller (line 1400) | |
| 203. Existing loan(s) taken subject to | | 503. Existing loan(s) taken subject to | |
| 204. | | 504. Payoff of first mortgage loan | |
| 205. | | 505. Payoff of second mortgage loan | |
| 206. | | 506. | |
| 207. | | 507. | |
| 208. | | 508. | |
| 209. | | 509. | |
| **Adjustments for items unpaid by seller** | | **Adjustments for items unpaid by seller** | |
| 210. City/town taxes to | | 510. City/town taxes to | |
| 211. County taxes to | | 511. County taxes to | |
| 212. Assessments to | | 512. Assessments to | |
| 213. | | 513. | |
| 214. | | 514. | |
| 215. | | 515. | |
| 216. | | 516. | |
| 217. | | 517. | |
| 218. | | 518. | |
| 219. | | 519. | |
| **220. TOTAL PAID BY/FOR BORROWER** | | **520. TOTAL REDUCTION AMOUNT DUE SELLER** | |
| **300. CASH AT SETTLEMENT FROM/TO BORROWER** | | **600. CASH AT SETTLEMENT TO/FROM SELLER** | |
| 301. Gross amount due from borrower (line 120) | | 601. Gross amount due to seller (line 420) | |
| 302. Less amounts paid by/for borrower (line 220) ( | ) | 602. Less reductions in amount due seller (line 520) ( | ) |
| 303. CASH ☐ FROM ☐ TO BORROWER | | 603. CASH ☐ TO ☐ FROM SELLER | |

HUD—1 (3-86)
RESPA, HB 4305.2

FTGIS-40 9/91

| | | | L. SETTLEMENT CHARGES | | Paid From Borrower's Funds At Settlement | Paid From Seller's Funds At Settlement |
|---|---|---|---|---|---|---|

**700.** Total sales/broker's commission based on price $            @         % =

Division of commission (line 700) as follows:

**701.** $                              to

**702.** $                              to

**703.** Commission disbursed at settlement

**704.**

**800. ITEMS PAYABLE IN CONNECTION WITH LOAN**

**801.** Loan Origination Fee

**802.** Loan Discount

**803.** Appraisal Fee

**804.** Credit Report

**805.** Lender's Inspection Fee

**806.** Mortgage Insurance Application Fee to

**807.** Assumption Fee

**808.**

**809.**

**810.**

**811.**

**900. ITEMS REQUIRED BY LENDER TO BE PAID IN ADVANCE**

**901.** Interest from              to              @ $              /day

**902.** Mortgage insurance premium for         mo. to

**903.** Hazard insurance premium for         yrs. to

**904.** Flood insurance premium for         yrs. to

**905.**

**1000. RESERVES DEPOSITED WITH LENDER**

**1001.** Hazard insurance         mo. @ $         /mo.

**1002.** Mortgage insurance         mo. @ $         /mo.

**1003.** City property taxes         mo. @ $         /mo.

**1004.** County property taxes         mo. @ $         /mo.

**1005.** Annual assessments         mo. @ $         /mo.

**1006.**         mo. @ $         /mo.

**1007.**         mo. @ $         /mo.

**1008.**         mo. @ $         /mo.

**1100. TITLE CHARGES**

**1101.** Settlement or closing fee         to

**1102.** Abstract or title search         to

**1103.** Title examination         to

**1104.** Title insurance binder         to

**1105.** Document preparation         to

**1106.** Notary fees         to

**1107.** Attorney's fees         to

(includes above items numbers:)

**1108.** Title insurance         to

(includes above items numbers:)

**1109.** Lender's coverage         $

**1110.** Owner's coverage         $

**1111.**

**1112.**

**1113.**

**1114.**

**1200. GOVERNMENT RECORDING AND TRANSFER CHARGES**

**1201.** Recording fees: Deed $         Mortgage $         Releases $

**1202.** City/county tax/stamps:   Deed $         Mortgage $

**1203.** State tax/stamps:   Deed $         Mortgage $

**1204.**

**1205.**

**1300. ADDITIONAL SETTLEMENT CHARGES**

**1301.** Survey         to

**1302.** Pest inspection         to

**1303.**

**1304.**

**1305.**

**1306.**

**1307.**

**1308.**

**1309.**

**1310.**

**1400. TOTAL SETTLEMENT CHARGES**   (enter on lines 103, Section J and 502, Section K)

Addendum to HUD-1
Settlement Statement

<u>NOTICE TO ALL PARTIES</u>: If information is obtained which indicates that the source of the borrower's financial contribution is other than from the borrower or other than stated by the lender in its closing instructions, the settlement agent is to obtain written instructions from the lender before proceeding with settlement.

Certification of Buyer in an FHA-Insured Loan Transaction

     I certify that I have no knowledge of any loans that have been or will be made to me (us) or loans that have been or will be assumed by me (us) for purposes of financing this transaction, other than those described in the sales contract dated _____ . I certify that I (we) have not been paid or reimbursed for any of the cash downpayment. I certify that I (we) have not and will not receive any payment or reimbursement for any of my (our) closing costs which have not been previously disclosed in the sales contract (including addenda) and/or my application for mortgage insurance submitted to my (our) mortgage lender.

_____    _____

_____    _____

Borrowers/Buyers                     _____
                                                        Date

Certification of Seller in an FHA-Insured Loan Transaction

     I certify that I have no knowledge of any loans that have been or will be made to the borrower(s), or loans that have been or will be assumed by the borrower(s) for purposes of financing this transaction, other than those described in the sales contract dated _____ (including addenda). I further certify that I have not and will not pay or reimburse the borrower(s) for any part of the cash downpayment. I further certify that I have not and will not pay or reimburse the borrower(s) for any part of the borrower's closing costs which have not been previously disclosed in the sales contract (including any addenda).

_____    _____

_____    _____

Sellers                                  _____
                                                        Date

Certification of Settlement Agent in an FHA-Insured Loan Transaction

     To the best of my knowledge, the HUD-1 Settlement Statement which I have prepared is a true and accurate account of the funds which were (i) received, or (ii) paid outside closing, and the funds received have been or will be disbursed by the undersigned as part of the settlement of this transaction. I further certify that I have obtained the above certifications which were executed by the borrower(s) and seller(s) as indicated.

_____

Settlement Agent                             _____
                                                        Date

[The certifications contained herein may be obtained from the respective parties at different times or may be obtained on separate addenda.]

WARNING: It is a crime to knowingly make false statements to the United States on this or any other similar form. Penalties upon conviction can include a fine and imprisonment. For details, see: Title 18 U.S. Code Sections 1001 and 1010.

FTGIS-42 9/91

# Arizona Real Estate Licensing Examination

The real estate licensing examinations for both salespersons and brokers are given to determine an applicant's eligibility to become licensed in Arizona. The appropriate examination is given after the applicant has met all of the requirements described in Chapter 10 of this text.

The examinations are designed to test the applicant's knowledge and reasoning ability concerning general real estate concepts and Arizona real estate laws and practices. (Obviously, the examination given to a broker license applicant will be considerably more difficult than the examination given to a salesperson license applicant.)

Currently, the examinations are prepared, administered and scored by Assessment Systems, Incorporated, a professional testing service in Philadelphia. Each examination contains 130 multiple-choice questions, and each question has four options as potential correct answers. Eighty of the questions are "uniform" questions, in that they address concepts accepted as fundamental to the practice of real estate throughout the country. Fifty of the questions are "state-specific" questions, in that they address the laws, rules and practices of the real estate profession in Arizona. The testing is completed electronically, and results are given before the candidate leaves the test center. (Details on both the examinations and the postexamination licensing procedures can be found in the *Real Estate Assessment for Licensure/State of Arizona Candidate Guide*, published by Assessment Systems, Incorporated.)

The questions in this text are primarily state-specific for Arizona. The 50 questions in the abbreviated sample examination that follows are also state-specific. They give a comprehensive representation of the types of questions found in many real estate licensing examinations. However, the reader should be advised that merely studying many different types of sample questions is no guarantee of success for any examination. If the concept, the law or the practice is known and understood, the applicant will be able to answer any questions asked on that particular topic.

## REAL ESTATE SALESPERSON LICENSING EXAMINATION
## ARIZONA SPECIFIC PORTION

Because ASI provides a score to you immediately after you take the examination, ASI needs to know how test questions perform BEFORE they are used to calculate your score. For this reason, ASI must pretest questions in order to evaluate their performance. If a pretest question is included in your examination, it will not be counted in the calculation of your score.

The examination contains 130 test questions that will be used to determine your score (80 general knowledge plus 50 state specific questions). The test may also contain 10 to 15 pretest questions mixed in throughout the examination. Pretest questions are not identified and you should answer all questions as if they were to be used in the calculation of your score. This will provide ASI with reliable performance data to provide valid and reliable examinations to future candidates. To assure candidates that the pretest questions will not reduce the time they have to take the examination, ADRE extended the test time by one-half hour, to a total of four (4) hours.

**General Test Content Outline**

**I. Real Estate Law**
  A. Contractual
    1. Encumbrances
       a. Priorities of liens
       b. Encroachment
       c. Restrictions/easements
       d. Mechanics' liens
       e. Attachments and agreements
    2. Contracts and agreements
       a. Characteristics of enforceable real estate contracts
       b. Elements of property descriptions
       c. Purchase price
       d. Standard printed clauses
    3. Options
    4. Deeds
  B. General practice
    1. Nature of real property
       a. Definitions
       b. Methods of legal description
    2. Parties dealing with interests in real property
       a. Legal capacity
       b. Individuals
       c. Corporations
       d. Partnerships
  C. Fair housing laws

**II. Ownership/Transfer**
  A. Land titles and interest in real property
    1. Estates in land
       a. Joint ownership
       b. Severalty ownership
    2. Fixtures/personal property
    3. Insurance
    4. Settlement procedures
    5. Lease and leasehold
  B. Voluntary or involuntary alienation of real property
    1. Dedication
    2. Adverse possession
    3. Sheriff's sale
    4. Foreclosure
    5. Escheat
    6. Condemnation
    7. Eminent domain
    8. Inheritance
    9. Gifts
    10. Taxation
  C. Public control
    1. Planning
       a. Urban
       b. Rural
    2. Zoning
    3. Property taxation
    4. Water rights
    5. Health and safety/building codes

**III. Brokerage/Agency**
  A. Distinction between agency relationships
  B. Agent responsibilities to principal(s) and or others
  C. Termination of agency
  D. Listing agreements
  E. Property management (residential/commercial)
    1. Management contracts
    2. Rentals and leases
    3. Repairs and maintenance
  F. Investments

**IV. Concepts of Appraising**
  A. Concepts and purposes of appraisal
  B. Appraisal techniques
  C. Elements of depreciation
  D. Principles of real property value
  E. Approaches to value
    1. Cost
    2. Income
    3. Market data
  F. Economic trends
  G. Neighborhood

Broker examination only:
H. Site analysis and valuation
I. Gross rent multiplier
J. Principles of capitalization
K. The appraisal report
**V. Finance**
A. Methods of financing
   1. Government
   2. Other
B. Truth-in-Lending and RESPA
C. Financing instruments
D. Financing terminology
**VI. Mathematics of Real Estate**
Basic mathematics to calculate solutions to the following problem areas:
A. Financing
B. Tax assessment
C. Commissions
D. Area calculations
E. Settlement statements
F. Profit and loss
G. Tax ramifications
H. General

**State Test Content Outline**
**I. Real Estate Law**
A. Judgments
B. Legal descriptions
C. Mechanic's lien
D. Purchase contracts
E. Recovery funds
F. Subdivision laws/time-share
**II. Ownership/Transfer**
A. Deeds
B. Homestead rights
C. Property taxation
D. Settlement procedures
E. Community property
F. Water rights/environment hazards.
**III. Brokerage/Agency**
A. Arizona revised statutes
B. Commissioner's rules
**IV. Finance**
A. Financing instruments
B. Foreclosure and Forfeiture
**V. Arizona Residential and Landlord & Tenant Act**

## SAMPLE EXAMINATION

1. When involved in a real estate transaction, a licensee is authorized to draft or complete any documents pertinent to the transaction by the

   a. Statute of Frauds.
   b. Arizona Constitution.
   c. Commissioner's Rules.
   d. Arizona Revised Statutes.

2. All of the following statements regarding the Real Estate Advisory Board are true except the members

   a. are appointed by the commissioner to serve six-year staggered terms.
   b. receive no compensation, only reimbursement for their meeting expenses.
   c. must meet at least once every calendar quarter.
   d. are two brokers, two subdividers and three public members.

3. A licensee completes a listing contract but does not convince the seller to sign it. Subsequently the licensee obtains a purchaser who buys the property. In this situation,

   a. no commission is due as the contract was not signed and is therefore unenforceable.
   b. a commission must be paid by the seller based on the prevailing rate in the community.
   c. a commission must be paid by the seller based on the prevailing rate in the community.
   d. a commission is due because a listing contract is an implied contract.

4. In a foreclosure, the trustor must relinquish possession of the property

   a. when the notice of default is recorded.
   b. three months after the notice of default is recorded.
   c. not less than 90 days after the notice of default is recorded.
   d. after the trustee's sale is held.

5. The Statute of Frauds was enacted to prevent

   a. forgery.
   b. perjury.
   c. unenforceability.
   d. fraud.

6. Which of the following statements concerning agency relationships is true?

   a. Listing contracts can be assigned from one broker to another as long as both brokers agree; the client need not be involved.
   b. A licensee should not attempt to list a property that is already subject to an exclusive listing contract with another broker.
   c. A licensee must disclose that he or she is licensed when purchasing property but not necessarily when selling property.
   d. In the interest of providing the best service to a client, a licensee should reject an unusually low offer on behalf of the seller.

7. The successful bidder at a tax foreclosure sale will receive a

   a. treasurer's deed.
   b. trustee's deed.
   c. certificate of purchase.
   d. certificate of sale.

8. The purchaser of a property notices that a structure on the property appears to extend over the property line. She should

   a. notify the seller in writing.
   b. notify the broker in writing.
   c. have the property surveyed.
   d. obtain a title insurance policy.

9. For an option to be valid and enforceable, all of the following are required *except*

   a. recordation.
   b. competent parties.
   c. an expiration date.
   d. valuable consideration.

10. Before receiving a public report for his or her property from the Real Estate Commissioner, the only items that a subdivider can offer the public are

    a. estates of inheritance.
    b. undivided interests.
    c. option contracts.
    d. lot reservations.

11. According to the Commissioner's Rules, all listing contracts must contain the

    a. termination date of the contract.
    b. commission rate to be paid to the broker.
    c. legal description of the property listed.
    d. description of all of the property improvements.

12. If a dispute arises in escrow over a misunderstanding between the seller and the purchaser, which document will determine the settlement of the dispute?

    a. The listing contract
    b. The purchase contract
    c. The escrow instructions
    d. The settlement statement

13. A homestead exemption will protect a homeowner against which of the following?

    a. Tax liens
    b. Judgment liens
    c. Mechanics' liens
    d. Trust deed liens

14. If a business is sold, which document would be used to transfer only the seller's possessory rights in the real property?
    a.   A bill of sale
    b.   A land contract
    c.   A bulk sale affidavit
    d.   An assignment of lease

15. Determining the priority of a mechanic's lien would be based on when the

    a.   contract was signed.
    b.   work was started.
    c.   work was completed.
    d.   lien was recorded.

16. According to the Commissioner's Rules, which of the following must be included in a real estate purchase contract?

    a.   An indication of how title is to be taken
    b.   The notarized signatures of the seller and purchaser
    c.   An indication of the form of the earnest money deposit
    d.   The proration settlement between the seller and purchaser

17. By signing a listing contract, a broker would be creating which of the following types of agency relationships?

    a.   A universal agency
    b.   A general agency
    c.   A special agency
    d.   An ostensible agency

18. An owner-occupied residence has a market value of $105,000 and a full cash value for tax purposes of 87% of market value. If the tax rate is $10.36 per $100 of assessed valuation, what would be the amount of the tax installment due on October 1?

    a.   $79
    b.   $237
    c.   $473
    d.   $946

19. According to the doctrine of prior appropriation, when two persons own property on opposite sides of a nonnavigable stream, who owns the water in the stream?

    a.   Both persons own the water equally.
    b.   The holder of the dominant tenement owns more than half of the water.
    c.   The holder of the dominant tenement owns all of the water.
    d.   The state of Arizona owns all of the water.

20. A utility company has the right to use land for the installation of power poles and transmission lines. This is an easement

    a.   in gross.
    b.   appurtenant.
    c.   by necessity.
    d.   by prescription.

21. A judgment lien is a general involuntary lien that is valid for

    a.   three years from the cause of action.
    b.   four years from the filing of the suit.
    c.   five years from the entering of the judgment by the court.
    d.   seven years from the execution of the judgment by the sheriff.

22. All of the following are required for a claim under adverse possession *except*

    a.   license.
    b.   hostile use.
    c.   statutory time.
    d.   continuous use.

23. The seller accepts and signs a purchase offer. After the licensee gives a copy to the seller, he or she must then give a copy to the

    a.   listing broker.
    b.   selling broker.
    c.   purchaser.
    d.   escrow agent.

24. To place a sign on a property offering it to the public, the licensee must have

    a. a valid listing contract.
    b. an enforceable purchase contract.
    c. the verbal permission of the owner.
    d. the written permission of the owner.

25. The two classifications of water in Arizona are

    a. navigable and nonnavigable.
    b. static and dynamic.
    c. percolating and nonpercolating.
    d. surface and ground.

26. Unless otherwise specified, married couples who purchase real property in Arizona will receive title in

    a. tenancy in common.
    b. community property.
    c. severalty ownership.
    d. joint tenancy with rights of survivorship.

27. From whom could a salesperson receive a bonus for having completed a difficult sales transaction?

    a. From the seller with the permission of the listing broker
    b. From the seller with the permission of the employing broker
    c. From the escrow agent
    d. From the employing broker

28. After a foreclosure has been completed, any funds remaining after the debt and foreclosure expenses have been paid will be given to the

    a. lender.
    b. borrower.
    c. holder in due course.
    d. foreclosing entity.

29. To create a valid mechanic's lien, a subcontractor must file within

    a. 60 days of starting the work.
    b. 60 days of completing the work.
    c. 90 days of starting the work.
    d. 90 days of completing the work.

30. The vendee under a land contract has paid $1,500 as a down payment toward the purchase of a $15,000 property. He has also made three annual payments of $3,500 each, of which $1,150 per payment was interest. If he defaults on the contract, his reinstatement period will be

    a. 30 days.
    b. 60 days.
    c. 120 days.
    d. 9 months.

31. All of the following events will automatically terminate a listing contract *except* the

    a. expiration of the contract.
    b. destruction of the premises.
    c. death or incapacity of the broker.
    d. decision by the owner not to sell.

32. Under Arizona law, real estate agents may discriminate against those who

    a. have children under five years of age.
    b. are currently addicted to crack cocaine.
    c. require the use of a seeing eye dog.
    d. are female.

33. Licensee *M* negotiated a purchase contract between the *E*s and *S*, an unmarried minor who wished to purchase the *E*s's residence. After escrow had been opened, *S* notified *M* that he no longer wanted the property. Given these facts,

    a. *S* can demand the return of any money he has paid.
    b. *M* can demand the payment of his agreed commission.
    c. the *E*s can hold *M* liable for liquidated damages.
    d. the *E*s can hold *S* liable for specific performance.

34. Regarding property taxes, the first half payment becomes due and the second half payment becomes delinquent, respectively, on

    a. October 1 and May 1.
    b. October 1 and March 1.
    c. November 1 and May 1.
    d. November 1 and March 1.

35. The type of deed most commonly associated with the completion of an agreement for sale (land contract) is the

    a. general warranty deed.
    b. special warranty deed.
    c. quitclaim deed.
    d. disclaimer deed.

36. The Real Estate Commissioner has jurisdiction over all of the following *except* the

    a. drafting of rules.
    b. setting of commissions.
    c. investigation of licensees.
    d. auditing of brokerage firms.

37. The Real Estate Commissioner can do all of the following *except*

    a. investigate an individual licensee.
    b. employ people to work in the department.
    c. inspect the records at a real estate office.
    d. suspend a license upon receiving a complaint.

38. The statutory reinstatement period during a trust deed foreclosure is

    a. 30 days.
    b. 90 days.
    c. 6 months.
    d. 12 months.

39. The maximum amounts payable from the Real Estate Recovery Fund per claim and per licensee, respectively, are

    a. $10,000 and $30,000.
    b. $20,000 and $40,000.
    c. $10,000 and $100,000.
    d. $15,000 and $300,000.

40. A salesperson licensee receives a written offer from a purchaser on a property listed with another broker. The salesperson should

    a. present the offer to the seller after calling the employing broker.
    b. present the offer to the seller after calling the listing broker.
    c. have the employing broker present the offer to the seller.
    d. have the listing broker present the offer to the seller.

41. Should the Real Estate Recovery Fund balance fall below $600,000, a salesperson licensee will pay an additional amount of how much upon the renewal of a license?

    a. $10
    b. $15
    c. $20
    d. $25

42. The successful bidder at a mortgage foreclosure sale receives a

    a. certificate of sale.
    b. certificate of purchase.
    c. warranty deed.
    d. sheriff's deed.

43. A salesperson licensee can be employed by

    a. one broker only.
    b. different brokers in different transactions.
    c. the seller and the purchaser.
    d. the seller and the purchaser in different transactions.

44. An affidavit of property value is used to

    a. verify the sales price for the county assessor.
    b. verify the sales price for the lending institution.
    c. convey free and clear title to the grantees.
    d. identify the grantees for title insurance purposes.

45. A trust deed can be released by the recordation of a

    a. principal note.
    b. deed of reconveyance.
    c. satisfaction of lien.
    d. preliminary title report.

46. A valid listing contract on community property should be signed by the

    a. husband.
    b. husband and wife.
    c. husband or wife.
    d. husband, wife and broker.

47. The relationship between the broker and the client should be similar to that of the

    a. salesperson and the broker.
    b. salesperson and the seller.
    c. trustee and the beneficiary.
    d. vendor and the vendee.

48. Which of the following is a noncash expense for an income property?

    a. Interest
    b. Management
    c. Maintenance
    d. Depreciation

49. All of the following would be exempt from the real estate licensing requirements *except*

    a. a person employed to market a property for compensation.
    b. a person employed by an owner to manage one income property.
    c. an attorney at law in the regular performance of his duties.
    d. a person with a valid power of attorney in an isolated transaction.

50. A broker must review all contracts submitted through his or her office within how many days of the date on the contract?

    a. Five days
    b. Seven days
    c. Ten days
    d. Fourteen days

# Answer Key

## Chapter 1
1. a
2. c
3. d
4. d
5. d
6. b
7. c
8. a
9. c
10. d

## Chapter 2
1. c
2. d
3. c
4. a
5. b
6. d
7. d
8. c
9. a
10. a

## Chapter 3
1. b
2. c
3. b
4. c
5. c
6. b
7. b
8. c
9. c
10. a

## Chapter 4
1. c
2. b
3. a
4. b
5. d
6. d
7. d
8. b
9. a
10. d

## Chapter 5
1. c
2. d
3. b
4. b
5. b
6. b
7. b
8. a
9. d
10. c

## Chapter 6
1. b
2. b
3. d
4. b
5. c
6. a
7. d
8. a
9. c
10. a

## Chapter 7
1. d
2. c
3. b
4. b
5. c
6. c
7. d
8. a
9. c
10. d

## Chapter 8
1. b
2. c
3. d
4. b
5. a
6. d
7. c
8. d
9. d
10. c

## Chapter 9
1. d
2. a
3. b
4. b
5. a
6. b
7. d
8. b
9. d
10. a

## Chapter 10
1. c
2. d
3. b
4. c
5. b
6. a
7. d
8. d
9. d
10. c
11. b
12. c
13. c
14. c
15. d
16. a
17. c
18. b
19. a
20. d

## Chapter 11
1. a
2. b
3. c
4. c
5. b
6. c
7. d
8. d
9. a
10. c

## Chapter 12
1. d
2. a
3. d
4. b
5. b
6. d
7. b
8. b
9. d
10. b

## Chapter 14
1. a
2. b
3. b
4. b
5. d
6. b
7. d
8. b
9. d
10. d

## Chapter 15
1. c
2. b
3. a
4. a
5. b
6. b
7. c
8. c
9. b
10. b

Type **ER**

**EXCLUSIVE RIGHT TO SELL/RENT**
**(LISTING CONTRACT LEGAL LANGUAGE)**

Legal I.D. **196460**

THIS IS INTENDED TO BE A LEGALLY BINDING CONTRACT. NO REPRESENTATION IS MADE AS TO THE LEGAL VALIDITY OR ADEQUACY OF ANY PROVISION OR THE TAX CONSEQUENCES THEREOF. IF YOU DESIRE LEGAL OR TAX ADVICE, CONSULT YOUR ATTORNEY OR TAX ADVISOR.

1. **EXCLUSIVE RIGHT TO SELL AND RENT.** In consideration of the acceptance by the undersigned licensed Arizona real estate broker ("Broker") of the terms of this Listing Contract ("Listing") and Broker's promise to endeavor to effect a ☐ sale or rental  ☒ sale  ☐ rental  of the property described below ("Property"), I or we, as owner(s) ("Owner"), employ and grant Broker the exclusive and irrevocable right commencing on **July 5**, 19 **95**, and expiring at 11:59 p.m. **October 3**, 19 **95**, to sell, rent, exchange, or option the Property described in Paragraph 2.

2. **THE PROPERTY.** For purposes of this Listing, the "Property" means the real property in **MARICOPA** County, Arizona described below, plus all fixtures and improvements thereon, all appurtenances incident thereto and all personal property described in Paragraphs 4 and 9.

   **1234 EAST COPPERTOWN DRIVE  -    TEMPE, ARIZONA**
   Street Address                                                                                   City/Town

   **LOT 13, BLOCK B, PARADISE SANDS SUBDIVISION**
   Legal Description

3. **PRICE.** The listing price shall be:  Sale: $ **155,000.-**

   Rental: $ **N/A**  per month, plus all applicable lease or rental (transaction privilege) taxes to be paid as described in the Owner's Profile Sheet ("Data Entry Form"), or such other price and terms as are accepted by Owner.

4. **FIXTURES AND PERSONAL PROPERTY.** The Property includes personal property and excludes leased equipment as described in the Data Entry Form. Except as provided in the Data Entry Form, the Property also includes all of the following existing fixtures or personal property: storage sheds; heating and cooling equipment; built-in appliances; attached light fixtures and ceiling fans; window and door screens; sun screens; storm windows and doors; towel, curtain and drapery rods; draperies and other window coverings; attached carpeting; attached fireplace equipment; pool and spa equipment (including any mechanical or other cleaning systems); garage door openers and controls; attached TV antennas (excluding satellite dishes); attached plant watering, fire suppression and misting systems; water treatment systems; smoke detectors and fire warning systems; security systems and fences.

5. **ACCESS AND LOCKBOX.** Owner ☐ does  ☒ does not  authorize Broker to install and use, on the Property, a lockbox containing a key to the Property. Owner acknowledges that a lockbox and any other keys left with or available to Broker will permit access to the Property by Broker or any other broker, with or without potential purchasers or tenants ("Prospects"), even when Owner and occupant are absent. If the Property is occupied by someone other than Owner, Owner will provide to Broker the occupant's written permission for the installation of the lockbox and the publication and dissemination of the occupant's name and telephone number. Owner acknowledges that neither the Arizona Regional Multiple Listing Service ("ARMLS"), nor any Board or Association of REALTORS®, nor any broker, is insuring Owner or occupant against theft, loss or vandalism resulting from any such access. Owner is responsible for obtaining appropriate insurance.

6. **AGENCY RELATIONSHIPS.**
   a.  Owner understands that Broker is Owner's agent with respect to this Listing. Owner understands that a Prospect may also wish to be represented by Broker in connection with the purchase or rental of the Property. In that event, Broker would be serving as the agent for both Owner and the Prospect. Since Owner does not wish to limit the range of Prospects at this time, Owner agrees to work with Broker to resolve any potential agency conflicts that may arise.
   b.  Owner initially authorizes Broker to cooperate with other brokers ☒ in any manner whatsoever  ☐ as subagents only  ☐ without offering subagency . This election does not relieve Broker of his obligation to present all offers except as provided in Paragraph 28.

7. **COMPENSATION TO BROKER.** Owner agrees to compensate Broker as follows:
   a.  **RETAINER.** Broker acknowledges receipt of a non-refundable retainer fee of **N/A** payable to Broker for initial consultation, research and other services.
   b.  **COMMISSIONS.** If Broker produces a ready, willing and able purchaser or tenant in accordance with this Listing, or if a sale, rental, option or exchange of the Property is made by Owner or through any other agent, or otherwise, during the term of this exclusive listing, for services rendered, Owner agrees to pay Broker a commission of

   **Sale: 6% of the selling price**          **Rental: N/A**

   With respect to any holdovers or renewals of rental, regardless of whether this Listing has expired, Owner agrees to pay a commission of **N/A** . The amount of the sale or rental commission shall be due and payable to Broker if, without the consent of Broker, the Property is withdrawn from this Listing, otherwise withdrawn from sale or rental or rented, transferred, or conveyed by Owner.
   c.  **PURCHASE BY TENANT.** If during the terms of any rental of the Property, including any renewals or holdovers, or within **N/A** days after its termination, any tenant, or his heirs, executors, or assigns shall buy the Property from Owner, the sale commission described in Paragraph 7(b) shall be deemed earned by and payable to Broker.
   d.  **AFTER EXPIRATION.** After the expiration of this Listing, the same commissions, as appropriate, shall be payable if a sale, rental, exchange, or option is made by Owner to any person to whom the Property has been shown or with whom Owner or any broker has negotiated concerning the Property during the term of this Listing

   (1) within **90** days after the expiration of this Listing, unless the Property has been listed on an exclusive basis with another broker, or (2) during the pendency, including the closing, of any purchase contract or escrow relating to the Property that was executed or opened during the term of this Listing, or (3) as contemplated by Paragraph 7(c).
   e.  **FAILURE TO COMPLETE.** If completion of a sale or rental is prevented by default of Owner, or with the consent of Owner, the entire sale or rental commission, as appropriate, shall be paid to Broker by Owner. If any earnest deposit is forfeited for any other reason, Owner shall pay a brokerage fee equal to the lesser of one-half of the earnest deposit or the full amount of the commission.
   f.  **PAYMENT FROM ESCROW OR RENT.** Owner instructs the escrow company, if any, to pay all such compensation to Broker in cash as a condition to closing or upon cancellation of the escrow, and to the extent necessary, irrevocably assigns to Broker all money payable to Owner at the closing or cancellation of the escrow. Broker is authorized to deduct compensation from any rent or other monies received on behalf of Owner.
   g.  **OTHER BROKERS.** Owner authorizes Broker to divide all such compensation with other brokers in any manner acceptable to Broker.
   h.  **NO LIMITATION.** Nothing in this Listing shall be construed as limiting applicable provisions of law relating to when commissions are earned or payable.

8. **HOME PROTECTION PLAN.** Owner acknowledges that home protection plans are available and that such plans may provide additional protection and benefits to Owner and any purchaser of the Property. Owner ☐ does  ☒ does not  agree to provide at his expense a home protection plan for the purchaser that will be effective at the close of escrow.

9. **ADDITIONAL TERMS.** _____

_____

_____

_____

10. THE TERMS AND CONDITIONS ON THE REVERSE SIDE HEREOF PLUS ALL INFORMATION ON THE DATA ENTRY FORM ARE INCORPORATED HEREIN BY REFERENCE. COMMISSIONS PAYABLE FOR THE SALE, RENTAL OR MANAGEMENT OF PROPERTY ARE NOT SET BY ANY BOARD OR ASSOCIATION OF REALTORS® OR MULTIPLE LISTING SERVICE OR IN ANY MANNER OTHER THAN BY NEGOTIATION BETWEEN THE BROKER AND THE CLIENT. BY SIGNING BELOW, OWNER ACKNOWLEDGES THAT HE HAS READ, UNDERSTANDS AND ACCEPTS ALL TERMS AND PROVISIONS CONTAINED HEREIN AND THAT HE HAS RECEIVED A COPY OF THIS LISTING.

**George Cellars**                                    **Martha Cellars**
Print Name of Owner                                   Print Name of Owner

**1234 East Coppertown Drive  -  Tempe, Arizona**
Street                                    City/Town                  State              Zip

**N/A**                                    **N/A**
Phone                                      Fax Phone

11.  *George Cellars*                      *Martha Cellars*
Owner's Signature          Mo/Da/Yr        Owner's Signature          Mo/Da/Yr

In consideration of Owner's representations and promises in this Listing, Broker agrees to endeavor to effect a sale, rental, exchange, or option in accordance with this Listing and further agrees to provide this Listing for publication by a local Board or Association of REALTORS® and dissemination to the users of ARMLS.

**NEWHOUSE REALTY**                        **555-5297**
Firm Name (Broker)                          Office Phone

By: *Janet DeWinter*  7/5/95    **N/A**
     Agent's Signature          Date        Fax Phone

Copyright© February 1993 by Arizona Regional Multiple Listing Service, Inc.            For Use with Data Entry Forms 1, 2, 3.

For Broker's office use only:

Broker's File/Lot No.: _____  Manager's Initials: _____  Broker's Initials: _____  Date: _____

**BROKER**

**1** ⌂ EQUAL HOUSING OPPORTUNITY

## ARIZONA REGIONAL MULTIPLE LISTING SERVICE, INC.
### RESIDENTIAL PROFILE SHEET (CLASS 1)
PAGE 1 OF 3

Ⓡ REALTOR®

R Denotes Required Entries for Adding a Listing

**RAREA** [ ] Area    **RGRID** [ ] Map Code/Grid    **RTYPE** [ ] Type of Listing (ER/EA)

**RHSN** | 1 | 2 | 3 | 4 | House Number    **RCP** | E | Compass Pt    **RSTR** C O P P E R T O W N Street Name    **RSC** D R (ST/RD/LN/ETC) (See User Sheet)    **UN** [ ] Unit Number

**RBL** [ ] Hundred Block    **RBC** [ ] N/S/E/W    **RCT** T E M P E City/Town Code (See User Sheet)    **RZP** [ ] Zip Code Prefix    **Z4** [ ] Zip Code + 4    **RCOU** M County Code    **BU** [ ] Building Number

**RBK** 1 9 8 Assessor's Book Number    **RMA** 7 6 Assessor's Map Number    **RPN** 5 4 3 Parcel Number    **PL** [ ] Parcel Letter    **TWN** [ ] Township    **RNG** [ ] Range    **SCT** [ ] Section    **MPG** [ ] WWMAP Page    **MPX** [ ] WWMAP Top Coordinate    **MPY** [ ] WWMAP Side Coordinate

**RSBD** [ ] Subdivision Name/Balance of Legal (or Metes & Bounds)

**LT** 1 3 Lot Number    **BOOK_PG** [ ] County Record Book & Page #    **CTRCT** [ . ] Census Tract    **GLAT** [ ] Geo Sync Latitude    **GLNG** [ ] Geo Sync Longitude

**RBR** 3 Bedrooms (Studio=0)    **RBATHS** 3 . 0 Bathrooms    **SQ** 2 2 9 6 Approx. Square Feet    **RSS** M Source of Square Footage { T=County Assessor A=Appraiser M=Agent Measured B=Builder X=Blank SQ.    **LS** 1 0 0 x 1 2 0 Lot Size Dimensions (or IRR)

**RFE** F D X P S T H Q A L N Encoded Features (See User Sheet) (Insert Data or Circle When Applicable)    **RHORS** [ ] Horses (Y/N)    **RPHY** [ ] Physically Challenged Features (Y/N)

**MD** [ ] Model    **RYR** 1 9 8 5 Year Built (or NEW/UNK/UC)    **RBD** [ ] Builder

**PCN** [ ] Planned Community Name    **MNM** [ ] Marketing Name

**RES** [ ] Elementary School (See User Sheet for School Codes)    **RJH** [ ] Junior High School    **RHS** [ ] High School    **RESD** [ ] Elem. School District #    **RHSD** [ ] High School District #

**RMB** 18 x 16 Master Bedroom None = 0 x 0    **R2B** 14 x 12 2nd Bedroom None = 0 x 0    **R3B** 14 x 12 3rd Bedroom None = 0 x 0    **R4B** 0 x 0 4th Bedroom None = 0 x 0    **R5B** 0 x 0 5th Bedroom None = 0 x 0

**RLR** 20 x 14 Living Room None = 0 x 0    **RDR** 14 x 12 Dining Room None = 0 x 0    **RFR** 20 x 14 Family Room None = 0 x 0    **RKT** 14 x 12 Kitchen None = 0 x 0    **RDN** 10 x 8 Den/Other Room None = 0 x 0

**RLP** 1 5 5 0 0 0 List Price    **EQ=LP - TO** Computer will Calculate Equity    **RDP** 4 0 4 0 0 Down Payment For Assumption or Carryback Purposes Only (None = 0)    **RTA** 1 2 9 4 Total Assumable Monthly Payments (None = 0)

**R1E** 1 1 4 6 0 0 1st Encumbrance (None = 0)    **R1A** Y 1st Loan Assum. (Y/N) (None = N)    **R1Q** Y 1st Loan Qualify (Y/N) (None = N)    **R1R** 1 1 . 0 0 1st Interest Rate (None = 0)    **R1P** 1 2 9 4 1st Monthly Payment (None = 0)

**R2E** 0 2nd Encumbrance (None = 0)    **R2A** N 2nd Loan Assum. (Y/N) (None = N)    **R2Q** N 2nd Loan Qualify (Y/N) (None = N)    **R2R** 0 . 0 2nd Interest Rate (None = 0)    **R2P** 0 2nd Monthly Payment (None = 0)

**R3E** 0 3rd/All Encumbrances (None = 0)    **R3A** N 3rd Loan Assum. (Y/N) (None = N)    **R3Q** N 3rd Loan Qualify (Y/N) (None = N)    **R3R** 0 . 0 3rd Interest Rate (None = 0)    **R3P** 0 3rd Monthly Payment (None = 0)

**TO = 1E + 2E + 3E** Computer will Calculate Total Encumbrances    **TP** (P I T) H M F Monthly Payment Includes (Circle Where Applicable)    **RTX** 1 2 0 0 Taxes    **RTY** 1 9 9 4 Tax Year    **WK** [ ] Week Available (Timeshares)

**RHOA** [ ] Homeowner's Association (Y/N)    **RHO** 0 Homeowner's Association Fee None = 0    **HF** [ ] Paid M = Monthly Q = Quarterly S = Semi-Annually A = Annually    **RPD** 0 Pad Fee None = 0    **PF** [ ] Paid M = Monthly Q = Quarterly S = Semi-Annually A = Annually    **RLL** 0 Land Lease Fee None = 0    **LF** [ ] Paid M = Monthly Q = Quarterly S = Semi-Annually A = Annually

**RTN** [ ] Occupant { V = Vacant O = Owner T = Tenant I = Interim Occ.    **RON** [ ] Owner/Occupant Name    **OT** [ ] - [ ] - [ ] Owner/Occupant Phone

**RSBA** Y Subagents (Y/N)    **RCS** 3.0 Comp. to Subagent    **RBB** Y Buyer Broker (Y/N)    **RCB** 3.0 Comp. to Buyer Broker    **XC** [ ] Other Compensation    **RVCOM** N Variable Commission (Y/N)

**RLO** [ ] List Office Code    **OPH2** [ ] - [ ] Office Other Phone Number    **OFAX** [ ] - [ ] Office Fax Phone Number

**RLA1** [ ] Agent 1 Code    Janet DeWinter List Agent Name    **RLD** 0 7 / 0 5 / 9 5 List Date    **REXP** 1 0 / 0 3 / 9 5 Expire Date

**HP1** [ ] - [ ] Agent 1 Home Phone    **MB1** [ ] - [ ] Agent 1 Mobile Phone    **PAG1** [ ] - [ ] Agent 1 Pager Phone

**LA2** [ ] Agent 2 Code    **HP2** [ ] - [ ] Agent 2 Home Phone    **MB2** [ ] - [ ] Agent 2 Mobile Phone    **PAG2** [ ] - [ ] Agent 2 Pager Phone

MLS # _____ Field Entered Y _ N _ Legal ID

The undersigned Owner acknowledges and reaffirms that this Profile Sheet is an integral part of the Listing Contract between Owner and Broker, that all information in the Profile Sheet is true, correct and complete, that the Owner will promptly notify Broker if there is any material change in such information during the term of this Listing and that Owner will indemnify other persons for inaccuracies in such information as further provided in the Listing Contract. If there is a conflict between the Listing Contract and this Profile Sheet, the terms of this Profile Sheet shall prevail. Owner agrees to indemnify and hold Broker, all Boards or Associations of REALTORS®, ARMLS and all other brokers harmless against any and all claims, liability, damage or loss arising from any misrepresentation or breach of warranty by Owner in this Listing, any incorrect information supplied by Owner and any facts concerning the Property not disclosed by Owner, including without limitation, any facts known to Owner relating to adverse conditions or latent defects.

*George Cellars / Martha Cellars*          *7/5/95*
OWNER SIGNATURE                              DATE

The undersigned Broker represents and warrants that the information in and manner of execution of this Profile Sheet and the related Listing Contract comply in all respects with the Rules and Regulations of ARMLS and the Broker's Board or Association of REALTORS®.

_____          _____
BROKER SIGNATURE                   DATE

## 214 Arizona Real Estate Practice and Law

(FEATURES: For Adding a Listing, underline the proper feature selections. (R) denotes required entries for Adding a Listing. All required Features must be entered for a new listing.)

**RDTYP    Dwelling Type**
- A. Single Family-Detached (SF DET)
- B. Patio Home (PATIO)
- C. Townhouse (TOWNHS)
- D. Apartment Style (APT)
- E. Gemini/Twin Home (GEMINI)
- F. Mobile Home (MOBILE)
- G. Manufactured Housing (MNFACT)

**ROWNS   Ownership**
- A. Fee Simple (FEE)
- B. Leasehold (LEASE)
- C. Condominium (CONDO)
- D. Timeshare (TSHAR)
- E. Co-Operative (COOP)

**RARCH   Architecture**
- A. Single Level (SNGL)
- B. Multi-Level (MULT)
- C. Ranch (RNCH)
- D. Territorial (TERR)
- E. Spanish (SPAN)
- F. Contemporary (CONT)
- G. Other (See Remarks) (OTHR)

**BSTY    Building Style**
- A. 2-3-4 Plex (234P)
- B. Clustered (CLUST)
- C. String (STRNG)
- D. High-Rise (HRISE)

**RAPSF   Approx. Sq. Ft. Range**
- A. <1,000 (<1,000)
- B. 1,001-1,200 (1,001,1,200)
- C. 1,201-1,400 (1,201-1,400)
- D. 1,401-1,600 (1,401-1,600)
- E. 1,601-1,800 (1,601-1,800)
- F. 1,801-2,000 (1,801-2,000)
- G. 2,001-2,250 (2,001-2,250)
- H. 2,251-2,500 (2,251-2,500)
- I. 2,501-2,750 (2,501-2,750)
- J. 2,751-3,000 (2,751-3,000)
- K. 3,001-3,500 (3,001-3,500)
- L. 3,501-4,000 (3,501-4,000)
- M. 4,001-4,500 (4,001-4,500)
- N. 4,501-5,000 (4,501-5,000)
- O. 5,001 + (5,001 +)

**RMBTH   Master Bathroom**
- A. 3/4 Bath Master Bedroom (3/4 MSTR)
- B. Full Bath Master Bedroom (FULL MSTR)
- C. Separate Shower and Tub (SEP SH/TB)
- D. Double Sinks (2 SINKS)
- E. 2 Master Baths (2 MST BTH)
- F. Tub with Jets (TUBJET)
- G. Bidet (BIDET)
- H. None (NONE)

**BED    Additional Bedroom Information**
- A. Master Bedroom Split (MSPLT)
- B. Other Bedroom Split (OSPLT)
- C. 2 Master Bedrooms (2MBR)
- D. Master Bedroom Upstairs (MBRUP)
- E. Master Bedroom Downstairs (MBRDN)
- F. Master Bedroom Sitting Room (MBSIT)
- G. Separate Bedroom Exit (EXIT)
- H. Master Bedroom Walk-In Closet (MWLKN)
- I. Other Bedroom Walk-In Closet (OWLKN)

**RFP    Fireplace**
- A. 1 Fireplace (1)
- B. 2 Fireplaces (2)
- C. 3+ Fireplaces (3+)
- D. Fireplace in Family Room (FM)
- E. Fireplace in Living Room (LR)
- F. Fireplace in Master Bedroom (MB)
- G. Two Way Fireplace (2W)
- H. Gas Fireplace (GS)
- I. Freestanding Fireplace (FS)
- J. Exterior Fireplace (EX)
- K. Firepit (PT)
- L. No Fireplace (NO)
- M. Other (See Remarks) (OT)

**RPPOL   Pool - Private**
- A. Pool-Private (PVT)
- B. Fenced Pool (FNC)
- C. Diving Pool (DIV)
- D. Heated Pool (HTD)
- E. Play Pool (PLY)
- F. Lap Pool (LAP)
- G. Above Ground Pool (AGD)
- H. No Pool (NO)

**RPSPA   Spa - Private**
- A. Spa Private (SPA)
- B. Above Ground Spa (AGS)
- C. Spa-Heated (SPH)
- D. None (NO)

**CPOL    Pool - Community**
- A. Community Pool (PL)
- B. Community Pool - Heated (PLH)
- C. Community Spa (SP)
- D. Community Spa - Heated (SPH)

**RDIN    Dining Area**
- A. Formal (FORML)
- B. Eat-In Kitchen (EATIN)
- C. Breakfast Room (BRKRM)
- D. Dining in Living/Great Room (LR/GR)
- E. Dining in Family Room (FAM)
- F. Breakfast Bar (BRKBR)
- G. Other Dining (See Remarks) (OTHR)

**RKFEA   Kitchen Features**
- A. Range/Oven (RG&OV)
- B. Dishwasher (DISH)
- C. Disposal (DSPL)
- D. Microwave (MICRO)
- E. Compactor (CMPAC)
- F. Refrigerator (REFRG)
- G. Pantry (PNTRY)
- H. Kitchen Island (ISLND)
- I. None (NONE)
- J. Other (See Remarks) (OTHR)

**RLNDRY   Laundry**
- A. Washer Included (WASHER)
- B. Dryer Included (DRYER)
- C. Stacked Washer/Dryer Included (STACKD)
- D. Washer/Dryer Hook-Up Only (HOOKUP)
- E. Inside Laundry (I-LND)
- F. Community Laundry (C-LND)
- G. Laundry in Garage (G-LND)
- H. Coin-Op Laundry (COINOP)
- I. None (NONE)
- J. Other (See Remarks) (OTHR)

**RFEA    Features**
- A. Fix-Up (FIXUP)
- B. Remodeled (See Remarks) (REMODL)
- C. Skylight(s) (SKYLIT)
- D. Vaulted Ceiling(s) (VAULTD)
- E. Central Vacuum (CNTVAC)
- F. Wet Bar(s) (WETBAR)
- G. Intercom (INTCOM)
- H. Roller Shields (ROLLSH)
- I. Fire Sprinklers (FIRESP)
- J. Elevator (ELEVTR)
- K. Security System (Owned) (SECOWN)
- L. Security System (Leased) (SECLSD)
- M. Cable TV Available (CABLE)
- N. Furnished (See Remarks) (FURNSH)
- O. None (NONE)
- P. Other (See Remarks) (OTHR)

**RMS    Other Rooms**
- A. Family Room (FAMRM)
- B. Great Room (GRTRM)
- C. Library/Den (LB/DN)
- D. Basement (BSMNT)
- E. Game/Rec Room (GAME)
- F. Arizona Room/Lanai (AZ RM)
- G. Loft (LOFT)
- H. Guest Qtrs-Sep Entrance (GSTQTR)
- I. Exercise/Sauna Room (SAUNA)
- J. Separate Workshop (SEPWK)
- K. Clubhouse (CLUBHS)

**RXFEA   Exterior Features**
- A. Separate Guest House (GSTHSE)
- B. Tennis Court(s) (TENNIS)
- C. Handball/Racquetball Court(s) (HNDRAC)
- D. Sport Court(s) (SPORT)
- E. Patio (PATIO)
- F. Covered Patio(s) (CPATIO)
- G. Balcony/Deck(s) (BAL/DCK)
- H. Gazebo/Ramada (GAZRAM)
- I. Storage Shed(s) (STGSHD)
- J. Circular Drive (CIRDRV)
- K. Private Street(s) (PVT ST)
- L. Private Yard(s)/Courtyard(s) (PVTYRD)
- M. Yard Watering System-Front (WTRFRT)
- N. Yard Watering System-Back (WTRBCK)
- O. Children's Play Area (KIDPLY)
- P. None (NONE)
- Q. Other (See Remarks) (OTHR)

**MH    Mobile Home Features**
- A. Single Wide (SINGL)
- B. Multi Wide (MULTI)
- C. Built after 1976 (1976+)
- D. In Subdivision (INSUB)
- E. Affidavit of Fixture (AFFID)
- F. Mobile Home - 5+ Acres (5+ AC)
- G. Mobile Home - Waterline Hookup (WTRHU)
- H. Mobile Home - Financing Available (FINAV)

**RPRK    Parking**
- A. 1 Car Garage (1G)
- B. 2 Car Garage (2G)
- C. 3 Car Garage (3G)
- D. 4+ Car Garage (4+G)
- E. 1 Car Carport (1C)
- F. 2+ Car Carport (2+C)
- G. Detached (DETACH)
- H. Slab (SLAB)
- I. Assigned Parking (ASSN)
- J. Unassigned Parking (UNASN)
- K. Side Vehicle Entry (SIDE)
- L. Rear Vehicle Entry (REAR)
- M. RV Parking (RVPKG)
- N. RV Gate (RVGATE)
- O. Electric Door Opener(s) (ELEOPN)
- P. Separate Storage Area(s) (SEPSTG)
- Q. Other (See Remarks) (OTHR)

**RCNST   Construction**
- A. Block (BLOCK)
- B. Frame - Wood (FRMWD)
- C. Frame - Metal (FRMMT)
- D. Brick (BRICK)
- E. Slump Block (SL-BLK)
- F. Adobe (ADOBE)
- G. Other (See Remarks) (OTHR)

**RFNSH   Construction - Finish**
- A. Painted (PAINT)
- B. Stucco (STUCCO)
- C. Brick Trim/Veneer (BKTRIM)
- D. Stone (STONE)
- E. Siding (SIDING)
- F. Other (See Remarks) (OTHR)

**CSTA    Construction - Status**
- A. To-Be-Built (BEBULT)
- B. Under Construction (UNCNST)
- C. Completed Spec Home (SPECHM)

**RROOF   Roofing**
- A. Comp-Shingle (COMP)
- B. Built-Up (BLT-UP)
- C. All Tile (TILE)
- D. Partial Tile (P-TILE)
- E. Rock (ROCK)
- F. Shake (SHAKE)
- G. Concrete (CONCRT)
- H. Foam (FOAM)
- I. Rolled (ROLLED)
- J. Metal (METAL)
- K. Other (See Remarks) (OTHR)

**RCOOL   Cooling**
- A. Refrigeration (REF)
- B. Evaporative (EVAP)
- C. Both Refrig & Evap (BOTH)
- D. Window/Wall Unit (W/W)
- E. No Cooling (NONE)

**RHEAT   Heating**
- A. Electric Heat (ELEC)
- B. Gas Heat (GAS)
- C. Wall/Floor Heat (WFLR)
- D. No Heat (NONE)
- E. Other (See Remarks) (OTHR)

**EGY    Energy Features**
- A. Solar Hot Water (S-HWTR)
- B. Sunscreen(s) (SUNSCR)
- C. Ceiling Fan(s) (C-FAN)
- D. Multi-Pane Windows (MLTPAN)
- E. Load Controller (LDCONT)
- F. Multi-Zones (M-ZONE)

**RUTIL    Utilities**
- A. APS (APS)
- B. SRP (SRP)
- C. SW Gas (SW GAS)
- D. City Electric (C-ELE)
- E. City Gas (C-GAS)
- F. Other Electric (O-ELE)
- G. Other Gas (O-GAS)
- H. Butane/Propane (BUTANE)
- I. Other (See Remarks) (OTHR)

**RWTR    Water**
- A. City Water (C-WT)
- B. Private Water Comany (P-WT)
- C. Well - Privately Owned (WLPO)
- D. Well - Shared (WLSH)
- E. Hauled (HAUL)
- F. Water Softener (Owned) (WS-O)
- G. Water Softener (Leased) WS-L)
- H. Irrigation (IRR)
- I. Drinking Water Filtering System (FILT)

Owner acknowledges receipt of copy of this page, which constitutes Page 2 of 3 Pages. Owner's Initials (_____) Broker's Initials (_____)

## CLASS 1 - PAGE 3 OF 3

(FEATURES: For Adding a Listing, underline the proper feature selections. (R) denotes required entries
for Adding a Listing. All required Features must be entered for a new listing.)

**RSWR   Sewer**
A.   Sewer - Public (PUBL)
B.   Sewer - Private (PRIV)
C.   Sewer - Available (AVAL)
D.   Sewer in and Connected (SCON)
E.   Septic (SEPT)
F.   Septic in and Connected (SPIN)
G.   No Sewer/Septic (NONE)
H.   Other (See Remarks) (OTHR)

**SERV   Services**
A.   City Service (CIT)
B.   County Services (COU)
C.   Other (See Remarks) (OTHR)

**RFNC   Fencing**
A.   Block (BLOK)
B.   Wood (WOOD)
C.   Chain Link (LINK)
D.   Concrete Panel (CONC)
E.   Wire (See Remarks) (WIRE)
F.   Partial (PART)
G.   None (NONE)
H.   Other (See Remarks) (OTHR)

**PROP   Property Description**
A.   Borders Preserve/Public Land (PUBLD)
B.   Waterfront Lot (WFRNT)
C.   Lake Subdivision (LAKE)
D.   Golf Course Lot (GLFLT)
E.   Golf Course Subdivision (GLFSB)
F.   Hillside Lot (HILSD)
G.   Cul-De-Sac Lot (CDSAC)
H.   Corner Lot (CORNR)
I.   Desert Front (DSFRT)
J.   Desert Back (DSBCK)
K.   Historic District (HDIST)
L.   City Light View(s) (CTYVW)
M.   Mountain View(s) (MTNVW)
N.   Gated Community (GATED)
O.   Guarded Entry (GUARD)
P.   North/South Exposure (N/S)
Q.   Alley (ALLEY)
R.   Street(s) Not Paved (NOPAV)
S.   Adjacent to Wash (WASH)
T.   Borders Common Area (BDCOM)

**HRSE   Horses**
A.   Corral (CORL)
B.   Stall (STAL)
C.   Barn (BARN)
D.   Tack Room (TACK)
E.   Arena (ARNA)
F.   Auto Water (AWTR)
G.   Hot Walker (WLKR)
H.   Commercial Breed (CBRD)
I.   Commercial Board (CBOA)
J.   Bridle Path Access (BPTH)
K.   Other (See Remarks) (OTHR)

**LTSZ   Lot Size**
A.   1-7,500 (1-7,500)
B.   7,501-10,000 (7,501-10,000)
C.   10,001-12,500 (10,001-12,500)
D.   12,501-15,000 (12,501-15,000)
E.   15,001-18,000 (15,001-18,000)
F.   18,001-24,000 (18,001-24,000)
G.   24,001-35,000 (24,001-35,000)
H.   35,001-43,559 (35,001-43,559)
I.   1 to 1.9 Acres (1 TO 1.9 AC)
J.   2 to 4.9 Acres (2 TO 4.9 AC)
K.   5 to 9.9 Acres (5 TO 9.9 AC)
L.   10 + Acres (10+ AC)

**RSHOW   Show Instructions**
A.   Alarm Activated (ALRM)
B.   Call Lister (LSTR)
C.   Special Instr/Pets (CLO) (PETS)
D.   Call Occupant (OCC)
E.   Subagent-Use Lockbox (LBSA)
F.   Buyer Broker-Use Lockbox (LBBB)
G.   Lockbox-Occupied (LBOC)
H.   Lockbox-Vacant (LBVA)
I.   Lockbox - Not ARMLS (LBNA)
J.   Vacant (VAC)
K.   KILO or Courtesy Key (KILO)
L.   Key at Guard Gate (KAGG)
M.   Tenants Rights (TRGT)

**RPOS   Possession**
A.   By Agreement (AGREE)
B.   Close of Escrow (COE)
C.   Close of Escrow +2 days (COE+2)
D.   Tenants Rights (T/RGT)

**USTY   Unit Style**
A.   All on One Level (1LVL)
B.   Two Levels (2LVL)
C.   Three or More Levels (3+LVL)
D.   No Common Walls (NCMWAL)
E.   One Common Wall (1CMWAL)
F.   Two Common Walls (2CMWAL)
G.   Three Common Walls (3CMWAL)
H.   Neighbors Above (NABOVE)
I.   Neighbors Below (NBELOW)
J.   End Unit (END)
K.   Poolside (PLSIDE)
L.   Ground Level (GLVL)

**RFEES   Association Fees Include**
A.   Exterior Maintenance of Unit (EXTU)
B.   Roof Maintenance - Partial (ROFP)
C.   Roof Mainenace - Full (ROFF)
D.   Blanket Insurance Policy (INSR)
E.   Water (WTR)
F.   Sewer (SWR)
G.   Garbage Collection (GRBG)
H.   Pest Control (PEST)
I.   Air Conditioning/Heating (ACHT)
J.   Electric (ELEC)
K.   Gas (GAS)
L.   Cable or Satellite TV (CBTV)
M.   Front Yard Maintenance (FYRD)
N.   Common Area Maintenance (CAM)
O.   Street Maintenance (STMT)
P.   No Fee (NONE)
Q.   Other (See Remarks) (OTHR)

**RREST   Association Restrictions**
A.   Pets OK (See Remarks) (PETS OK)
B.   No Trucks, Trailers, or Boats (NO TRK)
C.   Separate RV Parking (SEP RV)
D.   HOA Approval of Buyer Required (HOA BYR)
E.   None (NONE)
F.   Other (See Remarks) (OTHR)

**RINFO   Associaton Information**
A.   FHA Approved Project (FHAOK)
B.   VA Approved Project (VAOK)
C.   Special Assessment Pending (SPASMPD)
D.   Professionally Managed (PRO-MGD)
E.   Self Managed (SLF-MGD)
F.   Not Managed (NOT-MGD)
G.   Club, Membership Optional (CLUB)
H.   None (NONE)
I.   Other (See Remarks) (OTHR)

**RLN1   Existing 1st Loan**
A.   FHA (FHA)
B.   VA (VA)
C.   Conventional (CONV)
D.   Farm Home (FMHA)
E.   Private (PRIV)
F.   Wrap (WRAP)
G.   Treat as Free and Clear (F&C)
H.   Other (See Remarks) (OTHR)

**TRM1   Existing 1st Loan Terms**
A.   Assume - No Qualify (NOQUAL)
B.   Assume - Qualify (ASSM-Q)
C.   Non Assumable (NOASUM)
D.   Balloon/Call Provision (BALOON)
E.   No Prepay Penalty (NOPRE)
F.   Interest Only (INTONL)
G.   Financial Information Subject to Verification (VERIFY)
H.   All Assumable Existing Encumberances-No Qualify (ALLNQ)
I.   Not Applicable (N/A)

**TYP1   Existing 1st Loan Type**
A.   Fixed (FIX)
B.   Adjustable/Graduated (ADJ)
C.   Not Applicable (N/A)

**TRMO   Existing Other Loan Terms**
A.   Interest Only (INTO)
B.   Balloon - Call Provision (BALL)
C.   Other (See Remarks) (OTHR)
D.   Not Applicable (N/A)

**MISC   Miscellaneous**
A.   Retirment Only (RETIRE)
B.   Owner/Agent (OWN/AGT)
C.   Court Approval Required (COURT APP)
D.   Lender/Corp Approval Required (LENDR APP)
E.   REO Property (REO PROP)
F.   Exclusions (See Remarks (EXCLUSION)
G.   Flood Plain (FLOOD PLN)
H.   Home Warranty (HOME WTY)
I.   Have 1st Right/Accepting Backups (1RGHT/BU)

**RNFIN   New Financing**
A.   Cash (CASH)
B.   CTL (CTL)
C.   VA (VA)
D.   FHA (FHA)
E.   Conventional (CONV)
F.   Farm Home (FMHA)
G.   Buy Down Subsidy (BUYD)
H.   Seller to Approve Points (SAPP)
I.   No Carry (NCAR)
J.   Seller May Carry (MCAR)
K.   Wraparound (WRAP)
L.   Lease Option (LSOP)
M.   Lease Purchase (LSPU)
N.   Also For Rent (RENT)
O.   Equity Share (EQSH)
P.   Exchange (EXCH)

**RDISC   Disclosures**
A.   Seller Disclosure Available (SPDS)
B.   Super Fund/WQARF/DOD Area (SFND)
C.   Agency Disclosure Required (AGCY)
D.   Special Assessment District (SAD)
E.   None (NONE)

**PHO   Photo Code**
A.   Take Photo (TAKE)
B.   Photo Submitted (SUBM)
C.   Sketch Submitted (SKTC)
D.   No Photo Requested (NON)
E.   Extra Photos/Sketches Submitted (EXTR)

**EXM:** | | | | |
For Office Use Only

**DIRECTIONS:** Enter up to 159 Characters Maximum (including spaces and punctuation) to detail directions to the property.

XST Cross Street

DIR1 (Line 1)

DIR2 (Line 2)

**REMARKS:** 560 Characters Maximum (including spaces and puntuation) to specify any additional information.

RM1 (Line 1)

RM2 (Line 2)

RM3 (Line 3)

RM4 (Line 4)

RM5 (Line 5)

RM6 (Line 6)

RM7 (Line 7)

Owner acknowledges receipt of copy of this page, which constitutes Page 3 of 3 Pages.   Owner's Initials (_____)   Broker's Initials (_____)

PAGE 1

# RESIDENTIAL RESALE REAL ESTATE
# PURCHASE CONTRACT AND RECEIPT FOR DEPOSIT

THE PRINTED PORTION OF THIS CONTRACT HAS BEEN APPROVED BY THE ARIZONA ASSOCIATION OF REALTORS®. THIS IS INTENDED TO BE A BINDING CONTRACT. NO REPRESENTATION IS MADE AS TO THE LEGAL VALIDITY OR ADEQUACY OF ANY PROVISION OR THE TAX CONSEQUENCES THEREOF. IF YOU DESIRE LEGAL, TAX OR OTHER PROFESSIONAL ADVICE, CONSULT YOUR ATTORNEY, TAX ADVISOR OR PROFESSIONAL CONSULTANT.

## RECEIPT

1. **Received From:** __Jay and Linda Binder, Husband and Wife__ ("Buyer")

2. **Agency Confirmation:** Broker named on Line 16 is the agent of (check one):
3. ☐ the Buyer exclusively; or ☒ the Seller exclusively; or ☐ both the Buyer and Seller

4. **Title:** The manner of taking title may have significant legal and tax consequences. Therefore, please consult your legal or tax advisor if you have any questions.
5. Buyer will take title as: ☒ Determined before Close of Escrow | ☐ Community Property | ☐ Joint Tenants with Right of Survivorship
6. ☐ Sole and Separate Property | ☐ Tenants in Common | ☐ Other: _____

7. **Earnest Money:** Earnest money shall be held by Broker until offer is accepted. Upon acceptance, Broker is authorized to deposit the earnest money with
8. any Escrow Company to which the check is payable. If the check is payable to Broker, Broker may deposit the check in Broker's trust account or endorse
9. the check without recourse and deposit it with a duly licensed Escrow Company. Buyer agrees that, if Buyer breaches this Contract, any earnest money is
10. subject to forfeiture. All earnest money is subject to collection. In the event any check for earnest money is dishonored for any reason, at Seller's option.
11. Seller shall be immediately released from all obligations under this Contract notwithstanding any provisions contained herein. Unless otherwise provided
12. herein, all earnest money is considered to be part of the purchase price for the Premises described below.

13. a. | Amount of | b. | Form of | ☒ Personal Check | c. | Deposited | ☐ Broker's Trust Account
14. | Deposit $ ____ | | Earnest Money: | ☐ Other: ____ | | With: | ☐ Escrow Company: ____

15. **Received By:** __Janet DeWinter__
(PRINT SALESPERSON'S NAME) (SALESPERSON'S SIGNATURE) (MO/DA/YR)

16. __Newhouse Realty__
(PRINT NAME OF FIRM)

## OFFER

17. **Property Description and Offer:** Buyer agrees to purchase the real property and all fixtures and improvements thereon and appurtenances incident there-
18. to, plus personal property described below (collectively the "Premises").

19. Premises Address: __1234 East Coppertown Drive__ Assessor's #: __198-76-543__
20. City: __Tempe__ County: __Maricopa__ AZ, Zip Code: ____
21. Legal Description: __Lot B, Block B, Paradise Sands Subdivision__

22. **Fixtures and Personal Property:** All existing fixtures attached to the Premises: including storage sheds, electrical, plumbing, heating and cooling equip-
23. ment; built-in appliances; light fixtures; ceiling fans; window and door screens, sun screens; solar systems: storm windows and doors, shutters, awnings:
24. water-misting systems; fire detection/suppression systems; towel, curtain and drapery rods; draperies and other window coverings; attached floor coverings:
25. air cooler(s) and/or conditioner(s); attached fireplace equipment; wood-burning stoves; pool and spa equipment (including any mechanical or other cleaning
26. systems (if owned by Seller); garage door openers and controls; security systems and/or alarms (if owned by Seller); timers; mailbox; attached TV
27. antennas (excluding satellite dishes); and all existing landscaping, including trees, cacti and shrubs shall be left upon and included with the Premises.

28. **Additional Existing Personal Property Included:** __GE Refrigerator (Model GS-5760); Maytag Washing Machine__
29. __(Model MRF-18026); Hotpoint Electric Dryer (Model HP-714-B)__
30. **Fixtures and Leased Equipment NOT Included:** __All draperies throughout the house__

31. **Addenda Incorporated:** ☐ AAR Addendum ☐ Other ____

32. $ __150,000.00__ **Full Purchase Price**, payable as follows:
33. $ __2,500.00__ Earnest money as indicated above.
34. $ __5,000.00__ additional earnest deposit to be deposited with the escrow company by the
35. $ ____ buyers upon the sellers' acceptance of this offer.
36. __27,900.00__ (approximate amount) additional cash to be deposited with the escrow company
37. ____ by the buyers on or before the close of escrow.
38. __114,600.00__ (approximate amount) by the assumable loan #987,654 with Mountain Valley Bank
39. ____ by the buyers as of the close of escrow.
40. ____
41. ____
42. ____
43. ____
44. ____

45. **Closing Date:** Seller and Buyer will comply with all terms and conditions of this Contract and close escrow on | __9/8/95__ (MO/DA/YR) | . Any earlier closing
46. date requires mutual agreement of Seller and Buyer. Seller and Buyer hereby agree that the Close of Escrow shall be defined as recordation of the docu-
47. ments. If escrow does not close by such date, this Contract is subject to cancellation as provided in Lines 348-356.

48. **Possession and Keys:** Possession and occupancy shall be delivered to Buyer **at Close of Escrow, or** ☐ ____
49. ____
50. Seller shall provide keys and/or means to operate all locks, mailbox, security system/ alarms, and access to all common area facilities.
51. **IF THIS IS AN ALL CASH SALE, GO TO LINE 194.**

# FINANCING OPTIONS

52. **This sale is contingent upon Buyer qualifying for a new first loan.**

53. **Loan Amount:** $ _____  **Term of Loan:** _____

54. **Type Of Loan** ☐ Conventional Fixed Rate  ☐ Conventional Adjustable Rate  ☐ Other _____

55. **Interest Rate:** Interest rate shall not exceed _____ % as an annual rate for a fixed rate loan or an initial rate for an adjustable rate loan.
56. Buyer agrees to establish the interest rate and "points" by separate written agreement with the lender at the time of the loan application.
57. **Loan Application:** Buyer agrees to file a substantially complete loan application within five (5) calendar days after the acceptance of this Contract and to
58. promptly supply all documentation required by the lender. Buyer agrees to pay such fees as required by the lender.

59. **Conditional Loan Approval:** Within **fifteen (15) calendar days or** ☐ _____ **calendar days** after acceptance of this Contract, Buyer must place in
60. escrow a written conditional (preliminary) loan approval from the lender based on a completed loan application and preliminary credit report. If such condi-
61. tional (preliminary) loan approval is not received within the time specified, then Seller may give Buyer a five (5) calendar day written notice to perform. If
62. Buyer does not deliver to Escrow Company written conditional (preliminary) loan approval within said five (5) calendar days, then this Contract shall be
63. deemed cancelled and all earnest money shall be released to Buyer without further written consent of the parties and without regard to cancellation provi-
64. sions provided for elsewhere in this Contract. Buyer instructs lender to send copies of such approval to Brokers and Seller. Buyer authorizes the lender to
65. provide loan status updates to Brokers.

66. **Loan Costs:** Private Mortgage Insurance is required for certain types of loans. The cost will be paid by Buyer at the Close of Escrow in a manner acceptable to
67. lender. The following may be paid by either party:
68. **Discount points paid by:**   **Discount points shall not exceed:** _____
69. ☐ Buyer  ☐ Seller  ☐ _____   _____ total points. (does not include origination fee)

|  | Buyer | Seller |  | Buyer | Seller |
|---|---|---|---|---|---|
| 70. | | | | | |
| 71. A.L.T.A. Lender Title Insurance Policy | ☐ | ☐ | Loan Origination Fee (Not to exceed ___ % of loan amount) | ☐ | ☐ |
| 72. Escrow Fees | ☐ | ☐ | | | |
| 73. Appraisal Fee | ☐ | ☐ | ...Paid by Buyer and | ☐ | ...Paid by Seller and |
| 74. | | | reimbursed by Seller at closing | | reimbursed by Buyer at closing |
| 75. Any additional costs not otherwise agreed upon by Seller shall be paid by Buyer. | | | | | |

76. **Appraisal:** This sale is contingent upon an appraisal of the Premises by an appraiser acceptable to the lender for **at least the sales price or**
77. ☐ _____ . The party responsible for paying for the appraisal shall do so within **five (5) calendar days of**
78. **Contract acceptance or** ☐ _____ . Buyer and Seller acknowledge that the appraisal is an opinion
79. of value for lending purposes only, and may be different from the full purchase price.

# NEW FHA FIRST LOAN OR VA FIRST LOAN

80. **This sale is contingent upon Buyer qualifying for a new FHA or VA first loan:**

81. **Loan Amount:** $ _____ (excluding MIP, or Funding Fee)  **Term of Loan:** _____

82. **Type Of Loan:** ☐ FHA    ☐ VA

83. **FHA Mortgage Insurance Premium (MIP) or VA Funding Fee:** Amount $ _____ To be financed by Buyer which will increase the loan
84. amount to: $ _____ , or to be paid by Buyer in cash at Close of Escrow.

85. **Interest Rate:** Interest rate shall not exceed _____ % as an annual rate for a fixed rate loan or an initial rate for an adjustable rate loan.
86. Buyer agrees to establish the interest rate and "points" by separate written agreement with the lender at the time of the loan application.
87. **Loan Application:** Buyer agrees to file a substantially complete loan application within five (5) calendar days after the acceptance of this Contract and to
88. promptly supply all documentation required by the lender. Buyer agrees to pay such fees as required by the lender.

89. **Conditional Loan Approval:** Within **fifteen (15) calendar days or** ☐ _____ **calendar days** after acceptance of this Contract, Buyer must place in
90. escrow a written conditional (preliminary) loan approval from the lender based on a completed loan application and preliminary credit report. If such condi-
91. tional (preliminary) loan approval is not received within the time specified, then Seller may give Buyer a five (5) calendar day written notice to perform. If
92. Buyer does not deliver to Escrow Company written conditional (preliminary) loan approval within said five (5) calendar days, then this Contract shall be
93. deemed cancelled and all earnest money shall be released to Buyer without further written consent of the parties and without regard to cancellation provi-
94. sions provided for elsewhere in this Contract. Buyer instructs lender to send copies of such approval to Brokers and Seller. Buyer authorizes the lender to
95. provide loan status updates to Brokers.

96. **Loan Costs:** When maximizing the Buyer's loan amount under FHA "acquisition method," the Buyer's new loan amount **may** be reduced and additional
97. cash required at closing from the Buyer if the Seller pays for any of the items on Lines 98-105. The following may be paid by either party:
98. **Discount points paid by:**   **Discount points shall not exceed:** _____
99. ☐ Buyer  ☐ Seller  ☐ _____   _____ total points. (does not include origination fee)

|  | Buyer | Seller |  | Buyer | Seller |
|---|---|---|---|---|---|
| 100. | | | | | |
| 101. A.L.T.A. Lender Title Insurance Policy | ☐ | ☐ | Loan Origination Fee | ☐ | ☐ |
| 102. Credit Report | ☐ | ☐ | Recording to Vest Title in Buyer | ☐ | ☐ |
| 103. Escrow Fees (V.A All by Seller) | ☐ | ☐ | | | |
| 104. Appraisal Fee | ☐ | ☐ | ...Paid by Buyer and | ☐ | ...Paid by Seller and |
| 105. | | | reimbursed by Seller at closing | | reimbursed by Buyer at closing |

106. **Mandatory Costs:** FHA regulations require the Buyer to pay for the following items: Reserves (impounds) for property taxes and hazard insurance plus adjusted
107. interest. Both FHA and VA require that the Seller must pay for the following fees, if applicable: assignment, flood certification, recordings to clear title, bringdown
108. endorsement, document preparation, photo/inspection, tax service and warehousing. In addition, VA requires the Seller to pay all escrow fees.
109. Any additional costs not otherwise agreed upon by Seller shall be paid by Buyer.

©AAR Form 1546-830 RPC 07/94

110. **Appraisal:** The party responsible for paying for the appraisal shall do so within **five (5) calendar days or** [_____ **calendar days**] **of** Contract
111. acceptance. Buyer and Seller acknowledge that the appraisal is an opinion of value for lending purposes only, and may be different from
112. the full purchase price.
113. **VA Amendatory Clause:** It is expressly agreed that notwithstanding any other provision of this Contract, the Purchaser shall not incur any penalty by forfei-
114. ture of earnest money or otherwise be obligated to complete the purchase of the property described herein if the Contract purchase price or costs exceeds
115. the reasonable value of the property established by the Veterans Administration. The Purchaser shall, however, have the privilege and option of proceeding
116. with the consummation of this Contract without regard to the amount of the reasonable value established by the Veterans Administration.
117. **FHA Amendatory Clause:** It is expressly agreed that notwithstanding any other provisions of this Contract, the purchaser shall not be obligated to complete
118. the purchase of the property described herein or to incur any penalty by forfeiture of earnest money deposits or otherwise unless the purchaser has been
119. given in accordance with HUD/FHA or VA requirements a written statement by the Federal Housing Commissioner, Veterans Administration, or a Direct

120. Endorsement lender setting forth the appraised value of the property of not less than [ $ _____ ] .The purchaser shall have the
121. privilege and option of proceeding with consummation of the contract without regard to the amount of the appraised valuation. The appraised valuation is
122. arrived at to determine the maximum mortgage the Department of Housing and Urban Development will insure. HUD does not warrant the value nor the
123. condition of the property. The purchaser should satisfy himself/herself that the price and condition of the property are acceptable.
124. **Notice To Buyer:** If the residence was constructed prior to 1978, the U.S. Department of Housing and Urban Development requires that the Buyer receive
125. and sign a copy of "Notice to Purchasers of Housing Constructed Prior to 1978" before signing any purchase contract contingent upon FHA financing. The
126. notice explains potential risks if the residence contains lead-based paint.

127. **Buyer agrees to assume the existing loan(s) and pay all payments subsequent to Close of Escrow.**
128. **Assumption:**            This sale  ☒ is   ☐ is not  contingent upon the Buyer qualifying for assumption of the existing first loan.
129. **Release of Seller's Liability:**  This sale  ☒ is   ☐ is not  contingent upon Seller being released by lender from liability for loan being assumed. If
130. Seller is not released from liability, Seller acknowledges that there may be continuing liability in the event of a Buyer default.

131. **Type Of Loan:**    ☒ Conventional    ☐ VA    ☐ FHA _____    ☐ Other _____

132. **Current Interest Rate:**                          **Current Payment Amount:**
133. ☒ Fixed  ☐ Adjustable    ___11.0___ %              $ 1246.00          ☒ PITI    ☐ PI    ☐ Other _____

134.    **Loan Balance:** $ ___114,600.00_____
135.    The balance of any encumbrance being assumed is approximate. Any difference shall be reflected in the:
136.    ☒ Cash Down Payment    ☐ Seller Carryback    ☐ Other: _____

137. **Impounds:**    Buyer shall    ☒ reimburse Seller for any impounds transferred to Buyer or  ☐ _____

138. **Loan Transfer and Assumption Fees:**  To be paid by  ☐ Buyer  ☐ Seller  ☒ ___Split___  [All other lender charges shall be paid by Buyer.]
139. If more than one loan is being assumed, go to Additional Terms and Conditions (Lines 194-205).
140. **Credit Evaluation:** This sale  ☐ is  ☒ is not  contingent upon Seller's approval of Buyer's credit.  If applicable, Buyer shall provide to Seller a current
141. credit report from a credit reporting agency and a completed loan application on the current FNMA form within five (5) calendar days after acceptance of this
142. Contract. Disapproval of Buyer's credit requires written notice from Seller to Escrow Company within five (5) calendar days after receipt by Seller of current
143. credit report and completed loan application. Approval will not be unreasonably withheld. Escrow Company is directed to record a Notice of Request for
144. Sale on behalf of the Seller and at Seller's expense.
145. **Lender Requirements:** Buyer and Seller agree to cooperate fully with lender and supply the necessary documentation to complete the assumption.
146. **Mortgage Insurance:** The loan amount assumed may include mortgage insurance, which Buyer also assumes and agrees to pay exclusive of life insurance.

**SELLER CARRYBACK FINANCING**

147. **A portion of the purchase price shall be financed by the Seller and paid by the Buyer as follows, with the first payment due** [_____ MO/DA/YR]

148. **Loan Amount:**    $ _____  as adjusted, if necessary, pursuant to lines 134-136.

149. **Priority Of Loan:**  ☐ First  ☐ Second  ☐ _____

150. **Type Of Financing Instrument:** Buyer shall execute a promissory note and deed of trust in favor of Seller and record the deed of trust against the Premises.

151. **Interest Rate:** The unpaid balance shall bear interest at the rate of  [_____] % per year,  beginning at the Close of Escrow.

152. **Payment Intervals:**  ☐ Monthly  ☐ Quarterly  ☐ Semi-annually  ☐ Annually  ☐ Other _____

153. **Collection Fees:** Collection setup fees and servicing costs shall be paid by  ☐ Buyer  ☐ Seller  ☐ _____

154. Collection account to be handled by  _____

155. **Payment Amount:**  $ _____  or more, including the above stated interest.
156. If an adjustment in the loan amount is necessary pursuant to line 148, parties agree to adjust the:  ☐ Payment amount  ☐ Term

157. **Loan Term:**  ☐ Amortizing over _____ years  ☐ If balloon payment, principal balance due on or before _____
158.          ☐ Interest-only payments, with principal balance due on or before _____

159. **Late Payments:** If late, Buyer shall pay late fees:  ☐ Yes  ☐ No   If "Yes", payments which are at least [_____] calendar days past due

160. shall be subject to a late fee of  [_____]   If any balloon payment is late, then the late fee per day will be  $ _____

161. **Default Rate:** If payment(s) are at least 30 calendar days past due, then the principal balance shall bear interest at a default rate of **five percent (5%) or** [____%]
162. over the interest rate of the carryback as stated herein. Said default rate shall begin on the 31st day following the due date of the payment(s) until payment(s)
163. are brought current. Payments are first applied to accrued interest and penalties, then to principal.
164. **Credit Evaluation:** This sale [☐ is] [☐ is not] contingent upon Seller's approval of Buyer's credit. If applicable, Buyer shall provide to Seller a current
165. credit report from a credit reporting agency and a completed loan application on the current FNMA form within five (5) calendar days after acceptance of this
166. Contract. Disapproval of Buyer's credit requires written notice from Seller to Escrow Company within five (5) calendar days after receipt by Seller of current credit
167. report and completed loan application. Approval will not be unreasonably withheld.
168. **Due On Sale:** Loan created [☐ is] [☐ is not] due on sale of the Premises. If loan created herein is due on sale of the Premises, and in the event that
169. the Premises is sold, transferred or conveyed in any manner, the promissory note and deed of trust shall provide that the promissory note and deed of trust
170. become immediately due and payable.
171. **Buyer's Liability:** On certain qualified residential property, the Seller understands that under Arizona law the Buyer may have no personal liability in case
172. of a default and that the Seller's only recourse may be to look to the property for the sole and exclusive source for repayment of the debt. Buyer shall furnish
173. to Seller, at Buyer's expense, a Standard Loan Policy in the full amount of any loan carried back by Seller and secured by the real property described in
174. Lines 19-21 of this Contract. Such Standard Loan Policy shall show that Seller's lien has the priority agreed to by the parties.
175. **Taxes:** In the absence of a tax impound account, Buyer shall provide and pay for a tax service contract over the life of this loan which will provide a delin-
176. quency notice to Seller, or any successor in interest to the Seller, of any unpaid taxes.
177. **Insurance:** Buyer shall provide, maintain and deliver to Seller hazard insurance satisfactory to, and with loss payable to Seller, in at least the amount of all
178. encumbrances against the Premises. This provision shall be made a part of the language of the deed of trust.
179. **Payments Through Servicing Agent:** Payments on this loan and all prior encumbrances shall be made concurrently through a single servicing account to be
180. maintained by a duly licensed account servicing agent. Payments on this loan shall be made at least ten (10) calendar days prior to the due date of any periodic
181. payment due on any prior encumbrance. The parties hereby instruct servicing agent not to accept any payment without all other concurrent payments.

### GENERAL LOAN PROVISIONS

182. **Occupancy:** Buyer [☒ does] [☐ does not] intend to occupy the Premises as Buyer's primary residence.
183. **Release Of Broker:** Any loan described in this Contract will be independently investigated and evaluated by Seller and/or Buyer, who hereby acknowledge
184. that any decision to enter into any loan arrangements with any person or entity will be based solely upon such independent investigation and evaluation.
185. Buyer and Seller further hold harmless and release Broker and acknowledge that no Broker is in any way responsible for Buyer's or Seller's decisions con-
186. cerning the desirability or acceptability of any loan or any terms thereof.
187. **Changes:** Buyer shall not make any changes in the loan program or financing terms described in this Contract without the prior written consent of Seller
188. unless such changes do not adversely affect Buyer's ability to qualify for the loan, increase Seller's closing costs or delay the closing date.
189. **Return Of Earnest Money:** Unless otherwise provided herein, Buyer is entitled to a return of the earnest money, if after a diligent and good faith effort, Buyer does
190. not qualify for a loan described in this Contract. Buyer acknowledges that prepaid items paid separately from earnest money are not refundable.
191. **RESPA:** The Real Estate Settlement Procedures Act (RESPA) requires that no Seller of property that will be purchased with the assistance of a federally
192. related mortgage loan shall require, directly or indirectly, as a condition of selling the property, that title insurance covering the property be purchased by the
193. Buyer from any particular title company.

# ADDITIONAL TERMS AND CONDITIONS

194. _____ N/A _____
195. _____
196. _____
197. _____
198. _____
199. _____
200. _____
201. _____
202. _____
203. _____
204. _____
205. _____

206. **Escrow:** The Escrow Company shall be: _____
207. [☐ This Contract will be used as escrow instructions.] [☒ Separate escrow instructions will be executed.]
208. (a) If the Escrow Company is also acting as the title agency but is not the title insurer issuing the title insurance policy, the Buyer and Seller hereby request
209. the Escrow Company to deliver to the Buyer and Seller upon opening of escrow a closing protection letter from the title insurer indemnifying the Buyer and
210. Seller for any losses due to fraudulent acts or breach of escrow instructions by the Escrow Company. (b) If Seller and Buyer elect to execute escrow instruc-
211. tions to fulfill the terms hereof, they shall deliver the same to Escrow Company within fifteen (15) calendar days of the acceptance of this Contract. (c) All doc-
212. uments necessary to close this transaction shall be executed promptly by Seller and Buyer in the standard form used by Escrow Company. Escrow Company
213. is hereby instructed to modify such documents to the extent necessary to be consistent with this Contract. (d) If any conflict exists between this Contract and
214. any escrow instructions executed pursuant hereto, the provisions of this Contract shall be controlling. (e) All closing and escrow costs, unless otherwise stat-
215. ed herein, shall be allocated between Seller and Buyer in accordance with local custom and applicable laws and regulations. (f) Escrow Company is hereby
216. instructed to send to Brokers copies of all notices and communications directed to Seller or Buyer. Escrow Company shall provide to such Brokers access to
217. escrowed materials and information regarding the escrow. (g) Any documents necessary to close the escrow may be signed in counterparts, each of which
218. shall be effective as an original upon execution, and all of which together shall constitute one and the same instrument.
219. **Prorations:** Taxes, homeowners' association fees, rents, irrigation fees, and, if assumed, insurance premiums, interest on assessments, and interest on
220. encumbrances shall be prorated as of [☒ Close of Escrow] [☐ Other: _____]

221. **Assessments:** The amount of any assessment which is a lien as of the Close of Escrow shall be [☒ Paid in Full by Seller] [☐ Prorated and
222. Any assessment that becomes a lien after Close of Escrow is the Buyer's responsibility. Assumed by Buyer]
223. **IRS Reporting:** Seller agrees to comply with IRS reporting requirements. If applicable, Seller agrees to complete, sign and deliver to Escrow Company a certificate
224. indicating whether Seller is a foreign person or a non-resident alien pursuant to the Foreign Investment in Real Property Tax Act (FIRPTA).

©AAR Form 1546-830 RPC 07/94

225. **Seller Property Disclosure Statement (SPDS):**
226. (a) ☐ Buyer has received, read, and approved the SPDS.
227. (b) ☐ Buyer waives review and approval of the SPDS. **(BUYERS' INITIALS ARE REQUIRED HERE TO WAIVE SPDS** _____  _____ )
     BUYER    BUYER
228. (c) ☒ Seller shall deliver the SPDS within five (5) calendar days after acceptance of the Contract, after which Buyer shall have five (5) calendar days after
229. receipt by Buyer to immediately terminate this Contract notwithstanding any other provisions contained herein by delivering written notice of termination to
230. either the Seller or to the Escrow Company, and in such event, Buyer is entitled to a return of the earnest money without further consent of the Seller. (AAR
231. FORM 1417, OR EQUIVALENT, SHALL SATISFY THIS REQUIREMENT.)

232. **Title and Vesting:** Escrow Company is hereby instructed to obtain and distribute to Buyer a Commitment for Title Insurance together with complete and legible
233. copies of all documents which will remain as exceptions to Buyer's policy of Title Insurance, including but not limited to Conditions, Covenants and Restrictions,
234. deed restrictions and easements. Buyer shall have five (5) calendar days after receipt of the Commitment for Title Insurance to provide written notice to Seller of
235. any of the exceptions disapproved. REFER TO LINES 283-291 FOR IMPORTANT TERMS. If thereafter the title is otherwise defective at Close of Escrow,
236. Buyer may elect, as Buyer's sole option, either to accept title subject to defects which are not cured or to cancel this Contract whereupon all money paid by
237. Buyer pursuant to this Contract shall be returned to Buyer. Seller shall convey title by general warranty deed. Buyer shall be provided at Seller's expense a
238. Standard Owner's Title Insurance Policy, or, if available, an American Land Title Association (ALTA) Residential Title Insurance Policy ("Plain Language"/"1-4
239. units") showing the title vested in Buyer as provided in Lines 5-6. Buyer may acquire extended coverage at his own additional expense.

240. **Seller's Notice of Violations:** Seller represents that Seller has no knowledge of any notice of violations of City, County, State, or Federal building, zoning,
241. fire, or health laws, codes, statutes, ordinances, regulations, or rules filed or issued regarding the Premises. If Seller receives notice of violations prior to
242. Close of Escrow, Seller shall immediately notify Buyer in writing. Buyer is allowed five (5) calendar days after receipt of notice to provide written notice to
243. Seller of any items disapproved. REFER TO LINES 283-291 FOR IMPORTANT TERMS.

244. **H.O.A./Condominium/P.U.D.:** If the Premises is located within a homeowners' association/condominium/planned unit development:
245. (a) the current regular association dues are $ ___N/A___ ☐ monthly, ☐ ___N/A___ :
246. (b) Seller shall, as soon as practicable, and prior to Close of Escrow, (1) disclose in writing to Buyer any known existing or pending special assessments,
247. claims, or litigation, and (2) provide to Buyer copies of Covenants, Conditions, and Restrictions, Articles of Incorporation, bylaws, other governing docu-
248. ments, any other documents required by law, and homeowners' association approval of transfer, if applicable, and current financial statement and/or
249. budget. Buyer is allowed five (5) calendar days after receipt to provide written notice to Seller of any items reasonably disapproved.
250. REFER TO LINES 283-291 FOR IMPORTANT TERMS. Any current homeowners' assessments to be ☐ paid in full by Seller; ☐ assumed by Buyer
251. Transfer fees, if any, shall be paid by ☐ Seller ☐ Buyer ☐ Other: ___N/A___

252. **Inspection Period (Physical, Environmental and Other Inspections):** Buyer has been advised of the benefits of obtaining independent inspec-
253. tions of the entire Premises in order to determine the condition thereof. In addition to the provisions regarding wood infestation, Buyer shall have the
254. right at Buyer's expense to select an inspector(s) to make additional inspections (including tests, surveys, and other studies) of the Premises. Buyer
255. acknowledges that more than one inspection may be required to perform the selected inspections. The inspections may include physical, environ-
256. mental and other types of inspections including, but not limited to, square footage, roof, designated flood hazard areas, structural, plumbing,
257. sewer/septic, well, heating, air conditioning, electrical and mechanical systems, built-in appliances, soil, foundation, pool/spa and related equipment,
258. cost of compliance with Swimming Pool Regulations, possible environmental hazards (such as asbestos, formaldehyde, radon gas, lead-based
259. paint, fuel or chemical storage tanks, hazardous waste, other substances, materials or products; and/or location in a federal or state Superfund area,
260. geologic conditions, location of property lines, and water/utility use restrictions and fees for services (such as garbage or fire protection). Seller shall make
261. the Premises available for all inspections. It is understood that this inspection requires that the utilities be on and the Seller is responsible for providing
262. same at his expense. Buyer shall keep the Premises free and clear of liens, shall indemnify and hold Seller harmless from all liability, claims, demands,
263. damages, and costs, and shall repair all damages arising from the inspections. Buyer shall provide Seller and Brokers, at no cost, copies of all reports
264. concerning the Premises obtained by Buyer. Buyer shall provide written notice to Seller of any items reasonably disapproved,
265. excluding cosmetic items, within **ten (10) calendar days** or ☐ ___N/A___ **calendar days** after acceptance of the Contract. Any repairs agreed to shall
266. be completed prior to Close of Escrow. REFER TO LINES 283-291 FOR IMPORTANT TERMS.

267. **SQUARE FOOTAGE: BUYER IS AWARE THAT ANY REFERENCE TO THE SQUARE FOOTAGE OF THE PREMISES IS APPROXIMATE. IF SQUARE**
268. **FOOTAGE IS A MATERIAL MATTER TO THE BUYER, IT MUST BE VERIFIED DURING THE INSPECTION PERIOD.**

269. **Flood Hazard Disclosure:** If the Premises is situated in an area identified as having any special flood hazards by any governmental entity including, but not limited to,
270. being designated as a special flood hazard area by the Federal Emergency Management Agency (FEMA), the Buyer's lender may require the purchase of flood haz-
271. ard insurance at the Close of Escrow or some future date. Special flood hazards may affect the ability to encumber or improve the property now or at some
272. future date. **Flood hazard designation of the Premises or cost of flood hazard insurance must be verified by Buyer during the Inspection Period.**

273. **Swimming Pool Regulations:** These Premises ☐ do ☒ do not contain a swimming pool which is defined as an above or below ground swimming
274. pool or contained body of water intended for swimming, exclusive of public or semi-public swimming pools ("Swimming Pool"). Seller and Buyer acknowl-
275. edge that the State of Arizona has swimming pool barrier regulations which are outlined in the Arizona Department of Health Services Private Pool Safety
276. Notice. The parties further acknowledge that the county or municipality in which the Premises is located may have different swimming pool barrier regula-
277. tions than the state. During the Inspection Period, Buyer agrees to investigate all applicable state, county and municipal swimming pool barrier regulations
278. and, unless disapproved within the Inspection Period, agrees to comply with and pay all costs of compliance with said regulations prior to possession of
279. the Premises. If these Premises contain a Swimming Pool, BUYER ACKNOWLEDGES RECEIPT OF THE ARIZONA DEPARTMENT OF HEALTH SER-
280. VICES APPROVED PRIVATE POOL SAFETY NOTICE AS REQUIRED BY A.R.S. 36-1681 (E) AND A.D.H.S.. RULE R9-3-101.
281. **(BUYERS INITIALS ARE REQUIRED)** _____  _____
     BUYER    BUYER
282. Buyer and Seller expressly relieve and indemnify Brokers from any and all liability and responsibility for compliance with the applicable pool barrier regulations.

283. **Buyer Disapproval:** If Buyer gives written notice of disapproval of items as provided herein, Seller shall respond in writing within **five (5) calendar days** or
284. ☐ ___N/A___ **calendar days** after receipt of such notice. Seller acknowledges that items warranted by Seller must be maintained and repaired as
285. provided in Lines 312-319. If Seller is unwilling or unable to correct additional items reasonably disapproved by Buyer, including making any repairs in a workmanlike
286. manner, then Buyer may cancel this Contract by giving written notice of cancellation to Seller within five (5) calendar days after receipt of Seller's response, or after
287. expiration of the time for Seller's response, whichever occurs first, in which case Buyer's deposit shall be returned to Buyer, without further written consent of Seller,
288. and without regard for the cancellation provisions in Lines 348-356. Notwithstanding the foregoing, if the items reasonably disapproved by the Buyer exceed ten per-
289. cent (10%) of the purchase price, the Buyer shall be entitled to cancel this Contract. **BUYER'S FAILURE TO GIVE WRITTEN NOTICE OF DISAPPROVAL OF**
290. **ITEMS OR CANCELLATION OF THIS CONTRACT WITHIN THE SPECIFIED TIME PERIODS SHALL CONCLUSIVELY BE DEEMED BUYER'S ELECTION TO**
291. **PROCEED WITH THE TRANSACTION WITHOUT CORRECTION OF ANY DISAPPROVED ITEMS WHICH SELLER HAS NOT AGREED TO CORRECT.**

292. **Home Protection Plan:** Buyer and Seller are advised to investigate the various coverage options available for purchase.

293. ☐ A Home Protection Plan with the following optional coverage _____ ,

294. at a cost not to exceed $ _____ , to be paid by ☐ Buyer, ☐ Seller, and to be issued by _____

295. ☒ Buyer and Seller elect **not** to purchase a Home Protection Plan.

296. **Wood Infestation Report:** ☒ Seller ☐ Buyer will, at his expense, place in escrow a Wood Infestation Report of all residences and buildings included in this

297. sale prepared by a qualified licensed pest control operator consistent with the rules and regulations of the Structural Pest Control Commission of the State of

298. Arizona. Seller agrees to pay up to **one percent (1%)** of the purchase price or ☐ $ _____N/A_____ for costs of treatment of infestation, repair of any

299. damage caused by infestation and correction of any conditions conducive to infestation as evidenced on the Wood Infestation Report. If such costs exceed

300. this amount that the Seller agrees to pay, (1) the Buyer may immediately elect to cancel this Contract, or, (2) Seller may elect to cancel this Contract unless

301. Buyer agrees, in writing, to pay such costs in excess of those Seller agrees to pay.

302. **Sanitation and Waste Disposal Systems:** Buyer is aware and Seller warrants that the Premises is on a:

303. ☒ sewer system; ☐ septic system. Comments: _____

304. **Seller's Obligations Regarding Waste Disposal Systems:** Before Close of Escrow any septic tank on the Premises shall be inspected at Seller's

305. expense by an inspector recognized by the applicable governmental authority. Any necessary repairs shall be paid by Seller, but not to exceed **one percent**

306. **(1%) of the full purchase price or** ☐ $ _____N/A_____ . If such costs exceed this amount that the Seller agrees to pay, (1) the Buyer may

307. immediately elect to cancel this Contract, or, (2) Seller may elect to cancel this Contract unless Buyer agrees, in writing, to pay such costs in excess of

308. those Seller agrees to pay. Seller shall deliver to Escrow Company, at Seller's expense, any certification and/or documentation required.

309. **Seller's Obligations Regarding Wells:** If any well is located on the Premises, Seller shall deliver to Escrow Company, before Close of Escrow, a copy of

310. the Arizona Department of Water Resources (ADWR) "Registration of Existing Wells". Escrow Company is hereby instructed to send to the ADWR a

311. "Change of Well Information". (ARS 45-593)

312. **Seller Warranties:** Seller warrants and shall maintain and repair the Premises so that at the earlier of possession or the Close of Escrow: (1) the Premises

313. shall be in substantially the same condition as on the effective date of this Contract, (2) the roof has no known leaks, (3) all heating, cooling, mechanical,

314. plumbing and electrical systems and built-in appliances will be in working condition, and (4) if the Premises has a swimming pool and/or spa, the motors, fil-

315. ter systems, cleaning systems, and heaters, if so equipped, will be in working condition. The Seller grants Buyer or Buyer's representative reasonable

316. access to conduct a final walk-through of the Premises for the purpose of satisfying Buyer that the items warranted by Seller are in working condition, and

317. that any repairs Seller agreed to make have been completed. Any personal property included herein shall be transferred in AS IS CONDITION, FREE AND

318. CLEAR OF ANY LIENS OR ENCUMBRANCES, and SELLER MAKES NO WARRANTY of any kind, express or implied (including, without limitation, ANY

319. WARRANTY OF MERCHANTABILITY).

320. **Buyer Warranties:** At the earlier of possession of the Premises or Close of Escrow, (a) Buyer warrants to Seller that he has conducted all desired independent

321. investigations and accepts the Premises, and (b) Buyer acknowledges that there will be no Seller warranty of any kind, except as stated in Lines 322-328.

322. **Warranties that Survive Closing:** Prior to the Close of Escrow, Seller warrants that payment in full will have been made for all labor, professional services,

323. materials, machinery, fixtures or tools furnished within the 120 calendar days immediately preceding the Close of Escrow in connection with the construc-

324. tion, alteration or repair of any structure on or improvement to the Premises. Seller warrants that the information on Lines 302-303 regarding connection to a

325. public sewer system, septic tank or other sanitation system is correct to the best of his knowledge. Seller warrants that he has disclosed to Buyer and

326. Brokers all material latent defects and any information concerning the Premises known to Seller, (excluding opinions of value), which materially and

327. adversely affect the consideration to be paid by Buyer. Buyer warrants that he has disclosed to Seller any information which may materially and adversely

328. affect the Buyer's ability to close escrow or complete the obligations of this Contract.

329. **Release of Brokers: SELLER AND BUYER HEREBY EXPRESSLY RELEASE, HOLD HARMLESS AND INDEMNIFY ALL BROKERS IN THIS TRANS-**

330. **ACTION FROM ANY AND ALL LIABILITY AND RESPONSIBILITY REGARDING THE CONDITION, SQUARE FOOTAGE, LOT LINES OR BOUND-**

331. **ARIES, VALUE, RENT ROLLS, ENVIRONMENTAL PROBLEMS, SANITATION SYSTEMS, ROOF, WOOD INFESTATION AND WOOD INFESTATION**

332. **REPORT, COMPLIANCE WITH BUILDING CODES OR OTHER GOVERNMENTAL REGULATIONS, OR ANY OTHER MATERIAL MATTERS RELAT-**

333. **ING TO THE PREMISES.** Neither Seller, Buyer nor any Broker shall be bound by any understanding, agreement, promise or representation, express or

334. implied, written or verbal, not specified herein.

335. **Default and Remedies:** If either party defaults in any respect on any material obligations under this Contract, the non-defaulting party may elect to be released

336. from all obligations under this Contract by cancelling this Contract as provided in Lines 348-356. The non-defaulting party may thereafter proceed against the

337. party in default upon any claim or remedy which the non-defaulting party may have in law or equity. In the case of the Seller, because it would be difficult to fix

338. actual damages in the event of Buyer's default, the amount of the earnest money may be deemed a reasonable estimate of the damages; and Seller may at

339. Seller's option retain the earnest money deposit, subject to any compensation to Brokers, as Seller's sole right to damages. In the event that the non-defaulting

340. party elects not to cancel this Contract, the non-defaulting party may proceed against the party in default for specific performance of this Contract or any of its

341. terms, in addition to any claim or remedy which the non-defaulting party may have in law or equity. In the event that either party pursues specific performance of

342. this Contract, that party does not waive the right to cancel this Contract pursuant to Lines 348-356 at any time and proceed against the defaulting party as oth-

343. erwise provided herein, or in law or equity. If Buyer or Seller files suit against the other to enforce any provision of this Contract or for damages sustained by

344. reason of its breach, all parties prevailing in such action, on trial and appeal, shall receive their reasonable attorneys' fees and costs as awarded by the court. In

345. addition, both Seller and Buyer agree to indemnify and hold harmless all Brokers against all costs and expenses that any Broker may incur or sustain in connec-

346. tion with any lawsuit arising from this Contract and will pay the same on demand unless the court grants judgment in such action against the party to be indem-

347. nified. Costs shall include, without limitation: attorneys' fees, expert witness fees, fees paid to investigators and court costs.

348. **Cancellation:** Except as otherwise provided herein, any party who wishes to cancel this Contract because of any breach by another party, or because escrow

349. fails to close by the agreed date, and who is not himself in breach of this Contract, except as occasioned by a breach by the other party, may cancel this Contract

350. by delivering a notice to either the breaching party or to the Escrow Company stating the nature of the breach and that this Contract shall be cancelled unless the

351. breach is cured within thirteen (13) calendar days following the delivery of the notice. If this notice is delivered to the Escrow Company, it shall contain the address

352. of the party in breach. Any notice delivered to any party must be delivered to the Brokers and the Escrow Company. Within three (3) calendar days after receipt of

353. such notice, the Escrow Company shall send the notice by mail to the party in breach at the address contained in the notice. No further notice shall be required. In

354. the event that the breach is not cured within thirteen (13) calendar days following the delivery of the notice to the party in breach or to the Escrow Company, this

355. Contract shall be cancelled; and the non-breaching party shall have all rights and remedies available at law or equity for the breach of this Contract by the breach-

356. ing party, as provided in Lines 335-347.

357. **Risk Of Loss:** If there is any loss or damage to the Premises between the date hereof and the Close of Escrow by reason of fire, vandalism, flood, earthquake or

358. act of God, the risk of loss shall be on the Seller, provided, however, that if the cost of repairing such loss or damage would exceed ten percent (10%) of the pur-

359. chase price, either Seller or Buyer may elect to cancel the Contract.

360. **Broker's Rights:** If any Broker hires an attorney to enforce the collection of the commission payable pursuant to this Contract, and is successful in collecting some

361. or all of such commission, the party(ies) responsible for paying such commission agree(s) to pay such Broker's costs including, but not limited to: attorneys' fees,

362. expert witness fees, fees paid to investigators, and court costs. The Seller and the Buyer acknowledge that the Brokers are third-party beneficiaries of this Contract.

©AAR Form 1546-830 RPC 07/94

363. **Permission:** Buyer and Seller grant Brokers permission to advise the public of the sale upon execution of this Contract, and Brokers may disclose price and
364. terms herein after Close of Escrow.

365. **Attorneys' Fees:** In any action, proceeding or arbitration arising out of this Contract, the prevailing party shall be entitled to reasonable attorneys' fees and costs.

366. **Mediation:** Any dispute or claim arising out of or relating to this Contract, any alleged breach of this Contract or services provided in relation to this Contract shall
367. be submitted to mediation in accordance with the Rules and Procedures of the NATIONAL ASSOCIATION OF REALTORS® (NAR) Dispute Resolution System
368. or, if not available, another mediation provider. Disputes shall include representations made by the Buyer, Seller or any Broker or other person or entity in connec-
369. tion with the sale, purchase, financing, condition or other aspect of the Premises to which this Contract pertains, including without limitation allegations of conceal-
370. ment, misrepresentation, negligence and/or fraud. Any agreement signed by the parties pursuant to the mediation conference shall be binding. The following mat-
371. ters are excluded from mediation hereunder: (a) judicial or nonjudicial foreclosure or other action or proceeding to enforce a deed of trust, mortgage, or agreement
372. for sale; (b) an unlawful detainer action; (c) the filing or enforcement of a mechanic's lien; or (d) any matter which is within the jurisdiction of a probate court. The
373. filing of a judicial action to enable the recording of a notice of pending action, for order of attachment, receivership, injunction, or other provisional remedies, shall
374. not constitute a waiver of the obligation to mediate under this provision, nor shall it constitute a breach of the duty to mediate. All mediation costs will be paid
375. equally by the parties to the mediation, unless otherwise agreed.

376. **Entire Agreement:** This Contract, any attached exhibits and any addenda or supplements signed by the parties shall constitute the entire agreement between
377. Seller and Buyer, and shall supersede any other written or oral agreement between Seller and Buyer. This Contract can be modified only by a writing signed by
378. Seller and Buyer. A fully executed facsimile copy of the entire agreement shall be treated as an original Contract.

379. **Time of Essence:** Time is of the essence.

380. **Arizona Law:** This Contract shall be governed by Arizona law.

381. **Severability:** If a court of competent jurisdiction makes a final determination that any term or provision of this Contract is invalid or unenforceable, all other
382. terms and provisions shall remain in full force and effect, and the invalid or unenforceable term or provision shall be deemed replaced by a term or provision
383. that is valid and enforceable and comes closest to expressing the intention of the invalid term or provision.

384. **Construction of Language:** The language of this Contract shall be construed according to its fair meaning and not strictly for or against either party. Words
385. used in the masculine, feminine or neuter shall apply to either gender or the neuter, as appropriate.

386. **Compensation:** Seller and Buyer acknowledge that Brokers shall be compensated for services rendered as previously agreed by separate written agree-
387. ment(s). Any separate written agreement(s) shall be delivered to Escrow Company for payment at Close of Escrow, if not previously paid and shall consti-
388. tute an irrevocable assignment of Seller's proceeds at Close of Escrow. **COMMISSIONS PAYABLE FOR THE SALE, LEASING OR MANAGEMENT OF**
389. **PROPERTY ARE NOT SET BY ANY BOARD OR ASSOCIATION OF REALTORS®, OR MULTIPLE LISTING SERVICE, OR IN ANY MANNER OTHER**
390. **THAN BETWEEN THE BROKER AND CLIENT.**

391. **Additional Compensation:** RESPA prohibits the paying or receiving of any fee, kickback, or thing of value for the referral of any business related to set-
392. tlement or closing of a federally regulated mortgage loan, including but not limited to, any services related to the origination, processing, or funding of a
393. federally regulated mortgage loan and includes such settlement related business as termite inspections and home warranties. RESPA does not prohibit
394. fees, salaries, compensation or other payments for services actually performed. If any Broker performs any such services for a fee, Seller and Buyer con-
395. sent to the payment of this additional compensation for such services actually performed as follows:
396. _____ N/A _____
397. _____

398. **Time For Acceptance:** This is an offer to purchase the Premises. Unless acceptance is signed by Seller and a signed copy delivered in person, by mail, or facsimile,

399. and received by Buyer or by Broker named on lines 15-16 | by _N/A_____ , 19 _____ at _____ AM/PM, Mountain Standard Time,

400. or unless this offer to purchase has been previously withdrawn by Buyer, this offer to purchase shall be deemed withdrawn and the Buyer's earnest money
401. shall be returned.
402. The undersigned agree to purchase the Premises on the terms and conditions herein stated and acknowledge receipt of a copy hereof.

403.
404. BUYER _____ MO/DA/YR     BUYER _____ MO/DA/YR
          314 Home Street                              314 Home Street
      ADDRESS                                      ADDRESS
405. ___ Tucson, Arizona _____            ___ Tucson, Arizona _____
      CITY, STATE, ZIP CODE                        CITY, STATE, ZIP CODE

## ACCEPTANCE

406. **Agency Confirmation:** The following agency relationship(s) is hereby confirmed for this transaction:

407. Listing Broker: _Newhouse Realty_____
                     (PRINT FIRM NAME)

408. Is the agent of (check one): ☒ the Seller exclusively; or ☐ both the Buyer and Seller

409. **Subsequent Offers:** Upon acceptance of this Contract, Seller hereby waives the right to receive any subsequent offer to purchase the Premises until after
410. forfeiture by Buyer or other cancellation of this Contract.

411. **Seller Receipt of Copy: The undersigned acknowledge receipt of a copy hereof and grant permission to Broker named on lines 15-16 to deliver**
412. **a copy to Buyer.**

413. ☐ **Counter Offer is attached, and is incorporated herein by reference. If there is a conflict between this Contract and the Counter Offer, the**
414. **provisions of the Counter Offer shall be controlling. (NOTE: If this box is checked, Seller should sign both the Contract and the Counter Offer.)**

415. The undersigned agree to sell the Premises on the terms and conditions herein stated.

416. *George Cellaro* 8/17/95     *Martha Cellars* 8/17'95
      SELLER                MO/DA/YR     SELLER                MO/DA/YR
417. ___ 1234 East Coppertown Drive ___            ___ 1234 East Coppertown Drive ___
      ADDRESS                                      ADDRESS
418. ___ Tempe, Arizona _____            ___ Tempe, Arizona _____
      CITY, STATE, ZIP CODE                        CITY, STATE, ZIP CODE

For Broker Use Only: Brokerage File/Log No. _____ Manager's Initials _____ Broker's Initials _____ Date _____
                                                                                                                          MO/DA/YR

## CLOSING STATEMENT SOLUTION

### Real Estate Tax Prorations:

In Arizona the tax year runs from January 1 through December 31. However, the first payment is not due until October 1. Since this sale is being closed on September 8, 1996, the purchasers receive a credit for that portion of 1996 during which the sellers owned the property, based on the 1995 tax bill of $1,200.

> January 1–September 8 equals 8 months, 7 days (as the closing date belongs to the purchaser, prorations are computed up to, but not including, the closing date)

> $1,200 ÷ 12 months = $100 per month
> $100 per month ÷ 30 days = $3.333 per day
> 8 months × $100 = $800
> 7 days × $3.333 = $23.33
> $800.00 + $23.33 = $823.33 credit to the purchasers (debit to the sellers)

### Assumed Loan Prorations:

The unpaid balance of the sellers' loan was $114,600 as of July 1 (the listing was taken on July 5). However, as the closing date is September 8, two more monthly payments were made by the sellers and the loan balance reduced as follows:

| Date | Balance | |
|------|---------|---|
| July 1 | $114,600.00— | $93.10 principal reduction from the August 1 payment [$1,143.60 – ($114,600.00 at 11% for one month = $1,050.50) = $93.10] |
| August 1 | $114,506.90— | $93.95 principal reduction from the September 1 payment [$1,143.60 – ($114,506.90 at 11% for one month = $1,049.65) = $93.95] |
| September 1 | $114,412.95 | |

Therefore, the unpaid balance of the assumed loan was the September 1 balance, and the prorated interest is based on that figure. The interest proration is for September 1 through September 7: 7 days.

> $114,412.95 × 11% = $12,585.42 annually
> $12,585.42 ÷ 360 days = $34.96 per day
> $34.96 × 7 days = $244.72 credit to the purchasers (debit to the sellers)

Since the purchasers have agreed to assume the sellers' remaining debt, the balance of the loan is credited to them, as well as the interest on that balance for that portion of September during which the sellers owned the property. The sellers are relieved of their indebtedness for both the principal balance and the interest due as of September 8; thus both amounts are debited to them. In effect, the sellers are paying off their indebtedness with part of the purchase price of the property.

A.   **Settlement Statement**

**⊞⊞⊞ ⊕ OLD REPUBLIC TITLE AGENCY**

U.S. Department of Housing
and Urban Development

OMB No. 2502-0265

B.   **TYPE OF LOAN**

| | | |
|---|---|---|
| 1. ☐ FHA  2. ☐ FmHA  3. ☐ Conv. Unins. | 6. File Number | 7. Loan Number | 8. Mortgage Insurance Case Number |
| 4. ☐ VA  5. ☐ Conv. Ins. | | |

C.   **NOTE:**  This form is furnished to give you a statement of actual settlement costs. Amounts paid to and by the settlement agent are shown. Items marked *(p.o.c.)* were paid outside the closing; they are shown here for informational purposes and are not included in the totals.

| D. Name and Address of Borrower | E. Name and Address of Seller | F. Name and Address of Lender |
|---|---|---|
| Binder, Jay & Linda | Cellars, George & Martha | |

| G. Property Location | H. Settlement Agent | |
|---|---|---|
| 1234 East Coppertown Drive Tempe, Arizona | Place of Settlement | I. Settlement Date |

| J.   SUMMARY OF BORROWER'S TRANSACTION | | K.   SUMMARY OF SELLER'S TRANSACTION | |
|---|---|---|---|
| **100.  GROSS AMOUNT DUE FROM BORROWER** | | **400.  GROSS AMOUNT DUE TO SELLER** | |
| 101. Contract sales price | 150,000.00 | 401. Contract sales price | 150,000.00 |
| 102. Personal property | | 402. Personal property | |
| 103. Settlement charges to borrower (line 1400) | 506.00 | 403. | |
| 104. | | 404. | |
| 105. | | 405. | |
| | | | |
| **Adjustments for items paid by seller in advance** | | **Adjustments for items paid by seller in advance** | |
| 106. City/town taxes          to | | 406. City/town taxes          to | |
| 107. County taxes            to | | 407. County taxes            to | |
| 108. Assessments            to | | 408. Assessments            to | |
| 109. Sellers' Impound Account | 1,617.50 | 409. Sellers' Impound Account | 1,617.50 |
| 110. | | 410. | |
| 111. | | 411. | |
| 112. | | 412. | |
| 113. | | 413. | |
| 114. | | 414. | |
| **120.  GROSS AMOUNT DUE FROM BORROWER** | 152,123.50 | **420.  GROSS AMOUNT DUE TO SELLER** | 151,617.50 |
| **200.  AMOUNTS PAID BY OR IN BEHALF OF BORROWER** | | **500.  REDUCTIONS IN AMOUNT DUE TO SELLER** | |
| 201. Deposit or earnest money | 7,500.00 | 501. Excess deposit (see instructions) | |
| 202. Principal amount of new loan(s) | | 502. Settlement charges to seller (line 1400) | 10,010.00 |
| 203. Existing loan(s) taken subject to | 114,412.95 | 503. Existing loan(s) taken subject to | 114,412.95 |
| 204. | | 504. Payoff of first mortgage loan | |
| 205. | | 505. Payoff of second mortgage loan | |
| 206. | | 506. | |
| 207. | | 507. | |
| 208. | | 508. | |
| 209. | | 509. | |
| **Adjustments for items unpaid by seller** | | **Adjustments for items unpaid by seller** | |
| 210. City/town taxes          to | | 510. City/town taxes          to | |
| 211. County taxes 1-1-95    to 9-7-95 | 823.33 | 511. County taxes 1-1-95    to 9-7-95 | 823.33 |
| 212. Assessments            to | | 512. Assessments            to | |
| 213. Interest: 114,412.95 @ | | 513. Interest: 114,412.95 @ | |
| 214.  11% from 9-1-95 to | | 514.  11% from 9-1-95 to | |
| 215.  9-7-95 | 244.72 | 515.  9-7-95 | 244.72 |
| 216. | | 516. | |
| 217. | | 517. | |
| 218. | | 518. | |
| 219. | | 519. | |
| **220.  TOTAL PAID BY/FOR BORROWER** | 122,981.00 | **520.  TOTAL REDUCTION AMOUNT DUE SELLER** | 125,491.00 |
| **300.  CASH AT SETTLEMENT FROM/TO BORROWER** | | **600.  CASH AT SETTLEMENT TO/FROM SELLER** | |
| 301. Gross amount due from borrower (line 120) | 152,123.50 | 601. Gross amount due to seller (line 420) | 151,617.50 |
| 302. Less amounts paid by/for borrower (line 220) | ( 122,981.00 ) | 602. Less reductions in amount due seller (line 520) | ( 125,491.00 ) |
| **303. CASH** ☒ FROM ☐ TO BORROWER | 29,142.50 | **603. CASH** ☒ TO ☐ FROM SELLER | 26,126.50 |

HUD—1 (3-86)
RESPA, HB 4305.2

FTGIS-40 9/91

| | | | | Paid From Borrower's Funds At Settlement | Paid From Seller's Funds At Settlement |
|---|---|---|---|---|---|
| **L. SETTLEMENT CHARGES** | | | | | |
| **700.** Total sales/broker's commission based on price $ 150,000 @ 6 % = 9,000 | | | | | |
| Division of commission (line 700) as follows: | | | | | |
| 701. $ 9,000 to NEWHOUSE REALTY | | | | | |
| 702. $ to | | | | | |
| 703. Commission disbursed at settlement | | | | | 9,000.00 |
| 704. | | | | | |
| **800. ITEMS PAYABLE IN CONNECTION WITH LOAN** | | | | | |
| 801. Loan Origination Fee | | | | | |
| 802. Loan Discount | | | | | |
| 803. Appraisal Fee | | | | | |
| 804. Credit Report | | | | | |
| 805. Lender's Inspection Fee | | | | | |
| 806. Mortgage Insurance Application Fee to | | | | | |
| 807. Assumption Fee | | | | | 25.00 | 25.00 |
| 808. | | | | | |
| 809. | | | | | |
| 810. | | | | | |
| 811. | | | | | |
| **900. ITEMS REQUIRED BY LENDER TO BE PAID IN ADVANCE** | | | | | |
| 901. Interest from to @ $ /day | | | | | |
| 902. Mortgage insurance premium for mo. to | | | | | |
| 903. Hazard insurance premium for yrs. to | | | | | 300.00 |
| 904. Flood insurance premium for yrs. to | | | | | |
| 905. | | | | | |
| **1000. RESERVES DEPOSITED WITH LENDER** | | | | | |
| 1001. Hazard insurance mo. @ $ /mo. | | | | | |
| 1002. Mortgage insurance mo. @ $ /mo. | | | | | |
| 1003. City property taxes mo. @ $ /mo. | | | | | |
| 1004. County property taxes mo. @ $ /mo. | | | | | |
| 1005. Annual assessments mo. @ $ /mo. | | | | | |
| 1006. mo. @ $ /mo. | | | | | |
| 1007. mo. @ $ /mo. | | | | | |
| 1008. mo. @ $ /mo. | | | | | |
| **1100. TITLE CHARGES** | | | | | |
| 1101. Settlement or closing fee to | | | | | 175.00 | 175.00 |
| 1102. Abstract or title search to | | | | | |
| 1103. Title examination to | | | | | |
| 1104. Title insurance binder to | | | | | |
| 1105. Document preparation to | | | | | |
| 1106. Notary fees to | | | | | |
| 1107. Attorney's fees to | | | | | |
| (includes above items numbers:) | | | | | |
| 1108. Title insurance to | | | | | |
| (includes above items numbers:) | | | | | |
| 1109. Lender's coverage $ | | | | | |
| 1110. Owner's coverage $ 150,000.− | | | | | 760.00 |
| 1111. | | | | | |
| 1112. | | | | | |
| 1113. | | | | | |
| 1114. | | | | | |
| **1200. GOVERNMENT RECORDING AND TRANSFER CHARGES** | | | | | |
| 1201. Recording fees: Deed $ 6.00 Mortgage $ Releases $ | | | | | 6.00 |
| 1202. City/county tax/stamps: Deed $ Mortgage $ | | | | | |
| 1203. State tax/stamps: Deed $ Mortgage $ | | | | | |
| 1204. Affidavit of Property Value | | | | | 2.00 |
| 1205. | | | | | |
| **1300. ADDITIONAL SETTLEMENT CHARGES** | | | | | |
| 1301. Survey to | | | | | |
| 1302. Pest inspection to | | | | | 48.00 |
| 1303. | | | | | |
| 1304. | | | | | |
| 1305. | | | | | |
| 1306. | | | | | |
| 1307. | | | | | |
| 1308. | | | | | |
| 1309. | | | | | |
| 1310. | | | | | |
| **1400. TOTAL SETTLEMENT CHARGES** (enter on lines 103, Section J and 502, Section K) | | | | | 506.00 | 10,010.00 |

FTGIS-3056A 9/91

## Sample Examination Answer Key

1.     b
2.     a
3.     a
4.     d
5.     b
6.     b
7.     c
8.     c
9.     a
10.    d
11.    a
12.    b
13.    b
14.    d
15.    b
16.    c
17.    c
18.    c
19.    d
20.    a
21.    c
22.    a
23.    c
24.    d
25.    d
26.    b
27.    d
28.    b
29.    b
30.    d
31.    d
32.    b
33.    a
34.    a
35.    b
36.    b
37.    d
38.    b
39.    b
40.    d
41.    a
42.    a
43.    a
44.    a
45.    b
46.    b
47.    c
48.    d
49.    a
50.    a

# Index

# Appendix: Legislative Update

Many of Arizona's real estate statutes were altered by Senate Bill 1133, which took effect on July 21, 1997. Specifically, provisions of the Arizona Real Estate Code (Arizona Revised Statutes, Title 32, Chapter 20) met with substantive changes in prelicensing requirements, licensee disclosure obligations, written employment contracts and continuing education renewal procedures, among others.

The following summary has been provided by the Arizona Department of Real Estate. It particularly affects Chapter 2, "Listing Agreements"; Chapter 10, "Real Estate License Laws"; and Chapter 14, "Property Development and Subdivision." Most of the information has a distinct impact on real estate licensees. Some of it addresses statutes that don't affect licensees quite as directly but touches on topics of which licensees should be aware.

# Summary of the
# 1997 Omnibus Real Estate Bill

### And other legislation affecting real estate licensees

This information has also been published in the
June 1997 issue of the *Arizona Real Estate Bulletin*

Senate Bill 1133, the 1997 Real Estate Omnibus Bill, which becomes effective July 21, 1997, makes significant changes to Arizona real estate statutes. The following is a summary of those changes. The complete text of S.B. 1133 may be obtained free of charge from the Office of the Secretary of State, 1700 W. Washington Street, Phoenix AZ 85007. Request First Regular Session, Forty-Third Legislature, Chapter 172.

## ADMINISTRATIVE PROVISIONS

**A.R.S. §32-2108(A)**
Gives the Department the authority to request a Superior Court to order a person to comply with a Department subpoena.

**A.R.S. §32-2108(B)**
Specifically authorizes the Commissioner to establish a certification and enforcement unit and authorizes the unit to have access to the Arizona Department of Public Safety criminal justice computer system.

**A.R.S. §32-2136(A), (B) and (C)**
Clarifies that the Department may not charge a fee for a broker audit clinic. It also specifies the subject matter to be taught in a broker audit clinic, provides for clinics which may be designed to address property management activities, sales activities or both. It requires a person who becomes a designated broker to attend a broker audit clinic within 90 days after becoming a designated broker, unless the broker has attended an audit clinic during the broker's current licensing period, and requires all designated real estate brokers to attend an audit clinic once during every four period after initial attendance.

**A.R.S. §32-2152(B)**
Prohibits the Commissioner from entertaining complaints regarding commission disputes [previously prohibited by Commissioner's Rule A.A.C. R4-28-701(B)].

## PROVISIONS AFFECTING LICENSEES

**A.R.S. §32-2121(A)(1)**
The amendment to this license exemption replaces "officer" of a corporation with "a person exercising control over the corporation" when exempting someone dealing in the entity's own property. The exemption will also no longer apply to someone acting on behalf of an entity when the preponderance of that person's activities would otherwise require licensure.

**A.R.S. §32-2121(A)(9)(b)**
Provides a licensing exemption for persons employed by a designated broker whose duties are limited to soliciting interest in engaging the services of a licensee or gathering demographic information for use by a licensee. Note: Although the language of this statute, and that of several others, refers to "persons employed by a designated broker," the Department maintains that persons can be employed only by an employing broker, and that a designated broker supervises employees of an employing broker, but does not employ them. The Department will attempt to correct the language of affected statutes in a bill to be introduced during the 1998 legislative session.

**A.R.S. §32-2121(A)(12)**
Provides a licensing exemption for a person who offers to sell or lease property that constitutes a security (as defined in A.R.S. §44-1801) if it is sold in compliance with the Arizona security laws, and the person is a registered securities dealer or salesperson.

**A.R.S. §32-2121(A)(13)**
Provides a licensing exemption for a person who manages a hotel, motel or recreational vehicle park. The exemption does not pertain to membership campgrounds or mobile home parks.

**A.R.S. §32-2121(A)(14)**
Provides a licensing exemption for a person who, on behalf of another, solicits, arranges or accepts reservations or money, or both, for occupancies of 31 or fewer days in a dwelling unit in a common interest development.

**A.R.S. §32-2123(B)(7)**
Applicants for a license issued by the Department are required to furnish their Social Security Number. This new provision permits a person who does not have a Social Security Number (for bona fide religious convictions or other bona fide reasons documented to the satisfaction of the Commissioner) to use a federal tax identification number in lieu of a Social Security Number.

**A.R.S. §32-2124(A)(4) and (5)**
Includes cemetery and membership camping license applicants among those who are disqualified from obtaining a license issued by the Department if they have been denied a license in the past year, or had a license revoked in the past two years, pursuant to Arizona statutes or a similar statute in any other state.

**A.R.S. §32-2124(M)**
Prohibits the Commissioner from issuing a license to a person convicted of a felony and who is currently incarcerated, paroled or under community supervision, or on probation as a result of the conviction.

**A.R.S. §32-2125(B)**
Provides that a real estate, cemetery or membership camping license will be issued to a professional corporation or professional limited liability company only if its shareholders, members or managers hold active and appropriate licenses.

**A.R.S. §32-2125(F)**
Clarifies that license fees and education credits are not required for entity licenses.

**A.R.S. §32-2125(G)**
This new statute incorporates existing requirements of the Commissioner's Rules for notifying the Department within 10 days when a corporation, limited liability company or partnership makes changes in its officers, directors, members, managers or partners or any change in control of the entity; any amendment to its articles of incorporation, organization or partnership agreement; and, if a corporation, when a person becomes an owner of 10 percent or more of the stock of the corporation.

**A.R.S. §32-2125.01(B)**
Allows real estate associate brokers and salespersons, through their employing broker, to engage in cemetery or membership camping sales activities without being separately licensed. However, a licensee may not be employed by more than one employing broker.

**A.R.S. §32-2125.01(C)**
Allows designated or employing real estate brokers to engage in cemetery or membership camping sales activities and allows them to employ cemetery and membership camping salespersons and associate brokers without being separately licensed as a cemetery or membership camping broker or salesperson. See note at A.R.S. §32-2121(A)(9)(b) in this summary.

**A.R.S. §32-2126(A)**
Provides for automatic severance of licensed employees if an employing broker abandons the broker's office.

**A.R.S. §32-2130(C)**
Provides that the license period for a late renewal license commences the day after the expiration date of the expired license.

**A.R.S. §32-2133(A)**
Authorizes the Commissioner to issue a temporary broker's license to a licensed or unlicensed person for the purpose

of winding up the existing or pending business of a licensed broker.

**A.R.S. §32-2135(B)**
Real estate schools will now issue certificates of attendance using a school form rather than a Department form. An applicant for license renewal will no longer be required to submit certificates of attendance; instead, the applicant must certify to the Department (under penalty of perjury) that he or she has attended the required number of hours of course of study in the subjects required for renewal. The applicant must retain the certificates of attendance issued by the school and used for renewal for five years.

**A.R.S. §32-2151.01(A)**
Employing brokers must keep employment records, including copies of employment status, for all current and former employees for at least five years after the date of termination of employment. Formerly, the records were to be kept by the designated broker.

**A.R.S. §32-2151.02(A)**
Buyer's broker employment agreements must be in writing and contain the same information as a listing agreement (seller's broker employment agreement). The Department interprets this amendment to mean that if a buyer's broker relationship is established, an "agreement" has been reached, and the agreement must:

- Be written in clear and unambiguous language.
- Fully set forth all material terms.
- Have a definite duration or expiration date, showing dates of inception and expiration.
- Be signed by all parties to the agreement.

The question has be raised regarding a situation where a buyer's broker relationship is disclosed in the sales contract or other documentation. The Department *requires* that a separate buyer's broker agreement, as described above, should be used whenever a buyer's broker relationship is established.

**A.R.S. §32-2153(A)(13)**
Clarifies grounds for disciplining licensees for promotional solicitations of a speculative nature involving a game of chance or risk, or through a lottery or contest, not specifically authorized by statute.

**A.R.S. §32-2153(A)(17)**
Clarifies grounds for disciplining licensees who fail or refuse to produce, on demand by the Department, documents in their possession as required by law.

**A.R.S. §32-2153(A)(25)**
A licensee can be disciplined for signing the name of another person on any document or form without the express written consent of that person.

**A.R.S. §32-2153(B)(9)**
A licensee can be disciplined for violating the terms of any criminal or administrative order, decree or sentence.

**A.R.S. §32-2156 (part of House Bill 2408)**
Amended to include property located "in the vicinity of a sex offender" among disclosures which are not required to be made by a transferor of real property or a licensee. See CRIMINAL CODE OMNIBUS BILL (Sex Offender Notification) below.

**A.R.S. §32-2165(A) and (C)(1)**
Unlicensed activity by a broker or salesperson remains a class 6 felony, but this provision no longer applies to a person who fails to timely renew because of "unintentional neglect" or administrative untimeliness by the Department.

**A.R.S. §32-2165(B)**
A person, other than a broker or salesperson, who performs acts which require a subdivision public report or other Department approval without obtaining the required report or approval, is guilty of a class 5 felony.

**A.R.S. §32-2165 (C)(3)**
Penalties prescribed by A.R.S. §32-2165 will not apply to a person who discovers a license, public report or other

approval is required, and before the issuance of a cease and desist order notifies the Department of the person's intent to comply, applies for the license, public report or other approval, and ceases the prohibited activity.

**A.R.S. §32-2175(A)**
The retention period for records of residential rental agreements and related documents is reduced from three years to one year.

## SUBDIVISION PROVISIONS

**A.R.S. §32-2151.01(J)**
If real property in a development is sold or leased by a developer without the services of a listing or selling broker, the developer shall keep all records required for five years.

**A.R.S. §32-2181(E)**
Clarifies that the exceptions to the public report requirements apply to the act of creating six or more lots, not to the lots themselves. Also clarifies that the language of the subsection includes "lots" and "parcels" as well as "fractional interests" to conform to Department interpretation.

**A.R.S. §32-2181.02(B)(4)**
This new provision automatically exempts from §32-2181, under certain conditions, the sale or lease by a person of individual contiguous lots or parcels that were separately acquired by the person from different persons.

**A.R.S. §32-2181.02(B)(5)**
This new provision exempts from the requirement of an Arizona public report, under certain conditions, the sale of an improved lot in a subdivision located outside of Arizona but within the United States. The primary condition for this exemption is that the situs state has required the subdivider to deliver a public report or its equivalent to the purchaser.

**A.R.S. §32-2183(B)**
Subdividers who offer for sale improved lots (lots with dwellings) have the option to prepare their own public report and provide a copy to the Department rather than obtaining a public report under existing law. If the subdivider chooses this filing option and so notifies the Department when making application, the Department shall have 15 business days in which to certify the application and public report as administratively complete or deny issuance of the certificate if it appears that the application or project is not in compliance with all legal requirements, that the applicant has a background of violations of state or federal law or that the applicant or project presents an unnecessary risk of harm to the public. The subdivider may commence sales or leasing activities after obtaining a certificate of administrative completeness.

The Department may examine any public report, subdivision or applicant that has received the certificate. If the Commissioner determines that the subdivider or subdivision is not in compliance with any requirement of state law or that grounds exist under Title 32, Chapter 20, Arizona Revised Statutes to suspend, revoke a public report, the Commissioner may commence an administrative action under §32-2154 or 32-2157. If the subdivider immediately corrects the deficiency and comes into full compliance with state law, the Commissioner shall vacate any action that the Commissioner may have commenced. Note that A.R.S. §32-2195.03(B) (below) makes the same provision for unsubdivided land.

**A.R.S. §32-2183.04(A)**
Makes requiring a surety bond from certain subdividers discretionary (on the part of the Department) rather than mandatory.

**A.R.S. §32-2185.04**
Violation of any of the subdivision laws is no longer a class 5 felony.

## CEMETERIES

**A.R.S. §32-2194.14**
Violation of any of the cemetery laws is no longer a class 5 felony.

**A.R.S. §32-2194.17**
Reworded to add authority for limited liability companies, in addition to corporations, to conduct cemetery business.

**A.R.S. §32-2194.24**
New cemeteries and those making a material change to the plan under which the plots are offered for sale are required to establish an irrevocable trust fund for the maintenance and operation of the cemetery.

## UNSUBDIVIDED LAND

**A.R.S. §32-2181.03(A)**
Allows lot reservations to be taken on unsubdivided land. A.R.S. §32-2195.03(B) Applicants for unsubdivided land public reports may prepare their own public reports (see A.R.S. §32-2183(B) above).

## MEMBERSHIP CAMPING

**A.R.S. §32-2198.12**
Violating any of the membership camping statutes is no longer a class 6 felony.

## TIME-SHARES

**A.R.S. §32-2197(8)**
Time-share projects are redefined to exclude a project divided into fewer than 12 use or occupancy periods.

**A.R.S. §32-2197(18)**
Violation of any of the time-share statutes is no longer a class 5 felony.

## DEFINITIONS

**A.R.S. §32-2101.1**
A new definition intended to clarify the meaning of "acting in concert."

**A.R.S. §32-2101.2(a)**
Press releases are excluded, under certain conditions, from the definition of "advertising."

**A.R.S. §32-2101.4**
Clarifies the authority of an associate broker.

**A.R.S. §32-2101.5**
Defines "barrier," which is used in the definition of "contiguous."

**A.R.S. §32-2101.16**
Expands the definition of "contiguous" so that lots, parcels or fractional interests are not contiguous if they are separated by a barrier, or certain types of roads, streets or highways.

**A.R.S. §32-2101.21 and 32-2101.22**
"Developer" and "development" are defined because of their frequent use throughout statute and rule, and by industry.

## EDUCATION

**A.R.S. §32-2124(B), (C)**
The number of Arizona specific course hours required for a waiver has been corrected from 12 to 27 to conform with other sections of the statute.

**A.R.S. §32-2124(L)**
A newly licensed real estate salesperson must complete a six-hour course in real estate contract law and contract writing before becoming actively licensed (employed by a broker). Previously the course had to be completed within 90 days of licensure. Technically, because continuing education courses may be taken for credit only during the

two-year licensure period, a person would have to pass the state examination, obtain an inactive license, take the contract writing class, then return to the Department to activate the license. In practice, the Department will honor a contract writing course taken before an applicant passes the state examination, enabling an approved real estate school to offer the contract writing course in conjunction with 90 hours of prelicensure education.

### A.R.S. §32-2135(B)
Real estate schools will now issue certificates of attendance using a school form rather than a Department form. An applicant for license renewal will no longer be required to submit certificates of attendance; instead, the applicant must certify to the Department (under penalty of perjury) that he or she has attended the required number of hours of course of study in the subjects required for renewal. The applicant must retain the certificates of attendance issued by the school for five years.

### A.R.S. §32-2136(A), (B) and (C)
Clarifies that the Department may not charge a fee for a broker audit clinic. It also specifies the subject matter to be taught in a broker audit clinic, provides for clinics which address property management activities, sales activities or both, and describes when a real estate broker must attend a broker audit clinic.

## RECOVERY FUND

### A.R.S. §32-2190 (Repealed)
It is no longer a class 2 misdemeanor to make a false or untrue claim on the Real Estate Recovery Fund.

## OTHER LEGISLATION AFFECTING REAL ESTATE LICENSEES

### HOME OWNERS ASSOCIATIONS
House Bill 2495, Chapter 40

### A.R.S. §33-1248(C)
Home owners association (HOA) condominium boards of directors must give members at least 48 hours advance notice of a board's planned meetings.

### A.R.S. §33-1256(B) and (I)
A HOA lien on a unit for failure to pay an HOA assessment is now subordinate to any first mortgage or deed of trust.

A HOA statement issued to a lienholder, unit owner or other person setting forth the amount of unpaid assessment is not required to be in recordable form, but must be provided within 15 days after the request for the statement is received. The statement is now binding on the HOA, the board and the unit orders only if requested by a licensed escrow agent. Failure to provide a statement within 15 days extinguishes any lien for unpaid assessments.

### A.R.S. §33-1260(A) and (B)
Changes requirements in the written notice to a purchaser to include a statement disclosing alterations or improvements to the unit in violation of the declaration in the past six years. The notice must include a copy of the most recent existing HOA reserve study, a copy of the most recent annual HOA financial report (or a summary if the annual report exceeds 10 pages) and a copy of the current HOA operating budget.

### A.R.S. §33-1803(A) and (B)
Presently, HOA assessments may not be more than 20 percent greater than the year before. This amendment provides that the assessment must be lower if "limitations in the community documents would result in a lower limit for the assessment..." Reduces the grace period for payment of an assessment from 30 days to 15 days before it is deemed late.

### A.R.S. §33-1803(A) and (B)
Planned community HOA boards of directors must give members at least 48 hours advance notice of board of directors' meetings.

### A.R.S. §33-1806
Mirrors A.R.S. §33-1260 (above) for planned communities.

**A.R.S. §33-1807**

(A) A HOA lien, which is automatically established when an assessment comes due, may be foreclosed in the same way as a real estate mortgage.

(B) A HOA lien is subordinate to a first mortgage or deed of trust.

(F) A planned community HOA lien is extinguished three years after the full amount of an unpaid assessment becomes due (was one year) unless the HOA institutes proceedings to enforce the lien prior to that time.

(I) HOA statement requirements for unpaid assessments are now the same as for condo HOAs. See A.R.S. §33-1256(I) above.

## CRIMINAL CODE OMNIBUS BILL
(Sex Offender Notification)
House Bill 2408, Chapter 136

**A.R.S. §13-3825**

Within 45 days of notification by the sheriff, a local law-enforcement agency shall (was "may") notify the community of an offender's presence in the community pursuant to the guidelines established by the community notification guidelines committee (described below).

**A.R.S. §13-3826**

A community notification guidelines committee is established to adopt community notification guidelines which shall provide for levels of notification based on the risk that a particular sex offender poses to the community, and describes the levels of notification.

**A.R.S. §32-2156(A)**

Presently, no criminal, civil or administrative action may be brought against a transferor of real property or a licensee for failing that the property being transferred is or has been the site of a natural death, suicide or homicide or other crime classified as a felony, or that the property was owned or occupied by a person exposed to HIV or diagnosed as having AIDS. This amendment adds property "located in the vicinity of a sex offender who is subject to notification pursuant to Title 13, Chapter 38, Article 3."

**A.R.S. §341-1719**

The sex offender community notification coordinator is established in the Department of Public Safety. It shall, among other things, oversee the Arizona sex offender community notification process, and provide information to the community notification guidelines committee on a quarterly basis including the number of sex offenders, type of offense, and the county and agency which entered the name in the Arizona Criminal Justice Information System.

**A.R.S. §41-1750**

Confidentiality and limitations on use of criminal history information maintained by the Department of Public Safety does not apply to "computer databases Éwhich are specifically designed for community notification of an offender's presence in the communityÉ"

## AIRPORT INFLUENCE AREAS
House Bill 2491, Chapter 163

**A.R.S. §28-8485**

The state, a city, town or county may establish an "airport influence area," (AIA) for any airport it owns or operates, including all property subject to an average day-night sound level of 65 or more decibels or which is exposed to aircraft noise and overflights.

If an AIA is established, details must be recorded with the county recorder and "shall be sufficient to notify owners or potential purchasers of property in the AIA that property in the area is currently subject to aircraft noise and overflights."

## PRIVACY RIGHTS PROTECTION
House Bill 2399, Chapter 38

**A.R.S. §32-3801**

This new statutes prohibits a professional board (the Department of Real Estate, for instance) from disclosing "a professional's residential address and residential telephone number" unless the address and telephone number are the only address and number of record. As a result, the Department will not disclose a licensee's home address or telephone number if the licensee has a business address and telephone number. This new statute, signed with an emergency clause, was effective April 4, 1997, and supersedes A.R.S. §32-2125.03 which granted such confidentiality to licensees who requested it for good cause. The residence address and telephone number of an inactive licensee will continue to be available upon written request or in person.

## LEAD-BASED PAINT ABATEMENT
House Bill 2032, Chapter 264

**A.R.S. §36-1671**

Many new definitions are added to clarify new lead-based paint abatement and certification requirements.

**A.R.S. §36-1677**

Directs the Department of Health Services to adopt agency rules for accreditation of training programs, work practice standards, administrative sanctions, violation investigation and correction, et al.

**A.R.S. §326-1678**

Outlines certification, training and accreditation requirements.

**A.R.S. §36-1679**

Directs the Department of Health Services (DHS) to establish rules for the assessment and collection of non-refundable fees for original and renewal accreditations and certifications for lead-based abatement personnel and firms.

**A.R.S. §32-1680**

A person performing lead-based abatement without DHS approval is guilty of a class 2 misdemeanor. Note: DHS shall implement lead-based paint abatement rules by September 1, 1998 and enforce the new statutes by rules by September 1, 1999. If the Legislature does not provide DHS funding for these programs, for fiscal year 1998-1999, the new statutes will be repealed on July 1, 1998.